Larson's Book of Spiritual Warfare

Larson's Book of Spiritual Warfare

Bob Larson

THOMAS NELSON
Since 1798

NASHVILLE   DALLAS   MEXICO CITY   RIO DE JANEIRO   BEIJING

PUBLISHERS NOTE: The purpose of this book is to provide biblically based information for those interested in the subject of spiritual warfare. It is not intended to replace proper medical consultation or appropriate psychological therapy. Readers are encouraged to consult physicians and professional counselors prior to drawing any conclusions about the demonic diagnosis of physical, mental, or emotional ills. In addition, anyone attempting an exorcism should be properly trained and should be subject to pastoral authority and review.

Published in Nashville, Tennessee, by Thomas Nelson, Inc.

Unless otherwise noted, the Bible version used in this publication is THE NEW KING JAMES VERSION. Copyright © 1979, 1980, 1982, 1990, Thomas Nelson, Inc.

Scripture quotations noted NIV are from the HOLY BIBLE: NEW INTERNATIONAL VERSION". Copyright © 1973, 1978, 1984 by International Bible Society. Used by permission of Zondervan Publishing House. All rights reserved.

Library of Congress Cataloging-in-Publication Data

Larson, Bob, 1944–
    [Book of spiritual warfare]
    Larson's book of spiritual warfare / Bob Larson.
        p.   cm.
    Includes bibliographical references and index.
    ISBN-10: 0-7852-6985-1
    ISBN-13: 978-0-7852-6985-4
    1. Spiritual warfare. 2. Devil. 3. Satanism. 4. Occultism-Religious aspects—
Christianity. I. Title. II. Title: Book of spiritual warfare.
    BT981.L35   1999
    235'.4—dc21
                                                                98–51360
                                                                CIP

Printed in the United States of America.
16 17 18 RRD 08 07

Dedication

To Brooke Laurel Larson, the newest addition of our family.
As I neared completion of this book you were taking your first
steps. This book was written, in part because of my concerns
about where these steps will take you in a world that marches inexorably toward Armageddon. Your beautiful, innocent smile
reminds me of the responsibility I bear to provide you with spiritual guidelines to protect you from the influences of evil. Some
day, the legs you wobble on now will run headlong into life. May
the Holy Spirit who guided me in every step of writing this book
lead you in the paths of righteousness for His name's sake

Contents

Acknowledgments   xv

PART I:
DEMONS, THE DEVIL, AND DELIVERANCE

1. A WINDOW ON THE WORLD OF SPIRITUAL WARFARE   1

2. CEREMONIES IN SINGAPORE   11

3. THE EVIL SPIRITS OF ST. LOUIS   17
   The "Show Me" State Showed Me

4. THE DEVIL MADE THEM DO IT   30
   Unsettling Events in the News
   What Is Evil—Do We Know Any Longer?
   Who Is Satan?
   The Value of Accurate Information

5. THE EVIL THAT DEMONS DO   40
    The World
    The Flesh
    The Devil and His Demons
    Character Overcomes the Devil

PART II:
SATANISM AND THE OCCULT IN
CONTEMPORARY SOCIETY

6. MUSICAL MESSENGERS OF SATAN   55
    Stalking Slayer
    Warriors of Hell in Hamburg

7. MURDER FOR THE DEVIL   64
    Sleuthing Satanic Slayings
    Satan's Sons and Daughters
    Satanic School-yard Slayings
    The Attraction of Evil
    Signs of Satanism

8. OCCULT ENTICEMENTS   74
    The Inducement of Psychic Phenomena
    Satan's PSI in the New Age

9. GHOULISH GAMES   80
    The Lure of Dungeons & Dragons
    Ouija Boards

10. THE HORROR OF HORROR MOVIES   89
    An Unlucky Friday the 13th
    One, Two, Three, Four, Better Lock Your
    Family's Door

11 DRUGS AND THE DEVIL 96

Drug-Dealing Murders in Matamoros
The Link Between Satanism and Drugs
Confronting the Drug Dilemma
Some Advice for Parents

12 SERVANTS OF SATAN 106

Killing for the Devil
Blood Rituals

13. STORIES OF SATANIC CULTS 117

The Sacrifice of Innocent Animals
The Satanic Abuse of Children
What You Can Do to Stop the Slaughter

PART III:
BEHIND THE BELIEFS OF SATANISM
AND THE OCCULT

14. MEPHISTOPHELES'S MANIFESTOS 131

Literature of the Lie
Satanic Groups

15. ALEISTER CROWLEY'S CREED 147

The Crucible of Crowleyism
Spiritualism and Theosophical Thought
The Power of Magick

16. THAT OLD BLACK MAGIC 156

Wicca, the Old Religion
Historical Responses to Witchcraft
Gardnerian Witchcraft
Modern Witches in America

Witchcraft and Radical Feminism
Witchcraft Beliefs and Practices
Halloween High Jinks
Witchcraft Gods and Goddesses

17. SATANIC FOLK RELIGIONS   **171**
Marketing Occult Folk Religions
Westernized Folk Religions
Voodoo
Santeria
Macumba

PART IV:
THE METAPHYSICAL WORLDVIEW IN OUR SOCIETY

18. LOOKING OUT FOR NUMBER ONE   **185**
The Human Potential Movement

19. THE OCCULT AND MIND CONTROL   **203**
Neurolinguistics
Visualization
Meditation

20. THE OCCULT ASPECTS OF ALTERNATIVE MEDICINE   **216**
Crystals
Electromagnetic Healing
Acupuncture
Therapeutic Touch
Music Therapy
Psychic Surgery
Pyramid Power
Macrobiotics
Homeopathy

Reflexology/Iridology
Polarity Therapy
Naturopathy
Miscellaneous Therapies
A Summary of Concerns

21. PSYCHIC PHENOMENA   **250**
Parapsychology
Psychics

22. DIVINATORY DEVICES   **259**
I Ching
Tarot Cards
Tasseography
Chiromancy
Nostradamus
Water Witching
Astrology
Biorhythms
Auras
Dreamwork
Runes

23. OCCULT CONSCIOUSNESS   **276**
Mysticism and Enlightenment

24. OCCULT SPIRITUALITY   **282**
A Course in Miracles
Urantia
Keys to Understanding Occult Spirituality
A Summary of Non-Christian Perspectives

**25. THE POLITICAL SIGNIFICANCE OF OCCULT
CONCEPTS**   **293**
Global Consciousness

Global Humanism
Global Pantheism
Global Sociology
Global Goddesses
The Spiritual Consequences of the
New World Order

PART V:
A SURVEY OF DEMONIC ACTIVITY IN OUR AGE

26. HARMLESS DEEDS, HARMFUL DEMONS   307
Innocuous Actions, Destructive Demons
How the Devil Got in May Not Be How He Stays
Deliverance

27. THE POWER OF THE DEVIL   324
What the Devil *Cannot* Do
What the Devil *Can* Do

28. SATAN DOESN'T PLAY FAIR   338
Tony's Story
Does Satan Abide by Human Standards?
Is Human Sacrifice Practiced Today
by Satanic Cults?
Understanding the Unpardonable Sin
Annulling the Seal of Satan
How Do Demons Interact with Other Demons?
The Smell of Satan
Where Does a Demon Go When He Is Cast Out?
Breaking Curses of All Kinds
Casting Out Tony's Demons

29. HOW SATAN STEALS, KILLS, AND DESTROYS   358

A Real-Life Meeting with a Dybbak

How Does Satan Kill His Victims?

Charlene Summons Her Husband

Can Someone Who Isn't a Christian
   Cast Out a Demon?

30. THE ENIGMA OF DEMONS AND MPD   372

What Kinds of Trauma Can Create Multiple
   Personalities?

How Is Multiple Personality Disorder Treated?

Randall's Dramatic Deliverance

31. WHAT I'VE SEEN THE DEVIL DO   387

Shocking Displays of the Devil

Things I Didn't Think the Devil Could Do

Attempts on My Life

The Story of the White Horse

A Postscript

PART VI:
HOW TO HAVE DELIVERANCE FROM DEMONS AND THE DEVIL

32. THE EXORCIST   407

Does the Exorcist Face Physical Danger?

Does the Exorcist Face Spiritual Danger?

Practical Considerations for an Exorcism

33. PREPARING FOR AN EXORCISM   419

The Danger of Diagnosing Demons

Can a Person Be Delivered Long-Distance?

Dependency on Demons

CONTENTS

Demons and Diseases
Can a Person Be Delivered Without Knowing It?
A Final Word

34. ANATOMY OF AN EXORCISM   432
Ten Rules of an Exorcism

35. RESTORATION IN THE NAME OF JESUS   449
What to Do When an Exorcism Has Ended
The Illusion of Continued Possession
The Patient Progress of Healing
Brenda's Epilogue

Notes   465
Index   475
About the Author   481

Acknowledgments

I am grateful for the individuals quoted below who carefully reviewed chapters 2-5 and chapters 26-35. Their scrutiny of these portions of the book should give assurance to any reader concerned about the theological and psychological aspects of confronting demons and the devil. Thanks as well to my wife who was understanding and patient during the solitude necessary for me to write this book.

"Bob Larson tells it like it is, just like the prophets of old. The devil and his demons are a reality and so are their intrusions in human lives. To believe otherwise is to be ignorant of biblical truth. This book is a must for anyone in Christian ministry."

JERRY MUNGADZE, PH.D., PRESIDENT
MUNGADZE ASSOCIATION, P.C.
CENTER FOR TREATMENT OF DISSOCIATIVE DISORDERS

In the future it will be important to have pastors, deliverance workers, and therapists on the same team, speaking the same language. I believe this book is a step in that direction. He came to set the captives free, and we are to continue His work, so thanks for the training manual"

DR. JIM FRIESEN, PSYCHOLOGIST
AUTHOR OF *MORE THAN SURVIVORS: CONVERSATIONS WITH MULTIPLE PERSONALITY CLIENTS*

"Bob Larson's knowledge of the Bible and his many experiences in counseling have equipped him to present a realistic procedure in dealing with demonized persons. His accounts of Christ's deliverance of the oppressed are vivid and encouraging. His grasp of our authority in Christ and his compassion for those hurting enable him to share many helpful insights for those who would help to set the captives free."

C. FRED DICKASON, PROFESSOR
MOODY BIBLE INSTITUTE

PART I

Demons, the Devil, and Deliverance

Chapter 1

A Window on the World of Spiritual Warfare

It sounded like an airplane.

Why was it flying so low?

Then, the rumble grew stronger and stronger, until it seemed that my whole being was trembling.

I wondered if something was going to crash into the building.

My body swayed. That's when I realized that this wasn't the sound of an aircraft buzzing over my head. It was the roar of an earthquake under my feet.

I was in the middle of an exorcism in a large church auditorium. It was taking place during a workshop I was teaching on spiritual warfare. The man I was ministering to, named Blaine, was seated in a chair at the foot of the platform, directly in front of the pews. I had walked into the front aisle of the auditorium to be nearer to the people.

As the earth shook, I turned to see what was happening around me. I glanced back at the huge platform area. About fifty feet behind the pulpit was an immense hanging backdrop, about twenty feet high and nearly a hundred feet long, which displayed a cross. The crucifix swayed back and forth in giant arcs.

I had never been in an earthquake before, and the ten seconds of the 5.0 tremor seemed like ten minutes. It was a memorable moment. But the most striking thing about the earthquake in Anchorage was what Blaine had explained just prior to the earth moving under my feet.

Blaine, thirty-five years of age and part Native American, had been a Christian since the age of seven. His great-grandfather was one of the first missionaries to the Alaskan Eskimos. Blaine's demonic possession resulted in part from a curse that a witch doctor had put on his great-grandfather.

He was a spiritually marked man because of the family curse. Blaine had also opened his life to demons through his own involvement in the occult. As a young adult he explored the development of highly advanced psychic abilities, drawing power from plants, animals, and the sun. For example, one of the most powerful demons I confronted was the evil spirit Ra, named after the ancient Egyptian god of the sun.

"I worshiped Ra by staring directly at the sun for many minutes," Blaine explained.

"But a person doing that would burn the retina of his eyes and perhaps blind himself permanently," I said. "How did you avoid any damage to your eyes?"

"Ra protected me. I suffered no ill effects whatsoever. In fact," Blaine explained, "I drew so much energy from Ra that I went on three hours of sleep a night. It was a great feeling, until things started turning on me."

"What caused that?" I asked.

Blaine cast his eyes down. "I guess Ra knew he had control of me and didn't have to give me the benefits of sleeplessness anymore. That's when my life turned into torment."

Blaine continued. "I believed I was in contact with universal energy, and that I could draw up power from the earth. I did. I felt the vibrations."

So did I, when the earthquake came. A coincidence? Maybe it was just a chance occurrence. But perhaps . . .

Earthquakes in Anchorage aren't frequent, but the city sets on a seismic fault line, and occasionally tremors occur. Consequently, everyone wasn't as shocked as I was, and they didn't leave the church auditorium en masse. In fact, those assembled were so interested in hearing more of my teaching on spiritual warfare, they elected to continue the workshop, and the exorcism. I turned again to Blaine and resumed confronting the forces of evil invading his life.

I led Blaine in a prayer to break the spiritual bondage over his family line: "I, Blaine, renounce the curse put on my great-grand-father. I subject this curse to the blood of Jesus, and declare it null and void. I claim a new heritage of faith in Christ. Because Christ was cursed when He hung on the cross, no curse of Satan has any right over me."

Blaine struggled to speak and retain consciousness. Suddenly, Ra interfered by manifesting his presence. That's when God spiritually impressed upon me that the important part of breaking the curse hadn't been completed.

"Do you have children?" I asked.

"Yes, two—a boy and a girl."

"It's Ra's hold over their lives that is the key to setting you and your entire family free," I explained.

When I said that, Ra came forth in rage. Several men quickly stepped forward to hold Blaine's arms and legs as he thrashed about violently. When he was subdued, I continued leading him in a confessional prayer.

"I, Blaine, bequeath to my children and to future generations, a new spiritual estate, an inheritance of faith in Christ. The curse passed on from me to my children is broken. Satan, you can't have my children. I give them completely to God."

Those words didn't come easily. Excruciating internal pain tore at his body. He struggled laboriously to form each word of the prayer.

"Ra, come to attention in the name of Christ," I demanded.

Blaine's body jerked violently. His head twisted from side to side, and his eyes slowly opened wide as Ra looked angrily at me.

"You've heard Blaine's confession. Is the curse broken?" I forcefully said to Ra.

"Yesssss!" Ra screamed, agonizingly drawing out the answer.

"Do you have any more legal authority to be there?"

"Nooooo!" The word came out as a growling sound.

"Repeat after me."

Hesitantly, under extreme spiritual duress, Ra recited the litany of his expulsion, repeating the words after me: "I, Ra, renounce my claims to Blaine and his children, and receive the judgment of God."

The men holding Blaine strengthened their grip as Ra made one last exertion to fight back physically and spiritually.

I commanded that the demon Ra continue to repeat the renunciation finalizing his doom: "I lie not to the Holy Spirit and go now . . ."

Ra resisted. He knew what I wanted him to say next and, with whatever strength he had left, he was determined to fight back. Blaine's face grimaced and his body contorted in anguish. Deep snarls rose from inside him. Blaine's teeth gnashed and his head snapped back and forth from side to side.

The final words of Ra's declaration of God's judgment were screamed with a supernatural intensity.

". . . to . . . the . . PIT!"

The word *pit* shrieked from every part of his body in one final upheaval of deliverance. Blaine's body went limp. The only thing that kept him from falling to the floor was the assistance of the men standing near him. A broad grin filled his face and he laughed in a way his tortured countenance could not have minutes earlier.

I prayed for him to be filled with the Holy Spirit in that part of his life vacated by Ra. But I sensed there was work yet to be done. As soon as things were settled somewhat from the dramatic circumstances of Ra's expulsion, I pressed on to see what other demons were in his life.

"I demand to know, by the authority of Christ, what other demon God has appointed to judgment!"

A snarling sound came from deep in Blaine's throat.

"Come to attention. Who are you!"

"Electricity."

In more than twenty years of dealing with demons I had never encountered a demon like this before. At first I questioned whether the name was legitimate, or an attempt to trick me into drawing some false conclusion.

"Why do you call yourself electricity?"

"Because I like to toy with it."

"Spirit, I command that you go down, I call Blaine back."

Blaine's head tilted back and rotated with several back and forth motions and his eyes rolled up in his head. Then he bobbed slowly forward. When Blaine's consciousness returned I questioned him.

"What kinds of things did you do with electricity?" I wanted to know.

Blaine explained. "Because I was in contact with universal vibrations, I could pull energy out of electrical motors. Just for fun, I used to focus my mind on them until they came to a halt. I could actually hear the motor grinding down. It was a trick I used to impress people. They were amazed I could stop and start an electrical motor."

I stepped back a few feet from Blaine and paused. I knew I was dealing with a powerful demon. For a moment I said nothing. Then I looked directly into Blaine's eyes and stared deeply into his soul, calling up the demon with the intensity of my gaze. For a moment the entire auditorium was starkly silent.

Then, as if the demon of electricity were appearing on cue, every fire alarm in the building went off simultaneously. Strobe lights flashed incessantly from every corner, and the piercing screech of sirens wailed at earsplitting volume.

The auditorium custodians ran frantically to check out the situation. Later, after the workshop was completed, they told me that the church, and accompanying educational facilities, had a hundred different fire zones, each with its own alarm. Every one of them had been triggered simultaneously and the only way they were able to stop them was to disengage the master switch by drilling a screw into it!

A coincidence, again? Perhaps. But the triggering of a hundred fire alarms and an earthquake in one day, within minutes of each other, stretches the statistical odds of happenstance. In addition, the "natural" events were closely related to the supernatural functions of the spirit forces I confronted.

If you find this story intriguing, it's one of many such accounts of Satan and the supernatural you'll find in this book. By the time you get to the last page, you'll be convinced, perhaps for the first time in your life, that there is a God, there is a devil, and the Bible is truly God's infallible, inspired Word. These three conclusions will forever change your understanding of the world around you. With new spiritual understanding you'll see what's really behind the headlines, what's actually motivating much deviant behavior, and what's compelling humanity in its inexorable march toward Armageddon.

This is more than a book. It's a window on a world most have no idea exists. Notwithstanding occasional inexplicable circumstances, the average person interprets life with a naturalistic point of view. Anyone who reads this book will have that notion severely challenged. When you finish reading *Larson's Book of Spiritual Warfare*, nothing will ever appear to you quite as it did before. Your life will experience its own earthquake that will shake your theology and your worldview to its foundation.

You may find areas in your own life that have experienced spiritual bondage, things you completely overlooked before. You will certainly be alerted to the conduct of friends and loved ones that you didn't expect to be of demonic origin. Your prayers will experience new urgency and your reading of the Bible will take on a new dimension. You may think such conclusions are radical, but wait until you've absorbed this book into your life.

Why write so much about demons and the devil? First, we have the Old Testament warning from God that "My people are destroyed for lack of knowledge" (Hos. 4:6). In the New Testament the apostle Paul admonishes Christians regarding the danger of being taken advantage of by the devil when we are ". . . ignorant of his devices" (2 Cor. 2:11).

To put it bluntly, I speak so much about demons and the devil because others speak so little. I have to overemphasize the realm of the satanic supernatural because it is a topic almost completely avoided in polite evangelical circles. The tragic information gap that exists regarding occult activity necessitates someone answering the call to fill that void with biblically sound facts that meet the scrutiny of serious theological review.

The preeminence of the deliverance ministry in the life of Christ can't be ignored, as portrayed in the Gospels. In Matthew we learn that believers will judge demons in the world to come (25:41; 1 Cor. 6:3), so much more so we ought to consign them to the pit in the world that now is. Indeed, we have the authority to bind them (Matt. 16:19) and demolish their kingdom (1 John 3:8). In Mark we see Christ commissioning the Twelve to cast out demons (3:14–15), an appointment also given to the Seventy (Luke 10:17–20), and to those he sent out two by two (Mark 6:7). Mark tells us that when Christ cast out demons, "the whole city was gathered together" (1:33), a strategy for mass evangelism often ignored by today's Christians. Luke shows Christ being tempted of the devil (4:1–13) and then immediately proceeding to Capernaum to cast out demons in the synagogue (4:33–35). John records the words of

Christ explaining to His followers the nature of Satan's character, that he is and always has been a murderer and a liar (8:44).

Whatever ideas you've had about demons, prepare to discard many of them. Consider, for example, a few common miscon ceptions:

Christ always cast out demons immediately. Read again the account in Mark, chapter 5. A dialogue with the demon named Legion *followed* the command of Christ for this evil spirit to leave.

Demons can always be overcome instantly. Paul declared in 1 Thessalonians 2:18 that Satan had repeatedly prevented him from completing a goal he had purposed.

Christians can't be demonized. This fallacy will be countered in detail by Scriptures such as 1 Thessalonians 5:23, which points out that part of a Christian's life may not be fully surrendered to God and thus may be a potential dwelling place for demons

The best-kept secret of Satan's strategy is what I call the "Salvation Settles It All Syndrome." This is the idea that when you become a Christian, there is nothing more you need to do to ensure your safety from Satan. Wrong! What salvation settles is your *positional* standing with God in Christ. When you are born again, the eternal spiritual state of your spirit is determined However, in your soul and flesh you may suffer *conditional* susceptibility to the devil and his demons. Your position regarding salva tion is settled, but your condition concerning vulnerabilities to demons may be a matter of question, especially if you have been involved in the occult prior to your conversion.

Do you need to know more about the devil and demonic activity? Absolutely! If you are to heed the whole counsel of God's Word, you can't ignore this important responsibility of every Christian. Furthermore, with the increased intensity of occult activity in these end times, it behooves every believer to be aware of the practices that lure unsuspecting souls into spiritual bondage. Likewise, the satanic cults and satanic systems of belief, which are glorified in popular entertainment, need to be examined from a Christian perspective.

Eventually, you or someone you know will be faced with all the evil of the satanic supernatural, and when it happens it will be too late to know how to respond with scriptural forcefulness. Every coach in professional sports studies the weakness of the opponent carefully, and devises a plan to offensively take control of the game. Sadly, many Christians take less seriously the spiritual warfare of life than the average sports team does its afternoon on the playing field.

To most effectively combat this weakness in the body of Christ and educate Christians regarding the nature of the conflict we are engaged in, I have divided this book into six sections.

The first section is a general survey of the devil, demons, and the spirit world. You'll gain insights into my calling to the deliverance ministry and learn about the nature of evil and its operation in humanity. Most important, you'll discover how to distinguish between the influences of the corrupt world system, the carnal nature of fallen humanity, and the supernatural intervention of demons in everyday life.

Section number two looks at satanism and the occult in contemporary society. Satanic crime, the effect of horror movies, the influence of occult games, and the lure of psychic phenomena will be exposed. You'll also gain insight into the clandestine activities of cults committed to the worship of Satan.

In the third section you'll gain a new comprehension of the various religious systems, and literature, behind today's fascination with satanism. Books like *The Satanic Bible* and cults such as The Church of Satan, along with lesser known cults and textbooks of evil, will be examined in detail. The world of witchcraft, and its variants of voodoo and black magic, will be disclosed in a way that will help you see the extent of occult beliefs in our current culture.

Section four lays out the various ways the occult has invaded all aspects of modern life, from business to medicine. A detailed overview of all forms of divination and psychic experimentation will point out practices many might consider harmless, but which are actually extremely spiritually dangerous, from runes to water witching, and from books like *A Course in Miracles* to psychic hot lines.

The fifth section is a detailed analysis of the actual operation of demons in everyday activities. What the devil can and cannot do, how Satan attacks and operates, and stories of events involving the supernatural I have personally witnessed will provide fascinating reading. This section will also offer useful advice on overcoming through Christ.

The final section will walk you through a deliverance session. You'll find out how to prepare for spiritual warfare, diagnose the presence of demons, and actually perform an exorcism. I will explain methodically what you do and what you don't do when a demon manifests and it is necessary to cast it out, in the name of Jesus. The book concludes with helpful thoughts on what to do once a person has been delivered from demons. As I repeatedly state to those who attend my conferences and workshops, deliverance from demons and the devil isn't an event, it is an ongoing process of restoring spiritual wholeness to those Satan has attacked.

This book will give you a clearer understanding of where the battle lines of spiritual warfare are drawn. You'll discover more about the devil can and cannot do, and how he is able to get by with things to which most Christians are oblivious. You'll learn what to avoid and what to hold fast to. And you'll see the supernatural as you've never seen it before. Get ready! An earthquake is coming that will jolt you to a new level of spiritual victory where you will overcome, as never before, all the evil of the devil, in the name of Jesus.

Chapter 2

Ceremonies
in Singapore

I first encountered a demon in 1967 in the city of Singapore during a trip that changed my life in many ways. I was a young Christian man, yearning to experience the exotic sights I had only seen on the pages of travel magazines. First I went to Europe, then the Middle East, and finally Asia. For a month I trekked across the India subcontinent, from Bombay to New Delhi and Calcutta. I ended up in Southeast Asia.

Of particular interest to me were the stories of supernatural occurrences in these areas, particularly a Hindu ceremony called Thaipusam. This ritual of self-mutilation occurs every year in only two places on earth, a rural section of Malaysia, near Kuala Lumpur, and the island city-nation of Singapore.

Even in Hindu-dominated India, this rigorous ceremony of piercing and lacerating one's body is outlawed. But in 1967 Singapore was not the modern financial metropolis of international trade that it is today. In the late '60s it was still a sleepy tropical melting pot of diverse cultures and religious beliefs. This multicultural environment adopted an indifferent attitude toward the Hindu minority who practiced Thaipusam. The leaders of Singapore believed this live-and-let-live stance helped maintain religious and ethnic harmony

I was curious to see if the descriptions I had read about Thaipusam, the act of *bloodless* self-mutilation, were exaggerated so I set out to find a way into this secret world. After going through the normal tourist channels and finding no one who would talk about Thaipusam—much less tell me in which temple it would take place—I met a missionary who had witnessed this ceremony several years before. With his directions in hand, and the help of a curious taxi driver, I finally found the temple.

The Tank Road Hindu temple complex covered half a city block. Six-foot-high whitewashed plaster walls surrounded the temple grounds, which were accessible by a single, narrow entry. I expected some kind of security check, but was surprised to find that no one seemed concerned about who came or went

I arrived at nine o'clock in the morning and the temple grounds were already a bustle of activity. A hundred or so penitents were in various stages of self-torture. One man had large hooks through the muscles in his back, from which he was pulling a heavy stone idol around the grounds. Another man looked like a human pincushion, with more than fifty safety pins inserted all over his face. Still another had wooden soles strapped to his feet with dozens of sharp nails hammered through and pointing upward. I grimaced as I watched him walk in circles around the compound.

In the center of the Tank Road temple was a small, ten-foot by ten-foot shrine. Half a dozen bare-chested priests, covered from the waist down with the flowing Indian skirts known as *dhotis*, scurried in and out of the shrine with flower and fruit offerings. I made my way toward them to see the object of their devotion: a three-foot-high stone pillar in the shape of an elongated cone.

I caught the attention of one of the priests and pointed toward the object. "What's that?"

"A *lingam*," he replied in a British colonial accent. The priest noted the confused look on my face. "It's a male phallus," he explained, "a representation of the male organ. It signifies fertility and life."

Ordinarily I would have been put off by this display of religious adoration of a sex object but my travels across India in prior weeks had educated me to the eroticism underlying Hinduism. I recalled the depraved stone carvings I had seen over the entry of a temple in northern India. Bestiality and unspeakable depictions of sexual perversion had been precisely sculpted into the stone archway so that Hindus entering the temple couldn't avoid seeing them

When I asked the attending priest why such immoral renderings were found at a religious site, he answered, "These images help worshipers get out all of their dirty thoughts before they enter the temple."

That questionable logic introduced me to one of the conundrums of Hinduism. In some Hindu disciplines, perverted sexual practices are combined with religious devotion, as in tantric yoga. This school of yoga teaches that religious and erotic ecstasy are reached when the mind, breath, and semen are stilled in a single moment of sexual and spiritual enlightenment. The pornographic temple sculptures I had seen weeks before helped me make sense of the offensive sight before me in Singapore.

"Are you enjoying our religious festival?"

I turned around to see who was speaking and saw a slight Indian man standing right behind me. I wasn't sure how to respond. "It's interesting," was all I could say. "What happens after these people have finished torturing themselves?"

The man motioned for me to follow him a few steps to the temple entrance. He stepped outside the temple compound and pointed down the street. "They will walk three miles in that direction and then have all the instruments of torture removed." A broad smile filled his face as he spoke with a sense of pride. "You will not see one drop of blood shed. This shows the great power of our gods."

This man, like everyone I met at the ceremony, was unusually cordial. Like a Christian witnessing for his faith, these people wanted to accommodate me so that I would be beguiled by their gods. There was no way I could question them about the logic of their ritual. They were sincere in their dedication and proud to display their devotion.

As I stepped back inside the compound a band of musicians began moving about the crowd. One man blew on a flute, which made a mournful, almost atonal sound. He was accompanied by several men with drums, hanging from slings around their necks. Each man had his fingers covered with hard, round cylinders that beat rhythmically against the heads of the drums. The almost mystical sound evoked images of a snake charmer, and I half expected to see a mesmerized cobra rise somewhere on the temple grounds.

What bothered me most about this religious spectacle was that children were allowed to be present and watch the events. A dozen or so of them imitated their elders. Although their self-mutilation wasn't as severe, it appeared to be no less excruciating. Their backs and chests were pierced with dozens of pins and their arms bore signs of painful slashes. Several of them sat passively in a circle, seemingly indifferent to actions that under other circumstances, in other cultures, would have constituted the most severe forms of child abuse.

I wandered about the Hindu temple grounds until I came upon a devotee named Raja. Raja, who had journeyed to Singapore from Madras, India, told me that the previous year he had prayed to the Hindu gods to heal his ailing father. When his father's illness had subsided, Raja vowed he would travel to Singapore and fulfill his pledge. To prove his piety, he had stripped to his waist and sliced his exposed body parts with sharpened knives. His tongue was pierced with a six-inch-long ice pick.

More than a hundred three-foot-long, pin-sharp skewers also

pierced his body. The skewers were supported by a device called a *kavadis,* which consisted of metal braces strapped to his shoulders. Though the skin was lacerated, true to the testimony of the penitents, not a drop of blood appeared. All this self-torture was done to honor the Hindu goddess Kali.

How could a person's skin be punctured in dozens of places without bloodletting? How could a person endure such pain and still function? Why was there no infection surrounding the wounds? My mind was filled with questions and horror, but I was left speechless by such human degradation in the name of devotion

I walked to one side of the temple grounds where a six-foot-tall stone idol of Kali stood before bowing worshipers. Kali's entire body was painted black. One of her feet was perched on a dead body, while she held the severed head of her victim in her left hand. Around her neck hung a necklace of human skulls, her other victims. Her eyes were enlarged and distended. like many other pagan idols I'd seen on my travels.

Passing Hindus expressed their adoration for Kali by draping her arms and neck with garlands of flowers. I shook my head in disbelief and ached in my heart for Raja, who had credited such a frightful goddess with supernatural curative powers.

As I made my way back toward Raja, I noticed that he was accompanied by a young Indian who held a copy of sacred Hindu scriptures and chanted from the text as an encouragement to his friend. This young man read with an enthusiasm that bordered on mania. Suddenly his face contorted, his eyes bulged out, his head jerked back, and he let out a deafening scream. He crumpled over in writhing convulsions, as if some force had thrown him to the ground. His eyes rolled back in his head as his limbs jerked and flung about in the dirt. Other Hindu supplicants rushed to his side. They shouted at one another frantically in their native Hindi language.

"What happened?" I asked a Hindu who was standing nearby.

"The spirit of the goddess entered him," the man answered. "We know, because Kali always affects us like this when she comes."

The young Hindu seemed to be in torment, and I couldn't help but notice his eyes! They looked like the eyes of the stone goddess. Now I understood why many of the heathen idols had such protruding eyes. It was a sign of the evil spirit's presence.

That look haunted me for months to come, and it became an important clue to detect spirit possession. In subsequent travels I saw it in the eyes of Haitian witch doctors during voodoo ceremonies when they called forth the *loa*. I saw it in the eyes of Brazilian macumba adherents as they aped the actions of animals. I spotted it near Kathmandu, Nepal, as *sadhus*, Hindu holy men, sacrificed goats to the Hindu god Siva. And I witnessed it in Fiji as firewalkers stood unharmed in the midst of flaming coals.

All of these ceremonies, though called by different names and separated by thousands of miles, served the same master: Satan.

That day in Singapore profoundly shaped my view of the spirit world. The fact that I saw hundreds of devotees pierce their bodies in the most grotesque ways *without a drop of blood being shed* showed me the power Satan has over those who willingly submit to his kingdom. And the way in which I reacted when faced with a soul-rending demon made me realize God's anointing—a unique deportment in the presence of evil.

I returned to the United States and devoted myself to an intensive study of demonic phenomena for the sake of communicating what I saw to the body of Christ. I devoured every theologically sound book on the subject and searched the Scriptures for biblical incidents that would shed some light on how to deal with demons. My prayers were an open invitation for the Lord to use me in confronting evil spirits, but it took three years before I finally encountered a demon on American soil. That happened in the city of St. Louis, Missouri.

Chapter 3

The Evil Spirits of St. Louis

One night in 1971, three years after my trip to Singapore, I spoke at a Youth for Christ rally in a suburban St. Louis church. At the conclusion of the evening, a group of teenagers surrounded me to debate certain points in my message. As the conversation was about to conclude, a fifteen-year-old girl named Ann approached me.

She was short, with cropped blonde hair. Her arms were folded. "I don't believe in your God," she challenged me. "I'm an atheist." Her voice sounded cool, confident, and determined.

Without thinking I responded, "Do you believe in the devil?"

"Yes!" she insisted.

"Why?"

"Because I *feel* him."

By now the other youth surrounding us had backed off, irritated by her intrusion. I motioned for them to leave us alone and pointed for Ann to step to the side of the church platform.

"What did you mean by saying you *feel* the devil?"

A leering smile crossed her lips. "I have sex with the devil," she answered.

I was unprepared for her answer. Back then, I had never heard of incubus, demonic sexual intercourse in which a spirit assumes male proportions and sexually stimulates a human female. Frankly, I thought she was trying to impress me by her impudence. Just in case there was any truth to her story, I decided to find out more. I asked her to follow me into a nearby Sunday school room, and sent someone to tell Bill, the Youth for Christ rally director, to join me.

Minutes later the three of us sat facing one another with our chairs in a triangular position. I began with a series of questions about Ann's spiritual condition. In contrast to her belligerence a little earlier, she seemed to alternate between intense antagonism and nonchalance, often staring into space as if I were not there. She would reply to my questions about her spiritual beliefs in words that carefully avoided the name of Christ.

If I had been more experienced in such encounters, I would have known several ways to expedite the proceedings. I would have kept my eyes on her and insisted, as politely as possible, that she not take her eyes off me. I would have used biblical phrases that could incite a demon in our conversation, such as "the blood of Christ" and "the victory of the Resurrection," along with testimonial references to what Christ meant to me.

After nearly an hour of fruitless dialogue, I decided that Ann's story was serious enough to warrant a final attempt to contact a demon. Like most people wondering if they might be on the verge of an exorcism, I was hesitant. Who wants to attempt such an incredible accusation and be wrong? However, it was worth any embarrassment to set Ann free.

"Ann, in the name of Jesus," I started, not really sure of the exact words to use, "I demand to talk to the devil within you."

The Youth for Christ director leaned toward me and whispered in my ear, "I've been through this sort of thing before, and I'll help in any way I can."

I looked at him, relieved. I was grateful to know I could get some coaching, but wished he had said something earlier.

At first my entry into the domain of exorcism seemed a failure. Ann showed little reaction to my demand. Maybe I hadn't spoken forcefully enough.

"Didn't you hear me?" I asked the unseen presence. Borrowing language from a couple of books I'd read about exorcisms, I insisted. "I told you to come forward and talk to me, whoever you are."

This time Ann's head jerked backward and her body stiffened, just like the young Hindu boy in Singapore. Her eyes closed, her face contorted, and her fingers flexed as if something inside her was trying to come out.

When Ann's eyes opened, they widened with that same fiendish look. "What do you want with me?" a deep, masculine-sounding voice replied. "Leave me alone. Her body belongs to me!"

What struck me immediately was that the voice was not her own. It had a clipped British accent. Three years earlier, on that trip around the world, I had stood in London's Hyde Park and listened to the Sunday afternoon soapbox speakers as they spouted obscenities, poetry, and blasphemies. As a result, I could detect a genuine English accent.

"Ask his name," Bill directed me.

I sat forward in my chair, drawing myself to my full height as if that might be more intimidating. "In Jesus' name, tell me who you are."

"Miss Love," the spirit replied with a smirk.

I looked at Bill. He shook his head.

"Well, whoever you are, are you British?"

"Oh yes. I've even inhabited royalty."

Whether or not the comment was truthful, it was still remarkable for a fifteen-year-old girl from a rural Missouri community to speak in a male voice that sounded like an actor in a BBC sitcom.

"Do you really love her?" I asked.

The hands of Miss Love seductively caressed Ann's legs and thighs. "Of course. She's married to me. She's mine, all mine."

"Bring Ann back," Bill whispered.

Acting as if I knew exactly what to do, I ordered, "Spirit, I bind you in the name of Christ and command you to go down. Let Ann come back."

Miss Love shot an annoying glance at Bill and then reluctantly acquiesced. After what appeared to be an internal struggle of some sort, Ann's body gradually relaxed, her face softened, and her personality returned. It was amazing to see the spirit's obedient response to the spoken authority of Christ's name.

"Ann, I believe what you told me about feeling the devil inside you. You're possessed by a demon, and I'm going to cast it out!" As I spoke those words, I realized I had never done this before. Cast out a demon named Miss Love? I wasn't even sure who Miss Love was, let alone know how to proceed further. But my mentor, Bill, was sitting calmly beside me. And I knew there was a connection between that day in Singapore and this night in St. Louis. Thaipusam was God's way of introducing me to the reality of the supernatural.

I expected Ann to resist what I had suggested. Instead she dropped her head and spoke softly, "It's no use. I'm married to Miss Love and he owns my body."

Why didn't the spirit call himself Mr. Love? I knew that in the Bible, angels and demons were always referred to in the masculine gender. *Perhaps Miss Love is the demon's way of referring to Ann, not himself?* I thought.

Ann jumped to her feet and began pacing about the room, wringing her hands and gesturing erratically. "Help me, help me!" she cried one moment, followed by, "I want Miss Love, I like what he does to me!" the next.

"Sit down," I finally demanded, and Ann plopped herself into the steel folding chair.

I decided more had to be known before we could get Ann's cooperation. Then I experienced something that in later years of conducting exorcisms I would covet prayerfully. God spoke through me without any deliberate forethought on my part. "Miss Love, you're going to kill Ann, aren't you?"

This time the demon abruptly manifested. "How did you know that?"

I didn't have an answer. The thought was not my own.

"How are you going to kill her?"

Miss Love raised one eyebrow and cocked his head haughtily. "She'll hang from a tree, just like your Jesus!"

"Does Ann know this?"

"Of course. I've convinced her she has to die like Christ. She already has the rope and knows where the tree is."

"When?"

"Soon, very soon," Miss Love bragged.

"You can't have her, and you won't kill her!"

Miss Love crossed one leg over the other and shifted sideways in the chair. "Well, well, well, look who's talking," he taunted me. "You don't even know what you're doing—without help from your friend over there," he said, gesturing toward Bill. "Anyway, I know all about you."

As a young Christian I was still sensitive about my failures before coming to Christ. This was my chance to stand on the promises of God's Word and let my faith speak for itself.

"You're right, I haven't always lived for God. But that's in the past, forgiven. Jesus did something for me at the cross you'll never experience."

"I don't want to hear about that!" Miss Love screamed, maintaining that same precise British accent.

"Fine, then get out of here!"

"I won't go. I don't have to go as long as she doesn't know about . . ."

"About what?"

The demon in his bravado had obviously said something he shouldn't have.

"In Jesus' name, tell me what she needs to know."

"That stuff."

"What stuff?"

"All that salvation stuff you're talking about."

Looking back on that night from the perspective of hundreds of exorcisms later, I still marvel at how God intervened to make the demon say what I needed to know. Discovering what the victim of possession needs to say or pray to be free is a key to victory in exorcisms, and the information is usually obtained only after a laborious interrogation. It's like assembling a puzzle, involving life-and-death pieces. In this case, God mercifully allowed a divine shortcut to set Ann free.

The demon, knowing he had spoken out of turn, glared at me and faded away. When Ann returned, she was even more docile. What had taken place internally had weakened Miss Love's dominance.

"Please help," Ann pleaded. "I don't want to die."

"Then you do know about the . . ."

"The hanging? Yes, how do you know?"

"Never mind. It's just important for you to know that you don't have to die. Christ has already died for you."

I took a Bible and started through the Scriptures, explaining how Ann could know Christ personally. As later exorcisms taught me, such a situation normally evokes disruption. God's Word will usually cause the victim severe internal pain or the person will try to flee. This time, God dramatically intervened, and the only interference I could see was the overwhelming feeling of sleepiness that overcame her.

I assumed this reaction was because of the late night hour, which neared midnight. I learned later that induced slumber or mental fogging is a common distraction used by demons. Ann fought the sleepiness and assimilated what I was saying. She acknowledged each scriptural step of salvation. She prayed, asking Christ to enter her.

The prayer didn't come easily. At one point, I had to lead her word by word to overcome Miss Love's hindrance. When the last words of Ann's salvation prayer were spoken, the demon abruptly returned.

Now the evil spirit was less defiant than before, knowing his hold on Ann's life had been broken. "Think you're pretty clever, don't you?" the demon said. "But you still don't know who I really am, do you? Miss Love is what I call myself. That's not the name given to me by my master. Why, you even talked about me tonight."

Tonight? That was an odd thing to say. I thought about what I had said in my message that night in St. Louis. The focus was on the rock opera *Jesus Christ Superstar*. To me, the musical was blasphemous, pure and simple. Its depiction of Judas as a hero and Jesus as an ambivalent messiah who was involved with Mary Magdalene and doubted His calling was evidence of satanic inspiration. Christian young people needed to reject the seduction of popular culture's portrayal of their Savior.

"What do you mean, I talked about you? Who are you? If you're not Miss Love, what's your real name?"

"You can read all about me in the thirteenth chapter of Revelation."

I reached for my Bible and read aloud: "I saw a beast rising up out of the sea, having seven heads and ten horns, and on his horns ten crowns, and on his heads a blasphemous—"

"Blasphemy!" the spirit broke in. He threw back his head and laughed sarcastically.

Blasphemy! That's why he said I spoke about him tonight. Jesus Christ Superstar *is blasphemous!*

As if he read my mind, the spirit said, "Would you like me to quote a few of my favorite lyrics from that sterling opera I helped inspire? You do recall that the men who wrote *Superstar* were British?"

Before I could react, Blasphemy began quoting line after line from at least a half dozen *Superstar* songs. I knew that this was not an act by a fifteen-year-old girl who had memorized song lyrics, learned to effect an upper-crust British inflection, and perpetrated a hoax on me. The demon who stared from Ann's eyes exuded hatred for God and all that was good.

The spirit continued. "Miss Love . . . even *she* thought that's who she was. She thought I loved her, so I nicknamed her Miss Love, and took the name for myself too." Blasphemy looked at me insolently. "Pretty ingenious, wouldn't you say, old chap?"

The demon's flippant attitude seemed odd at the time. Through the years I've learned that some demons like to brag about their trickery. Sometimes I allow them to boast. Often they become overly confident and reveal something I wouldn't have known otherwise.

"Check to see if Blasphemy is the only demon," Bill said to me softly.

I demanded that Blasphemy tell me what other evil spirits were inside Ann. Reluctantly he divulged that there were six others. Ann's demons of lust, murder, and incubus each had names personifying their purpose. A demon named Monica puzzled me. Why did it have a human name? When we called Ann from the demon's trance, we learned that Monica was a girlfriend who had introduced Ann to the occult through the Ouija board and satanic rituals.

Bill taught me to start with the weakest demon and work upward, thereby depriving the top demon from drawing strength from those under him. (This may not be the most efficient way, but it works well in some cases.)

He also showed me how to cross-examine each spirit to find out its name, how it entered Ann, and then finally to lead Ann in a prayer, renouncing the sin of entrance. We then forced each spirit to pronounce his own doom by saying his name and declaring, "I renounce my claim to Ann, I obey the judgment of God, and I go to the pit." The entire procedure took hours.

Throughout the process, Blasphemy continually intruded,

knowing we were closing in on him. When all those under him were gone, we faced Blasphemy.

As a novice, I asked the demon if he was indeed the actual demon described in chapter 13 of the book of Revelation.

Blasphemy found my ignorance amusing. "Thanks for the compliment," he responded. "No, that one is yet to come, but my deeds have earned me the right to bear that name."

In subsequent exorcisms I have encountered demons named Satan, Lucifer, Beelzebub, and a host of other names taken from Scripture. What I learned that night in Missouri revealed to me that certain names in Satan's kingdom refer to a rank the spirit holds. Satan has apparently arranged a hierarchy like that of the military, with sergeants, lieutenants, generals, and so on. At the top of these levels are often the powerful demons: Lucifer and Satan. They are fallen spirits that have excelled because of their successful debaucheries. (Apart from Judas and the Antichrist, there is no biblical evidence that Satan ever possesses a person.)

Weakened by the lack of assistance from those under his authority, Blasphemy left more easily than I had anticipated. When he was gone, Ann jerked suddenly and came to her senses, with a look on her face we had not seen all night, an angelic serenity. Gone, too, were the sultry demeanor and the contentious attitude. She had only the sketchiest idea of what had happened and wasn't even sure where she was.

What struck me most was the ease with which she spoke the name of Jesus. When I had led her in a confessional prayer at the start of the exorcism, four hours earlier, she was only able to utter the name of Jesus, syllable by syllable. Now she said "Jesus" with a joy that came from her deep spiritual yearnings.

THE "SHOW ME" STATE SHOWED ME

That night in St. Louis taught me valuable lessons. Most important, God didn't allow me to encounter the evil spirits alone.

Without Bill at my side I certainly wouldn't have proceeded with confidence. And the exorcism might have lasted much longer than it did, so long that Ann might not have obtained full freedom.

Since then, I have been involved with hundreds of exorcisms. Some have lasted no more than a few minutes, while others have gone on for hours, weeks, months, and even years. Some demons have been almost benign to the point of wanting to leave rather than risk being battered by a servant of God. Others have fought vigorously and violently. Still others are bewildered by why they possessed their victims. Most fought skillfully and determinedly.

As you read this book and wonder if you might ever be thrust into a circumstance similar to the ones I will describe, I can assure you that God will not allow you to entertain such evil unaware of what to do. Furthermore, the purpose of this book is not to train you in deliverance, but to help you with your everyday Christian life. By understanding how Satan operates in the arena of the supernatural, you will be better prepared to thwart his advances.

I invite you to follow me into a realm few Christians dare to enter. You'll explore the meaning of *evil* and discover the best ways to resist cults and the occult. You'll learn how to wage spiritual warfare by confronting Satan's kingdom. As a practical matter, you'll find out how to bind evil spirits, loose angels, and cast out demons. You'll read many stories about actual exorcisms I've encountered, so we can demystify the procedure of deliverance.

Be careful not to presumptuously engage in spiritual warfare. If you do, the protection of God's guidance might be excluded, as it was with the seven sons of Sceva (Acts 19:14–16). These arrogant exorcists tried to cast out demons without the apostle Paul's knowledge and authority. They didn't know Christ and acted in self-confidence. Demons attacked them and physically overpowered and disgraced them.

My prayer is that you'll understand that spiritual warfare isn't the exotic stuff of missionary stories, and it isn't the distorted caricature of Hollywood horror films. It's the command of Jesus and a privilege every Christian can experience. When you realize what Jesus meant by trampling on serpents and scorpions (Luke 10:19), you'll uncover a new life of faith in our God—who is big enough to handle anything the devil can do!

Before you read on, let me comment on some important guidelines I have followed in writing this book. This was a risky book to write. It was risky because some might use this information with the wrong motives or wrong assumptions. I've done my best to avoid that happening. This book is also precarious for those who want to blame their emotional problems on the demonic. They may forego appropriate counseling and embark on a fruitless round of exorcisms at the hands of well-meaning but misguided exorcists. This book is also hazardous for those who think every spiritual difficulty can be corrected by delving into deliverance. Pursuing such a misdiagnosis could result in irreparable mental harm to those who seek freedom from imagined evil forces.

This book is also risky for me. I have placed myself in jeopardy of having my motives and theology misunderstood. It would be safer to stay silent, but I've spoken for the sake of those who agonize alone because few dare speak about this unique area of ministry. Victims of unspeakable demonic torment must know that others like them have suffered, and that men and women of God will place their lives and reputations in peril for them.

Empathetically embracing victims of demonic possession involves more than heeding St. Augustine's plea to hate the sin and love the sinner. It requires understanding the human fault of underestimating the devil's cunning, and thus being fooled by his strategies. Don't despise those who have fallen prey to possession by devilish powers. You may think they are morally weaker or less spiritually cautious than you, and you may be right in some cases. But remember, their story might be yours, "but for the grace of God."

The narratives I have chosen were selected because they illustrate examples of the various ways demons operate. They were not picked because they represent any particular point I wish to make or any certain doctrinal position I want to proclaim. They were the best anecdotes I could recall to emphasize what I considered important to this study.

Please note that references to demons are made in the masculine. This is appropriate with respect to biblical terminology, although a certain androgyny is inherent to the character and function of evil spirits.

Don't think that by meticulously noting the circumstances of each account of deliverance, you can decipher any specific person's case history. In the interest of confidentiality, and out of respect for those who so courageously presented themselves for ministry, I have altered certain details surrounding each person's story. In all cases names have been changed. When it did not affect the authenticity of the description, I sometimes changed the sexual identity of the person. On occasion I also modified the geographical location and other factors, while always seeking to maintain essential scriptural and factual accuracy. The basic information of each case is faithful to the original occurrence. Above all I have made certain that the spiritual dynamics of each exorcism remained exact.

In some ways I regret referring to those possessed by demons as victims. I fear it could connote a certain helplessness, which might evoke a disdainful opinion from some readers, or it may suppose a lack of personal responsibility for their state. I finally settled on using the term *victim* because I frankly could not find another suitable word. I apologize to any "victims" of demonization who may be offended by this expression. These people are gallant warriors in the struggle against evil, and their lives have been battlefields.

I say in advance to those who will microscopically inspect every Scripture I quote and each story I tell: This book is not the final word on spiritual warfare. It is the record of my journey from the safe confines of traditional ministry into uncharted realms of offering hope to the hopeless. I've made mistakes along the way, but I have done what I could, when I could, to set at liberty those who have been bruised by Satan (Luke 4:18).

If you find what's written on these pages difficult to accept, please don't judge me. Pray for me. I'm still struggling to discern God's purpose in calling me to such an awesome task. I aspire not to be an expert on demons and deliverance, but a student of the Holy Spirit, always seeking to learn more about His love for fallen humanity.

I don't have all the answers, but I do know that the spiritual battle lines of our age are not between believers of different persuasions. Christians are combatants in a conflict between good and evil, light and darkness, God and the devil. This war, against all the evil being done in the name of Satan, has already been won in the name of Jesus.

Chapter 4

The Devil Made Them Do It

Henry Lee Lucas's life of crime began when he stabbed and strangled his seventy-four-year-old mother before raping her dead body. By the mid-'80s, Lucas was considered one of the most notorious serial killers of our time. He claimed to have killed 360 people using, as he said, "most every way but poison." He admitted to shooting, stabbing, burning, beating, strangling, hanging, and crucifying his victims. Yet Henry was convicted of only three murders, including that of his common-law wife, Becky Powell, whom he killed when she was only fourteen.

He now claims 600 murders he confessed to was a number inflated to titillate authorities. The truth will probably never be known, but Henry knows why he did what he did. He says the devil made him do it. At least that's what he told me face-to-face.

Before Lucas was remanded to the Texas state penal system, he was housed for a short while in a small jailhouse in central Texas. Lucas heard my nationally syndicated radio broadcast and asked to meet with me.

Sitting in the cell with a condemned killer, without anyone in sight, was one of the eeriest experiences of my life. Lucas had nothing to lose by harming me, so I was understandably uneasy. I listened for hours as this uneducated drifter spun yarns about child abduction and white slavery cults.

Though Lucas said he never went beyond grade school, he seemed quite bright. He described in detail the way he dispatched various victims, and how underground satanic death cults trained him. I didn't know then—and I still don't know—how much of that is to be believed. But the one thing I do believe is that Satan controlled Henry Lee Lucas's life. He said so unequivocally, and his life of crime bears testimony to some out-of-control malevolent force within him.

Henry told me how he would murder one victim after another for days on end. He was indiscriminate in his targets. Some were children he'd abducted from playgrounds. One woman was raped and killed in a shopping center parking lot. Hitchhikers were the easiest to kill, and Lucas had forgotten how many of them had died at his hands. Lucas killed men, women, and children of all races and classes.

Henry put it this way. "At the time of the murders I was completely numb. I was like an ice cube. It was like being out of my body, almost like being unconscious. It felt good. I couldn't even see the person's body lying there. All I could see was an image.

"As long as I was near the body, I couldn't get my feelings back. So, to keep on killing without remorse, I would cut off part of the body and carry it with me while I went on to commit other crimes. One time I drove for days with a man's head, covered by a coat, lying on the passenger seat of my car."

I wanted to call for a guard, I was so repulsed by what he was saying, but I stayed because Henry said I was the one person he wanted to know the whole story.

"I would kill as many as ten people in one day," he continued with an icy stare. Henry looked at me to see my reaction to his revelation. He had an eerie gaze, since one eye was fake. I had trouble believing that he could muster the energy and the evil cunning to kill ten victims in one day! When he murdered, Henry must have been truly a crazy, demon-possessed man.

I glanced around the room to see if there were any sharp objects at his disposal.

Lucas must have known what I was thinking. "Don't worry," he said. "They won't even let me have a mirror in here." He pointed to a polished piece of flat metal hanging on the bars. "That's what I use to see myself when I shave . . . and I have to return the razor they give me when I'm finished."

I motioned for him to go on with his story.

"I went days without sleeping," he continued. "Then, when I got rid of the body part, I could finally quit killing and go to sleep."

"Why did you do it, Henry? Was it for the thrill of killing or was there some larger purpose?"

"I didn't mean to kill my mother. She tried to hit me, and I struck back. It was the same thing with Becky. I was overcome with rage . . ." His voice trailed off in a tone that sounded like regret.

"What about all the others you killed?"

"They were different." Henry leaned forward, and his voice lowered to nearly a whisper, as if he were afraid someone might hear him. "All the others I killed were done for the satanic cult I became part of."

I sat back in my chair, somewhat skeptical. Serial killers like Henry Lee Lucas are notorious con artists and telling the truth isn't something they do with consistency. Typically, they deny the evil they do and the pain they cause their victims.

"You have to kill to get into the cult," Henry explained. "As a satanic ritual, a child was kidnapped once a year and crucified alive. Our purpose was to reincarnate the devil as the ruler of earth. In exchange, the devil allowed me to go undetected. I even passed lie detector tests. I would sit across the street and watch the police investigate my victims, but no one ever questioned me. I wouldn't be in this cell today if I hadn't turned myself in."

Henry wasn't the first person to tell me about the murderous activities of secret satanic cults. His details of ritual killings squared with everything others had related. He described how victims were systematically tortured to prove the loyalty cult members had to Satan. The particulars about certain sexually depraved ceremonies were so similar to narratives I'd heard from ritual abuse victims it was uncanny.

Psychiatrists and even playwrights have come up with their own explanations for Lucas's crimes: suppressed homosexuality, the abusive upbringing of his prostitute mother, and his penchant for attention, which could only be satisfied by being exceedingly bad. Yet during the long hours we conversed, Henry returned again and again to the theme that Satan had made a pact with him, and he fulfilled his part of the agreement by murdering his fellow human beings.

Others insist that Lucas is just a storyteller, cleverly attributing the responsibility for his murderous actions to an unidentifiable cult. That may or may not be true, but I believe some want to ignore what Henry says because they can't admit that more than genetic and social influences skew certain people toward the dark side. No one could kill his mother and wife in cold blood and not have a serious evil influence.

As I spent those long hours in Lucas's cell, one thought came to me again and again. *Henry Lee Lucas was at one time a harmless child.* What made him a merciless killer? Are there other Lucases growing up in homes where the evil around them is indoctrinating them into a life of aberrant behavior? What makes them become so disturbed in their minds, emotions, and spirits?

There are answers for some of these questions. Other potential serial killers are just waiting to happen. They are consumed with a combustible mixture of anger and rage, and who knows what spark will ignite their crime spree. The absence of love in some families is so heartrending that one instant of rejection, one blow to the body, one rebuff at a time of emotional vulnerability, one employer termination is all that's needed to create another Henry Lee Lucas. No one will ever know what goes on inside the homes and hearts of these people, the full extent of the evil that is harbored there.

I found three recent stories in the news especially troubling.

UNSETTLING EVENTS IN THE NEWS

In Silsbee, Texas, eleven children, ages eight to fourteen, harassed and chased a horse in a pasture for hours until he dropped from sheer exhaustion, tangled in barbed wire. Mr. Wilson Boy was an old brown horse that no one would normally think of harming. No one, that is, except these eleven youngsters. When the owners of Mr. Wilson Boy arrived on the scene, they found their beloved quarter horse lying on the ground with a broken leg and sharp sticks rammed up his nostrils as the children's final bit of torture.

The youngsters, who clubbed the horse to death, returned to their elementary and junior high classes the next day and laughed about what they had done. They even thought it was "cool" to be arrested at school. Their remorselessness shocked the 6,300 residents of Silsbee, where the most common offense was a traffic ticket.

This cruel and senseless slaughter of a beautiful quarter horse raises the disturbing question: How were these children raised that they would do such a thing? Residents claimed they were all from "normal" homes.

The same question might be asked of thirty youths at a Castle Rock, Colorado, keg party. Tanked on beer, a group of teenagers stumbled upon what they thought was an unconscious, injured man. Unbeknownst to them, the person they abused was already dead. One of the group even urinated on the corpse, and then they left it without notifying anyone. Not one of the youngsters called to get help.

The local sheriff commented, "I've been in this business twenty-eight years and this is shocking. It really makes you wonder about kids today." In the aftermath, the only thing that could be done was to charge one of the participants with the abuse of a corpse. Again, these were the children of upstanding families.

Another more serious case involved two teenagers in White Cloud, Michigan, who killed a seventy-three-year-old man, then partied and showed his body to at least ten friends. The police didn't learn of the incident until four days later when relatives discovered the remains. The citizens of White Cloud were left to wonder how so many kids could have seen a murder victim's body and not told the authorities or even their parents.

I am bothered, of course, by the serious crimes involved in these incidents, especially the murder of the man. I am also concerned about the apathy exhibited by the young people who saw the evidence and did nothing. Such flagrant disregard says something dangerous about the rationale these young people live by. Can you imagine what reaction you would expect from your child if someone showed a corpse to him or her?

Most who hear about such horrible deeds point a finger at the home. They say there is a breakdown of the family. That's true, but we need to be more specific. The heart of the problem is the dismissal of God from the daily lives of parents and children. That is the true evil among us.

Confronted by the problems of the family, politicians blame a broad array of national ills and promise more money, at taxpayers' expense, to right such wrongs. Psychologists fill the news reports with sound bites about abuse statistics and grim deductions forecasting social disintegration. Reporters and columnists suggest any number of solutions.

Some point to the influence of the media and Hollywood, which have certainly stoked the fire by making heroes of villains. But if Hollywood cleans up its act, will that alone heal the home? I don't think so. Unfortunately, the problem is rooted deep in our society.

WHAT IS EVIL—DO WE KNOW ANY LONGER?

Horrific occurrences like those in Silsbee, Castle Rock, and White Cloud get buried in the back pages of our newspapers because the idea of evil is not easily accepted by today's culture. The mention of it does creep into our language occasionally. For example, President Bill Clinton called the Oklahoma City federal building bombers "evil cowards." In another instance, President Ronald Reagan was at first vilified, and then lionized, for helping to bring about the downfall of what he called the "evil empire"— the Soviet Union. Shakespeare scripted Mark Anthony's speech over Julius Caesar's body with the words, "The evil that men do lives after them." His audience of Londoners probably understood the notion of evil better than most psychiatrists—and most of us—do today.

Even the dictionary is no help in clarifying the word *evil*, for it uses synonyms such as *sinful* and *wicked*, words that are equally taboo in our age.

It's not enough to talk about evil in ambiguous terms, like Supreme Court Justice Stewart Potter, who defined *pornography* by saying, "I know it when I see it." A humanistic culture may never put its finger on what makes men do evil things. Still, that doesn't stop most from concluding that men do evil, and something—or someone—encourages them to do so.

The real tragedy is that few of the custodians of our culture are willing to say conclusively what is right and wrong. None will suggest there is anything like ultimate truth. They avoid using absolute moral terms like *evil* and *sin* because they are believed to be too judgmental for our "enlightened" culture.

When considering the behavior of the youth in Silsbee, Castle Rock, and White Cloud, I am bold enough to suggest that the devil made them do it, and their parents allowed the devil to do so!

This doesn't exonerate the youth from responsibility for their actions. "Each of us shall give account of himself to God," Romans

14:12 reminds us. To credit Satan as the origin of evil isn't the same as conceding to the comedic quip, "The devil made me do it." Instead, it gives the devil his due by admitting that human depravity alone can't account for the sheer outrageousness of some sinister deeds.

The higher-self advocates of our modern world have convinced many that cruel insensitivities are more the failure of people not yielding to the better angels of their nature than their being tempted by an evil adversary. I often wonder what these "seek your inner divine consciousness" types would say to the victim of satanic ritual abuse who told me of being buried alive in a coffin filled with snakes, surviving only by the use of a breathing tube sticking out of the ground.

What about the five year old who told me that satanists held her hands tightly around the handle of a dagger, which was plunged into the heart of her playmate? Her innocence was destroyed by the demon-possessed members of a generational Luciferian cult whose leaders believed such depravity was the only way to please their lord, the devil. These satanists were driven by the indwelling presence of evil, not merely the absence of good.

To the non-Christian, cruelties like the Cambodian killing fields are beyond rational accountability. The thought of three million people being genocidally slaughtered and their corpses hurriedly thrown in mass graves is unfathomable. The nonbeliever can only conclude that someone like Pol Pot, the deceased communist Khmer Rouge leader who perpetrated this evil, was insane or genetically aberrant. The humanists who dominate our age cannot bear to think that someone who directed the torture and murder of millions was inhabited by dark forces.

As for me, it's obvious I believe Satan is real. Whether or not our society chooses to acknowledge him doesn't change the fact that evil is ultimately embodied in a personal, malignant creature who tempts, torments, oppresses, and possesses humans.

WHO IS SATAN?

The identity of the devil is shrouded in myth, often eclipsing the biblical reality of a personal creature devoid of goodness. In literature and legend he is known as the Adversary, the Prince of Darkness, Slewfoot, Mephistopheles, and Old Scratch. The Bible refers to him as Satan, Lucifer, and the devil, the progenitor of pride, instigator of avarice, font of folly, source of seduction, origin of temptation, and evocator of evil. Human language seems inadequate to characterize what is unthinkable to the human conscience: absolute immorality incarnated in depravity.

Ezekiel 28:13–17 describes in detail his original state. He was exquisitely clothed, a master musician, and an anointed angel of the cherubim class who walked in the presence of God. He knew the perfection of Eden before the Fall and caused the stars to dance with his symphonies of adoration before God's throne. He was so beautiful that his very radiance became the source of pride that led to his fall.

From Isaiah 14:12–15, we learn that sometime after Creation, the idea lodged in Satan's heart to be like God, the Most High. As a result, war raged in the heavens, and Satan was successful in persuading at least one-third of heaven's angels to concur with his insurrection (Rev. 12:4). Since that time the devil has roamed the earth seeking vengeance upon the Almighty by tempting and ravaging man, the beloved of God's creation. Lucifer's emissaries of evil, the corrupted angels who rebelled and fell with him, are demons doing his bidding to oppose God's eternal purposes.

THE VALUE OF ACCURATE INFORMATION

My goal is to provide you with inside information on how the devil's kingdom of darkness operates so that you can effectively combat him when the need arises. In the world we live in today, you can be sure that someday, somewhere, that time will come.

In the heat of the spiritual warfare of an exorcism a demon once taunted me, "You'll never be able to speak about what went on tonight. No one would believe you, and that's our most powerful tool." If I have learned anything in all my years of dealing with demons it is that satanic spirits count on the human incapability of imagining anything being as evil as they are.

What starts out as just a little evil, like the killing of Mr. Wilson Boy, the quarter horse, can eventually grow to gigantic proportion. We cannot let "the devil made them do it" be the final spiritual epitaph of this generation. If we as a society can comprehend the cause for some of the outrageous behavior pervading our culture, we can begin to cure it.

Chapter 5

The Evil That Demons Do

Fifteen-year-old Andrew Merritt calmly loaded a shotgun in his upstairs bedroom, then tiptoed downstairs where his mother lay sleeping on the couch. He placed the barrel of the gun to her head and shot her twice. Then he and a friend left her body where it was and fled in her car to Mexico.

Only a few miles into the trip, one of the car tires blew out and stranded the boys in the middle of a field. Andrew used his mother's car phone to notify authorities about what had happened. Police found him looking at the photo on his mother's driver's license, with tears streaming down his cheeks. "The devil made me do it," was all that he muttered as they handcuffed him and took him to jail.

Andrew told his lawyer that Satan had appeared to him out of a fireball, which came from a black hole, as he listened to a death metal band singing a tune entitled, "Go to Hell." ("My only friend's the goat, with 666 between his horns.") The devil told Andrew to hasten his demonic return to earth by killing all

Christians, and to begin with his mother, who was a devout Christian.

His lawyer, a man who personally explained the case to me, put it this way: "Whether or not Andrew saw the devil, or thinks he did, really makes little difference. The music made him think he was in contact with something evil that took control. He believed it enough to kill for it. I'm faced with the fact that the influence of Satan can't be considered a mitigating influence in a court of law, and we have no effective defense for the case."

Today, Andrew languishes in a mental institution. His suicidal impulses are controlled by daily drug injections, and his hallucinations about the devil are stronger than ever. If he ever sees the outside world again, it won't be until after his forty-fifth birthday. He will certainly need extensive spiritual counseling to heal his troubled soul if he is to survive on the outside.

Andrew was a seemingly normal boy from a good Christian home. He may have had deeper psychological problems with one or more members of his family; but on the surface, we assume this tragedy should not have happened, not in this family. However, I believe other forces were at work in the Merritt household, undermining all the good intentions of Andrew's Christian upbringing.

I've met many young people who have been swayed by Satan. They are primed by adolescent rebellion and fueled by the antiparental invectives of some rock and rap lyrics; sometimes they fantasize about eradicating their parents so they can gain control over their lives. Most youth pass through this dangerous phase and move on to a more sane outlook. A dangerous few allow these obsessions to dominate their thinking.

In the hundreds of cases of demon possession I have dealt with, I can cite several dozen that involved teenagers who seriously considered killing their parents. When I faced their demons directly, the evil spirits told me of the detailed murder plans. Was there a man or woman of God who missed the chance to intervene in Andrew Merritt's case?

I met Andrew's pastor, the minister whose church Andrew's mother also attended and the man who conducted her funeral. I believe he was sincere when he told me, "I never saw anything that could have warned me of such consequences. If Andrew's mother could speak from the grave, I'm certain she would warn Christian parents not to assume that what happened to her couldn't happen to them."

I believe that crimes like those of Andrew Merritt could be curtailed if we understood how evil influences our lives. It's so simple if we just face it directly! Evil comes from the influence of the world, the flesh, and the devil and his demons.

THE WORLD

In spite of his diligence to oppose God's kingdom, Satan isn't sufficient in himself. The adversary is limited in time and space and he isn't omnipotent, so he must use a number of fallen spirits to do his bidding. He's playing for big stakes and may not send a particular demon on a mission to seduce one human. Therefore, he relies on the evil influence of his extended world system to pervert human behavior.

Christians often refer to the influences of "the world" as "worldliness" and quote as their pretext: "Do not love the world or the things in the world" (1 John 2:15). Friendship with the world is enmity with God, James 4:4 tells us.

When asked what the "world" is, most Christians respond with specifics, referring to whatever behavior their particular religious tradition has labeled as worldly. But specific behavior, such as drinking, smoking, dancing, and substance abuse, does not represent the world's system of spiritual conflict.

The true battle with evil is described clearly in the Bible. Ephesians, chapter 6, tells us that "principalities," "powers," and the "rulers of the darkness of this age" are in charge of our world. This Scripture refers to Satan's system of supernatural activity, which is organized spiritually and geographically. Certain principalities control particular countries and cities. (For example, Daniel 10 refers to the spirits "prince of Persia" and "prince of Greece.") Other powers direct their attention to designated sectors of society, such as the political and academic realms. Rulers of darkness focus on certain industries like entertainment and pornography. Demons with specialized abilities work their evil where they are most effective.

THE FLESH

The devil often sits back and lets the flesh do his dirty deeds. Unrestrained human sexuality can turn the beauty of intimacy into something ugly through pornography. In this case, the fallen nature of man's evil desire turns humanity toward evil without any active intervention from Satan. As James 1:14 points out, "Each one is tempted when he is drawn away by his *own* desires" (emphasis added).

Blaming everything on the devil is a precarious cop-out. The flesh—man's own lust—can accomplish much evil without active demonic intervention. On death row, serial killer Ted Bundy confessed that the influence of pornography had driven him to murder. When the homes of child molesters are raided, the police seldom find stacks of the *Wall Street Journal*. What they discover is hard-core porn, the obvious link to their perverted behavior.

The temptation of Christ in Matthew 4:1–11 clearly shows that the devil also directly appeals to our human weaknesses. Jesus had fasted forty days and forty nights when Satan tempted Him by suggesting that He turn stones into bread. This was a straightforward appeal to His hungering body. Today, men and women with human weaknesses are tempted by the images of erotic sexuality that flood our newsstands and saunter across the screens of our television sets. "Sex sells" isn't an advertising slogan born on Wall Street; it's an epigram conceived in the depths of hell based on temptations of the flesh.

In order to ward off the seductive appeal of the flesh, we need to lean on the promises of God to overcome our internal propensity to sin. The murder of Andrew Merritt's mother might have been prevented if young Andrew had truly understood the significance of 1 Corinthians 10:13: "No temptation has overtaken you except such as is common to man; but God is faithful, who will not allow you to be tempted beyond what you are able, but with the temptation will also make the way of escape, that you may be able to bear it." But then again, he may have committed his mind to Satan beyond the normal ability to resist temptation.

As I've just pointed out, some will sin as a result of the world's wretched standards of ethics and morals. Others will yield to temptation because their own flesh draws them inexorably toward depravity. But some may not fall into Satan's plans, even though the world and the flesh tempt them. These are the ones who need an extra inducement from the devil and his demons.

THE DEVIL AND HIS DEMONS

I believe that much of the degeneracy of our age is the direct result of the devil and his demons, who are dedicated to the goal of arousing desire for the forbidden. So what are these demons like?

WHAT IS A DEMON?

The very mention of the word *demon* conjures images of gargoylish creatures of the night—complete with fangs, claws, and backs hunched by the weight of depravity. Many victims of possession claim they can see such creatures. Whereas our "normal" eyes cannot behold the spirit world, those who give themselves to the occult can somehow see beyond this veil or else have demon-induced visions.

On some occasions when demons have appeared during an exorcism, the victim has described the spirit as incredibly beautiful. This reminds us of Paul's warning in 2 Corinthians 11:14 that when it suits his purposes, the devil can transform himself into an "angel of light."

But this visible manifestation of a demon says nothing about the actual nature of these fallen angels. Both secular and religious history are filled with references to demons. The ancients, who were untouched by the Jewish scriptures, held demons in superstitious esteem. Animists placated them as capricious forces to be appeased, lest they retaliate in mischievous ways. The Greeks believed demons were the spirits of departed wicked men.

Three theories: Pre-Adamic race, mongrels, or fallen angels Some Bible scholars say that demons are either the spirits of a pre-Adamic race or the offspring of evil angels who cohabited with human women (the Gen. 6 theory).

The pre-Adamic theory states that in Genesis 1:1 God created a perfect earth at some indistinguishable point in the past According to the theory, between verses 1 and 2 of the first chapter of Genesis, a cataclysm occurred, which was God's judgment on evil humanity. The spirits of this wicked race were disembodied and roamed the earth seeking humans to possess.

The cohabitation hypothesis is based on a unique interpretation of Genesis 6:1–2, which theorizes that evil fallen angels sexually commingled with certain human females before the Flood. This perverted union resulted in mongrels who were part human and part demonic, the genetically mutated giants of Genesis 6:4. The Flood subsequently destroyed the natural bodies of these monsters, leaving their spirits to seek human possession and habitation.

I agree that Genesis 6 describes a sexual linkage between demons and humans, which produced humanoid offspring. That is one reason for the severity of God's judgment in destroying the earth with a worldwide flood. However, I also believe that the death of these creatures at that time ended both their physical existence and their spiritual freedom. They were sent to a special prison (2 Peter 2:4; Jude 6).

In all my years of dealing with demons, I have never encountered a case that contradicts my conclusion about the origin of evil spirits: They are angels who fell from their estate as did Lucifer (Ezek. 28:11–19; Isa. 14:12–15). Approximately one-third of all created angels succumbed to the devil's pleas of insurrection against God (Rev. 12:4), and they are now his emissaries of evil (Matt. 25:41—"the devil and his angels").

Free vs. confined to hell. There is some evidence that the angels who fell with Lucifer are relegated to one of two states. Some appear to be free to roam the earth in search of human prey, while others are confined to Tartarus, or hell (2 Peter 2:4). The sin that confined these demons isn't clear from Scripture. Perhaps Jude, verse 6, refers to these demons ("angels who did not keep their proper domain . . . He has reserved in everlasting chains"). This may indicate that they are the ones who sexually cohabited with humans in Genesis 6.

The question "What is a demon?" must also address the nature of its character.

THE UNIQUE DEGENERACY OF DEMONS

Demons were created in God's image as was man, who is "a little lower than the angels" (Ps. 8:5). Consequently, demons have intellectual prowess and a will that determine their conduct. This individual distinctiveness extends to their personal identity. Each demon has a name and the capacity to speak (except in the case of mute demons). They also possess considerable emotion. James 2:19 describes them as not only believing in God, an indication of intelligent conviction, but also trembling at the thought of divine existence.

Wherever demons are spoken of in Scripture, they are depraved —"unclean" (Matt. 10:1); "wickedness" (Eph. 6:12); "evil" (Luke 7:21). Even though I've heard the voices of thousands of demons as they responded to my demands in the name of Christ, not one has ever expressed any desire to be different from what he is. Demons have listened while I led their victims to Christ, but no demon has ever asked to be a recipient of God's grace. Their condition is obviously one of unique degeneracy, a predicament that consigns them to a permanently unclean condition. In short, no demon can ever be saved from sin. Demons have no equivalent payment for sin on their behalf. Furthermore, not one has ever expressed any regret for his actions.

The moral nature of demons compels them to ceaselessly oppose God's kingdom and fight against His redeemed servants. They do so as invisible creatures, even though they may manifest visibly on occasion, just as the angels of the Lord appeared to man (Gen. 19:15; Luke 1:26). Though they may assume a mask of righteousness and beauty, the Bible illustrates that their true image is ghastly and abhorrent (Rev. 9:7–10).

THE SUPERNATURAL POWER OF DEMONS

As you will discover in this book, demons have extraordinary supernatural powers. Their physical strength far surpasses that of mortals. The demoniac of Gadara was so strong that shackles and chains couldn't confine him. He broke them in pieces and "neither could anyone tame him" (Mark 5:4).

This supernatural power extends itself to acts that seem to defy all natural laws of physics. Second Thessalonians, chapter 2, warns of the "power, signs, and lying wonders" that demons will manifest during the Tribulation. These paranormal phenomena include the healing of a wound that inflicts death (Rev. 13:12), creating fire that falls from heaven (Rev. 13:13), and animating a material object so that it speaks as if it were human (Rev. 13:15).

Demons are not bound by physical barriers. A legion of demons dwelled inside one man (Luke 8:30), indicating that thousands of them can coexist in the same confinement. Perhaps they are no more than minute dots in space, lending some credibility to the ancient conjecture that many angels can dance on the head of a pin.

Demons are obviously not bound by spatial limitation since

they can enter the material body of a victim. They can also travel from one location to the next almost instantaneously. I have dealt with demons who summoned assistance from spirits in other countries and these unclean spirits appeared almost instantaneously.

The most important thing to note about the nature of demons is their consistent devotion to Satan's purposes and their unilateral opposition to God. Because of this, they express complete certitude about spiritual matters. No demon I've dealt with has ever denied that the Bible is God's inerrant Word. None have ever questioned the deity of Christ or His authority over them. Their character is consistent: utter contempt for their victims, bitter hatred for the person ministering deliverance, and absolute loathing for Jesus and the Holy Spirit.

Demons incite sin in the hearts of the morally weak: lust, homosexuality, pedophilia, and adultery. That's not to say that every such vice is necessarily demonic, but it may be more times than we are willing to admit.

I have an important question for every parent reading this book: When was the last time you talked to *your* children about the devil? Could it be that Satan and sex are the two most taboo subjects in the Christian home? I'm not suggesting that Christian families be preoccupied with negative discussions about what the devil does; however, most Christian parents will have to admit they seldom, if ever, take time to tell their children there is a real devil who seeks to seduce, especially those who follow the Lord.

Our children must have a sense of sin and a comprehension that Satan is seeking to steal, kill, and destroy. They need to be told how despicable Satan is, and how clever he is in his plans to deceive them. The purpose for such a conversation is not to have our children focus on evil things. Our emphasis should be to keep the eyes of our families on things that are "true ... noble ... just ... pure ... lovely ... praiseworthy" (Phil. 4:8). But the Bible also commands us to "expose" the "works of darkness" (Eph. 5:11) and be "wise as serpents" (Matt 10:16).

Children need to know that evil spirits sometimes cause perverted behavior. It's not enough to warn them to avoid immoral actions.

CAN SOMEONE HAVE A DEMON WITHOUT KNOWING?

"Can a person have a demon and not know it?" may be one of the most fundamental questions asked about deliverance. The answer is yes. In fact, when people calmly ask me if they have a demon, their inquiry is usually an indication that they do not. While demons may feel obligated to challenge me while I am praying with a person, they will not normally advertise their presence if they are not threatened.

Some who are possessed *do* know that they have demons because they have seen them. These people usually have come out of a background in the occult where specific demons were summoned and appeared upon invocation. Others may know they have demons because they hear voices in their heads. Certain individuals can actually hear conversations between various demons. Others lose time because of demons having put them in a trance, and they wonder if such oblivion is the result of an evil spirit's presence. (Hearing voices and losing time can also be a symptom of dissociative disorder, which will be discussed later in the book.)

Generally, the person who has a demon knows he has serious spiritual problems that have defied all of his efforts to rectify. He may even have wondered if the root of his difficulties might be demonic. Most have never given serious consideration to the chance they are possessed. After all, who would really want to contemplate such a conclusion?

CHARACTER OVERCOMES THE DEVIL

One of the things that has amazed me about demons is that some people have committed inconceivably immoral acts without being controlled by demonic forces. I have known individuals who have gone so far as to offer human sacrifices in the name of Satan—yet demons, it seems, were never able to enter them. Other victims of the devil became possessed through seemingly lesser sins. Eric was one of them.

I encountered Eric while I was speaking at a strict fundamentalist Baptist church. He approached me, saying that an unusual anger had overcome him as I spoke. He wondered why he hated me so intensely, when as a devout Christian he should have been pleased by my presentation.

Later as I spoke to him I caught a flash of the demonic look in Eric's eyes, and found it a strange contrast to his reticent demeanor. Eric was slightly built and seemed to lack self-confidence. The demon's gaze was belligerent and spiteful. The change was so complete, no actor could have mimicked such a radical personality transformation. With Eric in a trance, the evil spirit defiantly confronted me with a loathing I have seldom seen, even in the cases of outright satanists.

The most curious thing that I discovered about Eric's possession was how it occurred. Months earlier, on his high school prom night, he lost his virginity in the backseat of a car. "That's when I entered him," the demon of lust explained.

I realize that many other teenagers have fallen into sexual sin and in some cases lived inordinately promiscuous lives, without ever granting a demon the right of entry. Why was Eric so easily overcome by such a common sin? I'm convinced the answer was his lack of moral fortitude and submission, perhaps, to the spirit inhabiting his sex partner.

If the core of a person's identity is strong-willed, it seems harder for a demon to take over, no matter what that person does. On the other hand, some people are "easy." Easy to talk into anything. Easy to bend the rules, easy to hang out with the wrong crowd, easy to compromise a principle, even though they may not actually step far over the line of transgression.

Why hadn't Eric's demon spent its time inhabiting a child

molester or a porn star? Because Eric was easy to invade, and the others who committed more heinous sins may not have been so compliant. That thing we call character, the defining force of our soul's will, is the final gateway to the human spirit. When the soul and character of a person have not been strengthened by a positive self-image, the constitution of that person is more vulnerable to not only the world and the flesh, but also the devil.

Parents can't supervise their children twenty-four hours a day, but they *can* instill in them a sense of godly character, a gift their children can carry inside their hearts all their lives. In a world that extols getting ahead at any cost, we must emphasize the value of ethics and absolute standards. From babyhood on, children need to be positively reinforced with a sense of their value as creations of God who are destined for spiritual greatness. They need to know they are loved and accepted for who they are in God's eyes. And they need to be prayed over, and with, on a daily basis. They will then be less susceptible to the influence of demons.

This affirmation needs to come from their parents. I believe that fathers and stay-at-home mothers play a crucial role in protecting our children. I know it is not always possible for parents to be with their children as much as they would wish, but when there is a choice between working to acquire things and spending time with one's children, the answer is easy. Spending time with your children is the best investment you can make to ward off supernatural evil influences.

I don't want to stir up unwarranted alarm by suggesting that Satan can influence any emotionally disturbed Christian kid to commit murder, as Andrew Merritt did. My goal is to speak to those who may think their rebellious offspring is just going through a phase, when the child may be in urgent need of spiritual counseling.

To protect ourselves and our children from the devil, we need to have a more perceptive understanding of what evil is all about. Evil is a matter of conduct, not just a state of mind. We must see the signs that Merritt's mother missed, and not be blind to a loved one's aberrant behavior.

My guess is that a closer examination of Merritt's life and surroundings would have produced additional clues. Most rebellious youth cover their bedroom walls with posters of satanic rock bands. They often keep a journal of occult sayings, rituals, and deeds. Their rooms may contain paraphernalia such as daggers, bones, skulls, chalices, and black candles. They may experiment with drugs and dress in black. They're especially fond of T-shirts with gruesome artwork about death and torment. This is not to suggest that any one or more of these indicators mean a teenager is about to commit a heinous act. But these warning signs should prompt parents to take immediate inventory of the emotional and spiritual health of their child.

Teenagers could be overcome by evil impulses, even to the point of contemplating parricide, without realizing how truly satanic such thoughts really are. The devil hears when they snarl under their breath, "I wish you were dead!" They may entertain thoughts of getting even in violent ways without considering that those thoughts are demonic.

We must never forget that evil is a real threat to us, and that the devil is constantly seeking to devour God's children (1 Peter 5:8)— in the name of Satan.

PART II

Satanism and the Occult in Contemporary Society

Chapter 6

Musical Messengers of Satan

I'll murder for the devil. I'm just waiting."

"Waiting for what?" I asked.

Unfortunately, David's boastful claim wasn't new to me. I'd heard the same swagger from other teenagers involved in satanism. My immediate response in such instances is to find out if the teenager is just bragging or if he really means it.

"I'm seventeen now. If the devil makes me happy and gives me what I want until I'm nineteen, I'll kill as many people as he wants after that. I'll keep on doing it until I'm killed."

David called my radio talk show, *TALK-BACK with Bob Larson*, which I have hosted for more than sixteen years. The show provides a forum for controversial issues seldom discussed elsewhere in the media. Satanism is one of those subjects.

David expressed his point harshly. "I'm a satanist. How can you worship Jesus Christ when He was a criminal dying for His crimes?"

"What crime is it to love people, to die for them, to shed your blood for them?" I asked.

"I've bled for the devil," David responded calmly. "I've cut myself. I've also offered Satan the blood sacrifices of animals. To show my dedication to the devil, I've carved pentagrams and upside-down crosses on my arms."

"How did you do that?"

"With razor blades and propane torches."

I kept probing David for more information, trying to discover how deeply he was dedicated to the devil. This knowledge would help me decide how to direct the conversation to counsel him.

"What else have you done for the devil?"

"Well," David answered, "I play in a black metal band called Eternal Death."

"What do you sing about?"

"'Unholy Rites' is one of the songs I've written. It's about sex with corpses," David told me. "Our satanic group digs up bodies in the graveyard."

"How did you hear about this show?" I wondered out loud.

"I was just flipping through the radio dial and heard you talking about Slayer. They're my favorite rock band. I heard you're going to be on tour with them next week."

"How did you start listening to Slayer?"

"When I was young, Slayer brought satanism into my life. It's because of their music that I worship the devil. Their lyrics introduced me to Lord Satan. They made me what I am. The words of their songs are the most important thing to me.

"A lot of other kids are like me. Slayer fans think the band members are gods. They worship them like crazy. If you want my advice, you'd better not go on tour with them. You might get hurt if their fans find out who you are.

"One more thing," David added. "Ask them if they're really satanists, 'cause if they're not, they're phony and I'm not going to listen to them anymore."

The account I will describe occurred ten years ago when the musical genre of satanic metal music was at the height of its popularity, and bands like Slayer were selling millions of records. I am including this narrative because it chronicles a critical phenomenon that introduced today's young parents to a musical immersion in the occult. The seeds sown by pop musicians extolling the vices of ungodliness influenced a generation whose easy acceptance of evil opened the door to our current climate of moral rootlessness.

STALKING SLAYER

A few days before David the satanist called, my secretary had buzzed my office intercom to convey an unusual invitation.

"Bob Guccione Jr., publisher of the rock magazine *Spin*, is on the phone," she said. "He wants you to fly to West Germany and tour with Slayer so you can write a cover story for *Spin*. Will you take the call?"

"He wants what?" I was astonished. It was hard to believe the son of *Penthouse*'s publisher, who was also the publisher of his own highly successful rock periodical, would ask me to tour as a journalist with the most notorious satanic metal band in the world.

Guccione and I had gotten to know each other well. We first met when *TALK-BACK* was doing a series of shows about pornography. Guccione was my guest to debate those who wanted warning stickers on record albums with questionable lyrics. He was a repeat guest on several subsequent occasions when *TALK-BACK* discussed censorship.

This time, Guccione was inviting me to be his guest for an all-expense-paid trip to West Germany. That part was intriguing. What perplexed me was touring with Slayer.

"Guccione, what are you trying to do to me?" I kidded.

"The staff of *Spin* thinks it's a great idea. It's the ultimate irony, you and Slayer. We originally thought about sending you on tour with a black metal band called Death. But they weren't bad enough. Slayer has the worst reputation as a satanic metal band.

"Everything is cleared with their manager and record company. We've told them this will be a *Spin* feature story. You'll have artistic freedom to write what you want."

The idea was mind-boggling. Me, writing a cover story for one of America's top rock magazines. Me, on tour with a band that sings about necrophilia and lyrically declares, "Praise Satan." A once-in-a-lifetime opportunity to go behind the scenes on a rock 'n' roll tour.

"You'll have an all-access pass to go anywhere you want with the band," Guccione promised. "Backstage, in the dressing room, on the bus, in the audience, even on stage."

"Will you do it?" Guccione wanted to know.

I thought about the teenagers, whose fascination with satanism had started with Slayer. Here was a unique opportunity to get the facts.

"Okay," I agreed. "Tell me when and where to meet Slayer."

"You'll leave Friday the thirteenth for Hamburg via Frankfurt. Don't let them sacrifice you on an altar to Satan," Guccione joked. *Friday the thirteenth*, I thought to myself. *Hmm.*

Seventy-two hours later, I was on my way to meet the boys in the band who sing, "Warriors from the gates of hell . . . In Lord Satan we trust."

Is Slayer serious about Satan? I wondered. *Do they look forward to partying with the evil one in the eternal inferno?*

I soon found out. That night in Hamburg I saw my first Slayer concert, and all hell broke loose.

WARRIORS OF HELL IN HAMBURG

To chants of "Slayer, Slayer," the band came on stage, appropriately dressed in black. Guitarist Kerry King wore a leather shin guard embedded with steel studs in the form of an inverted cross. Guitarist

Jeff Hanneman sported a T-shirt saying, "Slaytanic Wehrmacht" (war machine). Drummer Dave Lombardo wore a tank top and shorts. Vocalist Tom Araya's T-shirt declared, "Sex, Murder, Art."

Slayer picked a poor place to play for the devil. The hall was cavernous and cold. It had a thirty-foot ceiling and no heat. Inside, the temperature was about fifty degrees. Backstage, Slayer shivered, hunkered down like four lost sheep far from home.

Moments later onstage, they became fire-breathing demons from rock 'n' roll hell. In the midst of fog machines and the thunderous roar of three thousand fans, they exuded the embodiment of evil. They must have practiced for hours in front of mirrors to effect their snarls of contempt for decency.

"Guten Nacht!" Araya yelled, attempting a little German.

The fans roared approval. He could have spoken Swahili for all they cared. Slayer fans weren't there for small talk. They wanted to hear the songs of Satan sung syllable for syllable, note for note, just like on their records. The fans lip-synched the words, although the majority had no idea what they were saying.

No one in the band appeared nervous. They had obviously been through this a zillion times. The lighting man played his big board like a virtuoso pianist. First, the blue light on Araya, then the yellow spot on King. Next, Hanneman stepped to the foot of the stage at a spot marked "X," one of many locations on the floor where masking tape was pasted to show members of the band where to stand for the right spotlight. A red spot shone upward under Hanneman's chin creating eerie shadows, as he glowered menacingly.

The audience scowled back. They were a beer-buzzed, wasted bunch that the band referred to backstage as "German vermin." Their metal regalia openly invited evil. There were thousands of jean jackets, backs emblazoned with demonic depictions: horned goat-man (baphomet) symbols of Satan, gruesome images of devils, and more upside-down crosses than a denizen of demons could concoct in a month. One strange picture on the back of a jean jacket depicted a naked woman lying on her back, legs spread apart at the junction of an inverted crucifix. Black magic pentagrams declared, "Welcome to hell." Where else would Lucifer feel more welcome?

Behind Slayer, centered above the drummer, the stage backdrop featured their stylized pentagram logo. On each side of the satanic symbol were two six-foot stained-glass windows superimposed with a cross—upside down, of course.

The group began with "Hell Awaits." "Jesus knows your soul cannot be saved," they sang. "Crucify the so-called Lord!"

Next they sang "Black Magic," in which they claimed to be "captive of a force of Satan's might . . . Death takes my hand and captures my soul."

Later songs, such as "Evil Has No Boundaries," were overt invocations to the devil: "Satan our master in evil mayhem guides us with every first step."

No wonder teens like Dave began to worship Satan after playing these songs over and over again on their Walkmans and ghetto blasters.

The deafening roar of 120 decibels (112 is the pain threshold) was like standing next to a jet taking off. Slayer launched into "Spill the Blood": "Spill your blood, let it run on to me. Take my hand and let go of your life . . . You've spilt the blood. I have your soul."

How odd that the madness of black metal mania would strike in West Germany, a country that once boasted Europe's richest cultural heritage, the land of Bach and Beethoven. Before the parents of Slayer fans were born, however, Nazi insanity unleashed an onslaught of evil that knew no reasonable bounds. Demagogic rallies and sterile architecture promoted the Aryan ideal. Mass psychology triumphed over reason.

Clearly, Slayer's brand of black metal music was breeding the same insensitivity to logic. For the Nazis, it was the swastika. For Slayer, the pentagram. Another symbol of evil was once again inciting legions of the discontented to overthrow an existing order. What other conclusion could I draw, hearing Slayer sing "Altar of Sacrifice," which described the human sacrifice of a virgin with lines like, "Satan's slaughter, ceremonial death. Answer his every command. Enter to the realm of Satan . . . Learn the sacred words of praise, 'Hail Satan'"?

Fifty years ago Germans goose-stepped in exacting regimentation, stiff-armed salutes sanctifying der Führer. In Hamburg I watched German metal maniacs thrust satanic salutes upward and slam-dance to the fastest rhythms in rock. Their favorite was "Angel of Death," about Joseph Mengele, the butcher of Auschwitz, whom Slayer described as the "sadist surgeon of demise, sadist of the noblest blood . . . monarch to the kingdom of the dead." The song was an explicit account of Mengele's machinations. The crowd reacted violently.

In front of the stage was a location called the pit, a five-foot-wide section between the stage and steel restraining bars that held back the crazed crowds. One by one, various members of the audience headed for the pit. Fans at Slayer concerts didn't sit—because there weren't any chairs. They stood the whole night. Occasionally, one of them leaped into the air and somehow landed on top of the audience. Heads, shoulders, and outstretched hands supported him. Gradually, he made his way forward, pushing or being pushed. Crawling on his back and stomach, he surged forward like a fullback vaulting defenders at a goal line stand.

Eventually, he lunged toward the pit. Head over heels he somersaulted the last few feet until he landed head or feet first in the pit. Then security personnel ungraciously escorted him to the side of the auditorium. He was sent to the back of the crowd to try the same thing again.

Throughout the concert, the fans frowned constantly. Their expressions were intensely evil—except when I took their pictures. Then the tension in their facial muscles seemed to relax. They smiled. No one heard me say cheese, but the sight of a camera caught them off guard, and for a brief moment they appeared to forget where they were. After the flash went off, something seemed to click, and their eyes would narrow again. Curling their lips in contempt of propriety, they'd return to their devilish demeanor.

Everything Slayer did appeared contrived, even their onstage banter. During the next few days, I would learn that every comment of Slayer was canned. Night after night, they did the same introductions to songs. Nothing was spontaneous. Even Araya's right eyebrow, which arched slightly when he said "Satan," looked as though it had been choreographed. Every note of every riff, every scowl was the same, on cue, at the right bar.

The members of Slayer weren't satanists, and I told that to David when I returned from Germany. I explained that their songs about devil worship were only a gimmick. David was angry and disillusioned, but he wouldn't turn from the pathway of evil he had chosen.

Remember David's arms were scarred with pentagrams and inverted crosses. He played in a rock band called Eternal Death. Because he wanted to do a human sacrifice and others in his coven refused, David was kicked out of his own satanist group.

What father and mother could overlook blatant engrossment with the occult in view of such symptoms of satanism?

When I asked David, he responded quickly, "My parents think it's a phase I'm going through. But they're wrong. It's my religion!"

I asked David if I could send him a Bible so he could become acquainted with an alternative viewpoint about life. His response was chilling.

"I burn Bibles," David said. "When I don't burn them, I tear out the pages, chew, and swallow them, then puke them back up."

"What about satanists who renounce devil worship? You've heard me talk to them on the radio. What do you think of them?" I asked.

"Thanks for getting those wimps out of satanism," David

responded. "You're helping our religion. We only want the strong and true." David's response represents the tragedy of youth included in Satanism. Those who become ensnared in its seduction may become so spiritually blinded they are nearly incapable of escaping its enslavement.

Chapter 7

Murder for the Devil

They burned my girlfriend alive while I watched. She wasn't the only one they killed. Another friend of mine was forced to say 'Satan, I give my life to you now,' as they pushed him over a cliff."

Sarah was petrified. "I've never told anyone before," she confessed.

Why? Her answer was simple.

"What I saw was so inconceivable, no one would believe me!" fourteen-year-old Sarah said.

"How did they burn your girlfriend?" I asked.

"They tied her to a platform and lit a fire under her," she explained.

"Didn't she cry for help?" I wanted to know.

"She screamed, but no one would put out the flames. They were all wearing masks so no one could see who they were," Sarah sobbed.

"What did you do while all this was going on?"

Sarah continued. "I tried to stop them, but they held me back. They made me watch and then beat me afterward."

Sarah's involvement with satanism started with drugs, heavy metal music, and various forms of antisocial behavior. She did pot, speed, LSD, any drug she could get her hands on. She slept with every guy who would have sex with her. Soon the friend who was eventually burned alive invited her to a party, which turned out to be a satanic ritual. At first, it was an electrifying departure from her strict Christian upbringing.

Sarah didn't realize that killing a few animals preceded human torture and murder. The sight of seeing someone incinerated alive was so horrifying she later attempted suicide three times. She hadn't gone to the police because there was no proof. Of the two sacrifices she had seen, one body was charred beyond recognition and the other was drowned in the sea below a cliff. No traces. No evidence. Who would believe a teenager with a history of drug abuse?

"The burning sacrifice was reported in the newspapers," she acknowledged. "It was near some houses, and someone must have heard the screaming. But they never found who did it."

Why did I believe Sarah? With slight alterations, I had heard the same story from dozens of other youngsters. The similarities were singular. Gradual induction into the cult. Horrifying ceremonies designed to instill terror, guilt, and silence. Killings too bloody to imagine. No witnesses. No signs of the crime.

"Why haven't you told your parents?" I asked Sarah.

Her answer was a typical teen response. "I never tell them anything," she answered. "My parents and I never talk."

Don't imagine Sarah's tragedy couldn't happen to a child you know. Her parents are respected Christians in positions of church leadership. They are totally unaware of their daughter's involvement in satanism. They only know Sarah is rebellious and suicidal. Like most parents whose children explore the occult, they are excluded from Sarah's murky world of evil atrocities. They aren't alone. Even those whose job it is to investigate and prosecute crime are often in the dark about the devil's deeds.

SLEUTHING SATANIC SLAYINGS

Many law enforcement authorities ignore signs of occult crime—headless hens, spray-painted graffiti, decapitated animals, and mutilated bodies. But the times, "they are a changin'." In his book *The Ultimate Evil*, author Maury Terry writes, "There is compelling evidence of the existence of a nationwide network of satanic cults, some branched into child pornography and violent sadomasochistic crime, including murder. I am concerned that the toll of innocent victims will steadily mount unless law enforcement officials recognize the threat and face it."[1]

You may remember some of the murderers I am going to analyze, yet you may not know the satanic involvement of those criminals. The idea of organized satanic groups dedicated to violence and vandalism has largely been ignored by investigators and prosecutors.

CHARLES MANSON

There has been much to monitor in the short history of slaying for Satan. Some say the current craze started August 9 and 10, 1969, the nights Charles Manson and his "family" of followers murdered seven victims, including actress Sharon Tate. Manson had been seduced by an ideology suggesting Christ and Satan, no longer adversaries, had reconciled. Thus, worshiping Satan was the same as acquiescing to Christ. Charles Manson borrowed his insane ideas from Robert DeGrimston, founder of the Process Church, a '60s street cult.

According to Manson's prosecutor, Vincent Bugliosi, both Manson and DeGrimston preached "an imminent, violent Armageddon, in which all but the chosen few would be destroyed." As Bugliosi described it, Manson slightly altered the

Process theology that Jehovah, Lucifer, and Christ are all reconciled. "Manson had a simpler duality; he was known to his followers as both Satan and Christ," Bugliosi believed.[2]

THE NIGHT STALKER

In 1985 Californians locked their doors as the terrifying Night Stalker case dragged on for months. Residents feared they and their families would become victims of satanically inspired rape and murder. At least fourteen victims had been slain, and many more were robbed and sodomized by the Stalker. His victims were usually residents of yellow houses near freeways.

The Stalker's methods amplified the horror. In one particularly ghoulish slaying, the victim's eyes were gouged out. The Stalker often drew pentagrams at the crime scene. The wife of one of his victims declared he had forced her to "swear on Satan" not to scream for help. He favored no one. The Night Stalker molested children, murdered men and women, and used both guns and knives. Typically, his heinous work was done between midnight and 6:00 A.M., when he sneaked into darkened homes through unlocked doors and windows.

Police eventually arrested twenty-eight-year-old Richard Ramirez of El Paso, Texas. At his arraignment, Ramirez grinned and raised his arm to reveal an inked pentagram in the palm of his hand. Friends of Ramirez claimed he was fascinated with the music and satanic symbolism of the Australian rock group AC/DC. At a Rosemead, California, condominium Ramirez allegedly murdered thirty-four-year-old Dayle Okazaki and left behind a baseball cap emblazoned with the AC/DC logo.

The cover of the jacket for the AC/DC album *Highway to Hell* depicted the lead singer with satanic horns protruding from his head. He held in his hands a devilishly pointed tail. To investigators, AC/DC's song "Night Prowler" was chillingly similar to the activities of Ramirez. The tune vividly described a murderer lurking at night. "You won't feel the steel until it's hanging out your back," the lyrics warn. Sounding like a police profile of Ramirez, the refrain suggests, "I am your night prowler, I sleep in the day ... Suspended animation, as I slip into your room." After depicting the terror of a victim awaiting a homicidal attack, the singer said, "There ain't nothing you can do."

Ramirez's association with the occult was more than a passing fascination. He drew a satanic star on the upper part of his arm. Donna Myers, who knew Ramirez and eventually helped police finger him for the crimes, said he also etched a witch's star on his stomach. According to Myers, "He would say Satan is a supreme being, like we worship God. He would tell me that Satan watches over him, so he doesn't get caught or hurt."[3]

RICKY KASSO

The heinous criminal activities of adults like Manson and Ramirez were soon adopted by younger deviants like Ricky Kasso of Northport, New York, a Long Island suburb. With his blonde hair and blue eyes, Kasso could have been the kid next door. As an adolescent, he was an avid athlete, fond of early morning football practices. But at seventeen, he was underweight with slurred speech and no short-term memory. In his father's words, "All he thought about was drugs and rock music."[4] Kasso and his friends formed a self-styled, devil-worshiping cult they called the Knights of the Black Circle. On signs and walls, they spray-painted upside-down crosses, 666 to represent the Antichrist, inverted stars symbolizing the devil, and names of metal rock stars like Ozzy Osbourne and Black Sabbath.

Kasso scared his mother by smearing ketchup on his wrists, declaring she had driven him to suicide. He once wrote a song called "A Child of the Devil." Ricky's frightened parents told doctors about his suicide attempts, threatening behavior, use of hallucinogens, and arrest for digging up a grave. He was judged to be "antisocial" but not "psychotic."[5] A friend thought otherwise. He declared, "Ricky would talk to the devil. He said the devil came to him in the form of a tree, which sprouted out of the ground and glowed."[6]

Ricky Kasso exemplifies what happens when authorities fail to take serious note of satanic symbols and paraphernalia. For three years, Northport police had been finding remains of tortured or charred animals that appeared to have been victims of ritual sacrifice. The neglect to pinpoint the source of such devilry eventually led to the murder of seventeen-year-old Gary Lauwers.

Kasso blamed Lauwers for stealing from him $100 worth of PCP, the drug known as angel dust. With the help of an accomplice, eighteen-year-old James Toriano, Ricky tortured his victim for three hours. Lauwers was stabbed seventeen times, then Kasso gouged out his eyes while forcing him to say, "I love you, Satan." After his arrest, Kasso hung himself in his jail cell to his cellmates' chants of "Hang up! Hang up!"

In the cases of Kasso and many other youths involved in murder for the devil, satanism is far from an organized system of allegiance to Lucifer. Disaffected teenagers feel a sense of importance in satanism. It is the paramount perversion of all their parents hold dear, the ultimate rebellion. Satanism is a supreme cry for help, directed toward a society that gives youth everything materially, but no meaning for life.

SATAN'S SONS AND DAUGHTERS

Many teenagers involved in the occult are from broken homes where they were neglected or ignored. Most are extraordinarily bright and sensitive. Each harbors a deep, hidden hurt, often sexual or physical abuse. Generally, they have experienced disappointment with organized Christianity. Turning to the devil isn't their first choice. Suicidally inclined and overcome with a sense of worthlessness, they see Satan as their last resort to grasp a sense of personal importance.

How had Sarah merely become a daughter of the devil? Her parents divorced when she was a child, and she currently sees her biological father only once a year. Her youthful curiosity, fueled by parental indifference, propelled her into postpubescent crisis.

"I could say it was rebellion or demons that did it," she responded, "but it was my parents who drove me over the edge." Sarah explained to me, "My real father doesn't love me, and my stepfather doesn't have time for me. My mother acts like I don't exist. All she does is yell at me when she finds out I've done something wrong."

Charles Manson, Richard Ramirez, Ricky Kasso, and other killers for Satan were not born bad. They were bent bad by a society that neglected their basic human needs and substituted affluence for affection. In defiance, they became satanists, determined to exploit evil and get forcibly what they couldn't receive freely from those who should have loved them. A lack of self-esteem was the chief reason they exchanged virtue for evil. If being good didn't bring happiness, then being bad, exceedingly bad, would at least lead to power and lustful satisfaction.

SATANIC SCHOOL-YARD SLAYINGS

During the school year that followed when the doors on the first yellow school bus swung open at the first morning stop in the fall of 1997, at least a dozen students and two teachers were killed by schoolmates around the country in lunchrooms, in schoolyards, and at morning prayers. It all began on October 1, 1997, when a sixteen-year-old boy named Luke Woodham stabbed his mother to death, then fatally shot his former girlfriend and another girl at Pearl High School in Pearl, Mississippi.

The shooting deaths in Pearl were followed by other killings in West Paducah, Kentucky, Jonesboro, Arkansas and Springfield, Oregon. On December 1, 1997, fourteen-year-old Michael Carneal shot three high school classmates to death and wounded five others while they prayed at Heath High School in Paducah. Psychiatrists report that Carneal was tired of being picked on and teased, and confided that a gun he took to school made him feel powerful. Loitering in the hall, he waited for a prayer group of thirty-five students to lift their bowed heads and say "Amen." Then he pulled a semiautomatic .22 from his backpack and fired twelve shots at the victims, killing Kayce Steger, Jessica James, and Nicole Hadley. Carneal later told a teacher, "It was like I was in a dream." He pled guilty but mentally ill.

After Paducah came Jonesboro. On March 24, 1998, eleven-year-old Andrew Golden triggered a fire alarm to lure students at Westside Middle School outside, then opened fire with thirteen-year-old Mitchell Johnson from a nearby stand of trees. Four girls and a teacher were killed and nine other students and a teacher were wounded. The boys had bragged the day before that they were going to get even with enemies at the school.

After Jonesboro, Springfield, Oregon, was the site of another high school massacre. On May 21, 1998, fifteen-year-old Kip Kinkle shot his parents to death at their home and then opened fire in his school's cafeteria, killing two students.

The list continues. On June 15, fourteen-year-old Quinshawn Booker allegedly shot a teacher and a volunteer aide in a hallway at Armstrong High School in Richmond, Virginia.

The killings left the country scrambling for answers and a way to stop what seems to be a national trend. Perhaps what is most shocking are the youth of the killers and the brutality of the crimes. In each case, the killers were young males who either plotted to kill adversaries or really didn't care who they killed as long as they killed. Several of the killers claimed an occult connection. Luke Woodham stated in court that demons had driven him to murder.

THE ATTRACTION OF EVIL

Who are those deceived by the devil? By what means are they enticed? Why do they exchange truth for lies and beauty for ugliness?

Narcissism is the soul of satanism. The selfish satisfaction of vengeance and of carnal delights is a prerequisite for sorcery. Hatred, lust, and avarice are unsavory companions that repudiate God and all that is noble.

Satanists feel no gladness in the pulse of life. The heartbeat of hell deadens their capacity to be touched by human compassion. It all starts with a decision, a choice to turn from good and invite evil, trading decency for impropriety. They give up on goodness and seek instant gratification. Power over their lives and the lives of others is all that matters.

Although even satanists want to be loved, they believe love is unattainable; and so they opt for evil. In their lives, love has been capricious. To the satanist, hate is dependable and predictable. It's always there, and you know the effect of its application.

SIGNS OF SATANISM

If you work with teenagers or are the parent of a teen, your first question is probably, "How do I know if a teen is involved with satanism?"

Some telltale signs of youthful involvement in satanism are:

- An unhealthy preoccupation with fantasy role-playing games like Dungeons & Dragons (D&D).

- An interest in Ouija boards and other occult games.

- A preoccupation with psychic phenomena like telepathy, astral projection, tarot cards, I Ching, and parapsychology.

- An addiction to horror movies like the *Friday the 13th, Nightmare on Elm Street, Halloween,* and *Scream* series, whose main characters kill and maim.

- An obsession with satanic metal music, particularly

72

black metal bands and certain rap groups that promote antisocial behavior and evoke satanic symbolism.

- An affinity for satanic paraphernalia, including posters of black metal bands, skulls, knives, chalices, black candles, and robes.

- An inclination to write poems or letters about satanism or to sketch designs of upside-down crosses, pentagrams, the number 666, names of the devil, or skulls and other symbols of death.

- An attraction to satanic literature and such books as *The Satanic Bible*, the *Necronomicon*, the writings of Aleister Crowley, or keeping a private journal such as a *Book of Shadows* (a self-designed secret chronicle of satanic activities and ideas).

- An involvement with friends who dress in black, greet each other with the satanic salute (index and pinkie finger extended, with palm facing inward), speak and write backward, or organize secret meetings.

Beware of the temptation to anxiously search a child's room or screen his mail, which would breach his sense of trust. Don't suddenly demand that every offensive poster come off his wall and every distasteful record album go to the garbage. Precipitous action will instill further anger and rebellion. Instead, be alert for additional clues of satanic involvement. Ask prudent questions of your child's peers, teachers, and acquaintances. Above all, don't assume satanism can't intrude upon your family.

Chapter 8

Occult Enticements

Have you heard of the occult game Bloody Mary, Bloody Mary? Here is the chilling description given to me by a twelve-year-old boy named Chad.

"You go into a dark bathroom, stare into the mirror, and chant, 'Bloody Mary, Bloody Mary.' You wait until invisible claws scratch your face and you bleed. That's how you know Bloody Mary is there," Chad explained. "Now my friend Jamie and me are into more exotic stuff. We go through the mirror."

"Have you ever heard of astral-projection or out-of-body experiences?" I asked.

"Yeah, it's like that," Chad responded. "I look into the mirror and do the Bloody Mary chant. Then my mind goes into the mirror and travels to my friend Jamie's house. I got the idea from the movie *Poltergeist*."

"Does Jamie know when you're there?" I wondered aloud.

"Yes, if he does the right chants too. Sometimes I visit him when he doesn't know it, and I tell him later what I saw him doing."

"Chad, I want to ask you an important question. When you leave your body, who guards your soul while you're gone?"

Chad didn't know.

"There are two ways evil can overtake your soul," I said. "One is for you to sell your soul to Satan. The other is for you to do something in the occult that leaves your soul unprotected. When you leave your body, your consciousness isn't there to resist evil. When you visit Jamie, something else could invade your soul."

Chad was startled. He thought Bloody Mary was a lot of fun, a cute trick borrowed from Hollywood. The idea of the devil had never occurred to him. That's the way it is with most people. Casual clashes with the occult are commonplace in a society satiated with spiritism.

THE INDUCEMENT OF PSYCHIC PHENOMENA

For all the bad press Nancy Reagan got over her attention to astrology, and the séance-like sessions Hillary Clinton held in the White House solarium, they had company along the Potomac. One congressman who promotes the paranormal in Washington, D.C., says, "At any given time, about one-fourth of the members of Congress are actively interested in PSI [an acronym for psychic phenomena], healing, prophecy, remote viewing, or physical manifestations of psychic power."

Senator Claiborne Pell (D-R.I.), former chairman of the Senate Foreign Relations Committee, has been a vocal advocate of psychic research. The bookcase in Pell's private Capitol office was crammed with occult volumes, including *The Astral Body* and the works of Shirley MacLaine. He admitted consulting mediums to communicate with dead relatives.[1]

The Pentagon underwrites classified psychic research, and the CIA has used psychics to spy on Soviet weaponry. General Manuel Noriega, Panama's dictator, was the subject of governmental paranormal sleuthing. Some in the nation's capital have even suggested a spiritistic version of the nuclear Manhattan Project (the government's all-out attempt to invent the atomic bomb) to explore clairvoyance, lest Russia get a step ahead in the field of occult adeptness.[2]

The precincts of the paranormal have been extended to nearly every respectable constituency of life. At an international Transpersonal Conference attended by nearly two thousand participants, most of them Ph.D. psychologists, I listened to a lecture on what used to be known as occult metaphysics. The talk was delivered by Dr. Russell Targ, a staff physicist with the Lockheed Research and Development Laboratories. This distinguished scientist compared academic investigation into the paranormal with the phenomena experienced twenty-five hundred years ago by the oracles of Delphi.

With a bold face and without a blink, Dr. Targ discarded hundreds of years of scientific tradition by declaring, "Psychic function is a nonanalytic ability. [It can't be objectively investigated because] analysis is the enemy of psychic functioning."[3]

The scientist also described his testing of well-known spiritualist medium Ingo Swan, who "could put his consciousness anywhere on the planet." Under the guise of objective research, Dr. Targ told of testing psychics who received mental images from photographs unseen by them but secretly selected by the examiners. The audience was shown slides of a crude line drawing made by a psychic who supposedly telepathically obtained the likeness of a monument from a picture of Grant's tomb. Dr. Targ also suggested that prophecy could be practiced by anyone. He unequivocally declared, "You can experience now the experience you will have an hour from now."[4]

The introduction to satanism often comes from parapsychology. Not all casual investigators of the paranormal and are in league with the devil, but the arts they offer can open the mind to supernatural suggestions. Below is a brief description of PSI terms in case someone you know alludes to them.

PARAPSYCHOLOGY

By definition, *parapsychology* is that branch of the psychological sciences which deals with human faculties that are not operational within the limits of our five natural senses:

- *ESP* (extrasensory perception) is the catchall category for such abilities.
- *Clairvoyance* refers to paranormal information received by touching an object or focusing mentally on an event.
- *Telepathy* is the awareness of the thoughts or the mental state of another person.
- *Cognition* is the knowledge of an event as it occurs. Knowing about something before it happens is called *precognition*. Awareness of an event after its occurrence is known as *postcognition*. Those possessing such abilities admit they lack control over the reception of this information.
- *Astral projection* (soul travel out of the body) is a practice highly touted by parapsychologists. Chad and Jamie had never attended an occult conference or read a parapsychological journal. Their knowledge of astral projection came from their absorption with society's familiarity with the paranormal.

SATAN'S PSI IN THE NEW AGE

Players of the paranormal are no longer turbaned gurus gazing into smoky crystal balls. They don't claim to accurately predict the future or tell fortunes. Their occult outlook peers more directly into the soul. America is their metaphysical mecca. Rebirthers, numerologists, mind control metaphysicians, crystal experts, trance channelers, and bodywork authorities abound. In the opinion of one college professor who has studied the historical origins of the metaphysical movement, "It's really good old-fashioned occultism and superstition gussied up with pseudo-scientific jargon to give it an air of legitimacy."[5]

How does this cultural milieu of occultism affect those introduced to satanism? A subtle shift in societal attitudes has been occurring over the last decade. The New Age Movement and other popular mystical legacies have indoctrinated a generation to believe that self-preoccupation is an appropriate goal. Religious traditions based on Eastern modes of thought have gradually negated the Judeo-Christian concept of the conscience. Few today worry about the moral consequences of their actions.

This shift in cultural consciousness has removed an intangible inner barrier that guards against the occult. In prior generations, those who professed no religious faith were wary about demons and devils. They may not have believed in spiritualism, but they didn't mess with it, either. Today, people are no longer awed by evil and a fearsome door to the supernatural opens ever so casually.

Until recently, séances were shadowy, even shady affairs. Seekers of the supernatural circled a table with their hands placed lightly on its top, lowered the lights, and awaited signs of a spirit's presence. A flickering candle, a whoosh of wind, a slight tip of the table, or a wispy voice was enough to guarantee success. In some cases, a trumpet-shaped device appeared, and a voice was heard from the void. On rare occasions, an apparition manifested itself as a departed loved one or famous personage.

Shirley MacLaine and other occult proponents have refined the process and upped the ante on the entities. Darkened drawing rooms are unnecessary. Higher-consciousness seminars offer trance-channeled messages under the glare of klieg lights. The entire affair is videotaped in hotel ballrooms. Visitations of departed aunts and expired grandparents are too trivial. Present-day channelers are human radios, allowing the masses to tune in advanced spiritual information without an arduous search through sacred scriptures and ascetic disciplines.

Séances, frightful films, occult experimentation, sinister songs—these contemporary corruptions are luring many souls deep into demonic darkness. In the midst of such negativism, God promises those who sincerely seek truth and love that the power of good is greater than the essence of evil.[6]

Chad and Jamie's encounter with evil occurred so casually that parents should see how easily their children can become involved in the occult. Kids must know their parents love them unconditionally. If they wander into evil ways, they must be able to depend on their parents to respond quickly with alarm and concern.

A word of advice to parents: If your child embraces the paranormal, as Chad and Jamie did, quickly warn him that the idea of possessing boundless untapped powers of the soul is as old as Eden.[7] Admonish him against assuming such forces are a kind of biocosmic energy, like The Force of *Star Wars*. It doesn't matter whether psychic abilities come from the soul or Satan. Their lure of pride and power is self-destructive, occult enticements into more threatening facets of the slippery side of satanism.

Chapter 9

Ghoulish Games

My character is a priest. He uses supernatural powers just like the magic users do. But his alignment is lawful good, so there's nothing wrong with it," a Dungeons & Dragons player named Robert argued with me. "It's a game of fantasy. Playing D&D doesn't certify you as a witch."

Robert wasn't through leveling his salvo. "Dungeons & Dragons is one of the cleanest, funnest, and most mentally challenging games you could play," he insisted.

Robert is typical of Dungeons & Dragons players. His interest in fantasy role-playing games is fueled by an inquisitive intellect often left unchallenged by routine rigors of schoolwork. He escapes into a fictional realm by becoming absorbed in a fabricated world of medieval imagery, where his mind conjures heroics and adventure at whim.

"Isn't it dangerous to fool around with occult realities, even in an illusory fashion?" I countered.

"No," Robert said. "It's a test of your acting and imagination."

"But your character, the priest, uses occult forces."

"It's fantasy power," Robert responded. "There's nothing real in D&D."

People don't get involved in evil overnight. Many first encounter the occult in their homes as they crouch over game boards that answer questions or predict behavior. Games based on occult powers and principles are seldom taken seriously, but they do presume that consulting unseen forces is child's play.

THE LURE OF DUNGEONS & DRAGONS

Numerous case studies indicate that Dungeons & Dragons results in dangerous consequences. In the following criminal cases, the youngsters were all obsessed with Dungeons & Dragons, and critics blamed the game's influence for their violations:

- In California, the body of a bright seventeen-year-old boy washed up on a San Francisco beach.

- In Colorado, a twelve-year-old lad fatally shot his sixteen-year-old brother, then killed himself.

- In Kansas, a fourteen-year-old Eagle Scout candidate walked into his junior high school and opened fire with a rifle, killing his principal and three others.

- In Austin, Texas, a twelve-year-old boy jumped to his death from a hotel window.

The National Coalition on Television Violence says D&D is linked to more than fifty teenage deaths. One attorney, representing the family of a young suicide victim who was involved in D&D, declared, "It is a game that tells kids how to perfect the art of premeditated murder."[1]

THE STRATEGY OF D&D

Dungeons & Dragons began as a spin-off of war games. Gary Gygax, D&D's inventor, discarded familiar game components like cards, boards, and six-sided dice, and devised a game with no rules or time limits. A single game of D&D can last for hours, days, weeks, months, or even years. At least three people must play. One is the Dungeon Master, a controlling figure who devises the dungeon map and directs the game's flow. The other players are pitted against one another. They roll poly-sided dice to determine the various intelligence and dexterity ratings of their alter-ego characters, which are given fictitious names.

The players gather around a fictitious or roughly sketched map and set off on an imaginary odyssey through hazardous terrain created by the Dungeon Master. En route, they encounter obstacles, such as monsters and demons, which they thwart with violent tactics and occult spells. No one wins. The object is to survive the adventure and participate in the next game with an even more powerful character.

In my conversation with Robert, the teenager who defended D&D, I asked, "Isn't success in the game based on using treachery and violence?"

"Yes. In fact, my character got angry once and messed up some people. In my imagination he physically beat them up."

"How can you defend your character, a Christian priest, taking violent, revengeful action?"

Robert was cornered, and he responded protectively. "Christians aren't perfect. Anyway, the bad background of D&D is what makes it interesting. It shouldn't be played in church. It's okay, if you don't take it seriously."

The use of murder, arson, torture, rape, robbery, and the occult to endure the quest for the dungeon may not concern teens like Robert, but it does distress some. One former player admitted, "I derived a sadistic sort of pleasure from killing evil people in the game. If an evil character threatened me, I'd subconsciously treat him just like one of those junior high jokers who put me down. I was using D&D instead of the real world to work out my problems. In my D&D world, I had the power to alter events."[2]

SATANISM'S LINK WITH D&D

Some aspects of D&D are directly linked with satanism. The extent of occult collusion depends partly on the manuals selected to guide the game and formulate the dungeon master's strategy. Some manuals tell players how to summon demons and indulge in astral projection. At minimum, D&D replaces reality with a contrived universe where anything goes and moral absolutism is absent. Certain players may become so detached from the outside world that the death of their character triggers violent rage.

It is obvious that writers for the various manuals associated with fantasy role-playing games are well versed in the occult. Pentagrams and potions are frequently recommended. In the manual *Deities and Demigods*, the writer advises, "Serving a deity is a significant part of D&D, and all player characters should have a patron god."

Isaac Bonewits, a well-known practicing witch, considers Dungeons & Dragons such a good instructional mechanism to paganism that he has written a book showing players how to move from D&D into real sorcery. His special manual on demons describes the appearance and power of evil entities with accompanying sketches.

THE OFFICIAL ADVANCED D&D HANDBOOK

The *Official Advanced Dungeons & Dragons Player's Handbook*, written by game founder Gygax and published by the game manufacturer, TSR, Inc., is an explicit education in occultism. Gygax wastes no time informing his protégés, "The casting of spells, clerical and magical, is a very important aspect of play. Most spells have a *verbal* component, and so must be uttered ... Clerical spells, including the druidic [witchcraft], are bestowed by gods so that the desired . . . spell components will be placed properly in his or her mind." Gygax continues instructing players to memorize the appropriate spells to "impress the potent, mystical spell formulae upon the mind."[3]

Dungeons & Dragons' clerical spells are recited as bewitching chants. An opposing character may be dispatched by what is called a "necromantic slow poison." A "spiritual hammer" may be used to create a force field, striking any adversary in sight. The player may use divination spells to acquire "information regarding the relative strength of creatures in the area . . . and the relative chances for incurring the wrath of evil or good supernatural." Clerics can also perform "resurrections," bringing back to life imaginary characters that have been dead up to ten years.[4]

THE OFFICIAL ADVANCED LEGENDS AND LORE MANUAL

The official *Legends and Lore* manual explicitly describes a pantheon of pagan deities taken from the mythology of Native American Indian spirits, Babylonian gods, Celtic [witchcraft] deities, and Egyptian divinities. The manual warns, "The mighty evil gods, demons, and devils are prone to appear when their name is spoken . . ."[5]

Even out-of-body experiences are discussed. *Legends and Lore* explains, "When deities and their minions travel to planes other than their own, they are mystically anchored to their home plane by a metaphysical 'silver cord': this is similar to the one described for *astral spell* . . ."[6]

The specific instructions given to D&D players regarding demons and deities are alarming. Seekers of Indian spirits are told to dress their character in occult symbols to summon the serpents of the Snakeman. Those who evoke the Babylonian god Durga are warned he may "occasionally send a group of devils out to aid his worshipers, especially those that have recently sacrificed a virgin to their deity."[7]

The occult overtones of D&D are so explicit that virtually

nothing in the world of satanism is omitted. Players are told how to have their characters commune with nature spirits, consult crystal balls filled with human blood, and conjure the Egyptian deities that Moses opposed (Set, Ra, Isis, Osiris, Horus, Bes). Most disturbing are precise directions regarding Celtic human sacrifices. The place and manner of performing such sacrifices are detailed, along with the calendar dates for the appropriate high unholy days (including November 1, Samhain, the Lord of the Dead, Lucifer, as explained elsewhere in this book).[8]

Allegations of complicity with satanism so alarmed defenders of Dungeons & Dragons that the Game Manufacturers Association published a pamphlet responding to the objections. The writer argued, "Role-playing games no more make their players Satan worshipers than Monopoly makes its players slum landlords" Admitting D&D could be "a person's first exposure to the occult," and that some manuals contain information on satanism, the pamphlet counters that no game "assumes a player will actually try to . . . call up a demon."[9] As for the idea that vicarious sin equals actual sin, the writer concludes such a concept is "far-fetched," which is an unreserved denial of the teachings of Jesus Christ, who said that anyone looking with lust has committed adultery in his heart.[0]

Most D&D players do not pursue its more evil aspects and argue they shouldn't be penalized for indulging in fantasy rather than actual evil. What of the argument that D&D involves only imaginary evil?

Christian teaching underscores many objections to D&D, including the command to ignore evil imaginations and avoid "every high thing that exalts itself against the knowledge of God, bringing every thought into captivity to the obedience of Christ."[11] This injunction accepts the fact that creative imagination is an important part of spirituality. How else could the creation of the world and the wonders of heaven, from Genesis to the Revelation, be comprehended?

In the world of D&D, no morality parallels that of the real world. There is no theistic accountability or intrusion of a Christian worldview. Likewise, the motives of D&D characters indicate an exercise in expediency rather than moral perspective. The ancient writer of Proverbs warned, "For as he thinks in his heart, so is he."[12]

The link with satanism occurs when players use symbols and protective inscriptions associated with witchcraft and the occult. Necromancy (the biblically forbidden practice of communication with the dead) is sometimes used in D&D as a divinational means of deriving information. Such activity occurs in an imagined universe where the moral quality of the players' characters is often dichotomous.

One Dungeon Master I debated, named Charles, explained that the roll of the dice gave him a character who was "neutral-good" with "chaotic-lawful" attributes.

"That's contradictory," I challenged Charles. "In reality, good is not neutral. The very idea of ethical neutrality supposes that our world exists in a moral vacuum.

"The idea of someone being chaotic-lawful is equally bogus," I went on. "Chaos by its nature causes anarchy. How could that be lawful?"

Charles gave the stock D&D answer: "Dungeons & Dragons is in your mind, and you can do anything you want mentally without actually doing evil."

That questionable logic aside, the truth is that Dungeons & Dragons guides participants into a world of nonmaterial entities, forces, and spirits. Obviously, if such beings exist, the line of demarcation between fantasy and reality can easily be blurred. Warn anyone you know who plays D&D, "There is no assurance that conjuring an imagined entity will prevent a real spirit from responding!"

Every addiction to the devil is preceded by mental and emotional addiction to evil. The mere discussion of occult evil in D&D

manuals certainly doesn't condone exploring satanism, but it is a de facto endorsement of the occult.

OUIJA BOARDS

For many decades, the most popular occult game has been Parker Brothers' Ouija Board. The game's manufacturer is explicit about how to use this game. Players are admonished to take the endeavor seriously and not have a "frivolous spirit, asking ridiculous questions, laughing over it." The name Ouija comes from the French word for yes, *oui*, and the German word for yes, *ja*. Many players can tell terrifying stories associated with Ouija's accurate answers.

The Ouija board is a piece of pressed cardboard with the numbers zero through nine, the letters of the alphabet, and the words *good, bye, yes,* and *no* printed on the surface. The teardrop-shaped plastic planchette, or counter, is placed on top. Two players face each other with the board on their laps. Participants' fingers rest lightly on the counter, allowing it to move freely over the board. Questions are posed, and the counter eventually moves. A hole in the counter's center stops over the selected letter, number, or word.

When a letter is chosen, consecutive movements of the counter choose additional letters to spell out words in response to the players' inquiry. Instructions declare, "It gives you entertainment you have never experienced. It draws the two people using it into a close relationship and weaves about them a feeling of mysterious isolation. It surpasses in its unique results mind reading, clairvoyance, and second sight. Loaded with fun, excitement, and thrills more intense and absorbingly interesting than a mystery story."

I've talked with hundreds of people who have played with Ouija. Without exception, those who have asked the board to disclose its source of information have received the response: "demons, devils, Satan, Beelzebub, Lucifer," or a satanic equivalent.

Either unconscious assumptions were made by the players, triggering muscular responses to the question, or the reply was truthful. If the latter, the Ouija board is a spiritually dangerous tool of evil invasion. In an ironic admission, a television advertisement recently declared. "The Ouija Board—it's more than a game."

Chapter 10

The Horror of Horror Movies

W hat's so bad about horror films?" Jerry, a young man in his early twenties, began our conversation by defending slice-and-dice flicks. As the dialogue progressed, he admitted such movies affected him.

"My favorite is *Hotel Hell,*" Jerry said, "although it did make me barf up my popcorn. Some guy chops people up and makes fritters out of them.

"I don't know about other people, but these films make me want to act out what I've seen," Jerry conceded. "I used to come home and try weird things out on my wife."

"Like what?" I asked.

"The worst was the time I saw a Vincent Price film. Some guy discovered another guy didn't like him. So he found some dogs, killed them, and made pudding out of them."

"Dog pudding? You've got to be kidding."

"No. He made the other guy eat it."

"What's that got to do with your wife?"

"When I got home from seeing the movie, I got drunk and killed the family dog."

"Oh, no! . . . Let me guess. You made your wife eat it?"

"She didn't know what it was. I told her it was a special new recipe I made just for her."

I was grateful Jerry hadn't done anything worse. If he had really wanted to imitate horror film "art," his conduct could have been even more depraved.

Gross-out movies are big grossers on the screen and on video. Zombies, mutants, deranged murderers, and psychological torturers wreak wholesale havoc on a scale the gore industry calls KPMs—killings per minute. In today's horror genre, children possess psychic abilities to start fires at will. Nightmarish dreams turn into reality. Mutilated denizens of the deep crawl out of human flesh. Even automobiles come alive with demonic design, as Stephen King's deadly 1958 red Plymouth, Christine, illustrated in the movie of the same name.

This film trend started in 1974 with the horror classic *The Texas Chain Saw Massacre,* the story of five unsuspecting teenagers who became the main course for a family of homicidal cannibals. An ad for a horror movie reads, "This movie grabs you by the throat and stomps the life out of you. These are demons of death, vicious, bloodthirsty creatures who step from the screen into your lap. The worst part is, there's no way out. Unless, of course, you consider death a reasonable alternative."

Currently, horror movies make up a major portion of available video software.[1] Often a movie that bombs at the box office becomes a hit at home. Independent TV stations have launched a campaign of blood, sweat, and fear by airing blocks of scary syndicated shows on weekend nights. Critics call it "splatter" television, referring to all the blood spilled in living color.

Who watches such fare? While researching the phenomenon of horror films, I assumed the unpleasant duty of sitting through hours of ritualized satanic screen savagery. Most of these movies were R-rated. Yet almost always I was the oldest person and only adult in the theater. Average age? Approximately fifteen. The worst part was audience reaction as bodies were disemboweled and limbs amputated. Instead of hung heads and disapproving groans, the murderous mayhem met with cheers, laughter, and indifference.

"Chop his head off!" someone in the audience yelled as the movie portrayed a frightened, ax-wielding teenager turning on her tormentor.

A decapitated head dropped to the floor. "Slice him again!" another movie fan hollered in encouragement.

While blood streamed across the screen and a disemboweled body writhed in agony, a six-year-old in the audience nonchalantly asked his sister, "Would you get me some more popcorn?"

"Wow! That looked real," a teenager said to his friend as the spiny fingers of an armless hand ripped out a victim's eyeballs.

Blood, guts, and gore on the screen; popcorn, candy, and pop for the audience. No one gagged or grimaced. Beyond shock, the kids intently observed the wizardry of special effects that simulated savagery.

Since you weren't in the theaters to see for yourself, come with me on a spine-tingling journey through the world of horror films to consider their effect.

AN UNLUCKY FRIDAY THE 13TH

The *Friday the 13th* tetralogy was based on the character Jason, whose mother went on a vengeful killing spree in the first movie in the series. After his murderous mom was killed, Jason took over with a gusto that would do a psychopath proud, dispatching campers, vacationers, and anyone else who got in his way. The reward for such savagery? *Final Chapter*, the fourth in the violent *Friday the 13th* film series, grossed $11.2 million the first weekend it opened.

The outcome for others? Ask the parents of Sharon Gregory of Greenfield, Massachusetts. Mark Branch, a nineteen-year-old horror movie fan, killed their teenage daughter. The young woman, who was acquainted with Branch, was found in her bathtub. She had been stabbed repeatedly.

Branch had frequently rented horror films from local video stores, and police later found horror movie memorabilia at his home. Among the things they came across were videocassettes of *Friday the 13th* and a hockey mask—trademark of Jason, the movie's slasher. Police reported that Branch was so obsessed with Jason he "wanted to see what it feels like to kill."[2]

What fascinated Branch? In *Friday the 13th, the Final Chapter*, a carefree teenage boy searches a kitchen for a corkscrew. Suddenly the elusive utensil, wielded by an unseen assailant, flashes out of nowhere and impales his hand against the countertop. Then an ax cleaves his skull between the eyes. Unfortunately, the *Final Chapter* wasn't final. *Friday the 13th—A New Beginning* followed, featuring more than twenty killings.

The outcome for Branch? Police later found his dead body hanging from a limb in the woods near Buckland, Massachusetts.

ONE, TWO, THREE, FOUR,
BETTER LOCK YOUR FAMILY'S DOOR

No horror series has been more successful than the *Nightmare on Elm Street* sagas, starring incinerated child molester Freddy Krueger. In the original 1984 version, Krueger was a janitor at a small-town high school. After murdering innocent adolescents, Freddy was burned in the school furnace. Like *Friday the 13th*'s Jason, Freddy is dispatched at the end of each episode, only to return again, again, and again, his finger-knives poised to disembowel and decapitate.

Each time Freddy returns, he appears in dreams. But if Freddy kills you nocturnally, you're dead for real. Ironically, Freddy's rubbery, disfigured face, his glove with five-inch knife blades, and his tormenting terror constitute a de rigueur adolescent ceremony of satanism. Teenagers can unanimously cite Freddy's liturgy of atrocity: "One, two, I'm coming for you. Three, four, better lock your door."

No one anticipated that this grade-Z horror movie would turn into a cottage industry. The original version cost $1.8 million to make and earned $24 million. The first three installments of *Nightmare* brought in $103 million. Sales of ancillary merchandise topped $15 million. Freddy's mask still sells well at Halloween, and CDs, two *Nightmare* books, a board game, and Freddy dolls honor this suburban psychopath.

Condemning the criminal influence of horror films is made difficult by one simple fact. The perpetrators of emulated violence aren't around to confess. Mark Branch killed himself and can't tell us what motivated him. The same is true of Sean Helms. On January 28, 1987, the eighteen-year-old from Indianapolis, Indiana, was playing Russian roulette with his best friend when he pulled the trigger and sent a bullet through his own brain. Investigators reported the accidental suicide occurred after Helms had watched part two of the *Nightmare on Elm Street* series.

Friday the 13th and *Nightmare on Elm Street* are only two of many widely accepted horror movies that attract large audiences. The appearance of local video outlets, whose films are as dazzling as their flashing lights, has provided a new marketplace. Many such videos are low-budget flicks that never reach neighborhood theaters. Yet teens can rent and repeatedly watch these films in the comfort of their homes.

While splatter films cannot positively be blamed for increased interest in satanism, these movies have taken on new dimensions. In the '60s, horror films drew on such classic fiction as Frankenstein, Dracula, or Jekyll and Hyde. Today's movies and videos are more graphically sinister, concentrating on inescapable terror and ghastly revenge. The fixation is not on mythmaking and storytelling, but on death and destruction. Virtually without exception, the presence of human kindness and noble values is neither recognized nor desired in such films.

Some youth consider horror movies a rite of passage. Like riding a roller coaster, the trick is to see if you can take it. Some psychiatrists say it's a release for teenagers, a kind of primal therapy. Screaming at these escapades is a way of venting the frustrated forces of sex, violence, and hostility.

Horror flick director David Cronenberg argues that violence has a purpose beyond shock. Cronenberg says, "In a horror film, you invite people to confront some very disturbing things about the human body, disease, and death in the way they might confront them in a dream. It's an attempt to deal with realities that you normally refuse to face. Every time I kill someone in my movie, I'm rehearsing my own death."[3]

Some mental health professionals disagree with Cronenberg's rationalization. Reflecting on horror movie negativism, Los Angeles psychologist Marilyn Ruman declares, "Morbidity is the opposite side of optimism and hopefulness. We have a sense of not having control and celebrate death instead."[4]

The often chaotic plotlines and disjointed camera sequences of many horror films are randomly based. Instead of fostering mental stability, the cinematic techniques leave moviegoers wondering what will happen next. Such unpredictability enforces morbid fears that young minds cannot process.

The human mind can handle only so much stress before it becomes overburdened and desensitized. Scenes of gore galore can become so indelibly imbedded that the film becomes a living nightmare, triggering neuroses, trauma, and ongoing phobias. Something is tragically wrong with anyone who watches a movie for the thrill of watching blood flow.

Not everyone who watches slice-and-dice flicks cares to imitate them. Most will dismiss the vivid realism as clever photography and scintillating special effects. But a Jerry, who cooked dog casserole for his wife, or a Mark Branch, who apparently murdered to imitate his hero Jason, is one horror film fan too many.

Chapter 11

Drugs and the Devil

A woman named Nancy who approached me for help regarding her drug addiction illustrates the link between drugs and the influence of demons. "I need some help because I've been hooked on cocaine for over two years," she said.

"How do you get the money for the drugs? Steal?"

"Yes."

"Sell yourself?"

"That too. I also got busted for carrying a gun."

"Why were you carrying a gun?" I insisted upon knowing.

Nancy didn't respond. Then in barely audible sighs, she wept.

"Are you crying?" I asked.

"You asked where I got the money for cocaine. Well, most of the time I get the drugs for free. I know some guys involved in satanism. When I need some drugs, they come around. They take me places and get me stoned so I'll perform sexually for them."

"What kind of places?"

"Where they hold ceremonies."

Nancy's voice started to tighten. It was a difficult conversation for her. "What kind of ceremonies?" I probed.

"Animal . . . and human," she blurted out.

"When was the last time you saw them kill someone?"

"The first time, it was an infant. Two weeks ago, they sacrificed a six-year-old child. Afterward, they warned me they'd sacrifice me, too, if I ever told anyone."

DRUG-DEALING MURDERS IN MATAMOROS

The sobering reality of the connection between drugs and satanism was dramatically driven home a decade ago when fifteen bodies were unearthed in Mexico, across the border from Brownsville, Texas. A Matamoros, Mexico, drug ring had kidnapped and murdered innocent victims as sacrifices to Satan. The drug dealers hoped that in exchange the devil would grant them protection from the police and immunity from any bullets fired their way.

Police described the crime scene as a "human slaughterhouse." They discovered a cauldron containing blood and bones from the bodies. The heads of some victims had been cut open and the brains removed, to be mixed in the bloody cauldron. Before the bodies were buried, wires were attached to the spines, so that they could be pulled out later and made into necklaces.

The case cracked open when they abducted and sacrificed Mark Kilroy, a twenty-one-year-old student at the University of Texas-Austin. Kilroy was in Matamoros partying during spring break and was last seen drinking with friends. His parents searched for weeks, distributing more than twenty thousand handbills and offering a fifteen-thousand-dollar reward for information.

When the truth of his murder was finally known, Mrs. Kilroy concluded, "I think the suspects must be possessed by the devil. That would be the only explanation for such bizarre actions."[1]

James Kilroy said his son's death should show that even casual drug use can lead to deadly consequences. "Marijuana is what killed Mark,"[2] he told the press.

THE CHIEF DEPUTY'S VIEW OF THE MATAMOROS MURDERS

The day this story broke nationally, on my radio program I interviewed Carlos Tapia, Chief Deputy of Cameron County, Texas, where Brownsville is located:

LARSON: What startled you the most when you saw the crime scene?

TAPIA: I thought in my twenty-two years of law enforcement, I had seen everything. I hadn't. As we drew near, you could smell the stench . . . blood and decomposing organs. In a big, cast-iron pot there were pieces of human bodies and a goat's head with horns.

LARSON: What went through your mind?

TAPIA: When we saw the bodies, the suspects were laughing and making jokes. They had a very nonchalant attitude.

LARSON: Didn't they understand the gravity of what they had done?

TAPIA: In their wicked, distorted minds there was no seriousness. They thought they had performed some kind of heroic deed for the devil. They believed that by sacrificing innocent human beings, their loads of marijuana would have an invisible shield of protection from law enforcement officers. They were moving an average of one thousand pounds a week across the border.

LARSON: You must be incensed at what happened.

TAPIA: I was angry when I heard what they did to a private investigator working for the father of the American boy they murdered. They cut the skin off the bottoms of both his feet and made him walk on salt. Then they put him in a tub of water and boiled him alive. While he was screaming, they pulled pieces of raw flesh off his body.

LARSON: Any advice for our audience?

TAPIA: Don't get caught unawares like we did. If you see any signs of something that's out of the ordinary, notify your law enforcement officers. Do yourself a favor. Save your kids!

TEXAS STATE ATTORNEY GENERAL'S COMMENTS ON THE CRIME

I also talked with Jim Mattox, who at the time was the Texas State Attorney General in charge of handling the investigation of the Matamoros cult crimes.

"What about the link between drugs and this terrible tragedy?" I asked.

"Drug money provided the leader of his cult with the charisma and trappings of prosperity that attracted young men seeking to get ahead. Then, he used satanism to put some kind of spell on them. As a Christian, I believe that the devil possessed these murderers."

"Mr. Mattox, you've talked to the suspects. What are they like? What kind of person gets involved in drugs and satanism?"

"They came from fine families. One was head of a soccer team. Another, the head of an aerobics program. They did all the right things and appeared to be loving, kind, and generous people.

"What I saw in Mexico was unbelievable," Mattox went on. "My concern is for the growing influence of satanism. In a civilized nation, this should not be tolerated."

THE LINK BETWEEN SATANISM AND DRUGS

Drugs and satanism have been uniquely joined for centuries. Archaeologists note that pre-Columbian cultures forged a link between sadism, terrorism, and human sacrifice by taking drugs. The Meso-American folk religions of the Mayas and Aztecs required human sacrifices and used drugs to induce apathy in the victims.

The writings of the late Carlos Castaneda, whose books give glowing tales of pharmacological indulgence through the sorcerer

Don Juan, provide a societal backdrop for drugs and the occult. Castaneda, author of *Journey to Ixtlan*, *The Power of Silence*, and *The Fire Within*, idealized black magic practices of human-animal communication and spell-casting. He pointed out that all such occult procedures are possible under the influence of hallucinogenic drugs such as psilocybin and peyote. Many read his books and imitate Castaneda's fusion of the occult and narcotics.

For many participants in satanic ceremonies, the lure of drugs is an enticement attracting them to satanism. Once involved in the cult, the use of drugs, along with hypnotic suggestion, becomes a form of brainwashing. Satanic cult leaders know that even though their philosophy is based on moral anarchy, they must maintain cohesiveness with their followers. Drugs render the devil's devotees addictively dependent and less likely to abandon their allegiance to Satan.

Mind-altering substances, combined with the charismatic control of an influential cult leader, trap satanists, leaving them no way out. Ironically, the cult leader seldom uses drugs. To do so would put him at risk of losing control over members who are under the influence of drugs. By staying sober, he can better manipulate the group.

The lure of satanism is selfishness, the same gratifying impulse that causes many to turn to drugs. Thus, an unholy bond exists between drugs and the devil, narcotics being both a form of seduction and a means of continued entrapment. Some satanists avoid drugs after commitment to devil worship. To them, swearing allegiance to Satan is a more effective high than psychoactive substances. The result is what one social expert calls a "delusional habit of the mind."[3]

As with the Brownsville case, some clandestine devil worshipers become involved in drug trafficking. New inductees may serve as "mules," carriers who transport the drugs across borders and state lines. The illicit distribution of drugs generates an underground cash economy, enabling cult members to spend their time pursuing satanic activities.

A DETECTIVE'S VIEW OF DRUGS AND THE DEVIL

Detective Lt. Larry Jones, a police veteran and director of the Cult Crime Impact Network, strongly believes that drugs and satanism are inseparable. During an interview, he described to me why that link is so important.

"People with an inner pain often turn to drugs. But it doesn't work. It creates a bondage to the supplier," Lt. Jones explained. "If you have a satanic group supplying the drugs for you, it's easier to go to their meetings than steal the dope. Also, a certain amount of deadening of the sensibilities is necessary in order to get new cult members to go through what they have to endure."

Detective Jones talked about the use of drugs as a means of coping in cults. "Drinking blood is distasteful to any normal person, yet that's what is required to join some satanic cults. Drugs make it possible to do the unthinkable. Also, many new members have to cut or torture themselves to prove their devotion to the devil. Drugs help them withstand the pain.

"Once they become an active member of the cult, drugs become even more necessary to heighten the mystique of some ceremonies," Jones declared. "The more you do drugs, the less you are able to think clearly. Then you become less aware of what is being done to entice you into satanic activity."

DRUGS AND EVIL

Eugene Frank Thompson, age twenty, was a small-time burglar and a big-time cocaine addict. On March 23, 1989, Thompson injected cocaine twenty to thirty times during a four-hour period. Then, he armed himself with a semiautomatic machine pistol and went on a murderous rampage. A few hours later he ended his own life after killing two women, raping another, and wounding two police officers. Unquestionably, drugs pushed him over the edge of insanity into ultimate evil.

The evil of drugs often strikes the most innocent. According to the National Committee for Prevention of Child Abuse, more than twelve hundred children in the United States died at the hands of child abusers, many of them drug addicts. Of thirty-two states providing information about problems linked to child abuse, twenty-two cited substance abuse as "the dominant characteristic among their caseload." In the District of Columbia, almost 90 percent of reported child abusers are active substance abusers.[4]

The case of Douglas Alan Dale was particularly pathetic. Police found the eighteen-month-old boy screaming after eating four cubes of crack cocaine. The child's mother testified that the morning after a party in her apartment, young Douglas wandered into a bedroom where her boyfriend was sleeping with cocaine nearby. The child began hallucinating after stuffing the cocaine into his mouth.

CONFRONTING THE DRUG DILEMMA

Though the drug problem in America is tragic, the majority of people do not have serious problems with illegal substances. In fact, the most dangerous and widely used drug is alcohol. Advertisements depict beautiful women and athletic men drinking booze and seeming to get the most out of life. The result is a desensitization to abusive substances. Apart from such glamorization, most people, especially teenagers, use drugs for other reasons.

A published survey revealed that 50 percent of teenagers said they used drugs to experiment. Twenty-three percent said peer pressure was the main factor influencing them. Fifteen percent cited escapism. Ten percent blamed rebellion. Four percent said they turned on simply because drugs were readily available.[5]

If you're concerned that someone you love is on drugs, here are the main ones to look for:

- *Marijuana:* Made from the dried leaves of the Cannabis sativa plant. Smoked as a cigarette (joint). Tetrahydrocannabinol, the psychoactive ingredient. A gateway drug, introducing teens to other abusive substances. Impairs short-term memory and psychomotor functions. Contains cancer-causing agents. Psychologically addictive.

- *Cocaine/Crack:* Highly addictive and potentially lethal. Snorted, smoked, or injected. Stimulant. Affects blood pressure and respiratory system. When used as crack it causes hallucinations and seizures.

- *LSD:* Popular hallucinogen during the 1960s, enjoying a resurgence among today's teens. Purchased in dot form, blotted on a piece of paper, and swallowed. Causes panic, paranoia, flashbacks, and sleeplessness.

- *PCP (Angel Dust):* Hallucinogen that may cause violent behavior. Most often smoked, but also inhaled, injected, or eaten. Causes irrational behavior. Blocks pain receptors, sometimes resulting in self-inflicted injuries. Also known as Loveboat or Graveyard.

- *Uppers:* Stimulants such as speed (tablet, pill, or capsule) and crank (white powder and tablets). Sometimes in crystal form, such as crystal meth. Go by such names as Black Beauties, Footballs, Pep Pills, Bumblebees. Produces anxiety, sleeplessness, and blurred vision. Can cause heart failure.

- *Downers:* Capsules and tablets producing relaxation but also slurred speech and altered perception in large doses. Depression and comas may result. Both physical and psychological dependence. Go by such names as Blue Devils, Red Devils, and Yellow Jackets.

- *Designer Drugs:* Concocted by underground chemists using unique molecular structure to avoid illegality. May be stronger than the drugs they imitate. Includes synthetic heroin, Ecstasy, China White, and analogs of PCP.

Sold as white powder or tablet. Can cause uncontrollable tremors and brain damage.

SOME ADVICE FOR PARENTS

Here are some ways to take constructive action to get a teenager off drugs before such abuse leads to demonic subjection. Deal directly with the problem. The worst mistake is for parents to experience denial and presume the problem is a passing fad. But don't overreact. Calling the police at the first sign of drug paraphernalia or telling your child he has ruined the family's reputation could destroy any later attempt at reconciliation.

Be prepared for your child's vigorous denial. Get some facts from local drug treatment centers to help present your case. Drugs distort moral judgment. Your child's defense may seem preposterous (though it seems logical to him). Be patient. Explain your concerns. Your child may be more addicted than he realizes, and his response could be a distorted interpretation of his physical dependency. You may encounter irrationality and anger. Persist calmly to make your point.

Search your own heart to find your part of the problem. Has love been missing from your home? Is communication an obstacle? Does your child feel neglected? Has an emphasis on social status and materialism bred disrespect for moral convention? Have you blundered by providing inadequate supervision of your child's spare time? Has your family ignored spiritual values and the importance of regular attendance at church or synagogue?

When the time comes to broach the subject, begin by reaffirming your love. Assure your child that you want to be part of the solution. Ask him to point out your failures from his perspective. Inquire if he comprehends the real reason drugs seem attractive. Explain that you will not tolerate continued use of illegal and self-destructive drugs. Confirm your willingness to find the proper kind of therapeutic treatment to overcome the dependency.

Be ready for one of several arguments:

"The drugs aren't mine, they belong to someone else."

"I'm not hooked because I only use them occasionally."

"It's no different from the booze you drink or the pills you take."

"I only go along with it to be popular."

Drug abuse is a symptom, not a cause. Idle time is the devil's playground. Organize family activities to keep your child busy. Get him involved in community efforts to help the needy. Talk with your church about youth activities that combine spiritual and recreational interests. If necessary, insist that your child break off relationships with friends who use drugs. Go with him to concerts instead of dropping him off to see a rock band where drug use will be rampant. Talk with his teachers about special efforts to improve his poor schoolwork.

If your child is uncooperative, professional intervention or an austere rehabilitation program may be necessary. The situation may be too far advanced for parental intercession and require medical treatment and controlled supervision.

Remember, drugs can be an introduction to the occult, the doorway to the devil and death. Firm discipline, loving acceptance, and constant vigilance can prevent your child from getting hooked on Satan's opiate.

Chapter 12

Servants
of Satan

I renounce God! I renounce Christ! I will serve only Satan. Hail Satan! Those are the words I wrote in my own blood ... That night I did a ritual based on the pact and called up the spirits, asking them to enter my body when I went to sleep. I started having a dream about killing my parents. But when I woke up, it was no longer a dream. It really happened."

I had doubted similar stories, but there were no doubts this time. The person speaking to me was Sean Sellers, who was convicted in 1986 at age sixteen of three murders. At one time he was the youngest inmate on death row in the Oklahoma State Penitentiary.

I was most interested in talking with Sean because I had read about his trio of murders. He killed his first victim, a convenience store clerk, on September 8, 1985. The clerk, Robert Bowers, had once refused to sell beer to Sellers and a companion, Richard Howard. Howard stole his grandfather's .357 Magnum, and the two hunted Bowers down. Sean shot once and missed. He shot again and missed. Bowers tried to escape, but Howard blocked his way. The third shot hit and splattered blood against the wall and floor. Sean and Richard walked out, taking no money or merchandise—only the life of an innocent man.

On March 5, 1986, Sean shot his parents. Sean described to me the events of that night.

"I was very angry with them [my parents] about some problems related to a girlfriend," Sean said. "I went through my nightly satanic devotions by undressing and putting on black underwear and a black, hooded cape. I lit candles and incense. Then I invoked my main spirit, Ezurate, and fell asleep.

"I don't remember anything else until I walked into their bedroom. I had my stepfather's .44 revolver. I'm still not clear how I got it. I shot them both in the head."

He continued. "Then I left the bedroom. A little later I came back and turned the light on. I stood in front of my mother and watched the blood pour out of her onto the bed. Then I laughed and giggled. I felt like a big rock had been lifted from my shoulders—like a burden was finally freed from me."

Sean Sellers was introduced to satanism through witchcraft. The method of his induction contains some valuable lessons for parents and counselors seeking to avert youth from becoming involved in either witchcraft or satanism. I asked Sean to tell me about this part of his unfortunate pathway to devil worship and murder.

"It all started when a senior girl in my high school named Melissa gave a speech to the student body about witchcraft," Sean explained. "I have no idea why she was allowed to do it. She said she had witnessed a human sacrifice and had a piece of human skin to prove it.

"My girlfriend knew I was getting interested in this stuff so she contacted Melissa. Then Melissa called me. She told me, 'You can do black magic or white magic. But white magic is hypocritical. If you want real power, go with black magic.'"

"What did she suggest as a way to get started?" I asked.

"Melissa told me to get *The Satanic Bible* and some ritual paraphernalia," Sean said. "Then she gave me a crash course in witchcraft and satanism."

"Was she actively recruiting you?" I wanted to know.

"Yes, I think that was the reason for her speech at the school. She had been involved in witchcraft since the age of nine."

"Did Melissa ever mention being networked with any other witchcraft groups?"

Sean paused for a moment. "I think so, but I can't be sure. She was secretive. She controlled when she'd call me and where we'd meet. It seemed like she was in league with someone higher up, but I never met them."

"Do you know if there is any hierarchical structure in witchcraft?" I asked Sean.

"She was always talking about different levels. She said there were nine and that she was at level six. Melissa explained how I could go to higher levels on my own."

"What did she say about God?"

"She said that Christians were weaklings and she had more power through witchcraft," Sean explained. "I was mad at God because a girlfriend had dumped on me, so I accepted the idea. I even wrote a letter to my friends saying that the strength of one satanist equals ten Christians."

"Do you still believe that?" I inquired.

"No way!" Sean declared. "Satan is a created being. God is the Creator. The only power Satan has is the power we give him."

"Besides the influence of the witch, Melissa, what contributed most to your getting into devil worship?" I wanted to know.

"Every teenager I know involved in satanism has had problems with his father. Either their father wasn't there because of a divorce, or their father abused or ignored them. That's the way it was with me."

"Why is the influence of a father so important?"

"Because God is our Father in heaven," Sean explained. "Our human fathers represent to us what our Father in heaven is like. Those who don't have an earthly father who loves them may find it difficult to understand the love of God the Father."

"Was there ever a time after you got deep into witchcraft and satanism that you could have gotten out?" I asked.

"Yes. At one point I didn't want to be involved anymore. Melissa and other satanists told me there was no way out. But one day I got in trouble at school. The vice principal found my satanic books and called my mom. She came to school and took me home. My mother was so upset I finally realized how much I had hurt her.

"My stepfather told me, 'There were times I had to hold your mother crying because she was at work and couldn't make it home for your birthday. She would go without food so she could buy a present for you.'

"I felt terrible," Sean said. "I went to my bedroom and ripped up all my stuff on satanism. I decided that I loved my family more than satanism and wanted out. I went to a prayer group. I went to a priest. I went to everyone I could find, but no one took me seriously. No one had any answers for me.

"I would write poems and my thoughts about life and death. My mother read them, but she never really asked me what they meant.

"My parents began thinking it was no big deal and dropped the issue. That was their big mistake. By the time my parents started to realize that my satanism was serious, I had followed the devil's instructions to put bullets through both their heads!"

From his death row jail cell, Sean Sellers spoke forcibly about the devil's deception. I asked him what he says to those who have sold their souls to the devil. "I tell them the devil makes you do things that are alien to your nature," Sean said. "I was a sensitive kid who wrote music and poetry. I was a good student and an athlete. I loved nature and life and wanted to be a veterinarian. But Satan changed all that.

"The devil isn't *for* you, he's *against* you. Serving Satan sounds good at first. You can have anything you want. But in the end it's horrible. Satanists think they're looking forward to having fun in hell, but the devil makes a shambles of their lives before they get there. They end up in hell on earth!"

Sean described vividly the final effects of satanism that caused him to kill. "It took away the love for my parents and my girlfriend," he explained. "Eventually, I had no love. No mercy. No conscience. It was subtle. It happened little by little."

"What should parents do if they discover their child is interested in the occult?" I asked Sean.

"Don't panic," he advised. "That will turn them off. Find out if they've gotten occult paraphernalia out of curiosity or more serious reasons. If they're just experimenting, explain how dangerous it can be. Let them know it will destroy their lives."

"What if it's gone beyond that? Suppose a teenager is seriously involved in satanism?"

"First look for some hard evidence like scars, tattoos, demonic drawings, and satanic paraphernalia like bones and pentagrams," Sean counseled. "If you find that stuff, don't ignore it. It gets serious quickly. Get someone who can help you.

"If your child is involved because he isn't getting attention, start paying attention. Let your child know you love him." Sean went on. "Then start putting some limits on his behavior, who he goes out with, and where he goes. That may seem harsh and cause some rebellion at first, but you've got to do it. If you don't the outcome could be worse. Just look at me."

"What's it like on death row?" I asked Sean.

"My cell is seventeen feet long. It's got a desk, sink, toilet, a barred window, and a barred door," he answered. "The floor is cement and I sleep on a thin mattress. Once a day they let me out into the yard for an hour to exercise. The rest of the time I'm behind bars."

I still didn't fully comprehend why Sean Sellers had killed so brutally at fifteen years of age, so I questioned him further. "I understand that you've become a Christian. What's the difference between what you are now and what you were?" I asked.

"Well," Sean started, "I used to believe like most satanists that Satan is good and God is bad. I felt that Satan cared about all mankind. I loved Satan. I wanted to serve him. But after what's happened to me, I know Satan wants only to destroy mankind."

"Does satanism give you the right to get even with anyone you want?"

"It's the opposite of the golden rule," Sean responded. "I believed that if someone hurts you, you hurt them back. Satanism taught me that kindness is due to those who deserve it, instead of wasting love on ingrates. You should love only those who are deserving of love."

During Sean's trial he was silent, claiming he could not recall the crime. After the verdict, Sean's memory of much of the incident returned, a fact that clouds his days with inconceivable guilt. But Sean Sellers knows now beyond any doubts why he did what he did.

"Satan will never take anything you don't give him," Sean admits. "And I gave him everything. If I hadn't gotten into satanism, I would not be here today. Anyone who plays games with the devil is going to lose. The devil is going to use you and then throw you away."

Sean concluded with a lesson for parents from his own life. "After satanism affected me I couldn't go back to what I was before."

All that changed one day in March 1986 when Sean was in the Oklahoma City county jail two weeks after the murders. Free from drugs, Sean finally felt guilty about what he had done. Someone (he couldn't remember who) handed him a Bible. He opened it and began to read. Verses on love and forgiveness seemed to be on every page he turned to.

God might even forgive me, he realized. He fell to his knees, sobbing. He asked God to forgive him and to come into his heart and change his life.

When a local ministry came to the prison to lead a chapel service, a chaplain stopped by to see Sean. Every Tuesday Sean continues to meet with a group for prayer and Bible study.

"I've learned," Sean says, "that once the devil changes you, only God can restore you. Only He can reach into a heart the occult has destroyed."

Sean's story may be dramatic because of his age, but Sellers's methodical involvement in satanism and his brutal homicidal acts are not unusual in the annals of criminal satanism. Here are the stories of others who murdered in the name of Satan.

KILLING FOR THE DEVIL

Theron Reed ("Pete") Roland II was tall, dark, and handsome, and everyone considered him a basic all-around good boy. On December 6, 1987, Pete and three other boys, James Hardy, Ron Clements, and Steven Newberry, drove to a wooded area near Carl Junction, Missouri. They sacrificed a cat to honor the devil. Suddenly, three of them turned on Steven Newberry.

"Sacrifice for Satan," they chanted.

Frightened, Newberry started running. The three picked up baseball bats, which were part of the ritual, and began striking their comrade. One bat broke. Seventy blows later, Newberry was dead. Pete and his friends dragged the body to a cistern—"the well of hell," they called it. Along with the dead cat they had sacrificed earlier, the young satanic slayers tossed Newberry's body in the cistern.

One baseball bat belonging to Ron Clements had written on it "the ultraviolence stick," a phrase borrowed from the movie, *A Clockwork Orange*, about violent gangs in England. When it was over, Pete said he had expected the devil to appear and grant all of them great powers. Instead, Pete and his two friends got life in prison without possibility of parole. In court, the jury was shown a box with Pete Roland's prized possessions—a satanic notebook with demonic doodlings, a carved skull with a nail driven through it, and diabolical-looking rock posters and album covers.

TOMMY SULLIVAN'S SLIDE INTO SATANISM

One of the most celebrated stories of teenage satanism is the much-publicized account of fourteen-year-old Tommy Sullivan. Raised a devout Roman Catholic, Tommy was described by friends as a poetic person with deep feelings. In a special notebook, his very own *Book of Shadows*, he had written, "To the greatest of demons. I would like to make a solemn exchange with you. If you will give me the most extreme of all magical powers, I will kill many Christian followers. Exactly twenty years from this day, I will promise to commit suicide. I will tempt teenagers on earth to have sex, have incest, do drugs, and worship you. I believe that evil will once again rise and conquer the love of God."[1]

Friends say Tommy's descent into evil began when a teacher requested students to prepare a report on satanism. For Tommy, the assignment became an odyssey into the occult. The fourteen year old spent days listening to a growing collection of heavy metal records and became absorbed in playing Dungeons & Dragons. Tommy learned to write backward and inscribed in his *Book of Shadows* the words, "Evil of all mankind dwells within my soul. If you want in, let me know."[2]

His artistic side was visible in the sinister drawings in the *Book of Shadows*, which contained devilish creatures and scenes of sadistic rituals. One page was entitled "Come to Satan." On another page, a demonic figure held an upside-down cross, standing in front of a woman lying prostrate on a slab being lowered by pulleys into hell.

Finally, Tommy told his friends about a dream in which Satan appeared to him. "Satan had my face," the eighth-grader declared. "He was carrying a knife, and he told me to 'preach Satanism to other kids, and then kill everyone in your family.' I'm going to do this."[3]

One night shortly after, Tommy headed for the downstairs den to watch a horror movie. At 10:30, his father heard a smoke alarm go off and called the police. When authorities arrived, they found the house splattered with blood. Tommy's mother was discovered with her throat slit and dozens of slashes made with the thrust of a knife. Tommy had tried to gouge out her eyes, and her hands were partially severed.

The next day, authorities found Tommy buried in a snowdrift. His wrists were cut and his throat had been slashed ear-to-ear with an intensity that nearly decapitated him. Beside him lay the open Boy Scout knife that he had used to kill his mother and end his own life.

DERECK SHAW'S SATANISM

In another tragic case of teenage satanism, a Sackville, Nova Scotia, sixteen-year-old named Dereck Shaw phoned his girlfriend while her parents were out and told her that on the previous night he had been visited by Satan. According to Shaw, the devil appeared in a blue light and demanded his soul. After speaking with his girlfriend, Shaw told his half brother and stepbrother, both eight years old, to close their eyes while he went to his parents' bedroom and got his stepfather's hunting rifle. He carried the gun down to his bedroom in the basement and put the .30-.30 rifle barrel into his mouth and fired.

Dereck's parents bravely stepped forward to alert the press. They blamed their son's death on his two-year fascination with satanic worship and ritual violence. Just months before, they had confiscated Dereck's black candles, a hand-drawn pentagram, and instruction books by which he had apparently conducted rituals. The pastor of Dereck's parents, Reverend Hedley Hopkins, succinctly stated, "Young people who are bored are trying to make contact with evil. And if you try long enough, you eventually find something intelligent and malignant and destructive."[4]

Who are the youth most susceptible to satanism?

The devil's disciples are mostly middle-class and white. A high percentage are male because of the macho posturing required for blood-spilling rituals and acts of desecration. They are also often creative and intelligent. They are almost always victims of familial alcohol abuse, physical violence, and neglect. Some are leaders of cults, but most are influenced by older, big-brother figures who have already blazed a trail of devilish dissipation. Satanism supplies these young people with an anything-goes invitation. The occult world of mystery and magic becomes real.

SEAN SELLERS'S SAGA OF SATANISM

Why did Sean Sellers worship the devil? How did he become involved in satanism?

I asked him those questions.

He told the story of his childhood and gradual induction into the occult. Sean's parents divorced when he was a toddler. His mother, Vonda, married Paul Bellafatto in 1976. Vonda and Paul often neglected young Sean. They left him with family members as their transient lifestyle took them around the country.

Sean was an exceedingly bright student who read science fiction and supernatural tales. When he was ten, his baby-sitter checked out some satanic books for him at the library. In March 1984, when Sean was fourteen, he was uprooted again when Vonda and Paul deposited Sean with Vonda's sister in Okmulgee, Oklahoma.

"Like all teenagers, I was looking for acceptance," Sean explained. "At thirteen, I had a bad experience with a girl. I was mad at God and shortly thereafter was introduced to a witch who took me in as her apprentice. I ended up praying to Satan and felt a sensation like fingertips touching me everywhere.

"Then," Sean said, "I became obsessively involved with Dungeons & Dragons. I went frequently to the *Rocky Horror Picture Show* (a rock movie musical based on transvestism, sado-masochism, and other perversions). I met a lot of satanists there. I identified myself by wearing my left shirtsleeve rolled up and keeping my left pinkie fingernail unclipped and painted black. Through Ninjitsu, I delved into the violent aspects of the martial arts, learning how to conceal weapons and commit assassination. I once ate the leg off a live frog in biology class.

"Drugs played a role too," Sean went on. "I started out with marijuana. I had such a rigorous routine doing rituals at night that I took speed to keep me going."

BLOOD RITUALS

I asked Sean Sellers if he participated in the bloodlust aspects of satanism.

"Yes. I started carrying little vials of blood with me all the time," he answered. "I kept some in the refrigerator. I was working in a clinic on weekends and would steal needles for extracting blood and vials to carry it in."

"Did blood give you some kind of high? Where did you get the idea?"

"It was called for in some rituals we did," Sean divulged. "It gave me an eerie sensation. Like in the horror movies where people say that wickedness is 'delicious.'

"But that's not all. Part of the idea of drinking blood came from the attitude among satanists that the more bizarre something is, the more evil it is. Drinking blood was something that was disgusting, abhorrent, and condemned by God. So it fit in perfectly with the things I was doing. At first, it was like a thrill. As I got more into it, I began to crave blood." The testimony of Sean Sellers is a sobering reminder of the consequences of dabbling with the devil. The excitement he sought in Satanism cost Sean his freedom and his life. On February 4, 1999, Sean Sellers was executed.

Chapter 13

Stories of Satanic Cults

I'm Number One. That's what I call myself because I'm number one in my life."

Those words were spoken by one of the most cold-blooded individuals I've ever talked to. His comment came during a discussion about the criminal activities of satanic cults. I pressed Number One further. "Have you killed or would you kill for Satan?" I wanted to know.

"I'd kill instantly. It doesn't have to be for any reason. Not even the devil. Remember, I'm Number One."

"But have you ever killed anyone?"

"I plead the Fifth."

"Are you evil?" I challenged Number One.

"What do you call evil?"

"Like harming the innocent," I said. "For example, dealing drugs."

"If that's your idea of evil, I fit," Number One replied.

"How about stealing?"

"In a heartbeat. If I wanted something in your car, I would bust open your window and take it."

"Do you have any morals?"

"My only moral is that I'm Number One. If what I do is wrong, why do I feel so great when I kill? Why do I smile?"

I wasn't quite prepared for his follow-up question. "Have you ever tasted blood? Have you ever run your hands through warm guts?" Number One asked. "I kill animals. Cats, dogs, squirrels. Animals like that. Then I put my hands in their blood and lick it off my hands. It gives me a high and makes me smile. I'm teaching my six-year-old daughter to sacrifice animals and taste their blood."

THE SACRIFICE OF INNOCENT ANIMALS

Most instances of devil-worshiping animal mutilations and sacrifices are not uncovered, except when an ex–cult member comes forward. Those who once participated in satanic ceremonies unhesitatingly reveal that killing animals is an integral part of appeasing dark forces.

In the mid-1970s there were persistent reports about finding sheep, cattle, and horses whose reproductive organs had been removed and their blood drained. In the western United States from New Mexico to northern Alberta, Canada, talk of prize bulls and valued quarter horses being butchered was rampant. In 1980 *Newsweek* reported accounts of mutilated livestock in twenty-seven states.[1]

Those who scoffed at the satanic mutilation theory called the idea an example of mass hysteria, akin to a witch-hunt. They blamed preying animals, but their predator hypothesis couldn't explain some of the mutilations: needle marks in the animals' jugular veins, the surgical precision by which eyes and vital organs had been removed, the strange emphasis on dismembering genitals, the lack of body fluids and traces of spilled blood, the cleanly cut holes in the skull to extricate brains, and indications of burns on the hides.

Police files contain documented confessions of satanic involvement in animal mutilations. An Oklahoma woman, who spent five years in a devil-worshiping cult, said she made numerous forays to remote areas where cattle were killed and their blood removed by an embalming machine. Her wealthy cult used a helicopter and several trucks to avoid detection. The helicopter would transport the cow to a remote location or a truck with a telescoping lift would hold a cult member in the air while he performed the mutilations. Veterinarians instructed cult members how to acquire the needed blood and body parts. Large animals were selected because of the huge quantities of blood required for satanic baptismal immersion.[2]

My opinion, based on years of research and countless conversations with those involved in ritualistic sacrifices, is that during the 1970s when such activity gained attention, organized occult groups were indeed involved in the ceremonial slaughter of livestock. Though some instances could be attributed to predators, other cases bore clear trademarks of black magic killings. As more became known about the mutilations, the occult groups realized they would be discovered and, therefore, changed their ritualistic practices.

The use of cattle is particularly noteworthy. In the more advanced stages of Luciferian worship, cows play an important ritualistic role. Many groups trace their origins to ancient agrarian cults. Egyptians, Canaanites, and Babylonians had pagan religions that revered the cow as a mother goddess and combined bestiality with bovine genital veneration. Even today, tourists to the Egyptian pyramids can walk through subterranean passages and witness row upon row of elaborate stone sarcophagi used to entomb sacred cattle. The Valley of the Kings in Luxor contains five-thousand-year-old wall paintings that picture humans cohabiting with cattle and consorting sexually with other livestock.

Though organized satanic cults are a small part of the underground occult movement in America, their largely unknown presence is pervasive enough to account for the reported cases of animal mutilations. Without divulging confidences, I can reveal that I have personally counseled those who admit involvement in such cults. They are reluctant to acknowledge these crimes, fearing their stories would be discredited as outlandish fabrications of unstable minds.

THE SATANIC ABUSE OF CHILDREN

The ceremonial use of innocent animals is tragic, but nowhere near as abhorrent as the abuse, torture, and even murder of innocent children whose parents, mentors, and abductors offer them to the devil.

Dr. Gregory Simpson, a Los Angeles pediatrician, began looking into the ritual abuse of children after treating many scarred young patients. One dead girl's chest was carved with a pentagram. Dr. Simpson says, "The conclusion I reached is that satanic abuse of small children does exist, and it's something that needs to be dealt with by the medical community."[3]

Chicago police occult crime expert Robert Simandahl also expressed concern about ritual abuse of children. He said, "It's a subject that makes street gang activity look like a nursery school rhyme."[4]

In the words of Jeffrey Burton Russell, history professor and authority on the idea of the devil in Western civilization, "The rash of appallingly degenerative crimes, including the violation of children and the mutilation of animals, can be tolerated only by a society determined to deny at any cost the radical existence of evil."[5]

Only recently have human victims begun to reveal unbelievable tales of terror. They say ritualized murder begins with killing small animals, then larger ones. Next comes killing isolated adults who are kidnapped at random, followed by the systematic abduction, torture, defilement, and eventual sacrifice of children. Their incredible narratives reveal striking similarities. The statements by victims from different parts of the country tally with one another and are being corroborated by therapists.

Common elements combine to form a framework of evil. First a blood relative or trusted friend inducts a child. Secret ceremonies instill a ritualistic fear of evil, accompanied by robed and hooded figures, naked women on altars, hypnotic chants, goblets of animal blood, bottles of human flesh preserved in formaldehyde, and orgies between adults and children and children with animals. The eating of feces, drinking of urine, sacrifices of babies, and taking of pictures for pornographic purposes are other elements that law enforcement authorities and therapists have uncovered. Some cases of cannibalism have been reported.

Women previously involved in satanic cults tell of becoming brides to Satan. Others claim they were inducted to become baby breeders, to conceive babies for sacrifice without birth or death records. One woman claims she trained baby breeders, brainwashed from birth to believe such atrocities were normal. Her first two births from pregnancies induced by her stepfather were sacrificed, which she then considered an honor.

On one national telecast, a woman named Annette claimed breeders were sexually stimulated prepubescently in preparation for impregnation by age eight or nine. Another woman testified she was pregnant at ten, and the baby was sacrificed. At age eleven, she had another baby, which was sold to other cult members. In such cases, labor often was prematurely induced. A woman named Cheryl described her baby being impaled through the heart by an upside-down cross. To deal with the horror, baby breeders say they blocked out reality by multiple personalities and other forms of denial.[6]

MARKED FOR DEATH

Terrified youth have contacted me claiming they were marked for sacrifice at birth. One such teen was Joe, a young man who told a frightening story.

"I play in a black metal band called Lords of Darkness, and I've got a big problem," he declared.

"What's that?"

"Today's the twenty-eighth, right? Well, next month, on the eighth, I have a birthday."

"Happy birthday," I congratulated him.

"You wouldn't say that if you knew what's going to happen on my birthday. I just found out myself last Saturday. I'm going to be sacrificed to Satan."

"You're what!" I exclaimed. "Who's going to do it?"

"My parents. They've been into Satan worship all my life. I never thought much about it. It's just the way I was raised, you know, like some kids are raised Baptist. For me, my parents worship Lucifer."

"Why didn't you know before that you were destined to be sacrificed?"

"The subject never came up until I went to church. Several days ago, a girl I like asked me to go to her church. When I got home, my brother told my mother where I'd been. That's when she told me I'd have to be killed."

"How old are you?"

"Fifteen. I don't want to die. But it's all there in the black box."

"What black box?" I inquired.

"My parents have this black box they keep for the devil. It has several things in it—*The Satanic Bible*, a picture of my mother, black candles, goblets, daggers, and my birth certificate. Keeping my birth certificate in that box signifies a pact that I have to die some day. Now that I've been to a Christian church, my mother's guardian spirit has told her I have to die on my next birthday."

I directed Joe to professional counseling. Joe eventually took the black box from his home, smashed it with a hammer, and burned the contents except for his birth certificate. Then he started a new life free from his parents' satanic practices.

The primitive idea of human sacrifice has an ignominious history. Offering human victims in propitiatory rites reverts to the Canaanites of the Middle East and the Meso-American

Aztecs. The latter stained Huitzilopochtli temples with the blood of thousands of victims. The tradition is also found among ancient Greeks, Hindus, and druids. Such sacrifice was sometimes meant to atone for the wrongs of the entire group. Other times, human oblation was used to appease the gods after a natural disaster.

Human sacrifice among current satanic cults is often well organized and extremely efficient. Anticoagulants are used to store blood drained from a body, which may be disposed of in a portable crematorium. The idea of murdering another human for religious purposes is borrowed from black magic literature. Satanist Aleister Crowley wrote: "For the highest spiritual working, one must accordingly choose that victim which contains the greatest and purest force. A male child of perfect innocence and high intelligence is the most satisfactory and suitable victim."[7]

A book called *The Black Arts* states: "When the grimoires (black magic books) talk about killing a kid, they really mean a human child . . . there is a tradition that the most effective sacrifice to demons is the murder of a human being."[8]

MOLESTED AND MISSING CHILDREN

Some cult watchers and police agree that a large number of missing children are victims of human sacrifice cults. According to the few survivors, children are abducted and subjected to the terrifying intimidation of drugs and brainwashing before being sacrificed. They are warned that no one will believe them and that their parents will never want them back. Every technique of the cult is carefully planned to gain control of the youngsters' thoughts and behavior.

The defilement of children is important to satanists. The more helpless the victim, the greater proof of the cult members' devotion to the devil. They also believe that the more pure the sacrifice to Satan, the more power they obtain from the god of darkness. Innocent children and guiltless babies are perfect victims. Some law enforcement officials believe that many missing children are victims of occult-related abductions.

Throughout America, children are becoming victims of horrendous assaults. For instance, a thirty-seven-year-old California baby-sitter and her boyfriend were charged with sexual assault, lewdness with a child, and child pornography. Their victims, ages three, six, and eight, suffered nightmares, behavior disorders, and withdrawal after being held captive by satanists, who ritualistically raped them. Naked, they were forced to watch the sacrificial slaughter of cows, horses, cats, and birds.[9]

In another reported case of ritual abuse, investigators were told that victims were forced to drink blood and eat feces. One of the children said he watched a boy named Bobby, who had lived in a cage, participate in a ceremony before he was decapitated and cannibalized by adults. Seven children were treated for depression, suicidal feelings, and regressive development.[10]

One victim of ritualistic child abuse related to me an account almost too terrible to tell. At the age of five, she was taken to the room of the dying cult leader for a sexual initiation. A painful vaginal penetration was performed with the soon-to-be-corpse to ensure that his semen would be passed on ceremonially, a ritual designed to confer upon her the spirits he had conjured and served. When the leader died, she was ceremonially subjected to sadomasochistic violence too lurid to reveal. Suffice to say, her sexual organs were violated and abused in ways only a demented mind could conceive. Finally, she was forced to have anal, oral, and vaginal sex with every member of the cult, as well as several animals—all this at five years of age. To this day she remembers the orgiastic scene that followed, involving indiscriminate coupling of every sexual deviancy, including animal and human.

The ingestion of human waste products was often forced upon her. On one occasion she was buried alive for several days, breathing through a small air tube inserted into her coffin. To terrorize her further, nonpoisonous snakes were placed in her burial tomb.

Our conversation was the first time she had revealed what had happened to her. Why?

Suppose someone told you the story I've just related? Would you believe it? Do you believe what I've written above? Do I believe it? Yes, but I can't blame you if your credulity is stretched.

Law enforcement officials and the courts often feel the same way. In fact, the story of ritualistic abuse of children remains largely untold simply because it is so unbelievable. Satanic cults deliberately fabricate preposterous forms of child victimization, knowing that the more unthinkable their atrocity, the less likely the victim will be believed.

The easiest recruits for satanic groups are runaway teenagers. Often abused, neglected, and acquainted with the consequences of evil, they feel they have nothing to lose. They adopt the attitude that evil is pervasive and triumphant, so they might as well join it. Viewing themselves as victims of a competitive world and an adversarial society, they see satanism as a way to get what they want fast. Too late they learn that the price of getting out can be death. Some who would like to leave are presented with photographs taken of them during ceremonies, a convenient blackmailing technique. Hundreds of bizarre cults operate secretly. They are different from the more visible devil-worshiping cults like the Church of Satan, which repudiates all responsibility for the violation of minors.

Circumstantial evidence indicates that nationwide covens of child molesters are in touch with one another. Police have uncovered computer records linking child molestation rings, and the similarities of techniques used to violate the innocent indicate interaction between such groups. Investigators believe most networking is informal, extended by families and friends or from one generation to the next.

As with cocaine cartels, these satanic cults follow a hierarchical leadership. Leaders come from all walks of life, including the wealthy and influential. Victims I have counseled say one reason for their silence is that they would have to accuse powerful figures in the community whose credibility is much greater than teenagers who are caught up in such diversions as satanic metal music and drugs or alcohol.

Some investigators of satanic crimes suggest highly placed satanists have even infiltrated the criminal justice system. Law enforcement officials privately admit being ordered by superiors to cease investigations of satanic crimes. Others complain of political restrictions and unnecessary constraints.

There is evidence of nationwide connections between black magic groups and drug and pornography rings. Unfortunately, satanic crimes are often difficult to prosecute.

An occult crime is often hard to detect and to prove in a court of law. There is no pattern to these crimes for detectives to follow since victims are snatched at whim. Often all evidence is destroyed when victims are either burned or their bodies cut into pieces and buried. The most paradoxical obstruction to prosecution is our nation's criminal justice system itself. Courts often refuse to handle cases in which the practice of satanism alone is considered a sufficient criminal motive because satanism is an officially recognized religion.

If the state does prosecute, much evidence is not admissible in court since it involves religious ceremonies. Additionally, just performing a satanic rite is insufficient cause for prosecution. Constitutional rights of religious freedoms allow satanists free reign to worship the devil as they choose, so long as no law is violated.

Judges are reluctant to admit testimony of satanic abuse from small children in a court of law. Even in cases where medical symptoms indicate a crime has occurred, the veracity of the child's testimony is strained when he talks about being drugged and observing bloody ceremonies. The sacrifice of innocents continues because society is accustomed to Hollywood's horror genre. Thus, when a victim comes forward, especially a child, the account of abuse too closely resembles a fictional splatter film.

WHAT YOU CAN DO TO STOP THE SLAUGHTER

Ritualistic abuse of children can be halted if concerned citizens take action. Police, social workers, therapists, and parents must be aware of the symptoms of abuse and advise children on how to avoid being vulnerable. If your child needs day care, schedule unannounced visits to the center and demand entry anytime you wish. Teach your children that their bodies are their own and that no one, not even a family member or relative, has the right to touch them in a private place. Children should also be taught not to take rides, go on walks, or engage in any activity with someone they don't know, no matter how friendly and helpful the person may be. Saying "Don't take candy from strangers" isn't enough.

Consult a physician immediately if you detect unusual marks on your child's body, especially in the genital area. Be watchful for severe changes in childhood behavior surrounding sleep patterns, nightmares, toilet habits, and language. If your youngster suddenly begins using forbidden words or discusses sexual conduct in an unusually explicit manner, take special note of its cause.

Teach your child at an early age that horror movies and exploitative TV programs about the occult are off-limits because they are dangerous. Cultivate the concept of a loving, all-powerful God, not a cruel judge who sarcastically scrutinizes every action. Abductors attempt to brainwash their victims to believe that God will judge them for what they've engaged in so there is no point in trying to escape.

PART III

Behind the Beliefs of Satanism and the Occult

Chapter 14

Mephistopheles's Manifestos

I'm a satanist. I hurt people. I destroy them."

Kay wasn't the first seventeen-year-old whom I had heard say something like that. But the conversation took a strange twist almost immediately.

"Did you get the letter I wrote you?" she asked. "The one with the blood on it?"

"Yes. Your letter has an upside-down cross on the envelope. Inside it says, 'Satan rules!' You've drawn knives on it. They look like they're dripping in blood . . . Wait a minute! This looks like real blood . . . Is it?"

"Yeah," Kay confidently exclaimed. "My blood. I cut myself in a ceremony just for you."

"You've signed it, 'Yours truly, Lucifer.' Did you write this by yourself?" I inquired.

"With a little help from the demons in me, Lies and Hate."

"I suppose they helped you write the P.S.: 'If you don't devote yourself to Satan, watch out. This is not an empty threat but . . .'"

Kay interrupted, ". . . but rather a promise."

"You still remember the words?"

"I wrote them, didn't I? I meant it too."

Many teenagers are as ardent as Kay in their dedication to the devil and his lies. To understand why, we must probe the cultural seeds of satanism planted by occult religious movements. These sects extol the doctrines of hate that appeal to neglected and confused youth. The most basic question to be weighed in this section is a fundamental consideration of theology: Is the devil real? Is he a mythical monster? Or is he, as Carl Jung believed, an archetypal image of evil?

Does Satan really exist? John Wesley, the founder of Methodism, answered "Yes!" to that question. "There is no evil done or spoken or thought without the assistance of the devil, who worketh with strong though secret power. All the works of evil nature are the work of the devil," he said.

Many today, including some in the clergy, don't agree. They say that belief in a personal devil is a medieval fantasy constructed to anthropomorphically describe evil's existence. Society at large and youths in particular are desensitized to the authenticity of evil. Few realize an intense, intangible, spiritual struggle is taking place every day.

In his book *People of the Lie*, psychiatrist M. Scott Peck chronicles his pilgrimage from a skeptic who did not believe the devil exists to an active participant in exorcisms. Peck writes, "The spirit I witnessed at each exorcism was clearly, utterly, and totally dedicated to opposing human life and growth. It told both patients to kill themselves."[1] He concludes, "I know no more accurate epithet for Satan than the Father of Lies."[2]

Unfortunately, such absolute assurance concerning Satan and the reality of contact with the spirit world is not shared by the average American. One theologian has observed that the devil's cleverest wile is to convince humans he doesn't exist.

But the Bible strongly counters that assumption. Its pages are filled with references to Lucifer as a murderer, liar, adversary, and destroyer. He is alluded to as Beelzebub, Apollyon, and Mammon. He is described as being an angel of light when it suits his purpose, and a slanderer and tempter when that is convenient. For some, he is the ultimate cop-out to evade human responsibility for misconduct, as expressed in the quip, "The devil made me do it."

The biblical portrait of evil is much different from the perception held by satanists. The satanists I have confronted think of Lucifer as a chum who offers devilish delights. Hell is an eternal pleasure palace of endless orgasms. Evil is an impish indulgence met with a mischievous wink instead of divine disapproval. Above all, they see Satan as someone who cares more about them than God or their parents since he offers uninhibited gratification in place of sober moderation.

The devil appears as a friend who offers money, drugs, sex, excitement, and whatever their selfish desires fancy. When parents and society say no, the devil says yes. When God says "Wait," Satan says, "You can have it all, right now!"

Raised in an instant-everything society, teenagers think the devil delivers "microwavable" malevolence, quick fixes for long-term ills, and immediate satisfaction instead of delayed fulfillment. The '70s Rolling Stones's anthem, "You Can't Always Get What You Want," seems passé to today's youth. Madison Avenue has led them to believe their every whim deserves fulfillment, and worshiping the devil is a shortcut to gratifying every immoral instinct.

In an age of organized rebellion, satanism champions a creed of self-centeredness. Self-improvement books and motivational seminars have emphasized looking out for number one. Although muted, the underlying supposition of human potential courses has been "me first." Satanism condones such human frailties. Lying, cheating, gluttony, and greed are acceptable if they bring satisfaction. After all, the ultimate design of satanists is to become godlings, deities with all of Lucifer's passions and pursuits.

Another lure is the search for a nonnarcotic high. Satanists experience the raw essence of evil by participating in sacrificial ceremonies that seem to induce altered states of consciousness not unlike the psychoactive influence of hallucinogens. Also, in many solitary satanic cults, drugs play an important part in the ceremonies. In teenage cults, drugs and alcohol are integral.

LITERATURE OF THE LIE

Aiding the cultural climate of occult acceptance is a flourishing body of literature that exploits the darker side of human nature and the excesses of evil.

GRIMOIRES: BLACK MAGIC TEXTBOOKS

Grimoires, black magic textbooks for evoking demons, are the real thing. They are nonfiction, how-to books for the apprentice satanist. These manuals of magic have been ascribed to Solomon, Albertus Magnus, and assorted wizards. They describe rituals, ceremonies, and miscellaneous occult practices. Among the most notable are: *Liber Spiritum; Shemamphoras* (a Hebrew book); *Oupnekhat* (a Sanskrit manual); *Hell's Coercion* (attributed to Johannes Faustus); *The Key of Solomon* (ascribed to King Solomon); and *The Lesser Key of Solomon* (explaining the demonic hierarchy).[3]

THE KEY OF SOLOMON AND THE BOOK OF ENOCH

The Key of Solomon is the most famous book of antiquity extolling demonism. The Jewish historian Josephus in the first century A.D. referred to an occult book, supposedly written by King Solomon, with explicit instructions for incantations. This manual for summoning evil spirits was said to be composed by devils themselves. French and Latin versions abounded in the eighteenth century. The most popular version today was edited and embellished by Aleister Crowley.

The Book of Enoch is an apocryphal work attributed to the

biblical Enoch, composed in the second century B.C. It is based on an occult interpretation of Genesis 6:4. "The sons of God came in to the daughters of men and they bore children to them."

The Book of Enoch claims these "sons of Gods" were fallen angels who taught the powers of witchcraft to the beautiful women they seduced. Included in Enoch's book are the names of rebellious angels (demons) whose mission it is to torture mankind.

THE NECRONOMICON

The two most popular books representing the satanist genre are *The Satanic Bible* and *The Necronomicon*. The latter was the invention of American occult and horror-fiction author Howard Phillips Lovecraft (1890–1937). Lovecraft developed a mythology around the "dread Cthulhu," in which powers of evil and darkness from another time and space threatened to control the world. *The Necronomicon: The Book of Dead Names,* was their legendary occult text. Lovecraft claimed it was compiled by the "mad Arab Abdul Alhazred." In fact, the whole thing was concocted by Lovecraft, who cited references to it in his other stories.

A group of writers and researchers, headed by occult scholar Colin Wilson, collaborated to present *The Necronomicon: The Book of Dead Names* as a newly discovered masterpiece of occult literature. Wilson attempted to suggest that Lovecraft's invention may have had a historical basis in fact. Various occultists have claimed that a similar work has existed for centuries, rooted in *The Book of the Essence of the Soul* by an Arabian mystic named Alkindi. Others say *The Necronomicon* was truly based on *Al Asiz,* an ancient Arabic book on demons.[4]

The popular edition of *The Necronomicon* contains a dedication to Aleister Crowley. Credit is also given to "the demon PER-DURABO" (a name Crowley assumed). The preface ends with the appeal, "We enter the New Age of the Crowned and Conquering Child, Horus, not in a slouch toward Bethlehem, born within us at the moment we conquer the lurking fear in our souls."[5]

The Necronomicon is frequently quoted by self-styled satanists. Though they usually know little of its origins, the book's evil fascinates them. Reversing the biblical account of Lucifer's rebellion against god, *The Necronomicon* says the devil, the horned deity, SIN, was supreme among the Body of the ancient Ones.[6] The book warns that using its incantations, supposedly the oldest in occult history, may arouse demons that have not been summoned in six thousand years. Once called forth, the admonition declares, "ordinary exorcism and banishing formulae have thus far proved extremely inadequate by experienced magicians."[7]

In addition to an introduction and conclusion by the "mad Aran," *The Necronomicon* is divided into sections of line drawings of amulets and invocations. These are supposedly derived from the ancient Sumerians, a once-flourishing pagan culture in Mesopotamia, the site of Babylonia as well as Abraham's Ur of the Chaldees. Sumeria was ruled by seven cities, each with a different deity. The Sumerian civilization has been closely aligned with Aryan ideology, and their language resembles Hindu Sanskrit. Their religion was a complex system of ritual magic, including the summoning of evil powers.

Many of the amulets and invocations are in what is said to be the original Sumerian language. Some rituals, such as the conjuration of the watcher, require a preliminary sacrifice "in a clean and new bowl," though the nature of the "sacrifice" is not specified.[8] *The Necronomicon* concludes with the statement, "This is the book of the Servants of the Gods."[9]

Apart from its blasphemies and admitted "abominations," *The Necronomicon* is a primer for introducing students of the black arts to the methods of summoning the most foul spirits to accomplish evil bidding. Unfortunately, those who know nothing about *The Necronomicon's* background, undoubtedly overlook the possibly fictionalized origins of the book and take its invocations of evil seriously.

THE SATANIC BIBLE

The Satanic Bible, written by Church of Satan founder, the late Anton Szandor LaVey, is a 272-page diatribe for the devil. Published in 1969, it became an instant best-seller, topping the half-million mark. On some college campuses, it outsold the Christian Bible.

The book opens with LaVey's explanation of why he came to accept a hedonist philosophy. As a sixteen-year-old organ player in a carnival, LaVey says he observed "men lusting after half-naked girls dancing at the carnival (on Saturday night), and on Sunday morning when I was playing the organ for tent-show evangelists at the other end of the carnival lot, I would see these same men sitting in the pews with their wives and children, asking God to forgive them and purge them of carnal desires. And the next Saturday night, they'd be back at the carnival or some other place of indulgence. I knew then that the Christian church thrives on hypocrisy, and that man's carnal nature will [win] out!"[10]

Early in the book, the Nine Satanic Statements clarify LaVey's doctrines. I include them below so you can clearly understand the heinous basis for modern satanism. Being aware will help you recognize such ideas when revealed by someone involved in satanism.

1. Satan represents indulgence, instead of abstinence.
2. Satan represents vital existence, instead of spiritual pipe dreams.
3. Satan represents undefiled wisdom, instead of hypocritical self-deceit.
4. Satan represents kindness to those who deserve it, instead of love wasted on ingrates.
5. Satan represents vengeance, instead of turning the other cheek.
6. Satan represents responsibility to the responsible, instead of concern for psychic vampires.

7. Satan represents man as just another animal, sometimes better, more often worse than those that walk on all fours, who, because of his "divine spiritual and intellectual development," has become the most vicious animal of all.

8. Satan represents all of the so-called sins, as they all lead to physical, mental, or emotional gratification.

9. Satan has been the best friend the church has ever had, as he has kept it in business all these years.

Those who are familiar with the Bible will note that some of these statements are so diametrically opposed to Christian principles that they often twist biblical statements. Christ told His disciples to turn the other cheek.[11] *The Satanic Bible* says, "Satan represents vengeance, instead of turning the other cheek."

LaVey goes on to say, "Self-preservation is the highest law. He who turns the other cheek is a cowardly dog."[12]

In Proverbs and in Romans, readers are told: "If your enemy is hungry, give him bread to eat; and if he is thirsty, give him water to drink."[13] *The Satanic Bible* says, "Satan represents kindness to those who deserve it, instead of love wasted on ingrates."

"Why should I not hate my enemies?" LaVey asks. "If I love them, does that not place me at their mercy?"[14]

Since blasphemy is an integral part of worshiping Satan, LaVey includes outrageous invectives hurled against God. "I dip my forefinger in the watery blood of your impotent mad redeemer, and write over his thorn-torn brow: The TRUE prince of evil—the king of all slaves."

If that isn't offensive enough, he adds, "I gaze into the glassy eye of your fearsome Jehovah, and pluck him by the beard; I uplift a broad-axe, and split open his worm-eaten skull."[15]

Lying and indulgence and the seven deadly sins are condoned throughout *The Satanic Bible*, not just in the Nine Satanic

Statements. LaVey's ideology is based on immediate gratification. "Life is the great indulgence—death the great abstinence," LaVey proclaims. "There is no heaven of glory bright, and no hell where sinners roast . . . no redeemer liveth."[16]

Throughout *The Satanic Bible*, LaVey rails against God like a spoiled child resisting parental instruction. In addition to mocking every cardinal Christian doctrine, LaVey also ridicules white witches for not using their malevolent powers. He provides the "infernal names" of demons and proclaims that satanists condone any kind of sexual activity, so long as it "involves no one who does not wish to be involved."[17] Even the pain of sadism is endorsed.

Human sacrifice is indirectly condoned with a carefully worded qualification. LaVey insists he speaks of "symbolically" destroying the victim "through the working of a hex or curse, which in turn leads to the physical, mental, or emotional destruction of the sacrifice in ways and means not attributable to the magician."[18] Under no circumstance," LaVey insists, "would a Satanist sacrifice any animal or baby."[19]

In spite of such disclaimers, LaVey carefully describes the "ideal sacrifice" and says these "rabid humans deserve any clobberings they get." Further inflaming his readers, LaVey adds, "Mad dogs are destroyed, and they need help far more than the human who conveniently froths at the mouth when irrational behavior is in order . . . therefore, you have every right to (symbolically) destroy them, and if your curse provokes their actual annihilation, rejoice that you have been instrumental in ridding the world of a pest!"[20] After reading such words, individuals already steeped in resentment and rebellion could easily assume the right to harm, even murder someone.

The Satanic Bible concludes with detailed instructions on how to conduct a devil-worshiping ceremony. All sources of light, except candles, are prohibited. A nude woman usually lies prostrate, feet pointed north, serving as an altar. The air is purified by the ringing of a bell, and invocations to Lucifer are recited. *The Satanic Bible* includes all ritualistic utterances and paraphernalia, leaving no reader to wonder how he might pursue LaVey's infernal craft. LaVey also includes the "Articles of Faith" of satanism, the so-called nineteen Enochian keys, representing the "satanic paeans of faith."[21] LaVey gives his own interpretation of the invocation to these Enochian Keys as well as in the original Enochian language of evil.

THE SATANIC RITUALS

In 1972, as a companion book to *The Satanic Bible*, Anton LaVey published *The Satanic Rituals*, a how-to guide for satanists. Claiming that we are living in the Age of Satan, he promises followers the ability to "call the names of the Gods of the Abyss with freedom from guilt and immunity from harm."[22] By following the rites and ceremonies outlined, he offers the reader power and control over his destiny.

LaVey explains that "the productions contained [within *The Satanic Rituals*] . . . fall into two . . . categories: rituals, which are directed towards a specific end that the performer desires; and ceremonies, which are pageants paying homage to or commemorating an event, aspect of life, admired personage, or declaration of faith. Generally, a ritual is used to attain, while a ceremony serves to sustain."[23]

Embracing the ideologies set forth in *The Satanic Bible*, LaVey's *Satanic Rituals* compares ceremonies to a stage play. The ceremonial chamber, a dismal setting accented with demonic symbols, becomes the stage. Candles provide an additional mystic ambience. The priest and his helpers are the main characters, and the play's participants are the audience. They are often attired in dark, hooded robes. Success hinges upon the strength of the participant's belief and magical abilities. LaVey contends, "One of the most important 'commandments' of Satanism is: Satanism demands study—not worship!"[24]

In addition to blasphemy, there is blatant pornography and sexism throughout *The Satanic Rituals*. As noted before, the altar is often a naked woman. Sexual acts are common: "The (L'air Epais) ceremony of rebirth takes place in a large coffin. The coffin contains an unclad woman . . . whose task is to awaken lust in the 'dead' man who joins her . . . When the infusion is complete, the woman within shouts . . . 'Enough!'"[25] Perverted behavior is condoned: "An exclusively homosexual group can often conduct more fruitful rituals than a group with both heterosexual and homosexual participants. The reason is that each person in an all-homophile group is usually more aware of the individual active/passive propensities of his associates."[26] LaVey calls upon ancient, paganistic rites, such as the Seventh Satanic Statement in which participants "regress willingly to an animal level, assuming animal attributes."[27] LaVey also gives explicit instructions for conducting the black mass, made famous in the seventeenth century by drug peddler and abortionist Catherine Deshayes.

The Satanic Rituals concludes with a final commentary LaVey calls "The Unknown Known" in which he prophesies, "The twentieth century has prepared us for the future and the coming of the Age of Fire . . . The infant is learning to walk, and by the first Working Year of his age—he will have steadied his steps, and by the next—he will have attained maturity."[28]

LaVey's philosophy quite naturally leads to crime and violence. Satanists are determined to break all the Bible's Ten Commandments and promote the seven deadly sins: pride, lying, murder, a wicked heart, quickness to do evil, a false witness, and causing discord.[29] Consequently, ritual sacrifice (in which blood is consumed), uninhibited violence, and the celebration of selfishness are assiduously followed. Generally, such perpetrators aren't part of any organized satanic clique, but follow a self-styled route to evil.

SATANIC GROUPS

Adherents of satanism fall into two general categories. First are the psychotically and criminally inclined groups who appear to operate without external jurisdiction. These are the solitary satanists, who are usually responsible for grave-robbings, animal sacrifices, body mutilations, sexual orgies, church vandalizing, and blood ceremonies. They are more likely to have informal, evolving beliefs.

The second category is organized satanism, represented by cults such as the Church of Satan. Its philosophy centers on the ritualized catharsis of venting negative emotions to justify uninhibited conduct. Satanism is a religion that strikes back instead of turning the other cheek. Both self-styled and institutional groups use rituals to express their contempt for Christianity.

THE BLACK MASS

The best-known ritual is the black mass, which evolved during the Middle Ages as a parody of the Christian mass. A Mendes goat symbol or obscene figure of Christ is placed on the altar. Black candles are burned, and the chalice is filled with blood. A nude woman serves as the altar with the mass being celebrated on her buttocks or stomach. The host is desecrated, and backward prayers are offered. Traditionally the celebrants are nude except for robes adorned with satanic symbols. When a human sacrifice is offered, the blood of the sacrificial child is mixed with the chalice's contents and offered to the devil.

Some satanists prefer the spontaneity of self-styled ritualism as opposed to more formal adulation of Lucifer. They make up their own protocol of evil with only a general outline to guide them. Ceremonialism is usually not a high priority for informal occult groups. The intent of unaligned satanists is generally to provide an excuse to indulge in criminal and morally debasing conduct. Conversely, organized Satanists have as their ultimate aim the restoration of Lucifer to a position they believe is his rightful place as ruler of the universe.

THE CHURCH OF SATAN

Anton LaVey, a former animal trainer and carnival employee, gained a reputation as an expert in hypnotism and mentalism. On

April 30, 1966, the occult holiday of Walpurgisnacht (the witches sabbat announcing the transition from winter to spring), LaVey shaved his head and announced the formation of the Magic Circle, a secret ritualistic group from which he eventually organized the Church of Satan. Based on the disillusionment of his carnival years, LaVey, the "black pope of Satanism," declared, "Since worship of fleshly things produces pleasure, there would then be a temple of glorious indulgence."

LaVey studied the occult assiduously and began holding regular meetings to present his ideas about vampires, witchcraft, and sex. He gained national press by performing a satanic baptism on his three-year-old daughter and conducting the funeral for a sailor member. Celebrities started showing up, including Sammy Davis Jr., who wore a satanic medallion around his neck. LaVey claimed that actresses Jayne Mansfield and Marilyn Monroe were among his sex partners.

LaVey's brand of satanism was more theater than substance. He emphasized the drama of his ceremonies and disappointed those who expected membership in the Church of Satan to be a one-way ticket to orgiastic frenzy. True, there was a ritual nudity, but that, too, was showbiz. As LaVey told everyone all along, there really isn't a devil. Lucifer is only a metaphor for man's dark inner desires.

Church of Satan teachings resemble an indulgent form of psychotherapy more than any religious commitment to evil. To LaVey, man's true enemy is guilt, instilled by Christianity, and the path to individual freedom is through pursuing sin on a regular basis. LaVey admitted he regarded nothing as supernatural and leaned toward the Aleister Crowley school of magic, which is based on a scientific approach to the paranormal (see Chapter 15). Drawing members from various occult groups, the Church of Satan experienced rapid growth throughout the '70s with grottoes (local chapters) located in all major cities of the United States.

Since Anton LaVey's death, information about adherents and membership has been unavailable. Worship is led by a priest who is adept at performing rituals. The highest holiday is one's birthday. After that, Walpurgisnacht (April 30) and Halloween are the most important. In addition to the books of LaVey, members are encouraged to read the writings of Ayn Rand, Friedrich Nietzsche, and Machiavelli because of the emphasis these authors put upon excelling through human potential. Three basic kinds of rituals are performed:

1. Sexual rituals to satisfy eroticism.
2. Compassionate rituals to help someone.
3. Destructive rituals to get revenge.[30]

Rival organizations include the Church of Satanic Brotherhood, the Order of the Black Ram, the Ordo Templi Santanas, and the Temple of Set, which was founded by former LaVey follower Michael Aquino. Some followers exploited the totalitarian aspects of Church of Satan ideology and affiliated with extremist political groups. Eventually, LaVey closed down the grottoes and went into seclusion.

After years of heart problems, LaVey died on October 30, 1997, leaving unfinished projects ranging from a collection of essays to a novel and another album of organ music. Three months and a day after he died, his daughter Karla filed a petition for probate, seeking to administer his estate. Despite all the talk of being the Black Pope, the most evil and materialistic man in the world, at death the total value of his holdings came to $60,000, adjusted for annual book royalties. Several years of divorce proceedings and an ensuing bankruptcy had cleaned him out.

Blanche Barton, his biographer and mother of his child, filed an objection to Karla's petition, providing the court with a copy of a handwritten will signed with LaVey's distinctive forked-tailed signature. The Church of Satan has been besieged by bickering former adherents who insist that he was a fraud and that his institution does not properly worship the devil. Researchers have been unable to confirm, among other claims, Anton LaVey's rendezvous with Marilyn Monroe, his Clyde Beatty circus affiliation, his job as a San Francisco police department photographer, or the existence of any ballet symphony that LaVey might have played for as he claimed.

In addition, it was revealed that the black house on California Street known as the Church of Satan Headquarters was not a former brothel at all, but merely the home of LaVey's parents, who transferred ownership to him and his wife Diane in 1971. Even *The Satanic Bible* was conceived by Avon Books to cash in on the occult fads of the 1960s, and LaVey paraphrased much of it from books by Aleister Crowley and Ayn Rand.

According to family members, LaVey was not a millionaire possessing many homes and cars, but had relied on the generosity of friends and relatives since the mid-1970s. Since 1993 the black Victorian home was owned by hotelier Donald Werby, co-owner of Grosvenor Properties and a longtime LaVey friend from the old days of the Magic Circle. Werby paid $240,000 for the building as part of Anton LaVey's bankruptcy arrangement. The 1905 building had deteriorated beyond repair. It had no heat. All plumbing and electrical wiring were original and substandard. Perhaps the ultimate irony was the claim made by Anton's daughter Zeena, who was a guest on my national radio broadcast, the day after his death. Zeena, who was the first person baptized into the Church of Satan, declared that she had put a death curse on her own father and took credit for his demise

THE TEMPLE OF SET

The most active offshoot of the Church of Satan is Dr. Michael Aquino's Temple of Set. Taking the name of his organization from the Egyptian mythological god of death, Aquino is a highly visible spokesperson for satanism. Whereas LaVey avoided the public spotlight, Aquino frequents TV talk shows in the company of his wife and accomplice, Lilith Sinclair (Pat Wise). Aquino, a former lieutenant colonel in the Army Reserve with top secret security clearance, specialized in psychological warfare, an expertise that probably serves him well as a satanist. At one time a trusted ally of LaVey, Aquino was asked to organize special rituals for the Church of Satan.

Aquino claims Satan appeared to him as Set on June 21, 1975. Set, according to Aquino, was the spirit Aiwaz, who appeared to Aleister Crowley. Now, Set is inaugurating his own aeon, a time of satanic, spiritual, and intellectual enlightenment. Aquino has plucked his bushy eyebrows to form an evil stare and tattooed the number 666 on his head. That self-designation as the Antichrist claims the same identification as Aleister Crowley and picks up where the British satanist left off.

Whereas LaVey played the role of a huckster, disclaiming all affiliation with a literal devil, Michael Aquino takes Satan much more seriously. Aquino teaches that Setians may become gods through a process known as Xepering (pronounced Kepering or Kheffering from the Egyptian hieroglyphics for "to come into being"), a striving toward knowledge. Aquino attracts an upwardly mobile constituency, many of them coming from backgrounds of witchcraft and Christianity.

Chapter 15

Aleister Crowley's Creed

Do what thou wilt shall be the whole of the law," was the edict of the infamous Aleister Crowley and the creed of living for a young adult named Curtis.

"There are some things I want to make clear," Curtis told me. "Though you may call me a satanist, I'm not. I don't believe in the devil except as a symbol of raw creative impulses. I am a Fellowlight."

"But your late mentor, Crowley, was a satanist," I asserted. "He believed he was the Beast of the Bible's Revelation."

"Yes, but he wasn't a satanist," Curtis responded. "He didn't believe in the devil. And he had contempt for Ouija boards, séances, table-tapping, and trance mediums. He called it 'indiscriminate necromancy by amateurs.'"

"What paranormal powers do you contact?" I asked.

"Powers within me that are part of god."

"But Jesus said that the heart of man is evil and filled with murder, fornication, covetousness, and pride,"[1] I answered.

"What Jesus, Bob? I can list you fifteen different religious fig-ures who were all born of virgins and came back from the dead. Like Krishna, Jesus of the druids, Quetzalcoatl . . ."

"Wait a minute," I interrupted, "you're not going to compare Jesus Christ with Quetzalcoatl, the feathered serpent of human-sacrificing Meso-Americans?"

"Bob, your God has the manners and morals of a spoiled child. As a Crowleyite, I am the true Christian and you are a perversion of Christianity!"

"That's preposterous, Curtis. You're the one practicing black magic. After all, Crowley was kicked out of Italy for allegedly prac-ticing infant sacrifice. And one of his disciples there died from drinking blood."

"Yes, but he was never indicted for the supposed crimes."

"How did Crowley end up? A drug fiend. A heroin addict and a blithering idiot," I pointed out.

Since Curtis couldn't repudiate these facts, he did what most cornered debaters do; he changed the subject.

"The trouble with your kind of so-called Christianity is that you need some big daddy figure breathing down your neck, point-ing life out for you step-by-step," Curtis asserted.

"You're wrong. The Bible tells us God loved the world and sent His Son to die for our sins."

"That's a protection racket, Bob. If God made the rules, why should He expect us to be grateful?"

The question was ludicrous. Curtis was trying to bait me, and I wouldn't bite. So I changed the subject.

"What about Crowley's bisexualism?"

"Everyone should follow their own true will. Bob, if you tell your fellow human beings what's right and what's wrong, you're trying to interfere with their wills. You're a hideous blasphemer of Christianity."

Confused? You should be! Welcome to the world of occult ide-ology and satanic revisionism, where black is white and wrong is right. The world of Crowleyism, thelemic magic, wiccan worship, and assorted examples of occult black magic and sinister satanism.

THE CRUCIBLE OF CROWLEYISM

Born in England in 1875, Aleister Crowley became the most infamous black magician of all time. As a child he was so evil his Christian mother nicknamed him "The Beast," after Revelation's beast that came out of the sea with horns on its head, blaspheming God.[2] Ironically, Crowley's father traveled the English countryside preaching the Christian doctrines of a strict fundamentalist group known as Plymouth Brethren.

Crowley believed quite literally that he was the Beast of Revelation and declared open revolt against God. His writings, such as *Confessions* and *Magic in Theory and Practice*, stated his mission in life was to destroy Christianity and build the religion of Thelema (ritual magic based on the Greek word for "will") in its place.

Crowley was active in the Hermetic Order of the Golden Dawn, an English magical society he joined in 1898. The order taught how to consecrate talismans, set up magic circles, travel astrally, and study esoteric mysticism known as cabala (also kabala, Hebrew occultism based on numerological interpretations of Jewish scriptures). Like occult cabalists, Golden Dawn members believed they had power over demons through esoteric magical formulas. Members also believed they were governed by superior intelligences called Secret Chiefs. Crowley took the magical title of Perdurabo ("I will endure to the end"). He was eventually expelled from the Hermetic Order after gaining a reputation for breaking every moral law—from fornication to murder.

As a young man of twenty-eight, Crowley visited Cairo, Egypt. There a spirit appeared to him, which he referred to as his holy guardian angel, Aiwaz. The entity Aiwaz described himself as a representative of a great white brotherhood of ascended spiritual entities who ruled the earth. Aiwaz told Crowley a new aeon was

149

beginning that would last two thousand years. It would be founded on occultism.

Crowley's teachings were summed up in his Law of Thelema: "This Book lays down a simple Code of Conduct. / Do what thou wilt shall be whole of the Law. / Love is the law, love under will. / There is no law beyond Do what thou wilt."[3]

Crowley's philosophy was expounded in *The Book of the Law*, which taught that history can be divided into two eras. The first was the aeon of Isis, the Egyptian nature goddess, wife and sister of Osiris. During this time period, prior to 500 B.C., matriarchy and Egyptian mythology dominated humanity. The second epoch was Osiris, based on the Egyptian god of the underworld. During this time, coinciding with the period of Judaism, Buddhism, Islam, and Christianity, man dominated. In 1904, however, humanity supposedly entered the aeon of Horus, the Egyptian child-god of light, the son of Osiris and Isis. During this time, the true self of man would dominate, rather than any allegiance to external authorities, priests, or gods.

Crowley's creed was simple: "Be strong, O man! Lust! Enjoy all the things of sense. Fear not that any god shall deny thee for this." He lived what he preached. Crowley was accused of being a homosexual, a child molester, and a deviant of every sexual variation known to man. He borrowed the idea of sexual magic from Hindu tantric yoga and taught that sexual union reached its highest realm when the mind, the breath, and the semen were held still.

In Great Britain, Aleister Crowley became the head of a secret occult order based on thelemic black magic known as Argenteum Astrum (the Silver Star), the Inner Order of the Great White Brotherhood. Every member was required to go through a standardized test whereby he was supposed to interpret an unknown and unintelligible symbol through a vision or astral journey. If he passed, the candidate became a probationer. A year later, all orders being kept, the inductee could graduate to neophyte, acquiring control of his "body of light." The final state was that of a Zelator. In the

1920s and 1930s, Crowley accomplished with satanism in England what Anton LaVey did for devil worship in America in the 1960s.

During the First World War, Crowley transferred his activities to America. The press proclaimed him "the wickedest man in the world." He also spent time in Italy, but was expelled because Italian authorities accused his disciples of sacrificing human infants in occult rituals. According to one source, Crowley resided in the Abbey of Thelema near Cefalu, Sicily, and revived ancient Dionysian ceremonies. During a 1921 ritual, he induced a he-goat to copulate with his mistress, then slit the animal's throat at the moment of orgasm.[4]

Crowley insisted that divination be as precise as "scientific thesis," and declared that invoking spirits should not be a subjective phenomenon, but be accompanied by smells and visible forms. He dedicated his life to rescuing the occult from the "ill repute which . . . has made it an object of aversion to those very minds whose enthusiasm and integrity make them most in need of its benefits, and most fit to obtain them . . ."[5]

Toward the end of his life, Crowley was unable to communicate coherently. He died a poverty-stricken drug addict in 1947. Despite such an ignominious end, thousands in England and America still follow Crowley's teachings that uninhibited lust and licentious freedom are the way to spiritual truth. Ozzy Osbourne wrote a song dedicated to him. Renowned rock guitarist Jimmy Page bought his house, and the Beatles put his face on the cover of their album, *Sergeant Pepper*. Students and critics of occult literature agree almost unanimously that Anton LaVey's *Satanic Bible* draws heavily on the teachings of Crowley. His philosophy of "Do what thou wilt" has also inspired serial killers.

SPIRITUALISM AND THEOSOPHICAL THOUGHT

The development of Aleister Crowley's teachings can be understood in the framework of the evolving occult ideology and theosophical thought that preceded him. In the 1800s, a Russian psychic by the name of Helena Petrovna Blavatsky journeyed to Tibet and claimed to have met disembodied higher spiritual beings whom she called *mahatmas*. Her doctrine regarding communication with the spirit world was codified in her books *Isis Unveiled* and *The Secret Doctrine*. In 1875 she joined with two of her admirers, William Quan Judge and Colonel Henry Steel Olcott, to form the Theosophical Society in New York.[6]

H. P. Blavatsky determined to investigate the unexplained laws of nature and the latent powers of man. Her spiritual cosmology arranged deities under a Lord of the World, who commanded emanating spirits named Master Morya, Master Koot Hoomi, and Jesus.

Current advocates of Crowleyism continue to mix Christianity, the occult, and theosophical thought, as Blavatsky did. Consequently, the ideas of Crowley and other black magicians are presented in a light more acceptable to some Christians.

Eventually, the prestigious society of Psychical Research in Britain investigated Blavatsky's claims and found them wanting. She was accused of being a magician, hypnotist, and charlatan. Helena Petrovna Blavatsky died in disgrace as a lonely, obese, miserably sick woman.

SPIRITUALISM IN AMERICA

While Blavatsky and others explored mysticism in Europe, spiritualism in America was also having a heyday. Jackson Davis's book, *A Divine Revelation*, became a standard work for those seeking communication with the dead. Séances were organized to call forth ectoplasm, a foul-smelling, milky-white substance exuding like an umbilical cord from the mouth of the medium. Out of ectoplasm, apparitions were said to appear. Spirit messages, from the profane to the refined, were codified into the seven principles and nine articles of organized spiritualism.

The general conclusions of spiritualism ran counter to prevailing Christian doctrine. To the nineteenth-century occultist, infinite intelligence was god, original sin was a myth, and the crucifixion of Christ "an illustration of the martyr's spirit." Automatic writing, planchette-talking boards, trance-speaking, and materializations were sought by millions.

Contemporary satanism in America owes a debt of gratitude to the Fox sisters, Margaretta and Kate of Hydesville, New York. In 1848 their tales of tappings by a departed spirit swept the frontier. News of the phenomenon reached the White House. Abraham Lincoln appeared amused, but his wife, Mary Todd, persuaded Abe to invite professional mediums into the mansion. In vain they attempted to contact the president's late son, Willie, who had died at age eleven.

Others of the era followed suit. Poet Walt Whitman rhapsodized about being part of the eternal cosmic consciousness in "Song of Myself." Across the sea in the British Isles, Irish poet William Butler Yeats belonged to the secret occult society that had attracted Crowley, the Golden Dawn. Yeats attended séances, performed mystical experiments, and once tried to raise the ghost of a dead flower. Sir Arthur Conan Doyle, creator of Sherlock Holmes, was another firm believer in spiritualism.

THE POWER OF MAGICK

All schools of the occult share a common belief in the power of magick (spelled with a *k* by devout adherents of the craft). Magick is not new to mankind and has been the province of shamans, alchemists, and witches for centuries.

Modern groups tend to draw their inspiration from the Jewish cabalists of the Middle Ages. Cabalists believed that sacred writings could be secretly deciphered by understanding the hidden numerical meaning of letters. They traced their heritage to Babylon and to the thirteenth-century *Book of Zolar* of the medieval Knights Templar, whose first mission was to protect Jerusalem for

Christian pilgrims. Unfortunately, the Templars evolved into a magical society based on Gnosticism.

Following the Middle Ages, magical groups were persecuted by the Roman Catholic Church as heretical. With the rise of eighteenth-century rationalism, formerly esoteric associations began emerging again. The Societas Rosicruciana (Rosicrucians) appeared, and the cabalistic writings of Eliphas Levi surfaced. All insisted that ritual magick was the universal world religion, with entities on astral planes the source of undeniable spiritual truth.

The most pervasive secret orders of ritual magick have been the Ordo Templi Orientis (OTO) lodges, originally founded at the turn of the twentieth century by Karl Keller, and headed in England by Aleister Crowley. Scientology's founder, L. Ron Hubbard, also reportedly became associated with the Ordo Templi Orientis, although today's Church of Scientology disavows any association with the OTO.

Internal organizational structure of the OTO was based on Freemasonry-type degrees. To OTO's degrees, Crowley added an eleventh homosexual degree as part of the temple's ritual sex magick. Keller, a Viennese, toured the Far East and studied the Hindu tantric sex philosophy of yogis. He returned to combine them with Masonic rituals.

At OTO ceremonies, the baphomet symbol of Satan was openly displayed as a source of sexual power. Members believed that when their own sexual energy was aroused during magical ceremonies, they should identify with certain gods and goddesses as the source of their erotic enthusiasm. According to Crowley, the ultimate test of magical adeptness was to achieve intercourse with invisible astral beings, especially demon entities (incubus and succubus).

In America today, secret thelemic occult orders are currently enjoying a resurgence. One group publishes *The Newaeon Newsletter*, whose stated purpose is to "further the Great Work of the Beast 666, Our Father, Aleister Crowley, and to assist in the greater establishment of Thelema, whose Word is ABRA-CADABRA, and whose Law is Love."

Christians are warned by Thelemites, "Jesus shall never return for it was never meant to be. But the Christ, the Logos of the Aeon, the New World Teacher hath come already and his name was Aleister Crowley, the Beast 666!"[7] Other magical groups drawing on the traditions of Crowley and his followers include the Ancient and Mystical Order of the Rosae Crucis (AMORC—Rosicrucians), and the Ordo Templi Astarte.

Chapter 16

That Old Black Magic

She became a sorceress at sixteen. Her black cloak, dark eye makeup, and the magic wand she carried made her look the part more than most modern witches. For years, Laurie Cabot served as the official witch of Salem, Massachusetts. She constantly crusaded for her religion, as when I debated her on the *Oprah Winfrey Show*. On that telecast she claimed to be only a "white witch" who helped people. But Laurie Cabot was a media-manipulated caricature of the authentic article, unlike the reality of contemporary witchcraft. Today's media-savvy witches do their best to appear non-threatening.

WICCA, THE OLD RELIGION

Witchcraft is known by several names, including wicca (wise ones), the old religion, womanspirit, goddess worship, or simply the craft.[1] Witches may also be called druids, the Gaelic word for wise man or sorcerer. The term *witch* is generic, referring to both men and women. Though the word *warlock* generally is applied to male witches, adherents of the craft deny this distinction.

The history of witchcraft dates back to Paleolithic times and the worship of the goddess of fertility. She presided over a cult that celebrated the seasonal cycles of nature. More important, she provided a spiritual framework outside the patriarchal religions. The evoking of magical powers by wiccans for healing is found in the legends of Mesopotamia, Egypt, and Canaan.

As the children of Israel entered the promised land, Jehovah laid down strict injunctions against involvement with such practices.[2] Traditionally, witchcraft fell into two categories, white witchcraft practiced by tribal leaders who supposedly sought the good of the community, and sorcery that concerned itself with curses and revenge. In the Old Testament, both were presented as opposing God, and practicing witchcraft was punishable by death.[3] King Saul lost his life for consulting with the witch of En Dor.[4]

In ancient Greece and Rome, beneficent sorcery was officially approved. Certain goddesses, such as Diana and Hecate, were associated with malevolent magic and bloody sacrifices that occurred during the darkness of night. Hecate appeared in three forms: as Selene, the moon in heaven; as Artemis, the huntress on earth; and as Persephone, Queen of the Underworld.

When the Romans conquered England, witchcraft was already practiced there by the druids, who were well established throughout Britain and Gaul. The druids were knowledgeable in medicine and the use of herbs. Their universal remedies were mistletoe and serpent eggs, since both supposedly attracted astral light.

HISTORICAL RESPONSES TO WITCHCRAFT

Fear of witches was prevalent in medieval Europe, and such devilry was usually associated with women. Eventually, legal authorities instituted the death penalty for the practice of such superstitions. In the fifteenth century the church established dogma concerning demonology that linked witches to the devil, especially when they cohabited with him sexually (incubus). During the so-called Burning Times of A.D. 1300–1600, an estimated nine million people were killed because they were accused of witchcraft.

Ever since, witches have been trying to live down that reputation of devilish collaboration. The famous Salem witch trials in America were one of the last public outcries against the craft. In 1692 twenty supposed Salem witches were put to death and 150 were incarcerated. Ironically, this repressive response to witchcraft proved to be one of its biggest boons. Witches could claim they were unjustly persecuted and therefore deserved more rights than they might have been accorded otherwise, a kind of occult affirmative action agenda. Today witchcraft expert Margot Adler estimates fifty thousand to one hundred thousand neo-pagans or members of wicca actively practice witchcraft in the United States.[5]

GARDNERIAN WITCHCRAFT

Gerald Gardner, who was born in England in 1884 and died in 1964, did more than any other single individual in modern times to revive the ancient art of witchcraft. Gardner was an occultist his entire life, an initiate of the Ordo Templi Orientis, and a friend of Aleister Crowley, from whom he borrowed certain practices. Though poorly educated, Gardner studied anthropology on his own and was involved in the excavation of a site where the goddess Astaroth was worshiped. He studied occultism with the daughter of Theosophist Annie Besant and was eventually initiated into witchcraft. The publication of his book *Witchcraft Today* led to a revival of interest in the craft in England.

On the Isle of Man, Gardner operated a witchcraft museum and accepted initiates into training. Each coven was headed by both a high priest and a priestess. Membership was limited to couples. Worship occurred in the nude ("skyclad"), and power was raised by dancing, chanting, and meditative techniques. Gardner also incorporated ritual scourging, along with karma, reincarnation, three degrees of advancement, and the ritual known as Drawing Down of the Moon. Gardner revered two principal deities, the god of the forests and the god that lies beyond, known as the great Triple Goddess of fertility and rebirth.

Though witches delight in suggesting their beliefs have been handed down from preexisting traditions, the truth is most witches follow the Gardnerian legacy, which combines occultism with Eastern mysticism. By calling themselves Gardnerian, modern witches refer to specific covens that claim a chain of apostolic succession from Gardner's own coven. Even witchcraft leaders admit that Gardner had no access to an original coven or pagan tradition. Many of the craft claim that Gardner was sexually obsessed and fraudulently devised a system of occult succession. Alexandrian witches, closely related to the Gardnerians, follow Alex Sanders, a disciple of Gardner who claimed to be the "King of Witches" in England.

MODERN WITCHES IN AMERICA

Witchcraft in America was revived by Dr. Raymond Buckland, an anthropologist, and his wife, Rosemary, who studied under Gerald Gardner and brought his brand of wicca to America in the 1960s. Witch Sybil Leek, who started with Gardnerian rituals, also came to America in the 1960s and established several covens. The Religious Order of Witchcraft was incorporated in 1972 in New Orleans, Louisiana, by Mary Oenida Toups, its high priestess.

In the early '70s Gavin and Yvonne Frost of New Bern, North Carolina, opened the Church and School of Wicca, which has become one of the most visible and active witchcraft movements in America. The school has operated as a tax-exempt institution since 1972. Gavin and Yvonne pay less attention to traditional witchcraft deities and instead promote the development of psychic powers. Since the Frosts are of English origin, it's understandable that much of the school's doctrine is devised from the sexual ritualism of British magick traditions. Their basic message is that any suppression of the body's desires is unnatural and unwise. Drinking and sex are said to be morally appropriate and the precursors to a long and healthy life. The Frosts also endorse the Gardnerian concept of astral sex with spirit partners (incubus or succubus).

The Frosts insist their branch of wicca is nonthreatening, undergirded by the maxim, "Eight words the Wiccan Rede fulfill. If it harm none, do what you will." The Frosts insist their brand of witchcraft is benevolent because "any evil a witch does comes back threefold."

But when I debated the Frosts on *Larry King Live,* they admitted that it is all right to inflict physical harm on an enemy if by doing so a witch may be able to educate that person's soul. They even acknowledged that on the way to the television show they had put a hex on a taxi driver who irritated them.

In addition to the Frosts' Church of Wicca, several other witchcraft groups have gone public. The Church of the Eternal Source is an amalgamation of mystery cults centering on the culture and occultism of ancient Egypt. Members have generally been attracted by the archaeological significance of Egypt, which led them to some kind of spiritual encounter with Egyptian deities.

The Church of All Worlds is nature-oriented, promoting a symbiotic relationship between humans and earth. Instead of rituals, they promote sacralizing the planet as a form of pantheism.

The Radical Faerie Movement consists of gays and lesbians who see a connection between their sexual preferences and the old pagan nature religions.[6]

Other American witchcraft groups include the Church of Pan (espousing naturalist principles including nudity), the Church of the Wyccan Rede (founded on Celtic traditions), Circle (exploring shamanistic and neo-pagan paths), and the Covenant of the Goddess (a California group that has secured tax-exempt status for witchcraft groups).[7]

Witchcraft has experienced a rapid growth since the British Parliament repealed all antiwitchcraft laws in 1951. Witches no longer need to sequester themselves, worshiping silently under full moons. Now they can publish books and appear on TV talk shows to disclaim society's accusations that they are wrinkled hags spiriting through the night on broomsticks.

WITCHCRAFT AND RADICAL FEMINISM

Today, so-called Dianic cults (based on the ancient Greek goddess Diana) emphasize the traditional goddess of witchcraft. They believe this feminine principle of worship is a de-Christianized and backdated version of the Virgin Mary.

Margot Adler, a reporter for National Public Radio and author of the witchcraft tome *Drawing Down the Moon*, wrote, "In our culture, which has for so long denied and denigrated the feminine as negative . . . women will never understand their own creative strength and divine nature until they embrace the creative feminine, the source of inspiration, the Goddess within . . ."[8]

Feminist witches teach that their highest purpose in life occurs when they *become* the goddess, incarnated by the feminine deity they invoke. Elaborate rituals have been developed to achieve this state, often accompanied by trances and vocal elocutions from the goddess. Disagreements exist among feminist witches as to whether these utterances are actually messages from an entity or only the evoking of the archetypal goddess from within. In either case, the "Great Rite" employed to achieve this state is considered to be a divine union of the human and the spiritual. As a result, feminist witches believe they have been endowed with psychic powers.

WITCHCRAFT BELIEFS AND PRACTICES

Many witchcraft groups perform rituals that they say follow long-established traditions. They claim the leaders of current covens are descendants from earlier witches. Gone are the mystical miscreants of earlier times. Today's witches assert they are merely the counterreligion of Christianity, and they predate the Jewish faith. Rather than opposing Christianity, they prefer to adopt a position of superiority, saying they have selected an older form of worship.

Wiccan beliefs are rooted in ritualism designed to cultivate psychic powers. Their creeds are conveyed mostly in oral fashion with the assistance of the *Book of Shadows* (rituals hand-copied by each individual witch) and grimoires (books of spells such as *The Key of Solomon*). Witches organize in groups of thirteen people called covens, a term that was first used in 1662. The idea of a coven consisting of thirteen may have originated in prehistoric worship of the horned god when thirteen was the maximum number of worshipers to dance inside a sacred nine-foot circle. Some believe the number twelve was chosen to imitate Christ's disciples, with the coven leader making the thirteenth member and representing the devil. Each coven is usually autonomous except for those groups that owe their initiation to another witch assembly. Membership is by invitation, and progress occurs through degrees.

They meet regularly (usually on full moons) at gatherings known as *esbats*. Eight major festivals of the year occur seasonally, known as *sabbats* (the Latin spelling for sabbath was adopted in medieval times). These festivals are: *Samhain* on Halloween, the Celtic new year; *Oimelc* (also called *Candelmas*) on February 2, a festival of winter purification and the approach of spring; *Beltane* on May 1 (or April 30, May Eve), the fertility festival; *Lughnasadh* (also known as *Lammas*) on August 1, the festival of firstfruits; the vernal and autumnal equinoxes; and the winter and summer solstices.

During witchcraft meetings, various paraphernalia are employed, such as an athame (double-edged ceremonial knife used to raise the "cone of power"), chalice, sword, magic wand, crystal bowl with a rose (representing the sexual power of a woman's vagina), and pentacle (disk-shaped talisman). The five points of the star-shaped pentagram represent earth, air, fire, water, and spirit, and are used to cast magical spells. Unlike satanists, who invert the pentagram to place the two points upward (representing the horns of the goat-head image of Lucifer), witches rest their pentagram (pentacle) with the two points downward. Black clothes are worn to absorb energy during magical ceremonies.

Though ceremonies differ, a general pattern is found in most groups. A round table in the center of the room serves as an altar. An imaginary circle is made with the athame. The priest or priestess goes to each point of the compass to summon the four guardians symbolic of the four elements. Pan, or some coven deity, is invoked. The cone of psychic power is raised and the participants may dance, sing, or meditate. Some participants may face a magic mirror to receive messages. At the end, the circle is banished and the guardians are dismissed. A pentagram is inscribed in the air, and each person embraces the others with greetings of "Blessed be."

HALLOWEEN HIGH JINKS

For parents of younger children, one additional aspect of the cultural invasion of witchcraft must be addressed: Halloween. You may be surprised at the way October 31 has become a prologue to our acceptance of the occult. Believe it or not, Halloween has become the devil's day, ritualistically recognized by some devil worshipers and occult groups throughout the nation.

What are the facts about Halloween? Is it a time to invoke the ancient Cornish prayer, "From ghoulies and ghosties and long leggety beasties and things that go bump in the night, good Lord deliver us"? Let's take a brief look at the history of this holiday

THE DEVIL'S DAY

The Christian predecessor of Halloween, the Roman Catholic Church's All Saints' Day, was originally celebrated in May, not November 1. In A.D. 608 the Roman emperor Constantine appeased the populace of newly conquered heathen territories by allowing them to combine their ancient ritual of Samhain Day with the newly dated All Saints' Day. Rome's pantheon, a temple built to worship a multiplicity of gods, was converted into a church. While Christians celebrated the death of departed saints, pagans devoted the preceding night to their lord of the dead.

THE WITCHES' SABBAT

The choosing of the date of October 31 is no coincidence. October 31 is one of four major witches' sabbats, the four "cross-quarter" days of the Celtic calendar. The first, February 2, commonly known as Groundhog Day, honored Brigit, the pagan goddess of healing. The second, a May holiday called Beltane, was witchcraft's time to plant. On this day the druids performed magical rites to encourage the growth of crops. The third, an August harvest festival in honor of the sun god, commemorated the shining one, Lugh. These first three cross-quarter days marked the passing of seasons, the time to plant, and the time to harvest, as well as the time of the earth's death and rebirth. The last, Samhain, marked the coming of winter. At this time, the ancient druids performed rituals in which a cauldron symbolized the abundance of the goddess. It was said to be a time of "betwixt and between," a sacred season of superstition and spirit conjurations.

To the druids, October 31 was the night Samhain returned with the spirits of the dead. They had to be appeased or "treated" or the living would be tricked. Huge bonfires were set on hilltops to frighten away evil spirits and placate supernatural powers that controlled the processes of nature. More recently, European immigrants, particularly the Irish, introduced Halloween to America. By the late nineteenth century, its customs had become popular. It was an occasion to overturn outhouses, inflict property damage, and indulge in devilry that wouldn't be tolerated at other times of the year.

Today, Halloween is a banner day for merchants. It's a night when decent people become outrageous exhibitionists. Sixty percent of all Halloween costumes are sold to adults. On October 31, one of every four people between the ages of eighteen and forty will dress up as some kind of character.[9] For psychic readers, clairvoyants, and self-proclaimed visionaries, it's the busiest time of the year. Publishers of books on subjects ranging from astrology to witchcraft indicate a dramatic increase in sales. Salem, Massachusetts, home of American witchcraft, now celebrates a "haunted happening" at Halloween to expand its summer tourist season.

A spokesman for the National Retail Federation declared sales of Halloween candy reached $950 million in one recent year. Consumers spent another $1 billion on costumes, $500 million on holiday decorations, and $50 million on greeting cards.[10] That same year, 73% of adults participated in some kind of Halloween activity. "Grown-ups increased involvement is pegged to the holiday falling on a weekend for a second consecutive year." According to the American Express Retail Index, consumers were expected to spend an average of $81 on Halloween.[11] To capitalize on the occult and boost fall tourism, Universal Studios in Orlando has created "Halloween Horror Nights." The 19–night event features haunted houses and roving bands of chain saw-brandishing hoodlums and axe murderers that stalk customers.

HALLOWEEN'S SYMBOLS OF SATAN

The traditional practices associated with Halloween are easily identified with the occult. The jack-o'-lantern came from the tale of a notorious man named Jack, who was turned away from both heaven and hell. Consigned to roam the earth as a spirit, Jack put a glowing coal into a carved-out turnip to light his way through the night. This harbinger (which became a pumpkin) symbolized a damned soul. The colors orange and black can also be traced to the occult. They were connected with commemorative masses for the dead that were held in November. The unbleached beeswax candles used in the ceremony were orange, and the ceremonial caskets were covered by black cloths.

Other obvious ties Halloween has with the occult are:

- Halloween costumes are taken from the Celtic druid idea that ceremonial participants should wear animal heads and animal skins to acquire the strength of the beast they portrayed.

- Trick or treat came from the Irish tradition when a man led a procession to levy contributions from farmers, lest their crops be cursed by demons.

- Dunking for apples came from the old practice of divining the future. The participant who successfully clenched an apple between his teeth could count on a fulfilling romance with the lover of his choice.

- Cats represented incarnated humans, malevolent spirits, or the "familiars" of witches.

- Hazelnuts were used in romance divination. Some Halloween food had objects placed inside as a means of fortune-telling.

- Masks have traditionally been an animistic means of superstitiously warding off evil spirits or changing the personality of the wearer to communicate with the spirit world.

Halloween has other negative aspects besides a pagan background rooted in witchcraft and its emphasis on the devil and darkness. Some vandals are more interested in playing tricks than getting treats. Parents worry that a demented criminal will distribute poisoned candy or goodies containing pins and razor blades. There's also the danger that motorists won't see costumed kids walking on dark streets.

Such evil associations do not suggest that a parent permitting Halloween celebrations is in collaboration with the devil. But you would be hard-pressed to think of one positive virtue in Halloween. Its symbolism involves demons, ghosts, death, darkness, skeletons, fear, and terror.

CHRISTIANS CONFRONTING HALLOWEEN

Some anti-occult groups have successfully removed Halloween celebrations from public schools. Recently, an Arkansas minister filed a federal court suit, demanding that satanism-via-Halloween observances should not be tolerated in schools while prayer is banned. The Reverend Ralph Forbes named the devil as the defendant.

One mother, who led a similar fight to remove Halloween from the public schools, said she didn't mind the day being observed as a fall festival with children dressing up as characters from American history, but she drew the line at accenting the holiday's shadowy side. In her words, "If the principle of sectarianism has taken Christmas celebrations out of the schools, why not Halloween? If they can't honor God, why honor the devil?"

In this contemporary world of all-too-real satanic evil, many think it is time to cleanse Halloween of its unsavory elements. They feel a ban on official observances of Halloween would warn parents and children that Halloween's occult symbology celebrates dark and dangerous spiritual powers. At least parents could center family activities around wholesome fun. They could have a party, but condemn costumes that relate to evil. For instance, some churches celebrate All Saints' Day by having children dress as saints of the Bible. Children are never too young to learn that a day should not be dedicated to the devil.

WITCHCRAFT GODS AND GODDESSES

Worldwide, witchcraft is on the rise. In Swaziland, the king grants traditional healers the same status as graduate doctors. In Zimbabwe, the minister of health says witch doctors are as effective in healing as medical physicians. Nigeria has passed a law integrating spirit mediums into the state-run national health services.

Estimates regarding the number of witches in America are anybody's guess. Witches can be anybody. They don't have warts on their noses, and they don't spirit through the night on broomsticks. They are ordinary people who secretly practice their occult arts without fanfare. Many believe that man has lost spiritual contact with the cycles of earth and the rhythms of nature. Witches say their craft can heal this schism between man and earth through mystical truths and unleashing gods and goddesses who animate our world.

Mention black magic, evil spells, and devil worship to most witches and they respond with disgust or amusement. They dismiss all talk of Satan and diabolical deeds. Witches resent being lumped together with devil worshipers. For one thing, witches don't believe in a devil. They claim to be an elemental nature worship religion with roots in ancient agrarian cultures, which revered the earth as a mother goddess. Christians argue that the witchcraft deity is Lucifer.

The goat image of Lucifer (also known as a baphomet or goat of Mendes) found in witchcraft and satanism is taken from a biblical reference. Christ spoke of those who followed Him faithfully as sheep and those destined for damnation as goats.[13] Thus medieval black masses featured the worship of a goat, an animal then considered unclean. Satanists invert the pentagram, placing two points upward to represent a goat's horns. The single downward point is the goat's goatee. Though witches revere a goat as their horned god of the hunt and death (the lord of the forests, sometimes known as Pan), they deny the symbol equates to the Christian enemy, Lucifer.

Witches say they pay obeisance to principles of the Lady and the Lord. The Lord is a male deity of animals, death, and the beyond. The Lady is the triple goddess mentioned earlier in the discussion of Gardnerian witchcraft, manifesting in three aspects—maiden, mother, and crone. Each aspect of the goddess is symbolized by a phase of the moon: the waxing crescent, the full moon, and the waning crescent.[14]

The gods worshiped by witches and the ceremonial practices engaged in by wiccans vary from coven to coven. To some witches, the deities are thought forms developed over centuries. To others, they are archetypes. To many, they are actual entities. Self-styled adherents of satanism often draw no distinction between hardcore devil worship and wiccan ideals, often combining rituals from both in an evil amalgam.

Most witches today side with Freud who believed demons were products of the psyche and that demonic possession is rooted in the subconscious. Today's thoroughly modern witches are more likely to be New Age advocates who seek to evoke the god within. They read tarot cards, seek altered states of consciousness, pursue holistic healing, and practice hypnotherapy.

Witches have come a long way in their effects to glamorize the occult. The image of creepy crones has been replaced with the concept of an attractive spellcaster who is the envy of ordinary women. Witches today are younger and cuter. For example, Shannen Doherty stars in the WB–TV series, "Charmed." She and her fashionable friends fight evil warlocks with supernatural powers.[15]

ABC has promoted "Sabrina the Teenage Witch" (starring Melissa Joan Hart) as a show "the whole family can watch together." The program, features a teen witch with a talking cat named Salem. During at least one ratings period it was considered the number one show for children ages 2-11. The executive producer of the show attributed its success to kids' interest in magic.[16]

These more likeable witches appeal to larger audiences of women and children, especially teenage girls. The film "Practical Magic" starred Sandra Bullock and Nicole Kidman as glamorous spellcasting sisters. On opening weekend, the film conjured the top spot at the box office, grossing more than $13 million. After this success, Nicole Kidman immediately made plans with her husband Tom Cruise on a remake of the 1942 classic, "I Married A Witch," thus defining herself as the ultimate witch babe.[17]

Hollywood also cast a spell on young women with "The Craft," a movie which told the tale of four sexy young witches who used spells to get what they wanted. The image of the film was copied by Silver Ravenwolf, a Wiccan Priestess, on the cover of her book, "Teen Witch: Wicca for a New Generation." The artwork featured four young women (and one lone male) dressed in short, tight shirts and jeans, accessorized with a pentagram, stars and the moon, and the yin yang symbol. They were portrayed as powerful and tart. The verbiage on the back cover reads, "So you wanna be a witch? Come on, you know that you'd look glamorous and powerful in black ... that lighting candles and calling spirits would give you an aura of mystery . . . that life would be better if only you could turn your history teacher into a jiggling mound of orange (or maybe lime) Jello. Well, this book is here to let you know that wearing black clothing and threatening people with hexes and curses won't make you a witch ... what this book will show you is that how you live, how you deal with others and how you incorporate Wiccan laws into you life determines whether or not you are a true witch ..."[18]

Phyllis Curott, author of the best-selling autobiography *Book of Shadows* is a New York lawyer with her own legal practice and leads a high-profile coven. Her book was based on the ideal of being a witch as the feminist entree to success in the workplace.

Despite its newfound appeal, those lured to the occult should never forget the reality of witchcraft's evil aspect. In Bridgeport, Connecticut, a witch was convicted of statutory rape for seducing a 14-year-old boy and putting a spell on him, hardly the image invoked by Hollywood and network television.[19]

Chapter 17

Satanic Folk Religions

It was the first religion. It's 140 thousand years old. I spent five years in Haiti practicing voodoo." Those were the words of Gloria, an adherent of voodoo who vigorously debated me in defense of her craft.

"I've been to Haiti too," I responded to Gloria. "I've seen voodoo ceremonies, and they're not the benign religious exercises you make them out to be. I've watched people stand in fire, eat glass, push knives through their cheeks, and perform licentious ceremonies. And they claim to do it through the power of the devil."

"Oh, Bob," Gloria responded condescendingly, "what you call the devil, I call the Seven Great Powers. They live in Haiti, Brazil, and Mexico. The people rely on them. How can you say they're demons?"

"Who do you say they are? Mythological concepts?" I asked.

"The spirits of voodoo are reality, that's all."

"According to the Bible, all evil spirits are demons of the devil," I challenged Gloria.

"Well, I've met the spirits and I've never been possessed. And I've seen a lot more than you have."

"I'm not so sure of that," I said. "I've watched a voodoo priest put a follower into a trance and make him eat a live dove, shoving it into his mouth beak first. It's hideous."

"If he wants to eat raw bird meat, that's his business," Gloria retorted. "I've talked to the seven spirits of voodoo and they're not evil."

"Who do you think is behind the sexual rites in voodoo ceremonies? I've watched voodoo disciples bark like dogs, simulate copulation, and roll in the mud. They act like monkeys and mimic all kinds of animals. It's dehumanizing and degrading."

"Look, Bob, when they are possessed by a spirit, it's the spirit doing it, not the person. They're mentally blank. They don't even know what's going on."

"How can you be so sure these poor people in voodoo aren't being manipulated by some kind of evil power?"

"Well, I was raised a Christian. Then I went to a voodoo ceremony. The priest came to me, took my hand, and drew me into the center of the ceremony. Then they poured some rum into the fire pit. The flames leaped into the air. A spirit threw me into the fire and flames leaped around my entire upper torso. I didn't feel a thing. This convinced me of the power of voodoo," Gloria said.

"What kind of god would want to risk your safety by throwing you into fire?"

"It was their way of showing me they can protect me from anything."

"What did the spirits of voodoo say about spiritual things?" I asked Gloria.

"They told me there is no such thing as sin. No soul is ever lost. I make a mistake today, reincarnation says I can come back and do it over again."

"The Bible says we die once and then face the judgment of God," I insisted. "The idea that you can keep coming back to get it right is what the Bible in 1 Timothy 4:1 calls a 'doctrine of demons.' The voodoo spirits have lied to you, and that tells me they're from the devil."

"I've made my choice," Gloria insisted. "I believe what happened to me during the voodoo ceremony more than the Bible."

The roots of contemporary satanism can be traced to indigenous folk religions, some still practiced in Third World countries. Offshoots of these occult religions are also found in the United States. Participants are often influenced by these ideologies, either through family background or because of the media. Movies, television, and sensationalist paperback novels have popularized voodoo, macumba, Santeria, and other forms of occult ceremonialism.

MARKETING OCCULT FOLK RELIGIONS

Not all devotees of the devil are self-styled occultists. Behind today's faddish fascination with satanism lies a long history of folk religions that has enthralled the masses for centuries. Satanism in America is just one facet of the many-sided jewel of evil.

In Uganda, some military troops follow a twenty-eight-year-old priestess known as Mama Alice, who is determined to overthrow the government. Believers in her movement think they can ward off enemy bullets by coating themselves with the oil of a local tree. They think that by lobbing stones under Mama Alice's influence, the rocks will explode magically, as if they are grenades. Alice claims to be under the influence of a holy spirit she calls *lakwena*. Though she speaks only a smattering of English, Alice says her spirit can communicate in seventy-four languages. After some of her troops were killed in battle, Mama Alice offered to resurrect them from the dead.[1]

In America, we may not follow priestess leaders like Mama Alice, but folk religious beliefs are more pervasive than we realize. Tabloid advertisement headlines offer lucky rabbits' feet with the lure, "I personally guarantee you can be rich and have lots of money, and you can have it right now." Normally sane citizens adopt ridiculous superstitions. Flowers on an airplane are bad luck. Never talk about past accidents in an automobile. And if you must be admitted to the hospital, do it on a Wednesday.

Other Americans are obsessed with triskaidekaphobia—fear of the number thirteen, which folklore experts say developed from Christian symbolism (Judas, the thirteenth person to arrive at the Last Supper, betrayed Jesus).

Folk superstitions also appear in other developed countries. In Japan, a teenage girl wearing a Band-Aid on her arm hasn't necessarily cut herself. She may suffer a broken heart. Enlisting supernatural powers for the sake of love by using Band-Aids is a recent fad among Japanese schoolgirls. The girl writes the name of her heartthrob on the inside of her left arm and covers it with a Band-Aid for three days. Within a week, her wish to win over the boyfriend should be granted. Another Japanese superstition involves writing the name of a love object on a pencil eraser. If that fails, Japanese women draw a small white star on the nail of their left pinkie.[2]

Occult supernaturalism encompasses the three categories of hexes, spells, and magic. Hexes induce evil spells, sometimes through round hex signs with colorful geometric motifs. In much of eastern Pennsylvania, you can find farms with hex signs painted on barns to protect animals from disease and other misfortune. Spoken spells supposedly have magic powers, such as curses that cause harm or misfortune. These spells can be an oath, contract, or treaty directed against oneself or another person. Magic uses charms or spells to acquire power over natural forces and involves rituals or incantations.

When slave traders transported West African slaves to the Americas, they also uprooted a highly developed form of indigenous occultism. The African's world was inhabited by a pantheon of beneficent and malevolent deities, which were appeased and cajoled through elaborate ceremonies. To them, religion and magic were integral parts of daily life, not casual considerations. When doubt, fear, or decision was pending, West Africans looked to their gods for direction.

In the New World, slave masters who feared unifying forces among their subjects banished black magic and hereditary folk religions. To continue their forbidden relationship to the spirits, slaves developed a complex web of secret ceremonies, which they practiced clandestinely in the dark of night. Their objects of devotion were usually animistic spirits of nature, although they also revered their ancestors and continued to communicate with family members after their deaths.

BLACK MAGIC

Black magic, the ancestor of today's satanism, is the most violent and cruel of all pagan practices. It believes each person's desires for sex, revenge, anger, and power must be ritualized and released. Black magicians admit that some of the spirits they consort with are "lords of darkness" and must be approached cautiously. Once wrongly summoned, such an entity can be dangerous. Occult lore abounds with tales of alchemists and spiritists who conducted rituals improperly and invoked dark forces that drove the summoner to suicide or insanity.

Black magicians claim there are several means of protection against such pernicious forces. One is constructing a magic circle of security before you arouse discarnate beings. Fetishes and charms are also employed to ward off evil. Anthropologists who have studied endemic ceremonial magic in primitive cultures say that curses and spells can work if the persons to whom they are directed believe in their power. Followers of the black arts are always trying to counter the malicious intent of their enemies.

WESTERNIZED FOLK RELIGIONS

Voodoo, which was brought to the West Indies by African slaves, is the best known and most widely practiced black art in the

Western Hemisphere. Though usually associated with Haiti, it also thrives in America. In Florida, a third-grade student received official approval to skip school so she could participate in a ceremony to become a voodoo priestess.[3] In Vicksburg, Mississippi, a pharmacist's drugstore has offered potions to drive away evil spirits, lawsuits, and unrequited lovers.[4]

In Fairfield, Connecticut, police investigated the death of a baby whose body was disfigured and surrounded by black magic amulets.[5] In Beaufort County, South Carolina, a group of Harlem blacks has established the Yoruba Village of Oyo Tunji for practicing voodoo. Headed by Oyo Tunji, who traveled to Haiti and was initiated into voodoo in Cuba, the village contains temples dedicated to various deities.[6] In fact, there are more hard-core adherents of voodoo in New Orleans, Louisiana, than in Haiti!

VOODOO

Voodoo (known to anthropologists as *vodoun*, from the Dahomey West African word for "protective spirit") is more than a folk religion. It has played a powerful role in Haitian politics. The infamous Haitian slave revolt of 1791, led by Henri Christophe, began at a voodoo ceremony on a hot August night. In exchange for freedom from the French, participants pledged the ongoing allegiance of their nation to Satan. Observers of Haitian politics wonder if there might be some veracity to the pact.

For years François Duvalier, "Papa Doc," held dictatorial sway by intimidating the populace with his legendary voodoo powers. The common people believed he was the incarnation of Baron Samedi, the voodoo god of death. Duvalier named his security force after the legendary Haitian bogeymen who snatched away naughty children: Tontons Macoutes. To frighten enemies, Papa Doc kept the skull of a rival at his desk.

After Duvalier's death in 1971, Jean-Claude, "Baby Doc," took over. He changed the colors of the Haitian flag to red and black, the colors of voodoo secret societies. When "Baby Doc's" regime unraveled, he called on voodoo priests to help him control the unrest.

ZOMBIISM

The book and movie *The Serpent and the Rainbow*, which was based on the story of supposed zombie Clairvius Narcisse, alerted millions of Americans to the realities of voodoo. Narcisse was pronounced dead at the Albert Schweitzer Hospital in Haiti in 1962. Yet in 1980 a man claiming to be the deceased Narcisse introduced himself to the dead man's sister, Angelina Narcisse. She had been at her brother's deathbed eighteen years earlier. Angelina screamed in horror when the man used a childhood nickname only close family members knew and no one had used since her brother's death. The man said that his brother had attempted to kill him over a land dispute, and that a voodoo sorcerer turned him into a zombie after extracting him from his coffin. *The Serpent and the Rainbow* suggested that a powerful potion was the source of Narcisse's temporary trance.

Zombiism is the most extreme practice associated with voodoo. The state is induced by a powerful potion, which contains ingredients from a species of puffer fish and a specific toad. The chemicals contain hallucinogens, anesthetics, and other psychoactive substances that affect the heart and nervous system. Witch doctors say a zombie must be exhumed within eight hours or the body will die of asphyxiation. The zombie is exploited as a slave after retrieval from his state of intoxication.

VOODOO PRACTICES AND RITES

Voodoo priestesses (mambos) and priests (hougans) prepare gris-gris (pronounced gree-gree) bags for attracting love and prosperity. Voodoo dolls do exist, but are not commonly used as fetishes. Most voodoo priests do not admit to practicing black magic, although they say all hougans must first learn black magic to fully understand white magic. As a voodoo priest in Haiti explained to me, "To untie a knot, you must first know how it is tied."

Each voodoo believer is assigned a spirit at birth, his own guardian god who supposedly protects and guides him. The spirit's identity is revealed through an initiation ritual performed by a voodoo priest. The ongoing relationship with the god is intensely personal. A good life is ensured if the god is treated well. Most adherents set aside a part of their house for a small altar with a statue of their god. They constantly appease their spirit by placing his favorite food and drink on this altar.

The purpose of a voodoo rite is to summon the *loa*, or voodoo spirits, which then possess one or more of the congregants. Loa may be gentle if the *rada* rite is used, or bloody if the *petro* ceremony is employed. A grand master spirit, known as Damballah, is said to preside over all loa. Pentagrams are considered appropriate symbols for women and the Star of David for men.

One evening in Port-au-Prince, Haiti, I had the opportunity to witness an authentic voodoo ceremony. A full moon shone upon a calm, sultry night. When I arrived, the head voodoo priest invited me to take a front-row seat. I waited for more than an hour as a contingent of African-style drummers created an incessant beat. Then the ceremonial participants arrived. They danced erotically and frantically to the rhythms, gradually losing their inhibitions. A male and female dancer simulated acts of sexual intercourse.

One by one, the dancers became possessed as the evening neared its high point. Haitians refer to a voodoo celebrant who is possessed as being "ridden by a horse," literally "mounted" by the god. The person loses motor control and falls into what resembles a cataleptic seizure. Afterward he may perform seemingly paranormal feats.

A large black male, chosen to lead the ritual, stepped into a small fire built in the center. Then he picked up a red-hot piece of firewood and put it into his mouth, flames first. He bit off the end of the burning log and slowly chewed the glowing embers without any apparent pain or blistering. Next he took a dozen three-inch-long pins and pierced his cheeks; leaving them there, he resembled a human pincushion. Finally he took an empty glass and bit off a corner, chewed the glass, and swallowed it. I was no more than six feet away the whole time, taking photographs and carefully monitoring each part of the ritual to watch for trickery. To conclude the ceremony, the other participants danced wildly for at least an hour until the tortured leader fell into a deep trance and was carried away.

The rest of the ceremony was devoted to animal sacrifices and the eating of live doves and chickens. Most interesting was the final appeasement of the voodoo gods. The priest knelt with a bowl of powder. Taking a small amount in his hands, he gradually let the powder sift through his fingers, creating an intricate design on the ground. He saw the puzzled look on my face and explained, "I'm creating a symbol to invoke the goddess of water, Agua." He pointed to the clear sky above him.

Cr-r-rash!

Seconds after the priest finished his ritualistic motif, thunder exploded with a deafening roar and lightning struck a few yards away. Suddenly we were drenched in a torrential downpour.

As I quickly gathered my camera equipment to protect it from the rain, the voodoo priest smiled at me and said, "Don't be surprised. Agua always announces her arrival like that!"

SANTERIA

Santeria, an offshoot of voodoo, originated among black slaves in colonial Spanish territories, especially Cuba. Though they converted to Catholicism, the slaves insisted on retaining their African Yoruba spirits and identified them with Roman Catholic saints. Santeria thrives today in the United States among Cuban Americans and Puerto Ricans.

One of the Santeria's main doctrines teaches that the saint-gods must be appeased with blood sacrifices. So, *santeros* (Santeria priests) regularly slaughter animals, which has not gone unnoticed by police in Miami, Florida, who find goats' heads nailed to trees and bags of entrails strewn in pathways. Santeria shares several gods in common with voodoo, including Ogun, Damballah, and Erzulie. In all, seven deities are worshiped. A more sinister branch of Santeria, Palo Mayombe, unabashedly appeals to black magic.

Critics of Santeria are concerned that its influence is spreading to the hinterlands of America, attracting blacks, whites, and Spanish. Headless chickens are turning up in city parks and street corners in New York and Miami. *Botanicas,* Santeria stores, openly dispense cult supplies. A survey by the Roman Catholic Archdiocese of New York City revealed that thirty thousand people, at least 3 percent of the city's Hispanic population, sacrificed animals, and seventy thousand shopped in botanicas.[7]

In Hialeah, Florida, a Santeria center of worship known as the Church of Lukumi Babalu has officially opened its doors. The santero, the Reverend Ernesto Pichardo, said he would perform animal sacrifices for the church's three hundred members. Hialeah City Council members granted a permit for the building, and the U.S. Supreme Court, in a 1993 decision involving the Florida Santeria Church, sanctioned animal sacrifices.

MACUMBA

In Brazil, voodoo is known as *macumba* (or its variations, *umbanda* and *condomble*). In the sixteenth century African slaves were imported by the Portuguese to work the sugar plantations. The slaves brought with them an advanced system of witchcraft. Like Santeria, macumba melded with the Roman Catholic Church, and African deities were christened with Yoruba (West African) names. Today, as many as forty million Brazilians mingle Roman Catholicism with spirit cults.[8] Macumba and umbanda alone claim thirty million.[9] Government census forms include macumba as a religious affiliation, and there are umbanda radio stations, hospitals, and newspapers.

One evening in Rio de Janeiro, I attended one of the city's thousands of macumba churches. This one was a small whitewashed building on an obscure, narrow street. No one paid much attention when I entered. Apparently the sight of a curious tourist was nothing new.

I sat down on a rough-hewn wooden pew. In front of the church, an altar was crammed with intermingled statues of various orixa (African) deities and Roman Catholic saints. Devotees, dressed completely in white, venerated an idol of Orlorun, the supreme deity. The head priestess, Mother of Gods, watched over the proceedings, incessantly smoking a cigar. Occasionally she would approach a participant and blow cigar smoke all over him from head to feet.

To the accompaniment of beating drums, the worshipers danced far less frantically than voodoo participants. They swayed in time with the beat, periodically twirling like whirling dervishes. Once in a while the orixa would take control of a devotee to vocalize their message. The worshiper would enter a trance and speak in Portuguese, prophesying a message unknown to me.

At other times the orixa would seize violent control of their devotees. The possessed followers would thrash about wildly, barking like a dog. Some frantic devotees contorted their bodies as if imitating a monkey, making baboonlike sounds. No one in the building seemed amused or offended at such a degrading display of animalistic behavior.

The ceremony concluded when the Mother of Gods performed a healing ritual. Her followers lined up in front of her and approached one by one. They whispered petitions in her ear, and she responded by enveloping their bodies in more cigar smoke. Eventually the participants seemed to lose enthusiasm from exhaustion.

In macumba, good and evil are less distinct than in traditional religions. Moral directives are not sought. Instead, practitioners seek a benevolent equilibrium of spiritual harmony. As with voodoo, devout disciples may attempt supernatural feats such as walking on coals, swallowing razors, eating lightbulbs, or pushing nails and pins through their cheeks. Candidates for the condomble priesthood must live in seclusion for six months during their indoctrination. At the time of initiation, the candidates' heads are shaved, their scalps are nicked, and blood from sacrificed animals is poured over their heads.

Satanists borrow rituals from voodoo, Santeria, macumba, umbunda, condomble, and other Westernized folk religions. Self-styled satanists, on the other hand, use elaborate ceremonies, bloodletting sacrifices, psychic powers, and secret initiations inculcated by voodoo cults as a model for their rituals. These satanic folk religions often introduce those already alerted to the occult to darker, more powerful forms of evil.

PART IV

The Metaphysical Worldview in Our Society

Chapter 18

Looking Out for Number One

In Washington, D.C., a group of sober men dressed in military attire declare in unison, "I direct my thoughts to the world of my inner being. I see world leaders, friends, and adversaries joining together in fellowship to resolve issues, forgiving each other." The assembly of seventy-five people isn't a conclave of spiritualists or higher-consciousness seekers, but a band of Pentagon employees meeting for their weekly Pentagon Meditation Club. The club president advocates a new form of SDI (Strategic Defense Initiative), a "spiritual defense initiative" that will protect humanity by the "unified force" of a human "peace shield."

THE HUMAN POTENTIAL MOVEMENT

At the dawn of the computer age, "Don't fold, bend, staple, or mutilate" was the magnetic card instruction humorously applied to people. At the advent of the new millenium, seeking "transformational values" of "human potential" has become the battle cry of assorted higher-consciousness devotees. Through intuitional therapy, professional training courses, public education, and personal experimentation, a constituency has developed that believes mankind has a cosmic destiny. And through mystical examination and psychic development of one's human potential, superior beings who have undergone spiritual reconstruction will supposedly emerge as the new vanguard of the human race.

The same buzzwords and underlying values prevail: *human potential; practical spirituality; progressive politics; feminism* and *matriarchy; organic foods;* and *grassroots activism.* Apart from today's occult spirituality, these terms are spiritually neutral. Within the context of the current milieu they assume inherent definitions that convey a distinctive non-Christian ideology. Human potential advocates have utopian dreams of a world in which all humanity lives in harmony with earth and the cosmos. Instead of an apocalyptic Second Coming with dire events from without, a new spirituality is emerging from within. Even young children are being influenced. They may be asked to invent imaginary playmates or envision "helpers" who assist them in expanding their powers of fancy. They may lie on the floor, arms and legs outstretched, and pretend to become interrelated with one another or imagine they are animals in the forest or birds in the air. Such techniques are designed to separate their minds from their bodies, practices that can lead to occult, out-of-body experiences.

In one case, third graders concentrated intently, their little eyes squeezed tightly, their small brows furrowed. You could almost hear them thinking, *I wish I may, I wish I might.* But the power of imagination being employed had nothing to do with standard nursery rhyme fare. These diminutive students were on a journey of the mind to inhibit their negative behavior.

The teacher had told them to imagine tiny vultures living inside them. If they lost emotional control and were bad, the vultures would grow. If they learned to minimize conflicts with their fellow students, the vultures would diminish. Innocuously called an Autonomous Learner Model, the course had been developed to teach youngsters the mind's power to create reality.

Instead, it created a furor among parents. One mother reported her daughter couldn't sleep at night because she feared vultures were flying about her room. Another parent declared his son was imagining all kinds of monsters for the malevolent purpose of punishing his peers.

HUMAN POTENTIAL UTOPIANISM

The thrust of the Human Potential Movement, unleashing latent powers and abilities within man, is both socially utopian and spiritually idealistic. It supposes there are boundless capabilities in the human psyche and unlimited powers latent in the human spirit. All the dilemmas of mankind, from war to the environment to dysfunctional relationships, can be solved by an immense change in human consciousness. And the subconscious is the key. Subliminal and self-hypnosis tapes, along with visual stimulation devices, can unlock the solution to personal happiness and the power of the soul. Through positive reinforcement and restructuring the perceptual processes (that is, changing the way we look at the world), the innate force of the subconscious will conquer all foes and resist all negativism.

At the core of the Human Potential Movement is humanistic psychology, which places humanity at the center of the universe and denies the concept of original sin. Emotions are paramount, and traditional concepts of deity give way to "self-realization." A movement trademark is the eclectic borrowing of various disciplines, including gestalt awareness, transactional analysis, sensory awareness, primal therapy, bioenergetics, and biofeedback.

In business, traditional economic formulas such as time management, strategic planning, and carefully monitored cash flow are shunted aside in favor of "self-talk" and "centering." The market for spiritualizing business techniques is so lucrative that the Maharishi Mahesh Yogi's Transcendental Meditation Program (TM) has been adapted for corporate consumption under the name "One, Incorporated."

In 1993 Scientology officially became a religion in the United States when the IRS granted it tax-exempt status. Scientology continued to gain worldwide acceptance with celebrity endorsements from Tom Cruise, Lisa Marie Presley, and John Travolta. However, the German government denounced Scientology as an extremist, for-profit organization and refused to recognize it as a religion. German officials barred Scientologists from membership in major political parties, and placed the organization under surveillance. This prompted the church to compare its treatment to the persecution of Jews in Nazi Germany, which offended both survivors of the Holocaust and the German government.

America refuses to recognize Scientology as a dangerous cult. Los Angeles public school teachers have used Scientology teachings in classrooms, and President Clinton once told John Travolta he wanted to help out with the Scientology situation in Germany. In addition, a federal immigration court judge granted asylum to a German member of the Church of Scientology living in Florida who claimed she would be subjected to religious persecution if required to return to her homeland. Scientology established the World Institute of Scientological Enterprises and Sterling Management to invade the workplace with its science of the soul called Dianetics.

Silva Mind Control counsels businesspeople to solve work problems by projecting themselves out of their bodies. They are also told to envision their work environment complete with imaginary "counselors," entities who assist with improved profit-loss statements.

John Naisbitt, best-selling author of *Megatrends*, explains that mankind is shifting to a global economy. To assist the unwary, he and his wife have created their own metaphysical foundation called Bellweather. Naisbitt says, "We consider ourselves to be New Age entrepreneurs. Bellweather supports people creating new morals and new directions."

Innovation Associates of Framingham, Massachusetts, charges $15,000 for a four-day seminar designed to strengthen executives' commitment to a common purpose. Hoy, Powers, & Wayno, a New York firm, uses meditation, imaging, and intuitive thought to instill creativity and leadership among managers. At the Stanford Graduate School of Business, a professor uses Zen, yoga, and tarot cards as part of the instructive curriculum for the course "Creativity in Business."[1]

Consultants bill themselves as providing "stress management, employee assessment, and integrated strategies." One such consultant offers a psychotherapeutic assessment of professional potential by observing employees' "auras." Another "business analyst" advises Fortune 500 clients and trade associations with the assistance of channeling, psychic cosmic consciousness, "life-affirming" advice on "death and dying." One public relations firm offers "mainstream coverage for New Age ideas."

Typically, human potential groups meet for a weekend of training, which expands to a program designed to achieve personal growth and kindle latent abilities. Total attention is given to body awareness and impassioned feelings of the here and now. The purpose is to cultivate a less judgmental attitude about relationships and a less critical stance on conventional values.

In the beginning the Human Potential Movement attempted to emphasize credible leadership and cautious concern for group dynamics. That began to change when the movement adopted the Eastern mysticism popular in California. The goal of overcoming dull routines of everyday existence gradually evolved into pursuit of "self-transcendence" by merging with ideals of cosmic consciousness. Self-discovery for improvement of personal esteem unfolded into a form of metaphysical "self-actualization."

The roots of the Human Potential Movement can be found in nineteenth-century Theosophy and Emersonian transcendentalism, as well as Eastern mysticism. Biblically, Paul's letter to the Colossians addresses some pregnostic ideas similar to these. What's different today is the mass marketing and widespread acceptance of once-esoteric experiences. Scripture teaches that humanity in its fallen state cannot achieve reconciliation with God, and that salvation cannot come from works. The Human Potential Movement is a system of salvation that depends on what we can do for ourselves, not what God's grace can accomplish by faith in the redemption of Christ. The movement is humanistic, with humanity at the center of its hope to avoid fear and failure instead of centering on the help of the Holy Spirit. "I can do all things through Christ,"[2] the apostle Paul declared, the philosophical antithesis of developing human potential.

HUMAN POTENTIAL BUSINESS TECHNIQUES

In a competitive global economy, boosting company productivity and creativity takes a high priority. Many manufacturers are desperate to boost morale, spur inventiveness, and enhance profits. As a result, businesses are constantly looking for a new edge, and mind-control techniques are the latest fad to captivate corporate America. More than half the five hundred largest United States corporations, including Procter and Gamble, IBM, and Singer, have adopted some form of spiritual creativity training. These companies willingly pay anywhere from a few thousand dollars to a half-million dollars for product development sessions designed to reprogram employees' thinking.

Meditative techniques are used as part of stress-management strategies, including TM, self-hypnosis, guided imagery, yoga, and centering. Some techniques enhance intuitive creativity, such as visualization, Silva Mind Control, Dianetics, and focusing. Certain techniques heighten self-esteem by incorporating affirmations.

Visualization is a key word with many New Age business advisers. Employees undergoing training are told they must acknowledge their dreams and commit to realizing them. They're instructed to relax, take slow, deep breaths, and visualize a spacecraft taking them to another planet. Once there, the workers are to look back on earth to sense a oneness with the cosmos. The resulting visualization releases them from past limitations and restrictions. Psychotechnologies have invaded the workforce with the intent of "self-actualization" (otherwise known as "enlightenment" or "contacting one's inner divine nature"). Most occult influences enter through the human resources departments of large companies. Metaphysical seminars hide behind language chosen to obscure their religious nature. Such seminars make all the claims of religion, such as offering "transformational encounters" and "magical experiences." But to avoid the wrath of the IRS and the penalty of antidiscriminatory statutes, trainers consistently claim they offer no specific religious agenda. Any knowledgeable observer can readily recognize the Hindu concepts underlying the "cosmic consciousness" sought by human potential groups.

A Boston firm called Synetics offers to take employees on "mental excursions." Other entrepreneurs encourage businessmen to promote equality. Personnel might play with crayons, make up stories, or merely daydream. Programs like Transformational Technologies use meditation and hypnosis to promote common corporate visions. Employees are encouraged to think of themselves and the company as one, a unitary consciousness idea borrowed from Eastern mysticism.

Transformational Technologies is the stepchild of Werner Erhard's est and its successor, The Forum. Trans Tech sells its services apart from The Forum through franchise operations, with clients including RCA, Scott Paper Company, and Boeing Aircraft.[3]

Human potential concepts are not newly devised therapeutic tools, but are historically rooted in the ancient heresies of syncretism, Gnosticism, and Pelagianism. Syncretism, the melding together of unrelated ideologies, errs by failing to distinguish between God, His creation, and Christianity versus other religions. Just as early heretics sought to combine elements of paganism, Christianity, and philosophical thought, human potential groups use a variety of occult and mystical methods. Gnosticism, a heresy in the early church, was based on esoteric knowledge of the divine mysteries unavailable to the uninitiated. This information could be obtained if the seeker were properly guided by an intermediary. Groups such as Life Training and Lifespring carefully guard their group sessions and allow no public inspection of inner proceedings. With the aid of a gifted teacher, the training supposedly provides an awakened understanding of life. In the fifth century, Pelagianism denied the transmissible corruption of Adam's sin to all mankind and therefore held that human nature alone is capable of fulfilling the will of God. The ideas of self-discovery and self-betterment found in human potential groups extend this ancient idea.

The Human Potential Movement teaches that the mind/soul nature of man is God. Scripture teaches that God is the Creator of reality, not that He is our minds. All that exists was spoken into being by God, and we cannot deny or rearrange our objective material existence by a mere mental redefinition. Second, our misconduct cannot be justified by human efforts to do good. Only the grace of Jesus' redemption can provide atonement for erroneous action (sin). Finally, it is the Holy Spirit who progressively sanctifies us, not self-actualization facilitated by visualization procedures.

est

More than a half-million graduates were charged hundreds of dollars each to discover, in est's words, "You are part of every atom in the world, and every atom is part of you . . . the self itself is the ground of all being, that from which everything arises."[4] Such were the assertions of est, Erhard Seminars Training.

At age eighteen, Jack Rosenberg had an experience during which he says, "I lost the kind of consciousness that locates one in a certain place. I became the universe."[5] Later, while driving his wife's Mustang down a freeway, he declared, "I got it." What he got was a new name, Werner Erhard, and a system of philosophy rooted in yoga, Dale Carnegie, Mind Dynamics, Silva Mind

Control, Scientology, and Zen Buddhism. Erhard's arrogance led him to say, "How do you know I'm not the reincarnation of Jesus Christ?"[6]

Such preposterous claims were behind what some disgruntled ex-members said was a confrontational style of indoctrination that destroyed moral and emotional standards of coping. A former est worker now claims, "They said it was all right to sleep with your friend's husband because you can create the feeling of being guilty or feeling fine. You are your own God."[7]

After reading an *Esquire* magazine article about West Germany, Rosenberg borrowed the names of physicist Werner Heisenberg and German economics minister Ludwig Erhard. For more than a decade, he explored the then-developing Human Potential Movement, Zen Buddhism, hypnosis, Scientology, and California's Esalen Institute.

Erhard's seminar system involved a calculated process of breaking down the inductee's personality and rebuilding it by harassment and intimidation. The trainer verbally abused the audience with repeated obscenities. All ego defenses were ridiculed by hurling demeaning epithets at anyone who resisted the trainer's tactics. After hours of such manipulation, participants were supposed to "get it." For some, "it" became a way of overcoming introversion to assert themselves. For others, "it" was just another trip on the consciousness-raising express. By the time Erhard abandoned est in the mid-1980s, hundreds of thousands of graduates had been told that all religious ideas are meaningless. One's reality could be chosen at will, and gods could be invented as needed.

THE FORUM

"An expression of a breakthrough in transformation achieved by est"[8]—that's the self-congratulatory way The Forum describes itself. Unlike the est training format of lectures punctuated by personal confrontations between trainers and participants, The Forum is more casual and involved dialogue between leaders and audience. Whereas early est sessions prohibited bathroom breaks and involved verbal abuse, The Forum is more upscale than est and targets a corporate clientele. It even has a juvenile division, known as Young People's Forum, for children between six and twelve.

The Forum aims for "healthy, successful people, who are already effective in their lives."[9] Critics say that translates into those who can afford hundreds of dollars for four sixteen-hour sessions about "making it happen." Participants are assured that once they realize the benefits of The Forum, they will consider the cost "a joke."[10]

The Forum has convinced some chief executive officers that workers will produce more if they can contact their "sense of being." How is this achieved? The Forum ambiguously states that "being" is inexplicable, the "magic" of being trained in The Forum.

LIFESPRING

The U.S. Surgeon General's office once declared Lifespring "has considerable potential for emotional harm."[11] A Pennsylvania woman whose husband got a large settlement after suffering a severe psychotic reaction to Lifespring sessions said trainers told participants to slap the person with whom they felt closest. One session involved playing "Life Boat," a game in which trainees decided who deserved to enter a small boat to be saved from a sinking ship. Such criticism contrasted strongly with Lifespring's claimed benefits of "increased clarity on career direction, a deeper understanding of self, enhanced joy in relationships, and more fun in life."[12]

Founder John Hanley had been a trainer with Werner Erhard in Mind Dynamics courses during the early 1970s. Hanley left Mind Dynamics because he felt it emphasized too many abstractions and was too reflective. Hanley wanted to compel people to pursue a state of passion and "aliveness." His brand of self-awareness training took people through guided meditations and communication exercises. Hanley achieved financial success, but all was not well at Lifespring. When ABC-TV's *20/20* did an exposé, serious claims were leveled that Lifespring's "psychodramas" were morally questionable. Geraldo Rivera cited one case in which an ex-nun was told to go to a seedy bar and proposition the first man who spoke to her. On another occasion, participants were told to discuss their sex organs and describe their most bizarre and humiliating sexual experiences.[13]

When he founded Lifespring in 1974, Hanley presented his first training to twenty-three persons. By the '90s, he had centers in more than a dozen major cities. His expense budget exceeded $10 million, and he employed a full-time staff of over one hundred.[14]

Hanley readily paid homage to est and Erhard. He believed that est paved the way for the transformational training business. Hanley said, "The est course was a quantum shift in 'being' with people. We're all in Werner's wake." Any differences with est? "The est training focused on the fact that people were robots and on automatic pilot, while Lifespring was more concerned with personal relationships,"[15] he said.

Lifespring was unashamedly anti-intellectual. Feelings and experience were all-important. It was also strongly influenced by the ideas of Abraham Maslow, the late humanist psychologist. Hanley has explored the notions of philosophers Søren Kierkegaard and Martin Heidegger. Lifespring's basic idea has been that "personal growth and effectiveness are paramount," so that one may continue having "expanded choice, creating options and providing a supportive atmosphere for the examination of values and systems."[16]

Lifespring's goals have been achieved through gestalt awareness, encounter training, psychosynthesis, and Eastern meditation. Experimental learning methods included two people engaging in "communication exercises," guided meditations, and a variety of group exercises. Trainers presented brief "lecturettes," suggesting ways of testing beliefs and habits. The forty-five-hour Basic Course, sixty-hour Advanced Course, and ninety-day Leadership

Program focused on personal power, self-understanding, sexuality, communication, wellness, intuition, and spirituality.

LIFE TRAINING

Would you like to free your life of the fears, decisions, judgments, expectations, and beliefs that have "made your life into a drama, a series of habitual, automatic reactions to your problems"? Then Life Training is for you. Just devote seventeen-hour days on the weekend, from 9:00 A.M. to 2:00 A.M., to "processing" the experiences of your life. Why so much time so quickly? To quote a promotional piece, "The Training is designed to go very deep, very fast . . . It is this depth and rate of discovery that distinguishes this experience from other educational programs."[17]

Potential clients are told they will ease the effects of life's disorders by living in a new and "awakened" manner. How? By nurturing the "SELF . . . the capacity that the great religions have called the Soul."[18] Trainees are told that no particular religious belief system will be emphasized, but that Life Training is "spiritual . . . because it develops the capacity to live out of your spirit."[19]

Life Training was created in the late 1970s by two Episcopalian priests in San Jose, California. They borrowed the rational-emotive therapy of Albert Ellis, a noted humanist psychologist. His theory stated that all suffering stems from irrational thinking. But those who have participated in Life Training and are also familiar with est readily notice the similarities in the two-weekend format, the size of the groups, and the use of neutral hotel facilities. Other est resemblances include a controlled environment in which trainers verbally berate audiences, use of transformational buzzwords, group manipulation, and public exposure of painful past experiences. And as with est, the ultimate yardstick of all truth is the measure one takes of oneself.

Life Training sessions are so carefully designed that detailed instructions suggest how to be seated, when and how to talk, and what to do in the event of drowsiness during the marathon sessions. Watches, chewing gum, and outside reading materials are prohibited. Specific curse words are allowed in place of certain unacceptable epithets. The names God, Jesus, Christ, and Buddha are forbidden. Results of the training are held as confidential as information divulged to a priest.

MISCELLANEOUS HUMAN POTENTIAL
SEMINARS/ORGANIZATIONS

Insight Transformational Seminars (ITS): Founded in 1978 by John-Roger.[20] John-Roger was born Roger Delano Hinkins in a small Utah town. He says that in 1963, while in a coma, he became inhabited by a spirit identified as "John the Beloved."[21] John-Roger claimed to be the embodiment of the divine Mystical Traveled Consciousness, and headed the Los Angeles-based Movement of Spiritual Inner Awareness (MSIA).

His Insight Seminars brought in $8 million in one year.[22] His ministers have run productivity seminars for U.S. government offices and major corporations. Every year ITS presents an "Integrity Award" to "outstanding world citizens." MSIA's annual Integrity Days have given away as much as $10,000 to the favorite charities of celebrity honorees, such as Mother Teresa, Desmond Tutu, and Ralph Nader, most of whom have not been actively associated with John-Roger or his organizations.[23] Featured events are "Awakening Heart Seminars," costing $450, and "The Opening Heart Seminar" and "Centering in the Heart Seminar," which cost $775 each. His most recent book, *Forgiveness: The Key to the Kingdom,* was widely publicized by full page ads in magazines like *Time.* The promotional piece declared, "John-Roger with his depth of humanity and compassionate wisdom explains how forgiveness unlocks the imprisoned heart."

John-Roger states, "In awakening the heartfelt energies, you can't help but discover your own self-worth, your own magnificence." The targeted energy is defined as God, or "whatever you want to call it."[24] Mystical aspects of Insight Transformational

Seminars are underscored by the financial support of such groups as the Holistic Center for Therapy and Research and the Prana Theological Seminary.[25] (Prana is the Hindu concept of vital energy.)

Disaffected members have accused John-Roger of brainwashing his followers, seducing young male staff members with promises of promotion for sexual favors, and using electronic listening devices to preserve his reputation as a clairvoyant.[26] Former MSIA members report campaigns of hate mail and vandalism directed against them and their families.[27]

Perhaps his best-known proponent has been Arianna Huffington, ex-wife of Texas millionaire and politician Michael Huffington. Church members say Arianna was ordained a "minister of light" in the church, which required her to accept John-Roger as an entity higher than Christ. She reportedly donated $35,000 to one of his foundations. Arianna has denied being a member of MISA since 1986 but critics claim she has continued to use her wealth and political ties to promote the agenda of John-Roger. Ex-MSIA members accuse Roger of being a bisexual predator who bilks followers out of money and connections to support his teachings that his body contains the spirit of the Mystical Traveller, an eternal spirit that previously inhabited Jesus Christ.

Institute of Human Development: Offers a complete collection of metaphysical and self-improvement tapes for use in guided meditation, guided visualizations, and positive reprogramming. Complete freedom from sickness, fear, worry, and financial problems is promised. An additional "Cosmic Odyssey" offers the secret "why's of life and the universe" and the "highest New Age teachings." Tapes teach psychic self-defense against demon possession and negative energy fields, plus tutoring in past-life regression, future-life projection, cabala, awakening kundalini energy, developing ESP, commanding financial success, hypnotizing others by mental telepathy, Aquarian Age techniques of controlling the environment, universal binding laws of Egyptian mysteries, automatic handwriting from higher entities, talking with animals, and how to become a christ master.

Institute of Transpersonal Psychology: A Ph.D. program located in Stanford, California, offering bodywork, spiritual work, or psychological work that requires three to four years to complete. Courses include T'ai Chi, Aikido, Sensory Awareness, Zen Meditation, Hinduism, Astrology, the Tao of Physics, Arica, Hatha Yoga, Feldenkrais, Healing and Hypnosis, and Parapsychology. The institute claims to be on the frontier of psychology, uniting concern for the body, mind, and psyche. In addition to studies, daily one-hour sessions are set aside for yoga and jin shin jyutsu.

Arica: Named after a Chilean town where a Bolivian mystic named Oscar Ichazo lived. He founded what was called "scientific mysticism," borrowing from Hinduism, Zen, and Tibetan Lamaism (a form of occult spiritualism). Students are taught to hear music through their feet, develop breathing exercises, and engage in "mentations" (concentration on various organs of the body for specified time periods). Ichazo promotes Psychocalisthenics, a series of twenty-three movement-breathing exercises designed to awaken vital energy.

Esalen: Michael Murphy and Richard Price met Frederic Spiegelburg, professor of comparative religion at Stanford University, through whom they were introduced to the concepts of Eastern philosophy, yoga, and other subjects that eventually shaped their lives and work. They founded the Esalen Institute in 1962 at Big Sur, California.[28]

One element that made Esalen seem daring and sensual was its coeducational hot water, mineral baths in the 1960s. Exposed on one side to the sky and stars, some bathers experienced feelings of oneness with the universe that they claimed changed their lives.

The Esalen Institute preceded the Human Potential Movement and promoted early experiments with encounter groups and sensitivity training. In 1962, according to Michael

Murphy, "humanistic psychology was just beginning to take root. Gestalt therapy was virtually unknown outside narrow professional circles. Attending to the needs of one's body was reserved for athletes, dancers, and so-called 'health nuts.' Meditation had not been assigned a role in maximizing human potential, and anyone studying or claiming psychic insight was considered, at best, to be on the fringes."[29] All these disciplines were explored at Esalen.

By the mid-1960s, the Esalen seminars had shifted from ordinary didactic sessions to a newer kind of "experiential seminar," during which emphasis was placed on experiencing the theory being discussed. Psychotherapist Rob Gerard led his students in visualization exercises, while discussing the theory of psychosynthesis.[30]

Fritz Perls, the founder of gestalt psychotherapy, resided at Esalen when he was in his seventies. He disagreed with analytical explorations of a client's past, and advocated a kind of therapy that concentrated on the present. Clients were encouraged to exaggerate emotions, such as anger and fear, in a group environment.[31]

Sensory awareness courses required following a series of relaxation exercises designed to increase physical and mental awareness.[32] Bodywork, or "therapeutic manipulation," remains a staple at Esalen, where "skillful touching" is used to alter "the structure, the chemistry, the feelings, and the behavior of a human being."[33]

Today, the Esalen Institute defines itself as "a center to explore those trends in education, religion, philosophy, and the physical and behavioral sciences which emphasize the potentialities and values of human existence." Activities include seminars, workshops, and residential programs, as well as research and consulting.[34]

In February 1998 a mud slide nearly wiped out the Esalen bathhouse perched just a few hundred feet above the ocean. This prompted the nonprofit organization to issue a fund-raising plea for $2 million for reconstruction to continue to lure participants like mind-body guru Deepak Chopra and Eastern mystic and singer Joan Baez. The days when orgies were advertised on the bulletin board have been replaced with a sober reminder to incoming seminarians that "any substance that's illegal in the outside world is illegal at Esalen."

The Esalen group teaches seminars on topics like "The Pleasure Zone: Why We Resist Good Feelings and How to Let Go and Be Happy." A recent workshop featured teaching on "Techno-Pagans at the End of History: Psychedelics, the Internet, Virtual Reality, and You." When seminarians aren't attempting to heal childhood wounds or awaken the Buddha within, Esalen's participants sip herbal tea on the patio. Esalen's seminars include tuition, meals, and shared accommodations (two to a room) in sparse but comfortable redwood cabins and lodges.

CONCLUSIONS

This cultural milieu facilitating the rise of occult spiritualism erupted from the idealistic fervor and narcissism of the 1960s, but it is now encountering a midlife crisis. Suddenly, the limits of human mortality must be faced. Exploration of the spirit is a way of denying the reality of death by reconstructing materiality. One need only read a brief chronology of Homo sapiens to see how unscrupulous charismatic leaders have exploited such naïveté.

The onslaught of spiritualistic training in corporate America may signal its demise. Whatever short-term goals are achieved, future U.S. enterprise may be bartered away. Touchy-feely business techniques may temporarily increase sales, but unsuspecting individuals will be more vulnerable to altered states of consciousness and potential demonic possession. Placing mankind at the center of one's personal and corporate universe is blasphemy, a sacrilege promoted for corporate profit. Such pretentiousness may accelerate productivity momentarily through ego gratification, but eventually the idea that higher profits can be thought into being will be considered infantile.

Some occultists honestly admit that their goal of "unitary consciousness" and mass global "spirituality" can be achieved only if all hindrances to human potential are removed. New Age author and theorist John Randolph Price, in his book *Practical Spirituality*, described the elimination of two billion people with lower "vibratory rates."[35] Such apparently genocidal intent contrasts sharply with the claims of human potential champions. The reality of such propaganda is not global harmony and enlightened masses, but death, destruction, and the aims of the Antichrist.

A common theme of human potential cults is the supposed power in each of us to create our own reality. This viewpoint teaches that past events can affect us only according to the current meaning. Participants are told that reality is not what happened, but what one *thinks* happened. In contrast, Christianity teaches that the past is powerful and affects who we are today. Sinful deeds are not eradicated by ignoring them. They are forgiven by repentance and faith in Christ (1 Peter 2:24).

The underlying principle of the Human Potential Movement is that life must be experienced, not understood. In this psychological system, there is no right and wrong, only "what is." But avoiding the penalty for sin takes more than a few days at a transformational seminar. It requires the blood of Christ and His death on the cross (Eph. 1:7). Human potential philosophies may transform who we think we are and what we think may have happened. But the future of heaven or hell is an objective reality, and the judgment of God is an actual future event that cannot be wished away.

Chapter 19

The Occult and Mind Control

The pulse of rock rhythms blares from a speaker in the background. Dozens of people stand in obvious anticipation. Some breathe heavily. Others chant repeatedly, "Cool moss, cool moss." Finally, the group's leader steps onto a ten-foot-long path of glowing coals. The embers range in temperature from 1,200 to 2,000 degrees Fahrenheit. "We can do anything we want," the leader exclaims as he briskly traverses the fiery path.

Like lemmings, the others follow. Why not? They've shelled out $125 each and were told during the preceding five hours, "You can change fear into victory, limitations into freedom, doubt into certainty, and fatigue into energetic power." By the end of their sweltering stroll, they will believe the words of their firewalking instructor, who told them that every time someone creates a miracle, like firewalking, he transcends the accepted laws of the physical universe.

Firewalking began as a religious practice in the South Pacific and among the Hindus of India and other assorted idolaters around the world. Today's firewalkers are exploring psychological frontiers. They promise neophytes the ability to lose weight, conquer smoking habits, spell better, read better, and even achieve superior orgasms.

Manipulating the mind by orchestrating reality is a way to acquire "transformative" states of consciousness. To do so, one must overcome certain inhibitions of the normal mind-set, which include reserve and fear. Of the latter, a well-known firewalking teacher says, "Fear is just random energy. By changing our frame of reference, fear's power becomes personal power, the power to get things done."[1]

Power is much of what modern occult philosophy is all about: power to transcend time and space; power to defy presumed moral laws and known physical laws; power to do anything with one's mind; in short, power to become a god. In the words of one advertisement for a firewalk, "Experience a personal triumph. A deep belief in your ability to take action, to do what *you* want to do."

Will Noyes believes it. Crippled with arthritis, he couldn't stand straight or walk without crutches. After four months of firewalking, Will said he could walk upright and has taken dancing lessons. But professional medical journals illustrate different consequences. There are scores of documented hospitalizations and even foot amputations resulting from firewalking. At a recent convention of record retailing executives, 370 people were invited to march across twelve feet of burning coals to the theme from *Rocky*. An ambulance had to be called in, and many participants spent the rest of the conference on crutches after suffering second-degree burns.[2]

For the traditional firewalker in India or Asia, sacred devotion is part of the process. The walker may precede his feat by fasting, celibacy, and ritualistic purification. Western firewalkers make no such preparations. Instead, they speak of "anchoring, disassociation, and neurolinguistics." But a professor of anthropology observes of classical firewalking, "To my knowledge, there is always some supernatural overtone, some kind of relationship to a higher spirit. They're invoking a higher spirit or power and aligning themselves with this greater power. It almost always has cleansing properties."[3]

How can people walk on fire without injury? One firewalker claims that perspiration on the soles of the feet provides protection for a brief duration. The so-called Ledenfrost theory says the feet secrete an unidentified substance that shields them from injury. An instructor of firewalking claims that glands in the brain release protective chemicals called neuropeptides, and that positive thoughts about the walk encourage the secretion of this substance.

In one experiment, Bernard J. Leikind, a physicist, and William J. McCarthy, a psychologist, both from the University of California at Los Angeles, attended a firewalk led by Tony Robbins. Both men succeeded in crossing the bed of hot embers without injury, though Leikind had not attended the prefirewalk seminar, which was advertised as being crucial to the accomplishment.[4]

Their conclusions were that firewalking can be explained by a combination of physics and psychology. Leikind wrote that the secret to firewalking lies in the distinction between heat and thermal energy, the conductivity of different materials, and that "just knowing the temperature is not enough to decide whether something will burn us."[5]

Though firewalkers cross beds of the glowing embers, they are light and fluffy carbon compounds. Leikind reported darkened footprints where people had passed over the embers and pressed them down, cooling them so that the risk of injury was lessened. Even when the embers are glowing yellow—the hottest intensity—the thermal energy is not likely to burn a firewalker's feet. Serious injuries at firewalks have occurred when participants have spent more than the average 1.5 seconds needed to cross the bed of embers or have walked upon deeply piled, hotter embers.[6]

Leikind concedes that the Ledenfrost effect is a scientifically based explanation, since moisture does act as an insulator, but, he says, it is "likely to be helpful but not necessary for firewalking, provided the heat capacity, thermal conductivity, and temperature of the embers or rocks is suitably low."[7] He discounts various other explanations offered by firewalk theorists, ranging from protection by correct beliefs to a bioelectric field surrounding the walker as being "totally unsupported by any direct experimental data."[8]

McCarthy has theorized that psychology may explain why firewalkers sometimes feel no pain or heat. "Distraction can reduce the pain that people experience, because they can attend to only a few things at once."[9] At one firewalk, instructions were given beforehand that "actually seemed calculated to distract our attention from the sensations of our feet. Concentrating on the 'mantra,' looking up at the sky, hearing the applause and shouts of elation, and breathing in an artificial and forced manner, all served to distract the walker."[10]

Firewalking is scientifically possible without participating in mind-over-matter self-improvement classes. Firewalk instructors say that a person's subconscious mind may be at work even if the person is a doubter. But skeptics point out that if the instruction is not vital to the act of firewalking, then it is all a deception.

Can firewalking be removed from religious considerations by treating it as a mental and physical feat? Deuteronomy 18 refers to pagan fire purification ceremonies when it declares that the one who "passes through the fire" is committing an "abomination." Though devotion to an idol and spiritual purification may not be present during a Westernized firewalk, the inherent motivation is identical. Firewalkers worship the idol of self and seek to purify their insecurities and fears without turning to Christ, whose perfect love casts out fear. A study of the occult reveals that certain ceremonialism attracts evil spirits. Since fire purification ceremonies have been associated with entity possession and control (e.g., voodoo rituals), one can assume that a firewalk could be a denizen of demons.

Hypnosis could explain the absence of pain in firewalking

since its acute neurosensory response could be disassociated. But that could not explain the absence of blisters and burning experienced by some walkers whose faith apparently protects them. This seems to indicate a religious aspect, since "believing" is crucial to avoidance of harm. Hebrews 11:6 says it is impossible to please God without faith. Satan, who wishes to be "like God" (Isa. 14), may extract a commitment of "faith" to protect firewalkers and thus keep "true believers" from harm.

Christ reminded Satan of God's warning, "You shall not tempt the LORD your God."[11] Yet firewalkers do just that by suggesting they can think away the potential danger to which they subject themselves. God does vow, "When you walk through the fire, you shall not be burned."[12] But God's promise applies to inadvertent adversity.

God is faithful, but He is not obliged to intervene on our behalf when we frivolously place ourselves in jeopardy. The firewalker who seeks to alter his phobias and insecurities by threatening his own welfare blasphemes God, who offers His Holy Spirit for strength in our weakness and courage for our fears. Trust in God's Word is a more reliable guide to overcoming adversity than hot coals and hypnotic chants. God offers promises you can stand on without getting your "soul" burned.

NEUROLINGUISTICS

Firewalkers say that a successful firewalk demonstrates attainment of a higher consciousness. It's mind power at work at its most dramatic. That's why many firewalking instructors also teach neurolinguistics. Practitioners say they can cure phobias in minutes and enable clients to overcome any inhibition. Salesmen of the art claim they can induce an almost trancelike state in a potential client, causing him to respond affirmatively.

Neurolinguistic programming (NLP) is the brainchild of linguist John Grinder and Dr. Richard Bandler, a computer expert trained in gestalt therapy. It was developed at the University of California, Santa Cruz, and uses sophisticated techniques to establish rapport with a patient. The therapist scans a patient's body language and word patterns in search of underlying patterns. Hypnosis may be used, though some say the patient-therapist relationship itself can induce a natural trancelike state.

Dr. Bandler says NLP "teaches people to run their own brains instead of letting their brains run them."[13] The application of NLP also uses some techniques of so-called Ericksonian hypnosis (named after Dr. Milton H. Erickson). Erickson taught that psychotherapy could bypass client resistance by imbedding therapeutic messages during presumably casual conversations.

Some NLP therapists use a technique called "anchoring," the careful manipulation of voice changes and body movements for hypnotic effect. The use of hypnotic reinforcement is also prominent among NLP therapists. For example, a shy person may be asked to remember a time when he felt confident. He is then touched on the shoulder to embed or "anchor" that confidence. The mainstream psychological community is skeptical, viewing NLP as too manipulative. Studying how a person looks and sounds and treating him like a machine is considered too behavioristic and devoid of empathy between counselor and client.

VISUALIZATION

Visualization is another mind game. It also goes by other names such as "guided imagery," "dynamic imaging," or "positive imaging." The intent is the same: creating or re-creating physical realities with the mind's perceptual powers. Its roots are in Hinduism and modern Science of Mind sects. Hindus have a word for it: *maya*. All the universe is maya, or illusion, they say. Only spirit is substantive. Therefore, what common sense interprets as objective reality is really a figment of the mind. And if reality is an illusion, mental powers can alter it by visualizing something different.

The manipulation of maya is one way yogis seek to achieve union with their god, Brahman. For modern mystics, the purpose is more practical. Groups such as Christian Science and Unity teach that sin, sickness, disease, and failure are all products of the mind. None of these have tangible existence; they are only thoughts that can be dispelled by proper alignment of the mental processes.

Creative visualization involves a mind-body synthesis, beginning with relaxation techniques, followed by breathing exercises. Self-hypnosis procedures may also be employed. First, the desired image is centered in the mind and enforced with repeated affirmation. Contradictory thoughts must be allowed to float only fleetingly through the mind. At this point, any doubts about the visualized goal must be suspended. No outside authority is allowed to intervene, not even a transcendent God. At this moment, the one visualizing is thought to be in touch with his Higher Self, a projection of God, and therefore no harmful or selfish visualization is possible.

How does visualization differ from positive thinking and the homilies of Norman Vincent Peale? In brief, it is a big step beyond. It's more than mind over matter. Visualization claims to produce an entirely new reality. The message of its benefits is carried in workshops, seminars, books, cassettes, and videos, all available in scores of New Age catalogs and retail outlets.

In some cases visualization is used in attempts to cure disease by activating the immune system to increase the number of white blood cells. For example, the patient may be told to envision his cancer as a snake in his body being attacked by a giant eagle, which kills and carries it away. Subliminal voice recordings and consciousness-altering musical sounds of surf, wind, and rain may assist the mental voyage.

The health application of creative visualization has been its most readily received message. A promotional device marketing books and tapes to enhance visualization advertises: "Mentally and physically, begin the transformation you desire, whether it be improving appearance, alleviating illness or injury, easing discomfort from allergies or pain ... whatever you personally wish to alter and improve."[14]

Critics of visualization raise logical questions about its validity, even apart from the fantasies it engenders. Suppose two different people visualize competing realities? Which is entitled to preference? What structure of priorities guides such mental faculties? Suppose the reality sought is control over the lives of others? Who determines what selfish considerations are unfit for visualization? What kind of unconscious guide can circumvent self-indulgent goals? What if a critically ill patient tried to think away his condition instead of seeking appropriate medical advice? And for the Christian, what differentiates faith from visualization, since the former is declared in the Bible to be "the evidence of things not seen"?[15]

Visualization techniques open doors to the mind and spirit that the Lord intends to remain closed (see Gen. 1:27–29; 2:19–20). Adam apparently possessed incredible powers of intellect. But after humanity's fall, there is no indication God condoned the cultivation of psychic powers to alter reality. As for healing, visualization is particularly dangerous because real symptoms of serious illness could be ignored. Wishing away an organic disorder by psychosomatic manipulation could place the patient in greater danger as the disease progresses.

God alone is the Creator of all that exists. Satan is the master deceiver who manipulates our perception of reality. In Eden, he began this technique by tempting Eve with the question "Has God indeed said?"[16] In fact, God had not said what Satan suggested, but his implication distorted Eve's conception of God's character. Those who use visualization substitute an altered perception of reality for true repentance. They pretend that transgression does not exist, that evil and sin are unreal, to avoid facing their iniquity. Instead of seeking God's will, they rearrange unpleasant incidents.

Rather than allowing grace to make "all things work together for good,"[17] they make arrogant assumptions about situations in life and try to amend whatever they find unacceptable.

As a sales technique or a means of overcoming a negative self-portrait, a positive outlook is acceptable. But a fine line is crossed when mental depictions of success are sought by reconstructing reality. Visualization as a spiritual tool can become an Aladdin's lamp. It is particularly dangerous if one uses selfish mental fantasies to alter actualities. The Almighty becomes a mere spiritual vendor, dispensing products to the religious consumer upon demand, that *our* will instead of *His* might be done.

Once the visualization process begins, what authority will limit its application? Will a hazardous disease be thought away while the debilitation continues? Will financial failure be ignored while the visualizer dreams his way to riches and hastens the summons of the bankruptcy judge? Will Christ become an idealized icon, conveniently pictured in one's mind according to the human will rather than the prerogative of divine sovereignty? Could a visualized Jesus actually be a manifested evil spirit, invading one's mind with masquerading intentions?

Suppose a disease is caused by improper diet, unwarranted emotional stress, lack of faith in God, or personal sin. Can it simply be visualized as nonexistent, thus avoiding the penalty for sinful actions? Jesus offers mountain-moving faith, quite different from the entreaty of visualization, which says, "The mountain isn't really there." One has confidence either in a technique to alter what is, or in reliance on a higher power to take what is and render it as if it were not there. One's faith is in God, or one's faith is in faith.

MEDITATION

He's a professor at Harvard Medical School and the author of the renowned best-selling book *The Relaxation Response*—impressive credentials for someone who wants you to think yourself warm on a cold day. But Herbert Benson has done his research. Benson investigated Tibetan Buddhist monks in a cold Himalayan colony in the north of India. In deep states of what the meditative monks called "heat yoga," the devotees raised the temperature of their fingers and toes as much as fifteen degrees without changing their bodies' core temperature.

What other powers over mind and matter does meditation offer? Some advocates of the ancient art of meditation claim it can grow more brain cells, allow you to embody the consciousness of the true Messiah, and even enter the bodies of others to assist their spiritual quest. For eight dollars, one popular yoga instructor offers a course entitled "Contacting the Tree of Life and the Tree of Knowledge." A promotional brochure states: "While meditating with another person, you die and enter the Garden of Eden. You see the Tree of Life and the Tree of Knowledge, surrendering to the great evolutionary intelligence to give you what you need."

To most, meditation means prayer or deep contemplation. Others see meditation as an extremely private religious ritual. But the mystic who speaks of meditation seeks something far more tantalizing. He wants nothing less than to totally alter his state of consciousness in order to obliterate any sense of differentiated, or individual, self. The core experience to which he aspires may be called "detached alertness" or "passive volition," but the desired result is the same—achieving a state of unconcern toward all surroundings. Only then can the meditator hope to merge his mind with that of the "Universal Mind."

Several universally applicable techniques are used to enhance meditation. Some meditators suggest concentrating on the mystical "Third Eye" at the point midway between the eyebrows that supposedly coincides with the pineal gland. Some advocate riveting one's mind on a point in the abdomen about two inches below the navel, where the center of life is said to reside.

Another method involves using the yantra, the visual equivalent of a mantra, a geometric design on which the meditator can focus his attention. Other frequently used objects are an inscription, a flower, a statue, or a candle flame. Some use the mandala, typically a square or circle drawing designed in many colors, symbolizing unity of the macrocosm of the universe with the microcosm that is man. T'ai Chi, meditation in motion, is profusely practiced by the Chinese, who perfected the art. The purpose is to place the entire body and mind in harmony with the macrocosmic forces of the universe.

What are meditators getting for all those hours with eyes closed, concentrating on each breath and chanting mantras? Ardent advocates say it decreases tension, anxiety, and aggressiveness without use of drugs. Edgar Cayce, the occult mystic, described meditation as "an emptying of all that hinders the creative forces, rising along the natural channels of the physical man to be disseminated through those centers and sources that create the activities of the physical, the mental, the spiritual man."[18]

Whatever the side benefits, meditation is believed to be a pathway to "god-realization." Descriptions abound of what it's like to achieve that state. Meditators depict the ultimate consciousness acquired by their quest as a condition of unutterable bliss. Critics argue that such supreme detachment from reality might have such qualities, but part of the benefit comes from escaping all accountability for one's conduct and any responsibility to others. In fact, say the most vociferous detractors, that is exactly the kind of indifference one often finds in the contemplative countries of the Far East.

Some psychotics are relaxed and at ease with life. They have detached themselves from reality and are insulated from all that is unpleasant or perplexing. Yet they are considered mentally insane. Likewise, certain meditation disciplines may detach one from truth and create a fictional sense of serenity. The question is not how peaceful one feels, but whether that composure leads to constructive action. No one was more peaceful than Christ. But instead of retiring to a cave for contemplation, He actively sought instances of human need and "went about doing good."[19]

Certain techniques of inducing the meditative state may cause effects that should be avoided. For example, some yoga positions seem to attune the body's psychoneurological systems to automatically facilitate altered states of consciousness. Thus, merely practicing the postures could trigger undesirable results. Of course, if the motive is to affect the mind mystically, the outcome could be even worse. Some techniques, such as candle-staring or chanting, could disassociate the mind from reality to the extent that mental illness may result. That is why Christ warned against "vain repetitions"[20] not only because of its uselessness in pleasing God, but also because it shuts down the mind and increases vulnerability of the spirit. Christian meditation is the natural process of constantly acknowledging God's Word by focusing on the Lord's nature and His intervention in our lives. Occult meditation seeks to dull the senses and curtail the mental processes, to worship the self as an inner manifestation of the divine.

Meditation is not antithetical to biblical Christianity. In fact, the words *meditate* and *meditation* appear numerous times in the Old and New Testaments. But the Scriptures do lay down strict guidelines for meditation. The root word of *meditation* implies a process of slowly digesting God's truths, using concentrated thought patterns focused on the laws, words, and precepts of God.

In contrast to the mystical methods of meditation designed to still the senses and empty the mind, biblical meditation heightens the intellect. Christianity teaches that the mind is an avenue by which God reveals His laws and His love. The Christian meditator isn't trying to empty his mind but seeks to fill it with the knowledge of God without resorting to rigidly aesthetic disciplines. According to the Bible, meditation isn't an encounter with an overactive ego, but a natural flow of attention to the things of the Lord throughout the day.

The mystical meditator seeks a direct experience of "god-realization," achievable by circumventing the intellect's conceptualization processes. In that state, the answers to all life's questions will supposedly be intuitively revealed. This fourth state of consciousness is thought to be a higher condition of mind, offering uninterrupted communication with the divinity of one's higher self.

But the meditator may get more than he bargained for. Ironically, the Stanford Research Institute International, which often espouses metaphysical ideology, published a study warning against the dangers of intense meditation disciplines such as transcendental meditation. Researchers found that a form of psychological desensitization may occur, endangering those who are unable to control the release of large amounts of anxiety. Another study by the Illinois State Psychiatric Institute of Chicago concluded that certain forms of meditation are far less therapeutic than simply sitting daily and thinking about the expectation of relief.[21]

Christian meditation differs from occult meditation in its methods, motives, and result. "Let the words of my mouth and the meditation of my heart be acceptable in Your sight, O LORD,"[22] the psalmist said. Christians don't need to hyperventilate or encourage an insensible irresponsibility. Those who worship Christ eschew seeking an inner manifestation of self as God. They meditate instead on the transcendent God, who lifts us above our dilemmas to commune with Him. The kneeling position is not only more comfortable than the lotus position, but also more spiritually satisfying. Contemplating a risen Savior is considerably more uplifting than gazing at one's innie or outie!

Chapter 20

The Occult Aspects of Alternative Medicine

The patient lies on his back, naked from the waist up. First he engages in a series of breathing exercises and guided meditation. Then the healer begins the ancient art of laying stones. More than a hundred crystals are placed at various positions and angles on the patient's body. The healer says crystal power can soothe the mind, calm the spirit, and cure disease.

Just as modern science uses quartz crystals to drive watches and tune in radio stations, some psychic healers believe crystals are a powerful light force that can penetrate subconscious blockages in the body. They also work with other stones in the quartz family, including agate, flint, fossilized wood, onyx, opals, amethyst, and amber.

Desperate from pain and suffering, disillusioned with modern medicine, thousands turn to extraordinary healing techniques. American health care is increasingly seen as desensitized and impersonal. Doctors are viewed as part of a disease-oriented, technologically callous, and authoritarian health care system. Consequently, nontraditional forms of healing are making amazing inroads. A major New York medical center refers AIDS patients to spiritual healers. Many who are skeptical about the high cost of modern medicine turn to Dr. Feel Good, throw away their medicine, and wait for the healing hand of some unseen force.

Evidence of supernatural healing processes can be found in pictorial scenes on the walls of caves dating back fifteen thousand years. Egypt, Babylonia, Tibet, India, and China are among the cultures that adopted apparently effective means of nonrational healing. The modern trend toward holism had its genesis at the turn of this century. The New Thought Movement introduced metaphysical healing, based on the idea that bodily ills are the result of mistaken belief, a concept borrowed from mind science churches such as Christian Science.

Critics of alternative medicine say that, extravagant claims aside, no practitioner has yet opened blind eyes or cured an AIDS victim. Psychiatrists argue it's not unusual for a fleeting sense of well-being to follow an exotic healing procedure. They claim autosuggestion plays a big role in a temporary sense of euphoria. What worries doctors is that after the novelty wears off, the organic problem will once again be evident, and the person may be nearer death than before.

The diversity of alternative healing practices is astounding. Through visualization, healers teach terminally ill cancer patients to unleash their immune system by imagining the body's white blood cells as voracious sharks attacking cancer cells, envisioned as small, frightened fish. Some have adopted the Chinese practice of pulse diagnosis, by which the internal temperature of the body and the condition of five major organs are supposedly detected. Reiki, a laying-on-of-hands therapy, is based on the belief that healing can be psychically projected to distant locations.

The holistic health movement is based on the belief that all beings consist of cognitive, physiological, emotional, and spiritual qualities. Each of these must be integrated properly to bring health to the whole person. The universe is viewed as a supportive organism with a harmonious balance that can be duplicated in the body. By soothing body, soul, and spirit, holistic healers hope to restore the balance between the macrocosm of the universe and the microcosm of each individual's body.

This view contrasts sharply with traditional medicine. Historically, medical science viewed the human body as a biological machine, powered by energy released in the digestion of food. Health was considered the absence of pain and dysfunction. Sickness was thought to be the appearance of these symptoms. It was believed that illness usually originated from a single pathogen, such as bacteria or a virus, that invaded the body from without. The purpose of medicine was to identify and isolate the pathogen and destroy it with drugs or remove it by surgery.

Unfortunately, technological advances have altered the bedside manner of physicians so they are often detached, peering at patients through reports instead of a stethoscope. But the fact that alternative techniques seem more personalized does not necessarily mean they are more effective. The ultimate issue regarding health care should not be the patient's emotional comfort but the quality of the treatment he receives. From a natural standpoint, there is danger that a patient being treated with occult-style alternative medicine will accept the apparent absence of symptoms and presume a cure has been effected. Spiritually speaking, if the therapy is of the occult and administered by a healer under mystical influence, the encounter could result in psychic oppression.

Many Christians are attracted to alternative medical therapies, but they should consider that recognizing people have a soul and spirit does not mean those elements are properly acknowledged or treated with sanctity. Occult healers revere the spirit because they believe it is a spark of the divine, not because they honor biblical warnings against clairvoyant practices. Holism in medical treatment is good if conducted by a Christian therapist who treats the spirit as the eternal aspect God breathed into man.

When considering a healing therapy, it is crucial to consider its historical source. Job 14:4 warns us, "Who can bring a clean thing out of an unclean? No one!" James 3:11 adds, "Does a spring send forth fresh water and bitter from the same opening?" In some cases, a practice may be divorced from its pagan historical roots and redefined within a newly applicable frame of reference. If the practitioner makes no such distinction, there may be serious harm in store for those who are spiritually vulnerable. Thus, the advisability of receiving care from such a person is questionable.

The psychosomatic link between the body and mind is unquestionable. Thus, there is nothing inherently wrong with considering a "holistic" approach to healing, if by doing so one recognizes the trinitarian nature of man, knowing that healing must touch every aspect of one's life. Proverbs 17:22 says, "A merry heart does good, like medicine." But Christ did more than preach positive mental imagery. He didn't use autosuggestions to eradicate symptoms. Christ wasn't a placebo for the diseased and dying. Matthew 4:23 tells us He healed *all* forms of illness.

While there is nothing intrinsically evil about alternative medicine, its application should be viewed warily by Christians. For example, one occult healer described holism as "a point of view about the universe . . . the joy of creativity, the knowing of consciousness, the fulfillment of self-actualization." Obviously, the anatomical investigation of organic causes of illness has nothing to do with this philosophically stylized approach to health.

Supernaturalism has long been an arm of false religion. Jannes and Jambres withstood Moses with their miracles. The apostle Paul, in 2 Timothy 3:8, used these occult magicians as an example of those who "resist the truth." Thus, no matter how beneficial the deeds of occult healers seem, they ultimately oppose God's truth about the origin of illness and the identity of man's true Healer. They may call their healing arts holism, but the Bible calls it sorcery (see Deut. 18:10–11).

Satan is prepared to promise physical health in exchange for disobedience to God. In Eden he offered the ultimate incentive to

Eve: "You will not surely die."[1] But Satan's pledge of health and healing is bogus. He temporarily relieves physical affliction by transferring the malady to the emotional, psychic realm. Those who have been to psychic healers often experience assuagement of physical pain, but usually it is followed by emotional torment or an accentuated interest in the occult, drawing them deeper into the devil's snare. Thus, occult healing, which denies Christ as Creator, Redeemer, and Healer, merely exchanges an adversity on the organic level for torment on the spiritual level.

CRYSTALS

Some keep crystals in their refrigerator to prevent food from spoiling. Others sleep near crystals to facilitate pleasant dreams. Crystals are believed to be conduits of cosmic energy with the ability to cure Parkinson's disease, arthritis, chronic back pain, and even blindness. Psychics offer their services to program crystals so they will emote whatever qualities the users desire. As one psychic healer explained, "Your body is crystallized thought. Patterns are stored in the bones, and vibrations from crystals can replace a bad pattern."[2] An authority on crystals wrote, "Quartz originates as a thought form in the universal mind on higher levels of light, and it's projected down to the earthly substance that quartz is. Crystals are an access tool to other planes of awareness."[3]

Though several kinds of rocks are used to channel "biocosmic" power, most crystal champions prefer clear quartz. Because they are composed of silicon dioxide, a common component of the human body, quartz crystals and human beings are equated as brothers in earth's family. The clarity of crystals is thought to be a manifestation of their perfection. Their six sides represent the six chakras of the body's psychic energy as proposed by Hinduism. Crystals represent nothing less than a symbol of alignment with cosmic harmony.

Potential uses of crystals are bound only by the imagination.

Some bathe and sleep with crystals. Others lie silently on their backs with crystals strategically placed on their forehead, limbs, solar plexus, and chest. True believers in crystals have managed to stop smoking with their assistance. There are even mixing guides to crystalline nectars. Finely ground quartz is stirred into a glass in appropriate proportion with a liquid to bottom up and bliss out.

Crystals worn as pendants supposedly increase one's "auric field" (a term referring to the body's emanation of psychic energy). But they must be removed nightly or these "perfect" stones will pick up one's energy imbalances. During the night, crystals should be placed on top of a dish of dry sea salt, since salt provides an environment for the crystal to clear its energies. During the day, one supposedly can plant proper energies in his crystal by mental visualization. Affirmations are also used. One crystal patron suggests, "My life is one of total oneness with the God-force and Christed energies."[4]

The vibratory capacity of crystals is a fact of physics, but the concept of the body's compatible vibratory response is mere inference. Science has yet to prove that measurable electromagnetic or biocosmic forces resonate in the body. Thus, any suggestion of a sympathetic reaction between a quartz rock and human flesh is conjectural. None of the claims made by advocates of crystals have been accepted by the scientific community. Validation for such assertions rests solely on the questionable proof of personal testimony. It must be assumed, therefore, that the power of crystals is in the mind of the beholder. Anticipatory autosuggestion has a way of fulfilling self-made prophecies. If a person thinks a crystal will do a certain thing, in all likelihood such expectations will be satisfied, even if it means altering circumstances to produce "proof."

ELECTROMAGNETIC HEALING

Electromagnetic healing operates on the basis of the "unified field theory," which postulates that a subtle form of electrical stimulation occurs by the laying on of hands. In Sweden a well-known radiologist treats lung and breast cancer with electricity. Robert Becker, M.D., author of the book *The Body Electric*, envisions a day when electromagnetic healing will allow amputees to grow new arms and legs. English electromagnetic healer–psychic Kay Kiernan claims to have treated Queen Elizabeth II for a strained shoulder.[5]

Occult healer Olga Worrall claims to be a Christian and a carrier of healing energy. She says, "A healer is so constructed biologically that he or she transforms para-electricity into an energy that can be used by all living systems."[6] A psychiatrist hypnotized people to test the immune system's responsiveness to suggestion. He believes cancer cells can be confused by mental imagery and rendered incapable of defeating an attack by the immune system.

Until now, Western medicine has been based on technological therapies in conjunction with the latest pharmaceutical wonder drugs. Today, many are turning from mainstream medicine to those who offer alternative cures based on exotic beliefs rooted in Eastern mysticism. To those who question whether the source of a healing art should be considered before accepting any therapy, a famous psychic surgeon replies, "If the devil can relieve pain and remove an ulcer, then I prefer the devil."

Before seeking a non-Christian source of supernatural healing, an important question should be: "Where did the sickness originate?" While not every sick person has fallen under the attack of the devil, some sicknesses result from direct satanic assault. The Bible also points out that since in a broad sense all sickness is a result of sin, all disease is thus indirectly the work of the devil.

Acts 10:38 tells us, Jesus healed all who were "oppressed by the devil." Their relief came not by redistributing some form of bioenergy, but by removing Satan's domination over their bodies. Scripture says Christ healed because "God was with Him."[7] Before letting anyone lay hands on them, patients seeking solace should find out what god is with the healer and the source from which the psychic solicits healing.

ACUPUNCTURE

Shortly after the normalization of relations between the United States and China in the early 1970s, the practice of acupuncture began sinking its roots into American soil. Physicians traveled to China to study this ancient therapy, dating as far back as 2600 B.C. Some acupuncturists began hanging out shingles in the United States. One acupuncturist developed computer software that displays video charts of the human body, indicating acupuncture points for 627 medical problems that range from abscesses to yawning. The medical community took a cautious, begrudging look at the effectiveness of inserting needles at specified points to relieve stress, cure inner ailments, and induce analgesia.

Knowledge of acupuncture goes back nearly three thousand years in Chinese literature. Primitive societies practiced it hundreds of years earlier. Its most notable ancient description is in *The Yellow Emperor's Classic of Internal Medicine,* dated in the fifth century B.C. One legend claims that acupuncture arose when villagers noticed that a warrior's long-standing maladies were mysteriously cured by spear wounds suffered during a battle.

The term *acupuncture* comes from the Latin *acus,* meaning "needle," and *puncture,* which means "to prick." Originally, stone, bone, and bamboo needles were used. Ceramic, gold, and silver needles were introduced later. Their use is based on the philosophy of Chinese medicine, which is rooted in the religious tenets of Taoism. The primal energy of the cosmos, dubbed *chi* by Taoists, is thought to permeate all phenomena and instill life, vitality, and health in every living thing. Chi exists in the essence of yang, an aggressive male principle, and yin, a yielding female principle. Both flow through the body in defined pathways known as meridians.

Ideally, yin and yang are balanced in the body, but when a state of disequilibrium is introduced, the flow of energy is disrupted and disease occurs. Traditional Chinese physicians were not concerned with the symptoms of an illness, but turned their attention to constantly tuning up the energy balance. They believed that needles inserted at the proper points could disrupt the flow of yin and yang and thus restore a harmonizing balance to revitalize health.

Critics suggest otherwise. They insist that neither diagnostic nor therapeutic data prove that a special relationship exists between hypothetical acupuncture points and the function of internal organs. If nerve pathways are an explanation, why are the insertion points on acupuncture charts in epidermal areas completely unrelated to the afflicted organ? Fueling suspicion is the fact that the present system of acupoints numbers 365, based astrologically on the number of days in a year. Skeptics also ask how two separate dysfunctions can apply to the same point, such as the *zusanli* point, which is the accepted treatment point for both diarrhea and constipation.

Dr. Charles A. Fager, chairman emeritus of the Department of Neurosurgery at the Lahey Clinic in Burlington, Massachusetts, is an outspoken opponent. Dr. Fager argues,

> There is not the slightest shred of evidence to show that acupuncture produces any real physiological changes. The only people helped by it are those with pain and functional disorders. These people are very suggestive, and their cures are totally psychogenic in nature. There is no physiological reason why, if you stick a needle in somebody's ear, a pain in the small of the back will go away. The anesthesia is simply hypnosis. Acupuncture is basically a form of deception and fraud and should be against the law.[8]

Koreans have experimented unsuccessfully with injecting liquid radioisotopes into acupuncture points to trace the meridians. Kirlian photography has been used without convincing proof. Others have suggested that the needles stimulate secretion of cortisone, an internal painkiller. Additional research has focused on endorphins, internally produced neurotransmitters that can ease pain and create a feeling of euphoria.

One theory claims that human connective tissue forms a continuous network of molecules, which are semiconductors passing along energetic electrons. Collagen, which makes up the fascia (a layer of tissue below the skin), is a fibrous protein with enough crystalline structure to rapidly conduct electricity. Thus, meridians may be pathways of low electrical resistance in surface tissue, conducting a form of electrical energy the Chinese have called chi.

Meanwhile, several branches of acupuncture have developed. Acupressure supposes that intense pressure applied to a point using a thumb or elbow causes stimulation similar to an inserted needle. Ear acupuncture is based on the idea that all meridian channels meet in the ear. By triggering these points, such as putting a staple in the ear, the reflexes are triggered and the body's healthful balance of chi is restored. Critics, however, are persistent in claiming that the effectiveness of acupuncture requires an element of expectation on behalf of the patient, indicating that self-hypnosis may be the real effect of needle insertion.

Christians must ask whether the use of acupuncture can be divorced from its pagan and occult background. That depends on the practitioner's motives. Any act rooted in the occult and executed with that purpose opens one to spiritual danger. Certainly, one should not seek an acupuncture treatment from a Chinese Taoist, who could unwittingly invoke evil supernatural forces while attempting to bring physical relief. It is best to avoid such therapies as acupuncture until the medical community has had ample opportunity to perform further research. In the absence of any collectively acceptable anatomical explanation, the risk of engaging in an occult act suggests caution. Anyone desiring to pursue acupuncture therapy should consult a licensed practitioner, preferably one who professes faith in Christ and applies the technique on a purely medical basis.

The so-called nerve-gate theory is one possible explanation of acupuncture's effectiveness. This hypothesis suggests that needle stimulation affects synapses, the nerve junctions where pain impulses are transferred. Deriving a comprehensive hypothesis that accounts for both the remedial and analgesic benefits of acupuncture is difficult. Scientists are puzzled that a simple needle insertion seems to halt pain and also heal an organic disorder. One possible explanation with serious implications is that the force of chi is a form of alien supernatural energy that is invoked by a Taoist acupuncturist. The practitioner may be a mere technician, inserting needles according to a meridian chart with no commitment to a Taoist view of yin and yang. In that case, the risk is minimal, and the "remedy" may be psychosomatic. Danger is involved if the acupuncturist pays homage to the spiritualist tradition of his craft.

THERAPEUTIC TOUCH

One branch of alternative medicine teaches that the body is a manifestation of energy, and illness is the condition of poorly distributed quantities of this energy. Therapeutic touch suggests that a healer passing hands over the body surface in a circular, flowing motion can redistribute this vital energy. Such techniques have already been introduced into the curricula of nursing schools and medical colleges.

Belief in a nonphysical energy responsible for health and healing is common among occult healers. Rolling Thunder, a well-known American Indian medicine man, declares, "The Great Spirit is the life that is in all things—all creatures, plants, and even rocks and minerals." This power is said to be similar to the circulatory system. When it is unbalanced, illness results. The healer's job is to realign this energy with the equilibrium of the cosmos.

The practice of laying on of hands seems to serve two purposes. Some believe it draws energy toward the hands as they move across the body, so that balance is restored. Other holistic advocates suggest that the healer injects a kind of psychic energy into the patient. Most healers believe they are embued with a kind of power. Psychics assume that the same power responsible for touch therapy is also the source of psychic phenomena.

Dr. Delores Kreiger, founder of the Therapeutic Touch Movement, believes anyone can be taught to sensitize himself to the "unnamed and unmeasured energy." She insists that no religious faith is required by either the patient or the practitioner. Critics note, however, that Kreiger developed her theory after delving into Eastern philosophy and yoga.[9] While she claims no specific doctrine, she does admit application of therapeutic touch is similar to the ancient Hindu principle of prana, the so-called vital energy force of life.

What kind of energy do healers manipulate when they claim to redistribute an electromagnetic force in the body? In most cases, the energy is a figment of their minds. Psychic healers are elixir salesmen, dispensing hope in the form of exotic maneuvers of the hands. But it cannot be discounted that transcendental powers can be conjured, since occult healing aligns philosophically with the forces of Satan's kingdom.

Even if religious overtones are absent, that doesn't mean an act is irreligious. Contact with the spirit world doesn't depend on explicit overtures to demons. That's why biblical passages such as Deuteronomy 18 sternly denounce divinatory practices. Participation in such occult deeds may open one's life to deception. Consequently, if a healer is laying on hands in a similar fashion to that commanded in James 5, but without the restriction of a defined petition to Christ as Lord, the danger of acquiring demonic assistance is very real.

MUSIC THERAPY

Background music has long been used to reduce stress and provide a placid environment. Now, some healers say the right music can cure depression, diagnose mental illness, and reduce the effects of surgery. Their ideas are based on the theories of Pythagoras, the ancient Greek philosopher and mathematician. He taught his students to cleanse themselves of fear, worry, and anger by daily singing. Another example cited by music therapists is when King Saul's despondency was soothed by David's harp.

The curative power of David's music had nothing to do with the vibrations of notes on the shepherd's harp resonating with Saul's mind and emotions. Scripture plainly tells us that the king's desolation resulted from the influence of an evil entity. It was the God David worshiped and the Holy Spirit his music invoked who calmed King Saul's restless soul. Christianity recognizes the power of music to lift the human spirit in praise to God. But nowhere in the Bible is music presented as a sacred science to orchestrate health. This is an occult idea. Today's advocates of music therapy are sonic shamans who use musical magic.

Occult music therapists consider sonic vibration the creative force of the universe. Thus, appropriate application of specific tones, frequencies, and harmonic intervals is thought to evoke healing forces. The applications are many: reducing pain; inducing altered states of consciousness that release internal healing forces; accelerating the brain's directives to facilitate healing. Organs, bones, and various body parts are said to have certain vibrations responsive to relevant healing sounds.

Today's sound healers see themselves fulfilling the prediction of the psychic mystic Edgar Cayce, who declared that sound would be the medicine of the future. Some artists have written and recorded therapeutic music based on crystals, runes, tantric harmonics, and so-called spirit sounds. Dr. John Diamond, a holistic doctor and spiritualist healer, teaches that different pieces of music have the ability to raise one's "life-energy" and enhance the function of the thymus gland. Diamond combines his theory with acupuncture to stimulate certain meridians with particular tunes.

One psychic uses music therapy to treat headaches, stomach upset, and depression. The sound is directly applied to the body on the theory that each part of the physique vibrates at an audible frequency. Consequently, transmitting the correct frequency to a diseased organ supposedly restores its proper vibration. Because music is nonverbal and passes through the auditory cortex directly to the midbrain network governing our emotions, it is considered a short circuit that unleashes the healing powers of the mind. It is also considered helpful in regulating blood pressure and heart rate. Music therapy is believed to stimulate endorphins, natural opiates, and to alter the brain's alpha waves to produce deep relaxation.

PSYCHIC SURGERY

Andy Kaufman, the mechanic on the 1980s TV series *Taxi*, might be alive today had he not watched a prime time TV special on the paranormal. It was hosted by Burt Lancaster and featured a sequence on psychic surgery in the Philippines. Kaufman flew to Manila, where psychic surgeons operated on him. Two months later, he died at the age of thirty-five.

Psychic surgery presumes to be a bloodless method of operating without a scalpel. The patient lies on a table, and the surgeon makes an imaginary incision in the abdomen with his bare hands. Suddenly, some internal tissue appears, it's discarded, and the wound closes without scarring. The patient walks away without sedation or anesthesia.

One patient described his ordeal this way:

We attended a service with a hymn sing and a sermon, stressing the power of belief. We were taught a mantra to chant during the procedure. When they operate, they part the skin, stretching a pore. Their fingers are like laser beams. They feel the damaging clots, lumps, and scar tissue, and within 30 seconds they scoop them out, right in front of you. I got off the table, into my wheelchair, and had lunch. I felt fine.[10]

The Philippines is not the only place you can find psychic surgeons. A book entitled *Arigo: Surgeon of the Rusty Knife* heralds the feats of a Brazilian peasant who operated with an unclean pocketknife without pain, bleeding, or stitches. Those who observed him say he could stop the flow of blood with a verbal command. Arigo is also said to have had the ability to read blood pressure without instruments, though he never went beyond the third grade. Over three hundred patients visited him daily. The Brazilian claimed his powers came from the spirit of a German doctor who died in 1918 and returned to possess his body. Unfortunately, before scientific investigators could test him to their satisfaction, Arigo died in 1981.

Arigo was not alone. Brazil boasts thousands of psychic surgeons, some of whom are medical doctors. They believe they can contact the spirits of deceased physicians who operate through them, providing special skills. Most of their surgery is done in a trance state without using anesthetics or antiseptics. Though the practice is officially illegal, it still thrives. Brazilian healers are usually members of Cardecism, a spiritualistic sect. Unlike their Philippino counterparts, they seldom perform deep body operations, preferring instead to work on early breast cancer, skin tumors, and fleshy membranes over the eyes.[11]

Adept magicians, such as Henry Gordon, have easily debunked some psychic surgery. Gordon demonstrated for television cameras how he removed a huge piece of diseased tissue from the upper arm of a man, while a camera watched from two feet away. Gordon admitted later the "tissue" was a piece of chicken liver. The blood came from a tiny plastic vial broken at an appropriate time. Gordon's fingertips had pressed into the soft flesh so they disappeared from view, appearing to penetrate the skin without actually doing so.

The phenomenon of psychic surgery has never been demonstrated satisfactorily to critics. Such surgery is usually performed in dimly lit conditions where a high sense of expectation inhibits critical analysis of the event. Various kinds of witch doctors and shamans have claimed such abilities, and there is no reason to assume all of them represent a collective conspiracy of lies. Perhaps some occult practitioners possess the powers of materialization and dematerialization and can insert their hands into a person's body to remove something without signs of scarring or bleeding. Most psychic surgeons, however, probably rely on sleight of hand to accomplish their deeds.

PYRAMID POWER

Those not yet confident in crystals may opt for the power of pyramids. Not only can these triangular shapes be placed on one's body, but under a hollow version you can sleep more soundly, eat more nutritiously, and even achieve superior orgasms, say advocates. The philosophy of pyramidology is based on the idea that the ancient Egyptian pyramid of Cheops was built according to precise geometric measurements and alignments to channel an unexplained biocosmic force or electromagnetic field. Its power is said to work best when the pyramid is aligned along a north-south plain, either true north or magnetic north.

In 1970 Sheila Ostrander and Lynn Schroeder wrote a bestselling book titled *Psychic Discoveries Behind the Iron Curtain.* Their speculation about the power of pyramids began fueling a fad that has long interested occultists. Since the Greek historian Herodotus visited Egypt in the fifth century B.C., mysteries concerning the ancient land of the Nile have fed speculation that the early builders of the pyramids were privy to secret forces that could be harnessed by mankind.

In the philosophy of pyramidology, the triangular sides represent perfection, the square bottom embodies the four elements in

Egyptian mythology (earth, fire, air, water), and the apex signifies deity. Those who believe in the potency of pyramids say their form constitutes an amulet that provides precognitive and postcognitive knowledge. It may also be a point of contact with the world of higher consciousness.

Occult legend has it that Egyptian priests were initiated into their religion by spending a night inside a pyramid. In the morning, they exited, supposedly possessing the powers of a god. One promoter of pyramids suggests writing down what you desire on a piece of paper. Then place it under a pyramid for three to nine days. If your thoughts are properly focused during this time, the power of the pyramid will somehow psychically reply. Others claim to tell the past and future by placing a mirror under a pyramid.

Advocates of pyramid power claim proper use of these geometric forms can also sweeten water, mummify bodies, maintain the fragrance of flowers, sharpen razor blades, prevent foods from molding, and actually alter molecular structure. How? Pyramids are believed to be antennae that pick up frequencies of universal energy. The power is said to be most effective when the substance to be affected is placed a third of the distance below the apex.

The healing power of pyramids is supposedly based on the prismatic effect of certain rocks and the tiny electrical charge they emit when rubbed. Thus, rubbing a rock pyramid produces an electrical field that combines with the body's electrical forces to change cellular structure. The pyramid may be an open or closed structure composed of stone, wood, plastic, or metal.

Because of their size and age, the pyramids engender awe. After all, they are the oldest surviving man-made structures on earth. In addition, the religion of the ancient Egyptians was integrally tied to the pyramids, lending an aura of mystery. Thus, those involved in mystery school cults assume pyramids have secret powers known to the Egyptians of old and experienced by us today, though we cannot explain their power.

There is no evidence in Scripture or physics to suggest that the shape of an object inherently imbues it with supranormal powers. Shapes have an effect only if the one attaching such significance really believes power resides in forms. In that case, the convictions of the adherent produce effects, not the shape of the objects.

Occult alternative healing theories are based on several suppositions. First is the idea that the body will always naturally heal itself. No matter what the disease, restoring the body's energies to a proper equilibrium allows natural healing to occur. Second, negative physical realities are the result of projected thoughts. The particular therapy is not as important as the belief in its efficacy. In the words of one healer, "We have to work with both body and mind, so that the nonmaterial concept of health is manifested in our material being."[12]

Other approaches to alternative healing can be summarized in several categories:

Self-Healing: The patient's perception is considered more important than the viral nature of the disease. Laughter, courage, tenacity, and control are emotional factors governing the body's ability to self-heal. Maladaptive tension puts the body into a state of imbalance. Proper relaxation rebalances the body without intervention of outside chemicals.

Prevention: Proper diet is a major consideration, including some exotic advice. Many borrow from the Edgar Cayce readings and ingest ragweed for improving elimination and liver function. Dandelion leaves and roots are considered nutritive herbs. Three times as many vegetables that grow above the ground should be consumed compared to those that grow below the ground. They also say that mixing certain food types is taboo. For instance, meat and starch should never be eaten at the same meal.

Imagery: Just as placebos trigger positive mental attitudes toward certain therapies, so it is believed that an adjusted perspective can affect biochemistry. Simply said, the power of suggestion was the secret of shamans and the best way to facilitate the body's positive powers of health. Disease is seen as a necessary karmic force to teach those unprepared to leave the earthly plane of existence. Those who are ready to realize their personal responsibility for choices, including the option to accept the divine within, may no longer have need of sickness and can dwell in a continual state of wellness.

Nutrition: "You are what you eat." That adage literally guides the occult approach to cooking. Avoiding chemically treated foods and retaining nutrients in preparation are cardinal considerations. Packaging procedures, canning processes, and freezing techniques are all carefully monitored. The yin-yang quality of each food is also analyzed to examine its spiritual constituents.

Bodywork: This term refers to the necessity of an appropriate balance between the body and mind for continuing health. Its extreme form promises agelessness and youthful vigor. The body is seen as a reflection of life's experiences and spiritual progress. Techniques such as massage, yoga, aikido, T'ai Chi, and psychostructural balancing of the body are said to permit one's internal physiology to retain health.

MACROBIOTICS

Macrobiotics is an Oriental approach to eating organically. It comes from two Greek words: *macro,* meaning "large," and *bios,* referring to the science of life. Thus, macrobiotics proposes to blend eating with the macrocosmic order of the universe by carefully controlling food selection, preparation, and consumption.

Philosophically, macrobiotics is based on the idea that all energy in the universe alternates harmoniously between opposites—night and day, male and female, light and dark, yin and yang. This Taoistic approach supposedly applies to foods, harmonizing spirituality through diet. Preventing illness and arresting degenerative diseases are just two of the presumed benefits. There have been claims of heart disease and cancer cures.

Macrobiotics is more than a way to eat. It is a way of life. Its deference to ecological balance presumably achieves a oneness with the environment. This unity is precursory to a dynamic balance with other areas of life, including psychology, education, politics, and economics. The ultimate goal is world federalism and planetary unity. In the words of one macrobiotic proponent, "Planet Earth is surrounded by and immersed in a vibrational body of energy, which is conscious. The foci are 'power points' . . . sacred places, such as the pyramids, Stonehenge, etc." Eating macrobiotically places one in harmony with this "etheric web of consciousness."[13]

Macrobiotics suggests that 50 to 60 percent of the diet should consist of whole grains. Another 5 to 10 percent should include beans, bean products, and sea vegetables. Foods should be grown without chemicals and used in their natural state. This diet must be accompanied by daily exercise and spiritual practices of meditation and prayer, along with an appreciation of nature.

Most people become involved with a macrobiotic diet because of its philosophical approach to life, not for nutritional reasons. They tend to accept the larger approach to macrobiotics, which adopts a pantheistic worldview. This outlook is intrinsically federalistic because it denigrates individualism in favor of planetary oneness. Thus, the way one eats tends to influence the way one thinks.

One can eat macrobiotically without encountering any spiritual danger but still be at great risk. Macrobiotics is steeped in Oriental metaphysical ideas. Directives concerning macrobiotic cooking abound with testimonies about abatement of fears and phobias and the adoption of a more positive outlook on life. Such transformation ignores God's grace, received by repentance of sinful behavior. Instead, macrobiotics promotes almost miraculous well-being by achieving evolutionary spiritual consciousness. Further, the dualistic approach toward life and nature contradicts biblical principles of mankind's relationship to God and His environment. Those who eat macrobiotically often adopt a mystical worldview.

Documented testimony claims that properly balancing the yin and yang (acidity and alkalinity) of foods has brought cancer into remission and rejuvenated health. In a celebrated case, Dr. Anthony Sattilaro, president of Methodist Hospital in Philadelphia, claimed to be cured of prostate cancer that had metastasized to the brain. Such results are probably due to improved eating habits rather than harmony with biocosmic forces. The diet of most Americans is so abysmal that any use of organic vegetables and more sensible consumption of food are likely to produce health benefits.

There is a great danger that those who eat macrobiotically will also accept its attendant philosophy. The book *Macrobiotics: An Invitation to Health and Happiness* declares, "It is based on the realization that only you are the master of yourself—not bacteria, doctors, scientists, ministers, philosophers, or dieticians."[14] Those who wish to obtain the health benefits of macrobiotics must avoid accompanying non-Christian philosophical indoctrination.

HOMEOPATHY

George Guess was an M.D. until the North Carolina board of medical examiners revoked his license to practice medicine. A graduate of the Medical College of Virginia, Guess became the first American physician whose license was rescinded because of practicing homeopathy.[15] The result was a head-on legal collision between the medical establishment and this centuries-old therapy.

The principle of homeopathy is the paradoxical law of similars. Each physical condition is treated with a substance that, given in large quantities, could cause the condition. Most homeotherapeutics avoid antibiotics and allopathic drugs in favor of more than a thousand remedies of minute doses of natural substances from the plant, animal, and mineral kingdoms.

The English royal family consults homeopaths. In the 1930s King George was so enamored with homeopathy that he named one of his racing horses Hypericum, the name of a popular home-opathic medicine. Today, Queen Elizabeth II is the patron to the Royal London Homeopathic Hospital. In Germany the practice has been popular since the early nineteenth century. In France over six thousand physicians actively practice homeopathy, and at least eighteen thousand pharmacies sell homeopathic medicines. The Brazilian government requires schools of pharmacy to teach homeopathy.[16]

An eighteenth-century German physician named Samuel Hahnemann discovered that if too much of a substance caused a symptom, a minute dose of that substance sometimes cured the symptom. Under his care, patients who were dying (after receiving traditional medical assistance) were cured. It was Hahnemann who coined the Latin phrase *similia similibus curentur* ("Let likes be cured with likes"). It became known as homeopathy from the Greek words *homoios,* for "similar," and *pathos,* for "disease."

Homeopaths say their practice isn't unusual. Even medical sci-ence knows that inoculations against smallpox, measles, and polio involve small doses of the offending viruses. In homeopathy, other natural substances are used to stimulate the body into healing itself. The usual dose is either 6x or 30x, the x referring to the num-ber of times the substance has been diluted in a ratio of one part remedy to ten parts distilled water. The trick, say homeopaths, is finding the right medicine for each case. Also crucial is potentiza-tion, an exacting method of dilution that involves successive thin-ning of the substance, accompanied by vigorous shaking.

Unlike allopathic medical doctors, who see illness as a negative intrusion, homeopaths believe disease is a positive fight for health, the natural effort of the body to maintain a homeostatic balance. According to homeopathy, treating symptoms is bad because it suppresses the body's natural healing responses. The homeopath prescribes a catalyst that imitates the body's defenses and stimu-lates the body's responses. Unlike conventional drugs, which have a direct effect on the physiological processes related to the patient's systems, homeopathic medicines are thought to work by stimulating the immune system. Homeopaths also deny that a single virus is responsible for illness. Instead, they look to the holistic integration of mind and body to cure all physical and emotional states.

Homeopaths believe physical health is accompanied by mental health. They conclude, therefore, that organic disorders manifest emotional disturbances. While partially true, the exacting way homeopaths categorize such illnesses leads them to claim cures for conditions that demand spiritual healing. For example, heart ailments (physical dysfunctions) reportedly produce destructive delirium (emotional illness). Such an approach is too rigid in its direct connection between the physical and the emotional. It ignores certain mental-spiritual sicknesses that only the Lord can resolve, such as depression resulting from guilt due to sin.

Suppose a patient suffers from a headache, stomachache, and depression? Homeopaths commonly use a single medicine because the person is presumed to have one disease, an underlying susceptibility. This is based on the occult idea that well-being is a state of unitary harmony with a balanced cosmos. Homeopaths may ignore the actual viral intrusion that precipitated the disease and cause the condition to worsen by failing to treat it.

Homeopathy is definitely not scientific. The process of diluting by potentization is so extreme (sometimes as much as one thousand times) that it is unlikely any significant amount of the original substance remains. There is no proof that an electromagnetic discharge is released by the shaking procedure. Originally, homeopathy proposed an idea approximating the Christian idea of illness, that sin in fallen man causes spiritual estrangement from God, which triggers susceptibility to disease at the core of his being. Metaphysical homeopathy has slightly altered this concept to suggest that the core of illness results not from a person's being sinfully diseased, but rather from his alienation from his true self (i.e., the god within).

Many Christians are attracted to homeopathy. Its idea that all illness has a single, fundamental source squares nicely with the biblical stance that all humanity's dysfunctions have a single derivation, sin. In addition, many Christians are skeptical of the medical establishment because of its humanistic approach to behavior and its overdependence on mood-altering drugs. Because of the doubtful effect of homeopathy's diluted dosages, however, Christians must wonder if the effectiveness of homeopathy is due to a psychometric (placebo) cure, a medical response in which homeopathic medicine may serve the role of an occult talisman.

REFLEXOLOGY/IRIDOLOGY

"This little piggie went to market, this little—" Just then, your mother pulled the tip of your toe and you sneezed. Know why? Reflexologists have an answer. Your sinuses correlate to the reflex points on the extremities of your toes. If you believe that, there are even more fantastic accounts to dazzle your mind and tickle your toes.

Envision the sole of the foot as a microcosm of the body. Beginning at the big toe (the head), follow down the foot as if it were a corresponding replica of the thoracic and abdominal regions. Near the ball of the foot are the lungs. Farther down come the liver, gall bladder, and colon. Then assume that each sympathetic location of a body organ has a nerve ending at the exact representational spot on the sole. If the kidneys are near the arch and the coinciding nerve endings leading to the kidney are located there, a renal dysfunction can be treated by massaging and stimulating this part of the foot. This system is known as reflexology.

Iridology follows the same microcosmic principles. In this case, the eye's iris supposedly displays the status of every internal organ and records past and present states of health and disease. Though practiced in ancient societies and popular in Europe in the nineteenth century, Americans ignored iridology until the 1904 publication of *Iridology, the Diagnosis from the Eye* by Dr. Henry

Lahn. Until then, iridology had been considered irrational, akin to palmistry and phrenology. Today, it is a staple of naturopaths and many chiropractors and has gained considerable popularity.

Like reflexologists, iridologists consider the iris representational of all organs of the body. The top of the head is exemplified by the top of the iris, and the foot by the bottom of the iris. Other areas of the body are appropriately arranged with respect to their positions in the human physical structure. Instead of employing biopsies, blood tests, X rays, and exploratory surgery, the iridologist says he only has to examine the eye to pinpoint specific organs needing treatment.

Both reflexologists and iridologists are forced to admit there is no physiological basis for assuming that corresponding nerve pathways lead from the eye or foot to relevant body parts. How, then, are diagnoses made? Dr. James Carter, a noted iridologist who has researched the practice for fourteen years, says some conclusions are paranormal. Carter declares that perfecting the technique involves the use of "intuition . . . a kind of hyperconscious or ultraconscious state."[17]

Just how is the microcosmic representation and the corresponding organ or body portion connected? No one knows. Some kind of invisible pathway is assumed usually on the philosophical basis that all is God and God is all. But from the standpoint of neurology, such a pathway has never been confirmed. In spite of all this, reflexologists and iridologists concur that certain zones of the body (hands, feet, ears, eyes) are the loci for diagnostic intervention that circumvents intrusive, traumatic methods of traditional medicine.

Anatomically, the theories of reflexology and iridology are unproved. They operate on the basis of a schematic or homunculus approach, which considers certain portions of the human anatomy as miniatures of the whole body (the sole of the foot, eye iris, ear structure). Reflexologists sense tension or heat in the bottom of the foot, indicating dysfunction in the parallel portion of the body. Iridologists measure the texture, pigmentation, and density of the iris, which supposedly links to its corresponding tissue represented by this reflex. In short, each organ or tissue has a corresponding locus within the iris or foot that undergoes simultaneous change in conjunction with the affected organ. The long history of this theory began with pagan shamanistic (witchcraft) healing methods but has no verifiable basis in modern medicine. Ophthalmologists, certified eye doctors, never use iridology as a diagnostic tool, and reflexology has never been considered acceptable treatment by the mainstream medical community, including podiatrists.

POLARITY THERAPY

The patient lay on a cushioned table with pillows under his head and knees. Slowly, the therapist pressed his thumbs into the subject's feet, ribs, head, and stomach. At times, he used slow massage. Occasionally, his hands seemed to float over the patient's body. The practitioner explained, "Energy flows through your body, and energy controls the metabolism and the structure of the body. The body has an energy field around it. In Polarity Therapy, what we do is balance that energy."[18]

Polarity therapy, "acupuncture without needles," was started by Dr. Randolph Stone (1890–1981), chiropractor and doctor of osteopathy, who declared, "The art of the true healer must be to balance man with Nature, tune him into the greater energy field, so all the elements can flow and function. That is how Nature heals."[19]

In polarity therapy, the head and feet are considered positive and negative poles. Various other organs and tissues exist in polarity relationship. For example, the positive pole of the kidneys is the shoulder, while the negative pole is the ankles. During massage, tenderness or pain indicates an area where energy is blocked. As with acupuncture, polarity therapy has its own loci, where hand manipulation supposedly releases energy flow.

Polarity therapy is based on Stone's version of dualistic symmetry. To visualize Dr. Stone's theory, imagine the body as a long coil of electromagnetic wires. There are vertical currents running from head to foot, flowing down the right side of the body, then up the back, and up the left side and down the back. Horizontal currents flow east to west; dual, serpentine currents descend from the brain, crossing at different areas of the spine to form energy centers. In Dr. Stone's words, "The location of this energy is in the core of the brain and the spinal cord, where it exists as a highly vibrating, intense etheric essence of a neuter polarity as a molecular energy, this being the key to the entire structure and function of the body."[20]

When the body's energy flow is inhibited, polarity therapy teaches that circulation decreases, resulting in pain, tension, and emotional difficulties. The patient is encouraged to "go with nature" rather than running from pain. Polarity therapy practitioners carefully explain that "the techniques are not magical, psychic, or medical, nor are they tied to any particular religious belief."[21]

Such protestations aside, polarity therapy is distinctly Eastern. Dr. Stone has informed his students,

> The emoting done by the patient while you hold one of the polarity reflexes is the karmic result of previous actions lodged here as discordant energy factors and condenses crystallization. Tell the patient that it is literally paying for sins committed when one undergoes the treatment for the release of energy blocks accumulated, like unfulfilled obligations and debts.[22]

The basic training course for polarity therapy dwells considerably on metaphysical concepts. The energy therapists presume to balance what is called prana, the energy of the soul that originates in "the Spiritual Realms." Instructors teach how to "read" the body, noting the shape of the patient, to discern what energy imbalances are present. Students are advised to program the "Soul Energy" properly to appropriately influence the mind. Eventually, posturing exercises are taught, along with elimination techniques for the bowels, urine, sweat, breath, and emotions.

NATUROPATHY

The patient had little red spots on his ankles. At the local clinic, he was given a blood pressure test and precious little of the doctor's time. All the physician could say was, "You're a little hyper, aren't you?"

The patient then consulted a naturopathic doctor (N.D.). The diagnosis? Schamberg's disease. The N.D. recommended that the patient soak a cloth with witch hazel and apply it to the afflicted area fifteen minutes daily. The herb's astringent properties were supposed to strengthen the hemorrhaging capillaries. It worked.[23]

As with homeopathy, many proponents of naturopathy don't have anything to do with the occult. Naturopathy often is used by those with a metaphysical worldview but is not inherently anti-Christian.

Across the country, naturopathy is fast becoming a choice for the ill, especially those who have read glowing reports in various New Age journals. One reason for this popularity is the attitude of conventional physicians, who are trained for crisis intervention but have little regard for preventive medicine. On the other hand, medical doctors still view naturopathy as quackery and an insult to scientific medicine.

The term *naturopathy* was coined in 1895 by John H. Scheel, but the main proponent of the practice was a German named Benedict Lust, an osteopath, M.D., and naturopath. He primarily promoted hygienics and hydrotherapy. Lust wrote, "We plead for the renouncing of poisons from the coffee, white flour, glucose, lard, and like venom of the American table."[24]

In 1919, Lust founded the American Naturopathic Association.

His concepts remained popular until 1937, when sulfa drugs were used to fight infections. American fascination with miracle drugs and crisis medicine left naturopathy out of favor. Some states declared its practices a misdemeanor. Diploma mills and bogus naturopathic schools further tarnished the art's reputation. Much has changed since naturopathy fell into disrepute.

The return to less technologically sophisticated health remedies has spurred new interest in naturopathy. Predictably, many naturopaths employ an eclectic variety of disciplines, which can include homeopathy, hypnotherapy, acupuncture, and iridology. Though some naturopaths order blood or urine tests, most naturopaths disdain interventionism, preferring nonintrusive, preventive methods of dietary and herbal remedies. To quote one advocate, "Naturopathy is a method of curing disease by releasing inner vitality and allowing the body to heal itself."[25]

Naturopaths may be helpful under certain circumstances, but there are dangers. The disease may not have been detected in time to use naturopathic methods and could require immediate crisis intervention with antibiotics or surgery. Many naturopaths are unqualified to make complex diagnoses and thus render erroneous verdicts. Emphasizing diet and nutrition is good, but such advice must employ a complex knowledge of physiology, biochemistry, and pathology. Many naturopaths do not possess such information. They could recommend therapies of questionable value with possible occult connections. Because many naturopaths are firmly aligned with mystical ideology, only careful scrutiny of the naturopath's credentials and personal beliefs can minimize potential physical and spiritual dangers.

MISCELLANEOUS THERAPIES

Rolfing: Sometimes known as "structural integration," rolfing is a method of physical manipulation invented in the 1930s by a biochemist named Ida Rolf. By using hands and elbows, the practitioner maneuvers connective tissues to achieve "synchronicity" of the entire person—physical, emotional, psychological, and psychic.

Rolf therapists are trained at the Institute of Structural Integration in Boulder, Colorado. They are instructed in ten treatments designed to move the fasciae and reintegrate the head, chest, hips, and legs in a series of ten one-hour sessions. The patient is promised a more erect and supple body. Spiritually, rolfers believe that by removing distortions the body has acquired through aging, the subject may experience spontaneous flashes of intuitive insight and psychic phenomena. Some patients complain of intensive pain, which practitioners say is necessary to unleash the inner transformation.

Dr. Rolf's work evolved from years of studying yoga. Her philosophical basis for manipulation stemmed from the idea that the energy field of the body must be aligned with the earth's gravitational and energy fields. Just as Hindu yogis seek to properly align their chakras (psychic spiritual energy centers located along the spine), rolfing aims to properly sympathize the body with external, macrocosmic energy forces.

Chromotherapy: Color therapy has been used by psychics to view auras. Theosophists use it as a method of spiritual diagnosis. Some say it originated with Egyptian sun worship. In modern times, the idea has been popularized by Rosicrucians and spiritualists. Designers, doctors, and psychotherapists acknowledge that colors may indeed affect psychological (if not physiological) health. Some colors definitely are soothing, while others seem to invigorate. But color therapists carry these principles further to suggest that certain colors emit rays that seers and clairvoyants see spiritually to determine the condition of the body and soul. In addition to treating patients by discerning their response to certain colors, therapists may request the subject to hold an object of a specified color to alleviate an organic disorder.

The so-called gift of discerning the effect of colors usually rests with psychics or spiritists. The actual diagnosis is done by divination, a biblically forbidden practice. The color therapist may recommend use of astrology, mantras, and various forms of psychic phenomena. Some even suggest dietary considerations based on the colors of certain vegetables, according to zodiac associations.

Orgonomy: Developed by psychoanalyst William Reich, orgonomy proposes that all psychological disorders stem from blocked "orgone" energy. Reich taught that this energy was the biological form of a universal energy responsible for everything from the movement of the stars to sexual orgasms. He built what was called an orgone box, a cabinet made of layered steel wool and other materials, which he said would collect orgone energy and transmit it to the patients sitting inside. The federal Food and Drug Administration and other authorities eventually jailed him for distributing the device. Various techniques have been adapted from Reich's ideas, including Alexander Lowen's concept of "bioenergetics." Reich also taught that an invasion of UFOs was polluting earth's atmosphere. Reich's fascination with orgasmic energy has been resurrected by some New Age behavioral psychologists.

Herbology: In a world of health care dominated by harsh chemical drugs with serious side effects, some are returning to the idea that medicines from the earth are the best way to health and healing. Herbologists believe their prescriptions better support the body's natural immunization system and are preferable to drugs for the body to assimilate and use. Some herbs can treat several disorders, or the same herb can be used in combination with other herbs. Common uses are as decongestants (ephedra), laxatives (cascara, sagrada, and senna leaf), and digestive aids (papaya, ginger, and chamomile).

Though natural remedies should never replace synthetic drugs used in conjunction with modern medical technology, herbs can effectively treat minor illnesses such as colds, gastrointestinal difficulties, and influenza. But caution is advised when being treated by an occult herbalist. Some herbalists borrow the idea of the ancients that herbs have personalities and spiritual patterns of energy.

Shamans believed herbs were literal combatants in a war with the evil nature of illness. If the herbologist is merely concerned with the scientific description of a plant, no spiritual harm exists. But if the practitioner subscribes to the occult ideology of herbs, the treatment could result in demonic oppression.

Ayurveda: Widely practiced in India for five thousand years, Ayurveda is believed by many New Agers to be the first and most accurate form of holistic healing. The term *Ayurveda* comes from Sanskrit, meaning "science of life." Based on classical Hinduism, Ayurveda teaches that the individual existence of each life is indivisible from the "macrocosmic manifestation." Health and disease are considered in the broader context of the relationship between individual souls and the cosmic spirit.

According to Ayurveda, each person has four instincts: religion, finances, procreation, and freedom. Balanced health must fulfill all four. Once that is achieved through diet, yoga, and adherence to Hindu philosophy, self-healing balances the body's energies and retards the onslaught of illness. Ayurveda is often combined with Hindu tantric sexual philosophies to achieve ultimate union with truth. As acupuncture seeks to balance yin and yang, Ayurveda aspires to a symmetry between the Hindu god Lord Shiva (yin) and the goddess Shakti (yang).

A Summary of Concerns

It is strange that Christians are so prone to accepting therapies science disdains and occultists embrace. Practices such as macrobiotics and homeopathy adopt the idea that health is a state of equilibrium with the universal energy of the cosmos. Man is believed to be of divine essence, thus his pure nucleus affects perfect health if unhindered by blockages of disease. In contrast, the Bible teaches that man possesses an evil heart and a sinfully fallen nature, not infinite wisdom and divine perfection.

Undoubtedly, our bodies tell us something when we are ill.

Symptoms are a warning system designed by God to alert our immunological response. But it is dangerous to insist that a cosmic intelligence uses disease as a learning experience for mankind. Disease is an enemy, which may have physiological or supernatural origins. In the latter case, Christ healed those who were "oppressed by the devil."[26] Though manifestations of internal dysfunction could herald greater dangers to our bodies, there is no benevolent higher consciousness inflicting misery to correct errors of past incarnations.

While Christians have reason to be wary of science, which so often opposes faith, true science is the accurate examination of observable phenomena. Many alternative medical methods consistently fail the test of such investigations. For example, studies of the central nervous system have yet to produce reasonable explanations for iridology and reflexology. Still, well-meaning Christians sometimes respond vehemently when cautions are expressed concerning these practices. Their argument usually goes like this: "So-and-so is a Christian and has been treating me for years with iridology and reflexology. How dare you question his use of the practice and suggest he is part of occult medical methods?"

Because one part of the body connects to another does not indicate that a sympathetic system of healing therapy is valid or that physical well-being can be monitored by looking at a single segment of the physique (eye or foot). Alternative medical methods often function with circular logic, avoiding scrutiny by controlled study. Instead, they seek the validation of occult sources. As a case in point, Dr. Bernard Jensen, a foremost American proponent of iridology, in his textbook *Iridology: Science and Practice in the Healing Arts*,[27] credits for inspiration such metaphysical sources as *Isis Unveiled*, by medium and founder of Theosophy H. P. Blavatsky, and *The Aquarian Conspiracy*, by New Age idealist Marilyn Furgeson.

Satan, the author of all suffering, knows people want quick

answers and uncomplicated cures. Occult medical explanations offer immediate resolutions and seemingly practical conclusions. But the therapy usually requires an ongoing relationship with the healer, drawing the patient even deeper into a web of a non-Christian worldview. Other occult-holistic therapies are gradually introduced, further victimizing the sufferer. The body may indeed be relieved of its misery, but at the cost of eternal torment.

The web of occultism is carefully woven by beliefs in energies and undefined forces. Terms like *prana* and *chi* are seldom explained. Generalized references to life forces are employed, but philosophical assumptions about such energies are circumspectly guarded. Thus, the Westerner with a nominal Christian background may never suspect he is being lured into the trap of occultism, where self is exalted as divine. This singleness of reality makes all of creation part of God, the error elucidated in Romans 1, which describes man as culminating in depravity and indecency.[28]

Chapter 21

Psychic Phenomena

The message is the same, whoever the psychic you consult may be. Planet earth is undergoing fundamental changes that will profoundly affect the cosmos and the spiritual consciousness of humanity. Some say a quantum leap in elevated brainpower will result in an upward alteration in mankind's vibrational rate. Those who worship the globe as a goddess say a shift of earth's poles will occur, displacing present geopolitical alignments and geographical references.

Psychics say they are not the only ones with expanded forces of the consciousness. Others have the power. It's part of the human heritage. For example, you have a hunch and it pays off with emotional or financial success. You think the phone is going to ring, and it does. You go to the mailbox, and the letter you dreamed of the night before has arrived. You meet someone and know you have met him before. It doesn't involve the five senses, but the message comes through loudly and clearly.

Some say it's a special gift. Others claim it's standard, though underdeveloped, equipment of the mind and soul. Noted psychic the late Edgar Cayce said, "These [psychic powers] are latent in each and every individual, as has been given. It may be developed by application."[1]

The American Society of Psychical Research may not know where it comes from, but they certainly investigate psychic phenomena assiduously. Among their curiosities are telepathy, clairvoyance, precognition, hallucinations, dreams, psychometry, cognition, psychokinesis, poltergeists, ESP, and all other aspects of the paranormal. In 1882 the original version of the Society for Psychical Research was established in London. Those who joined were primarily men who had lost faith in religion but were averse to the prevailing view of the time, scientific materialism. The Society's stated aim is to "examine without prejudice in a scientific spirit those faculties of man, real or supposed, which appear to be inexplicable on a generally recognized hypothesis."

Psychic occurrences being taken so seriously is a relatively new chapter in the history of humanity. For centuries such speculation was considered the work of demons or eccentrics. Then, in the late seventeenth and early eighteenth centuries, traditional religious perspectives were subjected to the scrutiny of such secular philosophers as Hume and Voltaire. The nineteenth-century hypnotist Mesmer experimented with healing and astral projection. Spiritualism surged in popularity during Mesmer's time.

Today's psychic inquests occur not in the musty halls of academia, but on the highways of contemporary life. It even has an acronym, PSI, referring to that branch of the psychological sciences dealing with psychic ability and its phenomena. Psychic phenomena are definitely out of the closet. But many wish to once again inhibit this supposed sixth sense. Some are fundamentalist Christians who say such things are the work of the devil. But illusionists and practicing prestidigitators are equally antagonistic. Magician James Randi encouraged two of his protégés to infiltrate an experiment at Washington University's McConnell's Laboratory of Psychical Research. Randi claims that for four years researchers accepted trickery as proof of psychic powers.[2]

The faithful are undaunted. They claim to communicate telepathically with extraterrestrials, seek out-of-body experiences, aspire to know past lives, and dabble in clairvoyance. They are convinced that we can know the past, divine the future, receive information intuitively, send thoughts across distances, transcend space and time to recall incarnations, soul-travel beyond physical limits, and identify the unknown by the inexplicable powers of the mind.

PARAPSYCHOLOGY

As an *Apollo 14* astronaut, he walked on the moon. After leaving the life of an astronaut behind, Edgar Mitchell headed the Institute of Noetic Sciences, founded in 1973 and dedicated to the exploration of inner space. The term *noetic* was derived from the phrase "noetic quality" used by Harvard psychologist and philosopher William James, describing "mystical states of insight into depths of truth unplumbed by discursive intellect."[3] Mitchell's machinations represented the spectrum of interest in PSI phenomena. The institute examined near-death experiences, Tibetan meditation, clairvoyant remote viewing, remote healing, and mind-body links.

Generally, extrasensory occurrences are divided by categories. *Extrasensory perception (ESP)* is a catchall term that alludes to various kinds of paranormal curiosities. Clairvoyance involves receiving information from an object or event. Telepathy refers to the transference of thoughts, mind to mind, or being aware of the mental state of another person. Cognition means being conscious of events in the past (postcognitive), present (cognitive), or future (precognitive).

Parapsychology owes its popularity to a Swedish contemporary of Voltaire, Emanuel Swedenborg, who combined his scientific background with occult speculation and founded his own religion, Swedenborgianism. Modern parapsychology owes its impetus to J. B. Rhine, a biologist whose primary work was conducted at Duke University. Rhine began as a preministerial student but later declared, "I gave up the ministry when I found in psychology that there was no scientific basis for the existence of the will. Without free will, the ministry seems futile."[4] Today, Rhine's associates investigate card guessing, dice throwing, and other standard methods of testing ESP.

In addition to exploring extrasensory perception, investigators like Rhine also survey psychokinesis (PK), the exertion of influence on an outside physical object, event, or situation. The source of PK defies explanation, since there is no direct use of muscles, physical energy, or instruments. Psychokinesis is popularly displayed by such theatrical tricks as spoon bending, table tipping, and levitation.

What's behind it all? Some researchers look to Freud's contemporary Carl Jung for answers. As an investigator of the occult, Jung sought to explain astrological predictions and assorted divinatory developments, such as the I Ching. He proposed that coincidence links seemingly improbable events, something he called "synchronicity." This theory suggests that simultaneous occurrences of a certain condition can take place with one or more objective phenomena in what Jung called "another order of the universe."

Other explanations abound. One researcher says that when excited, the brain emits a cloud of particles of imaginary mass called "psitrons." Others think electromagnetic or gravitational fields are behind it all. Some subscribe to another of Jung's theories that refers to the "collective unconsciousness," a universal mind that connects all individual minds. Certain researchers acknowledge what they call the "subliminal self," a kind of psychic split personality that accomplishes phenomenal feats. Still others refer to unknown nonphysical entities capable of overcoming space-time restraints. Despite years of research and speculation, the elusive origin of psychic phenomena still lurks behind a big question mark that masks its derivation and intentions.

PSYCHICS

With more than one million teenage pregnancies a year, psychic Anna Harcourt's business is booming. For pregnant young women who fear an abortion, Anna claims she can make babies disappear from wombs. She calls it a "psychic abortion." An expert in black magic, Anna maintains she gives the souls of the unborn offspring to the devil in exchange for her services. In the last twenty years, she claims to have performed more than one hundred such abortions at her North England home.

Most New Age psychics who claim paranormal powers don't perform so malevolently. But their assistance is often unorthodox. A tabloid entitled *Astrology and Psychic News* contains some examples. Professor Amen-Ra says he has the ability to gaze into a person's eyes and predict his future. He wants only a photograph and $16.50 to ply his trade. Psychic E. B. Nathan is a palmist who requests that you photocopy both hands and send the sheet with $16 for what he says is "an honest, accurate prediction." Psychic Krishna Ram-Devi will meditate on your name for the same price and determine if your unhappiness and problems result from a wrong name given by your parents.

Throughout the centuries, psychic masters have been sought by the lowly and royalty alike. Capitalizing on superstition, fear, and grief, they have mixed charlatanism and entertainment to beguile the undiscerning.

On the more serious side, Uri Geller has fascinated millions with his purported ability to bend spoons. The United States Navy has employed psychics to track Russian ships, and the United States Air Force seriously considered developing a "psychic shield" for its missiles.

The bizarre side of psychics seems to interest people the most.

In Columbus, Ohio, newspapers reported the story of a fourteen-year-old girl living in a house with a garbage disposal and microwave that went into solo operation, along with a shower that started running unattended. News magazines featured photographs of a telephone levitating in the air, supposedly suspended by a poltergeist. Finally, a group of skeptics representing the Committee for the Scientific Investigation of Claims of the Paranormal checked out the situation. They discovered a surprisingly unsophisticated scam perpetrated by a clever, attention-seeking adolescent.[5]

Psychics come, and psychics go. So do their prophecies. Their success rate displays a minimal amount of accuracy except to the undiscerning, who rationalize failed predictions. The overactive imaginations of psychics leave followers cringing in fear of what might happen, and then depressed and disillusioned when nothing does.

Can psychic phenomena be scientifically examined without involving occultism? It's possible but improbable because of the lack of biblical guidelines within the scientific community. Unfortunately, many scientists ascribe to either atheism or humanist ideals of mysticism. In an issue of *The Humanist* magazine, it was revealed that two-thirds of all scientific researchers believe in ESP. Most scientists no longer argue about the validity of such phenomena. Instead, the current quest is to measure such forces and determine how they can be duplicated. How ironic that the best modern minds would fall prey to supernaturalism after expunging their cosmological views of all reference to Christian thought!

J. B. Rhine, mentioned earlier, posits a theory explaining parapsychology called "projection hypothesis," which assumes that an agency of the mind can function independently of the physical body. This agency supposedly has the capacity to project and contact an object beyond the organism it occupies. This is a scientific rationalization for what occultists call astral projection. Rhine strives to explain the phenomena of witchcraft without acknowledging existence of the supernatural forces propelling parapsychology. An important characteristic of psychic phenomena is the admitted lack of control over how and when the information is received. Accuracy and consistency are rare. Such randomness indicates the influence of a force outside human faculties.

In Colossians 2:18, the apostle Paul warns against bragging about mystical experiences and extrasensory communication. Psychics who boast of their abilities and offer their services to the public are described by Paul as being preoccupied with "idle notions."[6] Presumed psychic powers usually solicit spiritual pride and result in vain glorification of the carnal mind, as well as possible demonic influence. For the Christian, the power of Christ working through the believer is important, not some inexplicable force manifested arbitrarily.

Yet the masses follow the psychics with blind faith. From claiming to augment luck to improving libido, psychics stretch the imagination to prove their powers. Few followers evaluate the performance of psychics objectively, because people want to believe such powers are real and that benevolent fate controls their existence. To refute psychic claims is to deny a larger order and meaning in life. Those who refuse God His rightful place in their affairs substitute another principle of goodness and omnipotence, ignoring the logic that insists certain psychics are frauds. Take Uri Geller, for example. Debunkers who have investigated Geller's act suspect the spoons are made of nitinol, an alloy so sensitive to heat that the touch of a finger can make it curl. Several professional magicians have duplicated the trick by sleight-of-hand. According to magician Henry Gordon, the psychic secretly bends the spoon on the side of a table, a belt buckle, or a chair. Then he lets it slowly emerge between the thumb and forefinger, appearing to twist as it comes forth. In the absence of either explanation, one cannot discount supernatural demonic intervention to coerce the unwary into believing such powers prove the mind's power over matter. Consequently, some seek these powers and eventually pursue occult consciousness-raising techniques.

From the earliest recorded times, nonmaterial agencies and inexplicable forces have been credited with performing incredible feats. Some of those accomplishments were attributed to ghosts, demons, or mythological beings. In the last half of the nineteenth century, the spiritualist movement supported the idea that the departed precipitate such phenomena.

Christians must do more than speculate about the origin of such powers. When the paranormal occurs, the Bible mandates an explanation of the source. How? First, the Scriptures must be searched to see if such occurrences are forbidden. Second, the psychic gift must be subjected to the authority of Christ and compelled to cease if not from Him. Finally, its purpose must be analyzed to see if it truly exalts Christ. Such standards go far beyond scientific precepts of evaluation, because God's principles transcend the material and incorporate the supernatural, where demons and devils ply their wares.

Those who believe in psychic phenomena frequently dismiss any idea that these things could be of the devil, since some psychics appear to do good. But Matthew 7:22–23 warns us that on Judgment Day, some will say they did great things even in the name of Christ. The response of the Lord will be: "I never knew you; depart from Me." Remember, any supernatural occurrence has but two possible sources, God or the devil (or Satan's demons).

Some psychic feats are explicable. Those who say they can start stopped watches simply play the averages. One systematic study shows that 55 percent of stopped watches can be reactivated by the warmth of the human hand, which causes metal parts to expand and loosens internal mechanisms. Even so, some psychic powers are undoubtedly supernatural.

The lure of psychic abilities is rooted in Satan's appeal to Adam and Eve: "You will be like God."[7] The devil wants to convince sinners that they have boundless, untapped powers. Whether these psychic abilities are called biocurrents, brain waves, or biocosmic forces, Satan's demons externalize their psychic manifestation until they can take up residence within the person who thinks he possesses natural powers. Before assuming some psychic phenomenon is of God or man's mind, heed the words of 1 Thessalonians 5:21: "Test all things; hold fast what is good." Jesus displayed the supernatural and did deeds resembling psychic feats. But Acts 10:38 tells us how: "God was with Him." The same isn't true for psychics.

Chapter 22

Divinatory
Devices

They were awarded a Nobel prize for a breakthrough in particle physics. But the scientific investigations of Che Ning Yeng and Tsung-dao Lee were guided more by the hand of fate than the impulse of an inquiring mind. "Is there going to be a breakthrough in the next two years?" they asked. "Good fortune lies ahead. Persevere further," came the reply. The question wasn't posed to a committee of academic peers, but to a handful of yarrow sticks. Yeng and Lee had consulted the ancient Chinese divinatory device I Ching, the *Book of Changes*, a combination of hard science and soft irrationalism.

Psychic predictions and prophetic devices such as the I Ching, tarot cards, astrology, palmistry, runes, dowsing, and biorhythms have become symbols of certitude in a restless age. In spite of the capriciousness of such artifices, many who have rejected organized religion have turned to exotic occult instruments to direct their lives and offer advice about their futures.

To those interested in divination, intuition is the pathway to understanding life. Each person is believed to be part of a holo-gram. Each mind is a segment of this "collective unconscious." Divination is a means of tapping this universal bank of knowledge concerning the past, present, and future. Occult fortune-telling is a window opening to the self and the universal consciousness beyond. The key is to determine which system of divination will most quickly and clearly align one's higher self with the best avail-able channel of esoteric information.

Since civilization began, people have looked for ways to predict the future and uncover the purposes of the past. Some sought the significance of a single event, such as lighting a fire (capnomancy). Others studied causimomancy, the fate of objects thrown into the fire. Still others surveyed the entrails of animals or contemplated the bumps on the head (phrenology) or the moles on a face (moleosophy).

If they could know the future, people felt they could act on the information to better their circumstances or outwit the gods. Even today, nearly a million Frenchmen have paid twenty dollars each for a computerized translation of Nostradamus's *Centuries*, four hundred years after it was written.

Often forgotten is the poor track record demonstrated by psy-chics and diviners. Jeane Dixon, who has parlayed her prognosti-cations into millions of dollars, once said Jacqueline Kennedy would not remarry. Apparently her zodiac charts never consulted a Greek ship owner named Onassis. If psychics and fortune-tellers have anything in common, it is a studied ambiguity that circum-vents exacting scrutiny.

In this uncertain age, people are searching for patterns of secu-rity by which to live. They want to know what fatalistic forces guide the movements of men, the decisions of governments, and the des-tinies of civilizations. And they are willing to accept less than total accuracy. God is not. Deuteronomy 18:22 warns, "When a prophet speaks in the name of the LORD, if the thing does not happen . . . that is the thing which the LORD has not spoken." So stern was

God's view of psychic error that capital punishment was instituted for any self-proclaimed prophet whose prophecies did not come true.

Not all occult divination is inaccurate. Sometimes the law of averages prevails and a psychic prediction lucks out. In other instances, common sense succeeds and intuition triumphs to give the appearance of a portent. Sometimes, evil forces conspire to predict a course of action, then summarily fulfill it with seeming accuracy. But even when the information is unerring, God's principles cannot be ignored. In Acts 16, a damsel with a spirit of divination followed the apostle Paul for several days declaring that Paul was sent from God. But the apostle would not accept the praise and endorsement of a demon despite its apparent reliability. Deuteronomy 13 warns that even when a prophecy comes to pass, the prediction is not to be revered if the prognosticator is an idolater.

Why does the Bible have such exacting standards for evaluating prognostication? Psychic determinism and fatalistic chance lure people away from trusting God, whose mercy guides the affairs of humanity. In the process, volitional accountability is ignored. There is always someone or something else to blame: "My biorhythms weren't right" or "My horoscope chart said I could do it." If Eve had been a psychic, imagine how much more creative her excuse might have been!

I Ching

The I Ching originated during China's Han Dynasty and was intended to be a book of collective wisdom. Eventually, however, its sixty-four sections came to be idolatrously revered. Confucius is said to have studied the book so carefully that the thongs binding the tablets on which his copy was inscribed wore out three times from constant use. What fascinated Confucius was a doctrine teaching that the womb of the universe is a limitless, imperceptible void, T'ai Chi. All material objects have being and individuality due to a particular combination of negative and positive forces, the yin and yang. The I Ching hexagrams supposedly avoid mechanical answers in favor of promoting greater self-understanding so that one can interpret his own future.

Originally, the I Ching used yarrow stalks. Forty-nine stalks were thrown into two random heaps. These were then counted by threes and fives. Today, the most popular method is the tossing of coins. Three identical coins of any denomination are tossed six times. As the coins are laid according to the way they land, heads or tails, two trigrams form a hexagram. Each of the sixty-four possible hexagrams is believed to correspond to psychic principles. The *Book of Changes* is then consulted for the interpretation. Most practitioners of the I Ching acknowledge that the intuition of one's own spirit is the ultimate factor that governs this form of divination's interpretations.

By dislodging the active role of the conscious mind, the I Ching is supposed to reveal true, unconscious tendencies. Though the origin of the I Ching was Chinese, its prediction on principles of yin and yang is considered universal. It is also supposed to be a kind of spiritual training exercise to perfect one's ability to perceive accurately the essence of life However, the erratic forces of chance generally reveal only what is intuitively assumed. There is always a possibility, however, that evil, supernatural forces could manipulate the results to validate a preselected plan and lead the seeker spiritually astray. Even so, evil supernatural forces are neither omniscient nor omnipotent, having absolute control over the future.

TAROT CARDS

A popular divinatory device at psychic fairs is the set of tarot cards, consisting of the minor arcane and the major arcane with twenty-two cards, a card numbered 0, and the Fool. The four suits are designated wands, cups, swords, and pentacles, symbolizing the four elements of fire, water, air, and earth. Some historians say this system of occultism came from Chaldea by way of Alexandria and was used worldwide by occultists to communicate. (The name tarot comes from *taro-rota*, meaning "the will of the law, and the law of the will.") First used by a Frenchman in the eighteenth century, the term *tarot* has preserved its Francophile pronunciation, hence the silent final *t.*

The cards are said to be symbolic representations of reality. By reading them, one's unconscious powers are awakened. When this happens, the inner forces of fate can be controlled. The color, shape, and symbolic forms on the cards are to be studied intuitively. Some tarot guides provide meditations while concentrating on the cards.

The tarot is one of the least precise forms of occult divination. In fact, there are no standardized pictures appearing on the cards. Some adherents make up their own diagrammed figures and attach their own meanings to these designations. In addition, there are several methods of shuffling and laying the cards. Such arbitrariness ensures inaccuracy in determining crucial information. Consequently, tarot cards are only a psychic point of contact between the reader and the subject.

TASSEOGRAPHY

The ancient fortune-telling practice of tea-leaf reading has enjoyed a resurgence. No longer relegated to Gypsy tents at county fairs, this clairvoyant art attracts yuppies and serious businesspeople. The leaves are said to be a medium through which the reader's psychic abilities are stimulated to uncover hidden truths.

The usual method is to have the client invert an empty cup and turn it around three times. Then the reader places it on the saucer, tapping the bottom three times with the left index finger. In a light trance, the reader picks up the cup and turns it over to survey the lay of the leaves from all angles. Astrological considerations can be pondered, since occult lore holds that the bowl of the cup corresponds to the dome of the sky and the leaves are like the stars in their configurations.

Gravity determines how the leaves land. The variables of interpretation concerning the lay of the leaves are so erratic that almost any configuration could indicate something. For example, a triangular form supposedly indicates jealousy or rivalry. The tea-leaf reader would normally proceed to ask clever questions that the unsuspecting client would innocently answer, giving sufficient information to draw commonsense conclusions. If few leaves are left, it means direct action needs to be taken. An array of leaves without a pattern indicates confusion. Both are suitably ambiguous deductions to satisfy the patron that psychically derived data has been acquired.

CHIROMANCY

Palmistry is an equally popular psychic technique that predicts physical events, prognosticates financial success, and prophesies the possibility of dire circumstances. A recent issue of an in-flight magazine published by a major airline declared, "Relax your old prejudices and suspicions. Allow a practicing palmist to tell you what's in your hand."

Those adept at the art scan the dominant hand for the life line, indicating major physical events; the head line, revealing mental capabilities; and the heart line, illustrating events connected with emotional qualities of the individual. Additional consideration is given to the success line, the health line, and the mounts, that portion of each hand where calluses are located near the finger joints. These mounts are named after planets, including Jupiter, Saturn, and Mercury, and are said to reveal the qualities of leadership, reserve, artistic competence, and persuasiveness.

The color of one's hand lines also indicates certain qualities. Pale lines denote poor health. Red lines show an active temperament. If the lines are yellowish, one's nature is said to be proud.

When questioned about the prophetic abilities of palmistry, proponents caution that the practitioner of chiromancy can only issue warnings. It is the subject who must decide whether the predicted tendencies will be overcome.

The creases and patterns in one's hand exhibit vocational use more than reflections of the soul. The relationship of palmistry to astrological guidance further shows its whimsical nature. In most cases, the palmist is probably studying the customer's body language and listening carefully to answers of prudently worded questions. Thus, the indications of the fate line or the heart line are more likely an evaluation of the conversation than of the hand.

NOSTRADAMUS

A popular source of prophecy is the writings of Nostradamus, a sixteenth-century French medical doctor and avid occultist. His book *Centuries* consisted of a hundred verses composed in quatrains. Much of what he wrote seems a meaningless jumble, but some conclude his esoteric script predicted the rise of Hitler and other historical events, as well as still-future things. Most recently, Californians were alarmed by a video docudrama concerning Nostradamus that suggested a major earthquake was due near the San Andreas Fault—not exactly "earth-shattering" news.

Nostradamus was born of Jewish descent on December 14, 1503. He was raised on the classic languages and attained a doctor's degree, though his reputation as a physician went beyond anatomical boundaries. Nostradamus delved into alchemy, magic, and the occult to publish his *Centuries* volumes, which dealt with events from his time to the end of the world, predicted to come in 3797. He took the word *centuries* to refer to the one hundred four-line verses in which his prose was styled.

For those worried about nuclear war, there is this advice: "In the year 1999 and 7 months, there will come from heaven the great king of terror, to raise again the great king of the Mongols, before and after Mars shall reign at will."[1] Hitler himself was fascinated with *Centuries*. Others thought the French term *hister* in one of the quatrains was an anagram for Hitler. The wife of Goehhel (Hitler's propoganda minister) supervised the German printing of Nostradamus's writings. She believed they prophesied a victorious Third Reich. These predictions were dropped in pamphlet form from Nazi aircraft.

A reference to three brothers and the Antichrist's annihilating one of them led some in the 1960s to believe Nostradamus predicted the assassination of the Kennedys. Other followers of *Centuries* say he foretold air travel, the military use of aircraft, the space race, electricity, submarines, and even a bombing of New York City.

Critics of Nostradamus claim that even a cursory analysis of his prophecies reveals the quatrains were meant to apply to his time. They were particularly directed to the nobility of his age. Nostradamus apparently wrote in an obscure form of French that was mixed with his own unique linguistic construction. Consequently, his supposed predictions were virtually indecipherable to his contemporaries, let alone understandable centuries later. Most who read his *Centuries* fail to realize that each version has been heavily editorialized with the translator's own views. The colorful and highly metaphorical language employed by Nostradamus ensures a variety of translations. Anyone professing biblical allegiance cannot accept the predictions of his questions. To believe Nostradamus is to deny the scriptural premise that only the Lord knows the future because "the secret things belong to the LORD our God."[2]

WATER WITCHING

The caves of the Atlas Mountains in North Africa contain wall drawings of a dowser at work eight thousand years ago. The first modern authentication of finding water with a forked stick appeared in medieval Germany. But water witching isn't the only use of this occult craft. In the seventeenth century, William Lilly, an English astrologer, used what he called mosaical rods to discover buried treasure. Ritual magic textbooks of that era published elaborate instructions for preparation and use of divining rods. Today, dowsing rods are considered by some just one more component in the arsenal of articles available to the student pursuing nonrational means of obtaining information.

The American Society of Dowsers says everyone is born with the ability. Members search for lost articles, archaeological sites, missing persons, and downed aircraft, and they also track criminals and identify malfunctions in home appliances. One dowser says he witches for electrical shorts when his normal skills as an electrician don't suffice. Another dowser consults his pendulum to find out if girls in the office secretly love him.

The image of a dowser, forked hazel rod in hand, plodding over ground that conceals water is fading fast. Today, skilled dowsers stand at a field's edge and determine by remote conjuration the exact location of water. Other water witchers zero in on their targets using only a map of the location. Adept dowsers say they can witch for water from across the street or over the ocean with equal success.

The general technique is to hold a Y-shaped rod in one's hands. When the object or substance being sought is near, the end of the Y twitches downward. Dowsers say a sensation of tightness surges throughout their bodies, and a tingling in their arms precedes the rod's movement. What causes it?

Various theories have been postulated. One suggests that small magnetic field gradient changes (or electromagnetic radiations) stimulate sensors in the adrenal and pituitary glands. Stimuli are then transmitted to the brain, which commands the arms to twist. The minute movement is magnified by the length of the rod, which is a mechanical parametric amplifier. This theory claims that since the attracting field patterns are contingent upon their generator sources, dowsers can program their brains to respond to any kind of stimuli, including water, oil, pipes, or lost objects.

The spectrum of current uses of dowsing ranges from major oil companies to the U.S. armed services. During the Vietnam conflict, American Marines sometimes used bent coat hangers to detect mines, booby traps, and Vietcong tunnels. An advocate in New Zealand claims to breed horses by reliance on a pendulum to compile breeding charts. In France over a hundred medical dowsers are officially recognized as a professional group by the ministry of labor. Some dowse with crystals to locate disease. The crystal hangs from a string while a series of questions is asked. Pendular response guides the healer.

Various theories have been suggested to explain dowsing, such as molecular magnetism, the converging of some undefined bio-cosmic force, and electromagnetic attraction. One theory proposes that groundwater is positively charged and the dowser is negatively charged, converting the sap-filled dowsing rod into a conductor. Another hypothesis suggests the dowser receives undetectable extrasensory impulses, but there is no way to measure minute muscular movements that dowsers claim are subconsciously generated. Actually, there is no way to verify any of the explanations for water witching. In fact, many scientific reports show that dowsing never achieves any better than chance results, which cannot be predicted reliably in any single situation.

ASTROLOGY

Ms. Nevada Hudson, owner of a temporary employment agency, commutes to work like most other people in her Dallas suburb. But when Nevada arrives at the office, similarities end. Instead of visiting the coffee machine, she heads for her computer to punch in the numbers of her natal chart. In about forty-five seconds, a series of numbers and signs appears on the screen, giving Ms. Hudson all the predictive assistance she requests to guide her day. An Aries, Ms. Hudson is an astrologer who faithfully follows her horoscope.

According to the Gallup polls, fifty million Americans believe their destinies are determined by the movements of celestial bodies. Though astrology has been around for centuries, its popularity has grown remarkably in recent years.

Modern star-gazers have diversified the use of astrology. Some specialize in personal and corporate zodiac charts. Others give guidance on the stock market and recommendations on horse-track betting. Still others help select perfumes, diagnose disease, advise on choosing a pet, and meddle in the affairs of love and romance, telling customers who to love, mate, and bed, and not necessarily in that order. There are astrological greeting cards and perfumes, the latter a line of twelve zodiacal scents, including "Warm Leo," "Balanced Libra," and "Active Aries."

The gravitational pull of the moon on the tides, the energy-generating power of sunlight, and photosynthesis are scientifically measurable ways in which heavenly bodies affect life on earth. Other kinds of radiant and gravitational effects may be possible, but that is far removed from concluding that decisions regarding life and love can be influenced by Jupiter and Mars. The current zodiac charts were constructed prior to Copernicus, when an erroneous geocentric view of the cosmos dominated thought. Since the horoscope characteristics were assigned centuries ago, a gradual, slight shift on the earth's axis has resulted in the shift of an entire astrological house. Modern astrologers have never updated their blueprint of the heavens to include this alteration. Also, each religious branch of astrology assigns different characteristics to each house, so that a horoscope cast by a Buddhist in Bangkok will say something much different from the horoscope of a Hindu in Calcutta.

BIORHYTHMS

For nearly a decade, biorhythms have been lauded as an effective tool for revealing human potential. The concept goes back to a German nose-and-throat specialist named Wilhelm Fliess, a contemporary of Freud. Through his involvement with mystical speculation and numerology, Fliess became convinced that the number twenty-three contained physical significance. The number twenty-eight was designated to correspond with emotional cycles. He then added a thirty-three-day cycle pertaining to the intellect.

Starting the day a person is born, each of the twenty-three-, twenty-eight-, and thirty-three-day periods is plotted. When depicted on a graph, the modulating cycles are indicated as curves above and below a horizontal line at the center of each complete cycle. If the curve is above the line, high energy is expected. The person should be full of vitality in that area of his life. Creativity and cheerfulness can be expected. After passing the midpoint of the cycle, the line curves downward, signifying a recharging period. At this time, the person will likely be tired, moody, and unable to concentrate.

A critical day is revealed when the midpoint of the curve crosses the line, a transition day demanding attention. If two of these twenty-three-, twenty-eight-, or thirty-three-day cycles should cross at the same midpoint, it is known as a "double-critical" day. Watch out! If all three cycles cross at the same midpoint, a "triple-critical" day is at hand, and extreme caution should be exercised.

Biorhythms have attracted an unusual group of advocates. Consulting firms employ them. Special biorhythm calculators are available from mail-order houses. Sports enthusiasts and gamblers all have reasons to predict their winning days. It's claimed that about five thousand Japanese firms believe in the efficacy of biorhythms. Defenders and detractors square off with equal aplomb. Dr. Colin Pittendrigh of Stanford University says, "I consider the biorhythm theory an utter, total, unadulterated fraud. I consider anyone who offers to explain my life in terms of twenty-three-, twenty-eight-, and thirty-three-day cycles a numerical nut."

The author of a book on biorhythms says a large percentage of commercial and private airplane crashes is attributable to human error on a pilot's "critical" days; thus, many crashes presumably could be avoided if pilots refrained from flying on such days. A researcher at the University of Minnesota Chronobiology Laboratory dismisses biorhythms as a "silly numerological scheme that contradicts everything we know about real biorhythms with their dozens of variables."[3]

Advocates say proof of biorhythms' predictive power exists in the history of famous people. On down or critical days, Ted Kennedy experienced his misadventure at Chappaquiddick; Marilyn Monroe and Judy Garland poisoned themselves; Arthur Bremer attempted to kill Governor George Wallace; and Sirhan Sirhan assassinated Robert Kennedy.

Researchers acknowledge the body does have an inner clock that regulates sleep, another that calculates appetite, and a hormonal regulator that affects menstruation, hair growth, and fertility. The real rhythms of the body are circadian (twenty-four-hour cycles regulating sleep); ultradian (one-hundred-minute cycles influencing appetite and sex); circamensual (monthly cycles of hormones); and circannual (yearly clocks governing hair growth and menstruation). Scientists insist these somewhat predictable cycles are a far cry from the claims of biorhythm believers, who assert their ability to forestall death, destruction, heartache, and inefficiency.

The science of chronobiology recognizes the body does have biological rhythms that follow somewhat predictable, though variable, patterns. Blood pressure, respiration, temperature, pulse rate, blood sugar, hormones, and hemoglobin levels all conform to moderately definable configurations. One doctor who has studied chronobiology concluded that by charting rhythms of cell division in healthy and cancerous tissue, it may be possible to determine the most appropriate time to conduct chemotherapy. But assuming that human behavior can be controlled and anticipated by studying the body's internal rhythms leaves the arena of science and enters the realm of occultism.

AURAS

"Don't look for Sherwin Williams colors. Look past the person. Look for evanescent colors." That's the advice of one psychic who claims he can detect health, sickness, anger, and enthusiasm by the brightly glowing emanations surrounding a person's body.

Said to be a manifestation of one's higher self, auras are a field of multihued colors surrounding one's body, radiating from a few inches to several feet in every direction. The dominant color at any point in time is said to indicate the emotional, physical, and spiritual condition of the subject. Dark red shows anger, black indicates stress, and blue means a state of peacefulness. A smaller aura displays tension, while a more widely dispersed one demonstrates a relaxed condition.

Auras are said to exist in three zones. The first extends no more than a half inch from the body. This is the "etheric double" of one's physique. From that band, the inner aura extends an additional three inches. The outer aura expands a foot or more. Psychics generally contend that anyone can read these auras if he is attuned to them.

One auric teacher claims to use color readings regularly in the classroom to ascertain the capabilities of his students. Once, he witnessed a swirling, overly active aura and discovered the student was pregnant and worried that she wouldn't be able to finish school. The teacher was able to direct her to helpful counseling, which he says exemplifies how learning to read auras would create a more aware, compassionate world.

Science has yet to confirm that anything such as an aura exists. Kirlian photography has reproduced color emanations from fingertips, but some scientists insist this involves nothing more than the ionization of the air from warmth of the hand and is not internal radiation from man's soul. The phenomenon could be hallucinatory or spiritistic. In the latter case, it could be a demonic occurrence visible only to the eye of the beholder, who is experiencing satanic manipulation of his senses.

DREAMWORK

Who wrote *Dr. Jekyll and Mr. Hyde?* Robert Louis Stevenson? Wrong. The correct answer is the "brownies."

The brownies? That's what Stevenson called them. They were "little people" who appeared to him in dreams. Whenever he was running low on money and needed to write, he would sleep, dream, than ask the little people to spin stories for him. Edgar Allan Poe apparently also relied on dreams. The master of the macabre drew heavily on his nightmares to write chilling poems.

Jung, Freud, and the prophet Daniel would be amazed to witness how dreams are used today to guide human behavior. (All three were involved with dream interpretation.) The concept of dreamwork divorces dreams from a psychoanalytical and biblical framework. Dreams supposedly are honest indications of immediate predicaments. Some believe dreams link the subconscious with the Universal Mind. What one dreams is said to be a unified connection to the global and cosmic forces of clairvoyance. Dream guidance is suggested as a means of achieving future goals. According to one dreamwork advocate, "Dreams are among God's original blessings for those who are visionary enough to attune their innate wisdom to Divine Direction."[4]

Metaphysicians have adopted various forms of dream therapy, because they believe nocturnal fantasies are directly linked with the superconscious, one's higher spiritual self. They insist that supernatural revelation is not limited to religious teachers and sacred books, but that direct contact with "truth" is possible while asleep, when our cognitive inhibitions are at rest. Insisting that even the Bible uses dreams as a medium of revelation, they encourage direct communication with whatever being may appear in dreams, assuming the innate goodness and spiritual validity of any information received during slumber.

Some say that dreams reflect an unconscious response to waking reality. Dream analysts seek ways to translate that unconscious point of view into terms the conscious mind can comprehend. Dreams are a bridge between two states of mind, two ways of experiencing reality. They are also considered a precognitive key to warning against certain actions. In addition, some insist that dreamwork can actually change reality. By controlling dreams, one can manipulate real life.

Psychologists say dreams do reflect our inner thought life and may mirror repressed anxieties or inhibited desires. That deduction hardly assigns a predictive quality to dreams. It is true that in the Old Testament God sometimes revealed His will through dreams. But we observe no continuing occurrence of this practice in the New Testament, because the guidance of holy Scripture and the presence of the Spirit of truth abides with us to give continuing counsel day and night. When God did use dreams it was under His direction and at His prerogative. Such dreams could not be solicited, controlled, or interpreted without the Lord's guidance. Those who believe dreams provide access to psychic powers and are a means of guiding the future venture into the territory of divination, which God had forbidden. According to Scripture, interpretation of dreams belongs to the Lord. Nebuchadnezzar's occult soothsayers could not reveal his dreams, but Daniel declared, "There is a God in heaven who reveals secrets."[5]

RUNES

"Should I take that job? Am I ready for marriage? Will this venture make me rich? When in doubt, reach for your runes."

Runes? That's what the promotional brochure says. Previously, runes were known only to those interested in Scandinavian mythology. Today runes have become a major form of occult divination. Viking legend claims its supreme god, Odin, sacrificed an eye in his consuming passion to win the sacred knowledge runes contained.

Runes were originally characters of an alphabet used in an ancient form of Germanic writing. Consisting of twenty-four characters and typified by angular shapes, the earliest runes were credited with miraculous powers. They were thought to possess the ability to tell the future and were considered sacred talismans. It was common for those during the Viking epoch (about A.D. 800) to inscribe weapons and jewelry with runic symbols. To make the magic more potent, the inscription was frequently carved on the back of the object so the spell would work in secret.

Metaphysical shops sell these small clay or stone replicas as a means of interpreting dreams, attaining self-knowledge, and as oracles of the past and future. They are promoted as nothing less than a "personal adviser" contributing a dimension of "self-awareness."

Usage is simple. The rune stones (each inscribed with a letter from the Viking alphabet) are held or laid in front of the one seeking an answer. Gradually, a resolution is supposed to emerge from the core of the "listening heart." But where does the answer really come from? According to one advocate, runes will "put you in touch with your own inner guidance, with the part of you that knows everything you need to know for your life now."[6]

But runes are yet another means of exposing one's spirit to evil vulnerabilities and subjecting human inquisitiveness to fatalistic forces. No power of perception exists in a piece of rock. The only information comes from the imagination of the seeker or the imposition of information by demons.

Chapter 23

Occult Consciousness

Kathryn Lanza, a thirty-three-year-old Los Angeles legal secretary, knows what will happen when she dies. A hole will be cut in her skull, her brains will be removed, and the cavity will be filled with resins. Her internal organs, except her heart, will be extracted and placed in jars, and her body will be stuffed with herbs and submerged for two weeks in a preserving solution. She'll be coated with myrrh, scented with frankincense, and wrapped in silk and linen. Her bodily remains will then be placed in a noncorrosive metal sarcophagus lined with blue velvet. Kathryn Lanza will be mummified like the ancient pharaohs.[1]

In Salt Lake City, Utah, Summan Bonum Amen-Ra founded a cult dedicated to understanding the spiritual forces he believes governed ancient Atlantis and Egypt. Summan lifted rituals from the ancient *Tibetan Book of the Dead* to derive a mummification process that ranges from a no-frills $7,000 job to a $500,000 extravaganza that includes a sarcophagus encrusted with gold leaf and jewels. One of the fifty customers who have signed up declares, "I want to be at peace when I die. I am no longer scared of death."[2]

Immortality is a mainstay of humanistic futuristic thought. Unlike the scientific rationalists who have dominated the American mind-set since the 1950s, today's mystics are convinced there is life after death in one form or another. That's why cremation, cryonics, and even mummification attract an increasing number of customers who believe disposition of the body profoundly affects its immortal destination.

There are differing ideas determining which form of burial one should choose. Historically, cremation has been selected by those who believe the spirit should be released from the body for its next incarnation. Cryonics may be embraced by those who want their bodies reanimated at some later date. Mummification is picked as a way to prepare the body for its journey to the world of the afterlife where it progresses through various spiritual planes.

Cryonics is an increasingly popular, though expensive, means of ensuring an orderly transition to the next life—or a possible return to this one. One's dead body can be frozen with the hope it will be revived after science has learned to reverse death or repair damaged cells.

Cryonics involves putting the dead patient on a heart and lung machine to maintain a heartbeat and keep blood circulating. Ice is gradually applied around the body to lower the body temperature, while various chemicals are injected. Then the patient is taken to a laboratory where the blood is replaced with a balanced salt solution, which in turn is displaced later with a glycerol solution to minimize tissue damage. Finally, it's off to the warehouse, where the body is tucked into a cooling chest that resembles a coffin. The corpse is covered with dry ice until it reaches a temperature of −320 degrees Fahrenheit, after which it is covered with a foil material and put into a bag.

For those incapable of affording mummification or cryonics, the philosophy of reincarnation suffices. Mankind's most fundamental question has been transformed from "Who am I?" into "Who was I?" Consequently, various groups espousing reincarnation are enjoying a resurgent interest in their teachings. These organizations include The Association for Research and Enlightenment (Edgar Cayce's group), the Urantia Foundation, the Theosophical Society, and Unity School of Christianity. Their growing memberships are reflected in a recent study indicating that 60 percent of Americans consider reincarnation a reasonable probability.

Reincarnation is a serious consideration for some. Don't our souls need purifying? Why not let our existence continue until a state of perfection is finally reached and the soul can merge back into its source? Couldn't mental stress in this life be alleviated if the traumas of previous existences were identified? If a parent realizes a child had a history before conception, wouldn't that enhance respect for the newborn as an individual with a distinct chronology? Wouldn't everyone have an opportunity to finish every worthy goal left uncompleted at death?

Reincarnation insists there are countless opportunities for reformation. Christianity emphasizes the finished work of redemption achieved by Christ on the cross. Furthermore, reincarnation inhibits any choice of the will to determine a life of obedience to God's plan. Hidden in the implied merits of reincarnation is a selfishness that concedes no virtue in sacrificing for the welfare of others, since their lot in life is retribution for past sins. Reincarnation may seem reasonable until compared to a forgiving God who offers undeserved grace and mercy.

Though reincarnation was a popular theory among some sects of mystical Jews at the time of Christ, not a single Scripture exists to endorse this proposition. Some reincarnationists cite John 8:58 ("Before Abraham was, I AM") as evidence. But if Christ had suggested He was Abraham reincarnated, He would have been dismissed as a lunatic by His legalistic Jewish audiences. In fact, the Jewish leaders sought to kill Christ for blasphemy because they knew His statement was an assertion of His eternal deity (see v. 59; 10:30–33). Reincarnationists have claimed that Matthew 11:14 says John the Baptist was Elijah come again. But Luke 1:17 clearly explains that John came in "the spirit and power," the *style*, of Elijah's ministry.

Contrary to the exotic tales of past lives, the reality of why so many reincarnation accounts seem so convincing may be more mundane. Those with low self-esteem readily invent stories of marvelous past existences when they were persons of power, beauty, and nobility. These accounts are often conjured from the subconscious mind, which contains an incalculable record of sights and sounds, along with thousands of bits of long-forgotten information. Unrecalled movies, TV programs, photographs, songs, and literature may congeal into the "recollection" of an esteemed past life. Also, the influence of demons could concoct a past life scenario and hallucinogenically implant its fiction.

Unlike reincarnation, Christianity is not based on relativistic impressions of reality. It is founded on the teachings of Jesus and the doctrines of the apostles. It is what Jesus actually said and what His disciples really wrote that objectively guides the true follower of Christ. And no intermediaries are acceptable—not Buddha or Krishna, not angels, ascended masters, or channeled entities. Only Christ is the ultimate Authority because "all things were created through Him and for Him."[3] And the only enlightenment needed is to know Him and "the hope of His calling, what are the riches of the glory of His inheritance in the saints."[4]

MYSTICISM AND ENLIGHTENMENT

Exotic views of immortality are only part of this mind-set. Theories of enlightenment and mystical insights are abundant. *California Business* magazine asked state business leaders a series of questions regarding spiritual phenomena and discovered that 69 percent of Californians questioned said they were guided by a spiritual force, even though 30 percent said they never attended religious services. Interestingly more than 50 percent claimed their spiritual insights had come from various consciousness-raising techniques.

Science, behaviorism, metaphysics, psychology, and religion have been combined to navigate uncharted realms of human potential. The key to mysticism is discovering that reality depends upon the viewer's perspective. Since mankind is on an evolutionary course toward developing greater "potentiality," even the self can be re-created by an altered viewpoint.

Enlightenment in assorted occult models has become big business. And the search for these insights no longer requires years of arduous discipline in remote sanctuaries. The word is out that enlightenment is for everyone, quickly and reasonably priced. Various psychotechnologies and consciousness-altering devices claim to induce transformative states. Some use hypnotic regression. Others offer out-of-body experiences by listening to taped astral sounds. Still other techniques embrace flotation tanks, hyperventilation, and frenetic dancing.

The end product has several names. In Zen, it is *satori*. In Yoga, *samadhi*. In Hinduism, *nirvana*. In Sufism, *fana*. Some call it the "supreme consciousness." Others speak of "liberation" or "self-realization." To some it is the "mystic rose" or the "eternal flame." But whatever the intimation, it is a holy grail, the end of their spiritual search in this life. Becoming one with the pantheistic cosmos is their goal. In the words of one Eastern guru, Da Free John, "It is so direct, so obvious . . . [that] when you come to the point of acknowledging the Divine Identity and Condition of Manifested Existence, then you are enlightened."[5] If such doublespeak endorsing one's own ego as god doesn't make sense to the rationalist, the response is predictable: It works, therefore it must be right.

Today's explorers of truth are fond of contorting through postured positions and meditating to achieve deepened transcendental thought. As one spiritualist seeker said, "Enlightenment is the core truth of all religions. It is the essence of life. It is the discovery of the ultimate answer."[6] The search for ultimate reality instigated Jewish leaders to confront Christ in John 5. They demanded to know the authority by which He healed and forgave sins. Christ could have lured them down the road of spiritual introspection, but He did not. He might have told them to contemplate the cosmos, but He deferred. Instead, He offered Himself and His teachings, declaring, "He who hears My word and believes in Him who sent Me has everlasting life, and shall not come into judgment."[7]

Zen masters are fond of confounding their disciples with irrational behavior to help them break out of conditioned cultural states. They pose insoluble riddles or ask unanswerable questions. As one stated, "Enlightenment is beyond words and concepts. It cannot be grasped by intellect or any aspect of our rational, mental being."[8]

In contrast, Jesus never told His initiates to play mind games. He didn't instruct them to pursue an undifferentiated self that would dissolve their egos. Plainly and simply, He said, "I am the light of the world. He who follows Me shall not walk in darkness."[9] Those who explore the mystical may discover a form of enlightenment and a fleeting sense of well-being, but the darkness of their light cannot forgive sin.

The apostle John declared that Jesus is "the true Light which gives light to every man."[10] For the Christian, spiritual perspicacity is centered in a person, Christ, not an experience. In truth, the enlightenment of occult mysticism is actually the darkness of the devil, who has transformed himself into "an angel of light."[11]

Chapter 24

Occult Spirituality

No philosophy can exist in a vacuum, without a doctrinaire ideology. As eclectic as today's metaphysical milieu is, it nevertheless needs some sort of mooring. Several belief systems provide that anchor, cults such as Edgar Cayce's Association for Research and Enlightenment and the demonic document *A Course in Miracles*. Use of the term *cult* in this portion of the book is based on Webster's designation of a religious body that is "unorthodox" or embodies "devotion to a person or idea."

Despite their dissimilarities, metaphysical religious cults have a notable resemblance to one another. Most conspicuous is the idea that the subconscious dictates the active choices of life. Understanding its compulsions and achieving its enlightenment are fundamental objectives. These groups propose to understand hidden stimuli so that the subconscious can be reprogrammed with a redefined reality. Rather than delineating existence in relationship to an external deity, such cults are determined to launch adherents on the path of self-discovery.

The subconscious (often referred to as the higher self) presumably is a loyal guide to truth. To unlock such truths, the seeker must find a system to help him open the door to the path of spiritual innovation. Consequently, those involved in occult spirituality hop from one cult to another, constantly pursuing the ultimate key to getting in touch with their "ground of being."

Reliance upon intuitive confirmation of spirituality is a common denominator in these groups, since intuition is believed to be totally accurate. The aesthetic practices of these groups are designed to sharpen one's ability to hear the inner voice of intuition. Adherents are usually told that old ways of believing and programmed patterns of thought must be relinquished before hearing the inner voice. Thus, meditation, fasting, isolation, mantras, yoga, self-hypnosis, and other tools are employed to shut out the active world and enter the intuitive realm of passivity. Unlike traditional religious devotion, which focuses on the assistance of an external deity, cults promoting alternative spirituality encourage consulting the inner self and receiving words, images, feelings, and sounds that supposedly are guides of the soul. They purport to offer what traditional religions do not—a new way of perceiving reality. It is an unconventional way of interpreting our relationship to the universe. Whatever the codification of beliefs, the purpose is to prove and experience what mystics, shamans, and ancient seekers of the mysteries have always said.

Occult spirituality does not always represent aberrations of belief outside the mainstream of secular thought. The affirmation of reincarnation, psychic contact with the dead, and the survivability of the soul are supported by part of the scientific community. No less a source than the chief of brain biochemistry at the National Institutes of Health has said, "It is conceivable to me that the information stored in the brain could transform itself into some other realm. Matter can neither be created nor destroyed; and perhaps biological information flow cannot just disappear at death and must be transformed into another realm."[1]

The power of such a worldview could be underestimated. But consider that a National Opinion Research Council survey shows that nearly 50 percent of American adults believe they have been in contact with someone who has died. However one views this idea, its cultural acceptance signifies the demise of empirical science and the authoritarianism of established faiths. The revelation of the self, the idea that the soul is universal and the repository of ultimate reality, is a dominant presupposition of our age.

Occult spirituality thrives because it declares that mankind is undergoing a galactic shift in consciousness. The old ways of believing by means of creeds and ecclesiastical dogma are gone. Time, space, and human consciousness must now be viewed from a multidimensional level that can be understood only by communicating with the primordial vibration of life. From this verity, no cathedrals will be built to scrape the sky; we need only the worship of the inner self in the sanctuary of the soul. The Second Coming is no longer an anticipated event confined to limitations of time and space. Christ has come, and He dwells within all humanity in the consciousness of the Supreme Self. To help the reader better understand the way that occult spirituality may be organized into a cult system of religious thought, I will share a couple of examples. (Consult the author's other books for more detailed descriptions of similar cult groups.)

A COURSE IN MIRACLES

This huge, three-volume set reinterprets almost every orthodox Christian belief. Such doctrines as the atonement and the crucifixion of Christ are blatantly denied. Known as *A Course in Miracles*, it was dictated to a Columbia University psychologist, Helen Schucman, by an inner voice claiming to be Jesus. "This is a course in miracles," the voice began. "It is a required course. Only the time you take it is voluntary."[2]

Summing up the *Course*'s essence, the voice declared, "Nothing real can be threatened, nothing unreal exists." The entire *Course,* consisting of nearly twelve hundred pages, was acquired by a form of automatic handwriting over a period of seven years, between 1965 and 1973. It was eventually published in 1976 by the Foundation for Inner Peace, headed by parapsychological investigators Robert and Judy Skutch. The foundation also offers other books and pamphlets, as well as audio- and videocassettes.

Schucman admits the handwriting made her "very uncomfortable." After writing what the voice said, she gave the documents to her close friend Dr. William Thetford, professor of medical psychology at Columbia University's College of Physicians and Surgeons. Schucman, who died in 1981, was a religious skeptic with little regard for spirituality and mysticism. Thetford had been raised in the Christian Science church. He explained his personal theological views in a manner resembling pantheism: "Since all life stems from God and is one and inseparable, certainly the life force that animates animals and plants is the same as the life force that animates us."[3]

Schucman kept notepads handy to take down what the voice dictated. Messages came almost daily, sometimes several times a day. She gave the *Course* instruction to Thetford, who typed a manuscript. First came the 622-page text, then the 478-page *Workbook for Students,* followed by an 88-page *Manual for Teachers.*

Schucman's entity claimed to have an important message for our time, centered in the philosophy that guilt is absolved through forgiving others, not by seeking personal forgiveness from a loving God. The *Course* aims to correct what it says are errors of Christianity that overemphasize suffering, sacrifice, and sacrament. "Every religion . . . has been inspired by God. To believe in the God in everyone is the ultimate religion," the *Course* declares.

Such statements are typical of the *Course*'s unconventional approach to theology. Whereas most religions are concerned with the exculpation of sin and communion with God, *A Course in*

Miracles boldly proclaims, "It is impossible to think of anything God created that could need forgiveness."[4] Elsewhere, pardon for transgression is referred to as an illusion, a "happy fiction." Ironically, though the *Course* denigrates God's forgiveness, it conversely claims that personal peace is possible when humans forgive others.

As might be expected, Christ is stripped of His divinity. "The name of Jesus is the name of one who was a man but saw the face of Christ in all his brothers and remembered God," the *Course* alleges. For those Christians who find such comments to border on blasphemy, literature from the foundation that publishes the books pronounces: "The *Course* [lends] itself to teaching, parallel to the ongoing teaching of the Holy Spirit."[5]

Explicitly, the *Course* states its aims as: (1) "the undoing of our belief in the reality of guilt," (2) "emphasizing the importance of Jesus as our gentle teacher," and (3) "correcting the errors of Christianity." The foundation's statement of purpose certifies: "The corporation has as its specific aims . . . helping those interested to integrate the *Course*'s principles into their personal lives, that they may better realize their true identity . . . as children of God."[6]

URANTIA

Who is God? Why am I here? What happens after I die?

If those questions concern you, the *Urantia Book* claims to have the answers. God is the Lord of a universe containing numerous inhabited planets, it says. Man's purpose is to discover his pre-existence as a god. After death, developed souls may inherit their own planet over which they can reign as a deity. Among other Urantia rejoinders are these: The real name for earth is Urantia; Adam was sent here from another planet thirty-eight thousand years ago; Urantia's first human being was over eight feet tall and appeared as a god to biologically uplift the human race.[7]

The inventory of controversial Urantia doctrines doesn't stop there. Christ was not the creator of all that is, only the originator of our local universe, Urantia. This universe is said to consist of a thousand inhabitable worlds (i.e., solar systems), several super-universes, and a trillion inhabitable planets, one of which is Urantia. The Holy Spirit is actually the Mother Spirit, who was the sexual consort of Jesus Christ.[8] Additional details are available in the 503-page *Concordex of the Urantia Book*, which maintains that the Bible is "a magnificent collection of beautiful devotional, inspired writings, along with various human writings that are far from sacred or inspired."

First published in 1955, the 2,097-page *Urantia Book* was supposedly delivered to Dr. Bill Sadler by seven spirit beings. These entities claimed to be celestial creatures who communicated by automatic handwriting. They declared the Urantia revelation was "the finest worldview of religions available to contemporary man." According to these beings, man's ultimate guide to faith is reliance on what are called "Indwelling Thought Adjusters," presumably parts of divinity who advise people through successions of rein-carnated universes until they attain the presence of the "Paradise Father." A central theme is the hidden years of Christ, from age twelve to His public ministry. During that time, Jesus supposedly learned to develop His psychic powers by being tutored in the East's mysticism.

Many spiritual seekers have gravitated to Urantia in search of esoteric explanations for the serious issues of life. Its presupposi-tion that man is evolved from the animal kingdom and destined to be a god fits well into New Age concepts. The longing for arcane information renders these people susceptible to Urantia's bogus offer of the "finest major divine revelation since the coming of Christ to our planet."

The Bible views very sternly the communication of spiritual information not sanctioned by the Lord. Deuteronomy 18:20 insti-tuted the death penalty for false prophets. How can they be known? "When a prophet speaks in the name of the LORD, if the thing does not happen or come to pass, that is the thing which the LORD has not spoken," Deuteronomy 18:22 states. The apostle Paul affirmed the accuracy of his teachings by warning that if "an angel from heaven, preach any other gospel to you than what we have preached to you, let him be accursed."[9] God's principle of legal judgment and spiritual jurisprudence is that every truth must be established by two or more witnesses. At Christ's baptism, the Father spoke and the Spirit descended. A supposed revelation like Urantia, which disagrees with apostolic doctrine, has no objectively verifiable corroboration.

KEYS TO UNDERSTANDING OCCULT SPIRITUALITY

An important key to unlocking the essence of an occult worldview is knowing a definition of terms like *subconscious, intuition,* and *higher self.* Occultists confuse their reference to the subconscious with biblical indications that man's conscience helps guide moral decisions. The metaphysical concept of the subconscious and the Christian concept of the conscience are incompatible. The subconscious is the collective repository of personal and sensory experiences. It is an informational "computer bank." But it has no capacity to interpret that data in a morally qualitative sense. It is spiritually neutral and an inappropriate guide to virtuous behavior. The conscience, however, can be morally quantified. When the Christian speaks of conscience, he refers to one of two inner voices, God's moral law and the indwelling Holy Spirit. Romans 2:15 speaks of God's law being written on man's heart, his "conscience also bearing witness" to the moral message of divine directive. Furthermore, it is the assignment of the Holy Spirit, speaking through conscience, to "convict the world of sin, and of righteousness, and of judgment."[10]

What we commonly call intuition is no more than feeling strongly about something without conscious reasoning. Intuition is derived from an intellectual component, as well as a composite of life experiences. Its veracity is only as good as the person's powers of judgment and reasoning. Assigning to intuition infallible attributes of deity is idolatry. Replacing the role of a transcendent supreme being with ego is arrogance of the worst sort. It also leaves the evaluation of each action up to the individual instead of an external (biblical) moral code. The idea that the soul represents a supra-consciousness of ultimate reality is derived from the notion of self-deification. If the "higher self," or soul, is a spark of the divine, it must be the embodiment of supreme truth. In contrast, Christianity teaches that God is the ultimate reality, for only He has existed from eternity past. Scripture instructs that only the character of God is immutable. Even the cosmos as we know it will disappear, and only the Word of God will endure forever.[11] To liken the attributes of God to the soul is to indulge in idolatry by exalting man's mind to the status of sacredness.

Many who flirt with occult spirituality come from a Christian background and cannot totally jettison their beliefs in Christ. Thus, they seek systems that ignore such cardinal doctrines as hell, guilt over sin, and the blood atonement of Christ while maintaining reverence for Jesus the Man. They may be attracted to teachings like *A Course in Miracles*, with its platitudes about love and forgiveness that sound somewhat Christian while ignoring Satan as a personal source of evil and the need of divine redemption.

Normal Christians with a liturgical background may gravitate toward groups like The Church Universal or Nichiren Soshu, which practice chanting and repetitive decreeing. They may end up uttering affirmations that are blasphemous, such as the "I am that I am" decree whereby one claims for himself the title of God. Those who frequently indulge in decreeing enter trance states in which they involuntarily permit entities to enter them and display spirit possession. Devotees often practice affirmations for extended periods of time, during which they experience the yogic state of disengagement from reality, making them prey for cult indoctrination. Decreeing also increases the disciple's vulnerability to thought transformation, brainwashing, and demonic control.

Certain aspects of occult spirituality adopt the concept of "ascended masters," spiritual adepts who guide those on earth. Both Hinduism and Buddhism teach that the karmic cycles of reincarnation can be ended by enlightenment. The soul may then merge completely into the godhead and thus enter a state of impersonality. Such souls may also choose to retain their individuality as a means of guiding less spiritually developed souls on earth. Spiritualist trance mediums, who prefer to identify their entities, developed this doctrine to explain why beings on the other side wish to communicate across death's gulf.

How can one know if such ascended masters are of Christ or the spirit of antichrist? The formula is simple. First John 2:22 tells us, "He is antichrist who denies the Father and the Son." Some ascended masters actually claim to be Jesus Himself. How can we know if any such personage truly is the Christ? Consider the following biblical facts. Isaiah 9:7 says Christ must belong to the house of David. Micah 5:2 says He would be born in Bethlehem. Isaiah 7:14 prophesies that Christ would be born of a virgin. In the New Testament alone, over 550 references to the Christ refer specifically to the person of Jesus of Nazareth. As to the idea that there are many Christs, John 3:16 clearly states that Jesus is God's *only* begotten Son. Jesus' words in Matthew 28:18 settle the issue: "All authority has been given to Me in heaven and on earth."

A SUMMARY OF NON-CHRISTIAN PERSPECTIVES

Two cups of hope; two cups of altered consciousness; three tablespoons each of self-awareness, self-improvement, and self-esteem; one heaping teaspoon of peace; one generous pinch of humanism, Eastern mysticism, and occultism; one handful of holism; one scoop of mystical experience. Mix thoroughly together, bake in a warm, friendly environment, fill with your most appealing dreams, garnish generously with positive thoughts and good vibrations.[12]

That's the way one writer describes the current spiritual climate of Western societies. Our world starves for the reality and love proffered but seldom delivered by great non-Christian religions. The spirituality-searching public is easy prey for the message of replacing old sentiments and modes of culture with the theme that mankind can achieve global harmony by tapping into higher consciousness.

Such gullible acceptance of failed religious systems illustrates a poor sense of history. For millennia, metaphysical ideas have been age-old ideologies in the East. The result? Immeasurable poverty, indifference to human misery, and a fatalistic outlook that awaits the justice of Karma rather than inviting immediate human compassion.

In India a deformed beggar sits indefinitely in a gutter. A female child is allowed to die. A holy man streaks his hair with cow manure. And it's all done in the name of mysticism. The explanation? The beggar's bad Karma placed him in this position, and helping him could hinder the "Great Cause" of karmic fairness. The child came into a world where females are considered less desirable than boys. The holy man believes all creatures are extensions of God. The cow is the mother of life, thus its excrement is blessed.

Occult worldviews thrive in the atmosphere of Satan's lie, "You will not surely die."[13] It has taken form in films, the holistic healing techniques of mystical medicine, and the belief in energy dualities that has invaded the halls of academia. Occult spirituality is but a stage-stop in the Aquarian quest for man's evolutionary transformation to levels of consciousness beyond evil. What the initiate fails to see is that the holding pen is a pigsty, the devil's destination.

"For many deceivers have gone out into the world who do not confess Jesus Christ as coming in the flesh," Scripture warns.[14]

Many cults today offer alternative routes to God. They tender hopes that the earth will be beautified and man's soul purified. They propose a world in which guilt, fear, and selfishness will be things of the past Picean Age, unworthy of the new spirituality. While these cults may promise godhead, they deliver only the same lie sold by Satan in Eden.

Chapter 25

The Political Significance of Occult Concepts

Science has made unrestrictive national sovereignty incompatible with human survival. The only possibilities now are world government or death" (Bertrand Russell, writer and philosopher).[1]

"Unless the concept of planetary government is universally accepted, the human race must live with the perpetual threat of nuclear extinction" ("Letters to the Editor," *Time*).[2]

"We have an obligation to expose and attack the world of Bible worship, salvationism, heaven, hell, and all the mythical deities" (*The Humanist*).[3]

"One of these days I'll be so complete I won't be human, I will be a god" (the late John Denver, singer and composer).[4]

Musician John Denver, philosopher Bertrand Russell, a letter writer from Akron, Ohio, and the editors of *The Humanist* have much in common. All have enthroned man at the center of existence, and all have concluded that nationalistic sovereignty and patriotic pride are deadly foes to be extinguished. All ascribe to a form of political and social philosophy known as globalism, a worldview propelled by occult philosophy.

Delineating a term like *globalism* isn't easy. Definitions vary from one advocacy group to another, depending on whether their primary allegiance is to scholarly interests or one-world unity concepts. Despite their differences, globalists hold certain things in common. Ethnocentricity has to go. Believing that one's religious or cultural heritage is superior is a no-no. "Equivalency" is the goal—the idea that all governments, as well as all legal, spiritual, and economic systems, deserve identical international respect.

Among one-world aspirations are abolition of the traditional family structure, an international court of law to arbitrate worldwide disputes, and a common economic structure. Global laws would abolish war, hunger, and poverty. Extreme factions even suggest that children be produced by genetic control, with fertilization and gestation occurring outside the body. Most globalists favor unilateral disarmament.

Such suggestions sound like a speech of appeasement by England's prime minister prior to World War II, Neville Chamberlain. Hitler preached a one-world message, but his hidden goal soon demonstrated that lust for political control far exceeds altruistic desire for world harmony. Permanent disarmament would be unattainable, because some despot would seize the opportunity to arm and destroy the balance of impotency. After six thousand years of civilizations' carving up territorial perimeters, it would be folly to believe war and bloodshed to acquire territory would be unselfishly surrendered.

Occult principles are a key to achieving these goals. Political practicalities are possible in any society only if a corresponding ideology provides philosophical support. Metaphysical thinking furnishes globalism with an integrated values system drawn from various mystical religious traditions. This "new" spiritual perspective would replace belief in a transcendent deity with reliance on man's inherent goodness and wisdom. To oversee this arrangement, a more liberally funded United Nations, with greater powers of police enforcement, would be established.

According to occult thought, mankind's progress toward harmonious relationships has been slowly evolving. At the dawn of this new Aquarian age, a significant step forward will be taken, allowing humanity to break through to a new spiritual consciousness, a "quantum leap" or a "paradigm shift."

GLOBAL CONSCIOUSNESS

Widespread injustice. Nuclear arsenals and warheads in waiting. Famine of measureless proportions. Mankind on the edge of time. That's the way proponents of a New World Order see our planet, a place inhabited by a dangerous species called man. What's to be done? Achieve a state of inner peace, and reconcile differing political ideologies. Meditate. Smile peacefully. Become one with your adversaries.

A Zen master puts it this way: Imagine yourself as a swimmer in a river. Then imagine yourself as the river. Become the river to understand its perspective. Then imagine yourself as a world citizen. A new understanding of political consciousness will overcome you. As each citizen of the planet follows, the world will become one.

To the mystic, all of creation is an undivided unity. They believe the Bible presents a cosmos that consists of individual personalities, a diversity of events, and material objects that exist of themselves, apart from God. Though God has a purpose for all existence, His will for each person and circumstance differs, except for the ultimate goal of bringing glory to God. More important, God's moral qualities are intrinsic to His character. Human beings are not extensions of His nature but of a differentiated essence, with the capacity of moral volition to choose sin or obedience to the Creator.

One globalist organization, the World Peace University, envisions a world where "peace is the way of life, where hunger no longer exists, and where individuals achieve their highest degree of personal fulfillment."[5]

The techniques to accomplish world peace range from so-called citizens' summitry (promoting international personal diplomacy) to visualization and affirmation methods, which pursue peace by mentally creating a state of harmony. Visualize a world in which there is no right or wrong, politically speaking. There is no other side. No enemy. No inevitability of war. The planet is one, and we are one with the planet. This physical reality must become a political reality. And these aspirations can be achieved only when mankind acquires higher consciousness. Much focus is on anti-nuclear interests, supporting establishment of nuclear-free zones, where atomic weapons, facilities, equipment, and supplies would be banned. Some even suggest that countries renounce the right to be defended by nuclear weapons.

GLOBAL HUMANISM

If occult globalists have a creed, it is the tenets of humanism. As a man-centered "religion," humanism has drawn fire from Christian parents concerned about school textbooks, and from television evangelists who see it as the enemy of Americanism and evangelicalism.

Responding to assaults on humanism by the religious right, humanists have often allied themselves with atheists, secularists, and civil libertarians. Because of their eclectic social vision, they have found friends in globalists and all those committed to the idea of planetary unity and custodianship of the earth's monetary and environmental resources.

Prominent occult theoretician Dr. Robert Muller, former secretary of the United Nations Economic and Social Council, has said, "Humanity is evolving toward a coherent global form best described by a metaphor of the human brain; each person, young or old, able-bodied or handicapped, is an important neuron in the emerging planetary brain that is constituted by the meridian net-workings among people."

Such views represent an incredible shift in the thinking of Western civilization. For several centuries, a theocentric worldview has dominated nations of the First World. Now, an anthropocentric perception of society is gaining precedence. The earth itself is seen as a kind of living organism, demanding future citizens to oppose industrial development and nuclear power.

Traditional concepts of God have no place on the agenda of New World Order proponents. The *Humanist Manifesto II* states, "As nontheists, we begin with humans, not God, nature, not deity ... no deity will save us: We must save ourselves."[6] This fits well into the framework of occult ideology, since man is perceived as a god who is capable of saving himself. Likewise, the humanist condemns diversity of worship as an impediment to progress. In fact, humanists believe all religions are a disservice to the human species. Since syncretistic spirituality wants to synthesize all religious doctrines into an eclectic system, old orders of religions would be abolished and replaced with a globalistic set of beliefs acceptable to both humanists and those with an occult perception of internationalism.

GLOBAL PANTHEISM

Globalists have also advanced the idea of a universal interdependence in which God and nature are fused into one. The groves may no longer be worshiped, but the hills and trees are revered ("resacrilized," as some put it) to the extent that man is no longer a unique moral creature. Today, a merged perception of God's being and man's existence dominates Western thought, closely resembling Hinduism. God is seen as being at one with and pervasive in all matter. Thus, moral objectives are measured by their contribution to cosmological oneness, not personal moral accountability to a transcendent Creator. And if God is not out there looking down on each person's moral conduct, then right is what each part of the one perceives right to be.

Certainly Christians should be in the forefront of environmental concerns because of the biblical principle of dominion and stewardship over the resources of earth. The biblical ethic of man being given dominion over creation is an act of trust, not folly. The Christian who understands the sacredness of this stewardship over the environment is interested in safeguarding our natural resources. But what globalists propose is quite different. They seek "resacralization" of the environment and refer to the "enchantment" of the environmental ethic. These are religious concepts compatible with a pantheistic approach. Occult environmentalists often adopt a concept similar to aboriginals, who believe earth is our mother, imbued with a sense of sacredness. In effect, the soil and vegetation become gods to be revered. This sin is referred to in Romans 1 when it speaks of unregenerate pagans who "worshiped and served the creature rather than the Creator" and thus "exchanged the truth of God for the lie."[7]

Interdependence is a commonly heard term among one-worlders. In fact, they have drafted what they call a "Declaration of Interdependence" whose stated purpose is as follows: "To establish a new world order of compassion, peace, justice, and security, it is essential that mankind free itself from the limitations of national prejudice and acknowledge that the forces that unite it are incomparably deeper than those that divide it."[8]

Futurist, architect, and inventor Buckminster Fuller once said, "Cosmic evolution is irrevocably intent upon completely transforming differently competing entities into a completely integrated, comprehensively interconsiderate, harmonious whole."[9]

Scripture tells us the spiritual whore of Mystery Babylon foretold in Revelation 17 will be the ultimate culmination of all spiritual error, led by the Beast that ascends from the bottomless pit. With its blasphemous declaration of man as a god and its espousal of occult abominations, New World Order spirituality is an excellent candidate to be this false system of worship that is the "Mother of Harlots." The final purpose of global interdependence will be to deliver to the devil a deceived generation seduced by false science and indoctrinated by spiritualist mediums who call for peace and world harmony at the sake of people's souls.

GLOBAL SOCIOLOGY

Globalism's social agenda is guided by several presuppositions that are highly amenable to occultism. First, the entire earth, including its oceans and biosphere, is seen as the common property of mankind. Because the purity of earth's water and air affect all living creatures, globalists insist that all of nature be placed under international jurisdiction. Pagans readily accept this proposition because of their pantheistic principles. To them, nature is not only interdependent but also cosmologically interrelated because of its one source. To the humanistic globalist, there is no God. All that matters is, well, matter. If "all is one," as the mystic declares, that proposition can be easily ratified by legislative powers that are internationally binding.

The philosophy of holism also underpins this social agenda. If man, nature, Mother Earth, and the entire cosmos are interconnected, national sovereignty would be antithetical. The shared experience of oneness achieved in altered states of consciousness, plus the messages of trance-channeled entities and so-called guardian angels confirm unitary awareness and global interdependence.

But history shows that interdependence destroys the healthy economic competition upon which the advances of mankind have been based. Our current quality of health care, common conveniences, and food surpluses result from global rivalry that has spurred international inventiveness and productiveness. Removing that incentive would destroy the desire to generate wealth, which fuels productivity. Failed communist economies are excellent examples of what happens when a noncompetitive marketplace exists.

The scene of social engineering is the best place to observe the mutuality of globalism and humanism. Among the items on their bilateral agenda are abolishing traditional family structures, minority rights, and universal education. As for women's rights, both tend to see our male-dominated society as stemming from the West's Judeo-Christian heritage. The new spirituality tends to be more matriarchal. Some contingencies have resurrected ancient ideas of goddess worship, tracing their devotion to such archaic deities as Diana and Aphrodite.

GLOBAL GODDESSES

Fertility cults were common in ancient agrarian societies. People were close to the earth and especially conscious of reproductive cycles in their herds and families. Fruitfulness was crucial to survival, so female-oriented nature religions flourished. Idols of Artemis were depicted with multiple mammaries to nourish life. With such matriarchal emphasis came the belief that women were unusually gifted spiritually. Male dominance as a source of spiritual guidance and creator of the species' future was a relatively new cultural phenomenon that arrived with the supremacy of Christianity in the West.

European society viewed man as the creator and mythmaker of civilization. It is men who forge the way into the wilderness of economic competition. Men wage wars and build weapons of mass destruction. It is the virility of men that emblazons the silver screen. And it is men who serve primarily as our priests and pastors.

Globalists see this as a cosmic imbalance, the reason for the nuclear precipice on which humanity hangs. They envision a world led by women, with feminine spirituality and wisdom predominating over an elevated consciousness. This synthesis of feminism and spiritual devotion is known as Womanspirit, a resurgence of the "Cosmic Mother" to her rightful place as central in the earth's religion.

Certain feminists have resurrected the mysteries of goddess worship by erecting temples to the female deities of antiquity. Others committed to a matriarchal culture have instituted wiccan celebrations and rituals to raise the vibrations of Mother Nature and to usher in the age of Womanspirit. Occult feminists look for female principles of piety in astrology, tarot, mythology, and folklore. They see mystical significance in the announcement of Christ's resurrection to two women. Ancient mysteries are searched for hidden perspectives on feminine dominance as the source of social harmony.

Ancient goddess worship cults were incredibly licentious. Temple prostitutes served as an access to the matriarchal mysteries. Sexual fertility was emphasized, and ritual intercourse was an initiatory procedure. In Aphrodite worship, virgins were inducted into the cult by being deflowered with a male statuette bearing an oversized phallus. Goddess worship demonstrates this same preoccupation with sexuality. In addition, goddess worship is based on appreciation of feminine psychic inclinations. Advocates of goddess worship often align themselves with witchcraft and have been known to declare blasphemously, "In the beginning was the goddess."

THE SPIRITUAL CONSEQUENCES OF THE NEW WORLD ORDER

Globalism is altruism in action, noble but ignoring man's ignobility. It's also old hat. It was tried by Marx, Lenin, and Stalin. Like contemporary one worlders, they, too, longed for worldwide social and political dominion. But those systems cost the lives of millions who have died in gulags of horror. Why consider a concept that erected the Berlin Wall as an "economic barrier" to prevent East Berliners from fleeing globalistic communism?

Globalists have poor memories. They forget that many of their utopian models are also molded on the Third Reich's thousand years of predicted prosperity. Do the gas ovens of Buchenwald say nothing to the humanist who professes consummate faith in man's nobility? Perhaps we should ask the Jews of the Warsaw ghetto if globalism works. Maybe we should consult the citizens of Poland and Hungary about interdependence.

Globalism superstitiously assumes that abstractly articulated ideals will somehow hold in check man's voracious greed. History attests that man yearns for individuality, not the socialized sanctity of federal domination. He yearns to be a unique creature in the scheme of the universe, not an indistinguishable part of the whole. Globalism is also monism, the doctrine that all is one and that God, man, and nature are part of the same essence. This failed philosophy has produced only hunger, violence, and overpopulation in the Eastern societies where it has predominated.

The emerging world religion accompanying the New World Order insists that all religions teach basically the same truth. If Buddha and Jesus had differences, they were accidental doctrines, since both had the same intent. The goal of globalism is to minimize distinctions between religions and humanistically focus on the man-centered aspect of all world faiths. While globalists speak romantically of one planet, one people, one government, one currency, and abounding brotherhood, the Bible promises a city where these ideas will reign for eternity—the New Jerusalem.[10] While they speak of finding enlightenment through an altered consciousness that manifests itself in a transformed social structure, Jesus declares unequivocally, "I am the way, the truth, and the life."[11]

What would mainstreaming of transcendentalism on a global scale mean? For one thing, mystical fable would become more important than verifiable reality. Tough decisions and unwanted deductions would be harder for people to handle. Cultural escapism would increase. As cases in point, imagine a spiritualist who creates his own reality as an air traffic controller or a military negotiator at a summit conference, or a committed metaphysician in charge of an atomic reactor or a critical care ward. Each of these individuals would make vital decisions without the guidance of objective criteria.

Isis, Diana, Aphrodite, Artemis, and their ilk do not represent a golden age of feminine supremacy. That conclusion ignores historical and anthropological fact. Matriarchal religions of antiquity made possible patriarchal exploitation of women. In the name of religious devotion, ritualistic sex merely excused legalized prostitution. By deifying femininity, women were demoralized and exploited. They were demoted to sex objects and childbearers without regard for true feminine self-esteem.

Jesuit philosopher Teilhard de Chardin, revered by internationalists, proposed that mankind would eventually reach an "Omega Point" at which a world consciousness would unify all individualized thought. Who would choose to live in such a homogeneous civilization? Only those who espouse political socialism. What powers of state would be required to enforce such cooperation and unselfishness? Unthinkable forces of totalitarianism. What cost to personal freedoms would be required to establish communal consciousness? Complete loss of privacy and the ability to live and travel unrestricted.

"I am the Alpha and the Omega, the Beginning and the End."[12] Christ declared mankind's Omega Point is not a convergence with cosmic consciousness. It is Judgment Day when, according to Revelation 21:8, sorcerers "shall have their part in the lake which burns with fire and brimstone." The notion of global government and unitary spiritual consciousness, with its proclivity for the occult, is sorcery of the first order, punishable by eternal condemnation.

PART V

A Survey of Demonic Activity in Our Age

Chapter 26

Harmless Deeds, Harmful Demons

Demons pop up in unlikely places for the strangest of reasons. The demons I have encountered were not usually found in large cities where sin seems to abound; they often revealed themselves in out-of-the-way places, where you'd least expect to confront such hideous evil.

One such location was a rural Canadian community known best for its wheat crops and earth-solid prairie values. One warm spring afternoon, the churches of that area banded together and invited me to address a special youth rally. What I thought would be an ordinary day turned out to be a remarkable encounter with evil.

Almost the whole town, nearly a thousand people, turned out. They sat on wooden folding chairs arranged in front of a small stage at one end of the high school basketball gymnasium. The hometown team apparently didn't draw large crowds, so the gym had been constructed with little room on the sidelines for seats. Both sides of the court came within a few feet of abutting cement-block walls.

The crowd responded to my message in a typically Canadian manner: polite and quieter than U.S. audiences and with respectful attentiveness. I spoke about young people's need to fully surrender their lives to Christ. I barely mentioned the subject of spiritual warfare, giving only a brief warning.

"Avoid the occult," I warned them. "Even a slight brush with the things of Satan can bring lasting spiritual damage to your life. Remember, the devil plays for keeps, and he's always seeking the chance to lure you into a compromising situation. I've known teenagers who became demon-possessed by doing far less than they thought would lead them to satanic bondage."

At the end of my message, I asked people to bow their heads for a closing prayer. As we did, someone screamed from the center of the congregation. I looked up to see chairs flying in every direction. The clatter as they hit the floor was like a string of firecrackers going off. Some people panicked and ran for the doors.

I focused on the cause of the disturbance. A teenager was shouting obscenities and racing around throwing chairs. He lunged at one of the cement walls and tried to scale it, clawing at the masonry with his fingernails.

A dozen or so burly farmers converged around the young man and pinned him to the gym floor. Speaking over the public address system, I asked the crowd to remain calm and told the men who had subdued the teenager to bring him forward. Then I motioned for a pastor to come near, and whispered for him to take over and dismiss the audience once I was out of the building. Meanwhile, the young man who had caused the disruption was dragged backstage, kicking and screaming.

"Is there a church nearby?" I asked. A pastor who had given the afternoon's invocation told me that the young man attended his church, and volunteered his facility. Three other pastors agreed to meet us there. One pastor commented, "The scene in the gym will probably cause the biggest uproar this town has seen since the railroad bypassed our grain silos for larger markets to the south."

We put the youngster in the backseat of a car and drove him to a white frame building several blocks from the gym. Once inside the church, the teenager continued to thrash about, spouting obscenities. Two of the more muscular pastors pinned the teenager to the church floor just in front of the first row of pews.

"Does anyone have any idea why this young man went berserk?" I asked.

"Randy is a popular kid in town," said the pastor of the church. "He's usually cruising up and down Main Street picking up girls. He's quite the lady's man."

"He's captain of the football team," another minister added. "I just don't understand what this is all about. Randy is a quiet kid. He hardly ever says anything. Why would he act like a maniac?"

Everyone agreed that the outburst back at the gymnasium was something they would never have expected of Randy. That was sufficient evidence for me, and I took action.

I walked over to Randy, whose eyes were wild and dark. His expression looked vacant. I wasted no time confronting the devil. "In the name of Jesus, I demand to know what evil spirit made Randy act as he did."

The ministers looked surprised. My unabashed bluntness stunned them. Everyone suspected Randy's actions might be demonic, but confronting the demon head-on wasn't something they would have done. They just wanted Randy to come back to his senses.

(The reaction of those clergy is typical. I often hear preachers of the gospel refer to some heinous crime or outrageous action as "demonic." Even the secular press will sometimes refer to a particularly gruesome murder as "diabolical." But such adjectives are usually linguistic trips of the tongue, with no real intent of actually diagnosing what happened as coming from a supernatural source.)

"Now wait a minute, Mr. Larson," one of the ministers interjected. "You can't just come waltzing into our town and tell us that the most popular kid in our high school is demon-possessed. Why—"

"Hang on, Hank," Randy's pastor interrupted. "You and I both know Randy is not the kind of kid who would go berserk in public and cuss like he did. Maybe Larson senses something we don't."

I did, and it was because of that look in Randy's eyes, the same one I had seen so long ago in Singapore. I immediately challenged the spirit staring at me. "I demand again to know your name. In the name of Jesus, tell me who you are!"

The men holding Randy tightened their grip. The muscles of his athletic body flexed and Randy sat up on the floor. He rose to his knees like an animal about to pounce on its prey.

Slowly and deliberately a voice came from deep within his throat. "My name is Disobedience."

"How did you enter him?"

"Through the game."

"What game?"

"I don't have to tell you!"

"You have no choice. The Lord demands that you tell me, as do all these men of God."

The spirit Disobedience glanced around the room at the ministers. He locked his eyes on each of them, trying to find one he could intimidate. In spite of their earlier skepticism, they stared back at the demon with confidence. If any one of the preachers had backed off, I don't know what might have happened.

"We rebuke you in the name of Jesus," said the pastor who had at first questioned what I was doing.

"Amen," said another.

Every pastor confirmed his agreement, which left the demon little choice. "I entered through the 'light as a feather' game," Disobedience said in disgust. "His parents told him he couldn't go out that night, but he did. He disobeyed them, and that gave me my right. Now he belongs to me."

"Spirit, I bind you in the name of Jesus. Go down. I want to talk with Randy."

The eyes of Disobedience rolled back and Randy gradually came to his senses. "What am I doing here in my church? How did I get here?" He shook his head in amazement.

After a few minutes of explaining what had happened, I confronted Randy. "Tell me about the 'light as a feather' game. When did you play it?"

"I don't know what you're referring to," he answered. "I think it's a child's game."

"What's this all about?" his pastor inquired.

"'Light as a feather' is one of those so-called parlor-room games," I explained. "Someone lies down on the floor and the others gather around the person. They put the tips of their fingers under him and chant over and over, 'You're light as a feather.' They keep doing it until they lift him in the air. Sometimes they actually hold him over their heads."

Another pastor broke in. "Are you sure it isn't just a matter of the weight distribution on their fingertips?"

I shook my head. "That's what most people think. They suppose it's some principle of physics. But I've talked to scores of people who have done this, and everyone has told me they felt no real pressure on their fingertips. The person they were lifting really did feel light as a feather."

"I remember!" Randy said. "I played it when I was five or six ... Yeah, I was six. My parents told me I had to stay home that night, but I sneaked out after dark. I met some of my friends in the park and someone said he had seen other kids lift a guy into the air. I thought it was a really cool thing to do. It worked."

Randy jerked. His head snapped back, then forward. "Of course it did," Disobedience said. "But even if you get rid of me, it won't do any good. I may be the gatekeeper who let all the others in, but I'm not the one who keeps all of us here. And you'll never know who he is."

"Spirit, I bind you in Jesus' name, and I command that angels hold you in torment until such time as God has revealed how we can get rid of all of you. Go down, now!"

Disobedience offered little resistance. He was convinced that we wouldn't find the clue to how he and the other demons had managed to hold Randy under their control all these years.

I asked a couple of the pastors to stay near Randy and make sure he didn't try to run away. Then I called the others aside and discussed what had happened.

"Do any of you have an idea what else he might be involved in?" I asked.

They looked at one another for some recollection. His pastor declared that Randy attended church faithfully, always got good grades in school, and never gave anyone any trouble.

"The most striking thing about him is his popularity—and his car," his pastor said.

Something quickened in me at that statement. "His car?"

"Yes, Randy is always driving up and down Main Street, showing off his car. I suppose it's not much by big-city standards, but around here it's the best car any kid has. Bright red with fancy spiked hubcaps. Randy washes it almost every day, and waxes it once a week. Yup, he's more proud of that car than any teenager I've ever seen."

"What's he like when he's not driving his car?"

Randy's pastor thought for a moment. "Now that you mention it, he's a different person. Randy's a shy boy. He comes from a poor family; he worked hard to get the car. I suppose that driving it makes him feel special."

I had heard enough. The Holy Spirit had led me to figure out how the demons maintained control over Randy, but I needed to test my theory to prove that God really had disclosed the key to Randy's deliverance.

I motioned for the pastors to follow me to the front of the church. Randy was now sitting on the pew, breathing heavily.

Perspiration dripped from his brow. He grimaced and seemed to be in some kind of pain.

"Randy," I said, "if you want to be free from the demons who have you, there's only one way. You've got to give up your car."

"No! I won't do that!"

It was Randy speaking, not the demon, and I knew I had hit the most spiritually sensitive area of his life. "That car is an idol, and God will have no other gods before Him. If you want to be free, you've got to put the Lord first in your life."

"But He is," Randy argued. "What's my car got to do with it?"

"Randy, I don't want to talk to you now. Please cooperate with me. I call forth the spirit whom God has called to judgment, the spirit that controls Randy because of his car."

Randy looked at his pastor, who nodded his head. "Go on Randy. Do what Mr. Larson tells you to do."

Randy put his face in his hands. As he did, his body stiffened again, and his head pulled back. A demon manifested, but it wasn't Disobedience.

"You're the demon who has entered from Randy's obsession with his car, aren't you?"

"Maybe. What of it?"

"Do you want to be tormented like Disobedience, or are you going to cooperate?"

"I saw what you did to him. Just leave me alone. This body is mine. He wants me."

"Why? Because you help him become somebody he wouldn't be otherwise?"

"That's my function."

"And what's your name? Tell me before I call on the angels of the Lord to smite you."

"Nooooo! I'll tell you. My name is Pride."

"Are you chief among your kind?"

"Yes."

"And who is Disobedience?"

"He came in first and let the rest of us in. He's the gatekeeper. But you can't get rid of me. Randy likes me. I help him meet girls and stay popular off the football field. Because of me it doesn't matter that his parents are poor. When the two of us are in that car, he's the king of the road!"

Pride seemed calm and unperturbed, confident of his control over Randy. This story might have ended there except that God showed me what to do next.

I called Randy out of the trance and asked him to step forward with me to the altar rail at the front of the church. I told him to kneel in front of it, and I told his pastor to kneel on the other side of the rail, facing him. I asked the rest of the pastors to stand behind Randy and pray for what was about to happen.

"Do you have the keys to your car?" I asked Randy.

"Yes, in my pocket."

"Take them out and hold them in your hands."

Randy reached into his jeans and pulled out the keys. He clenched them tightly in his right fist.

"Randy, there's only one way you can be free from these demons. You have to donate your car to the church so it can be sold and the money given to missionaries. If you'll do that, give the keys to your pastor. You've got to be willing to walk the streets in humility until your pastor says you've made enough spiritual progress to drive again."

Randy tensed, but this time it wasn't the demon's reaction. His body shook almost uncontrollably, and he began sobbing. He buried his face in his hands. His right fist clenched the keys tighter and tighter.

"It's not fair! Other kids come from homes they can be proud of. Their moms and dads are important. My folks are just poor farmers. All my life the other kids made fun of me. It wasn't until I got that car that things were different."

He wept until I thought he would collapse on the floor. Then he slowly regained composure. "Mr. Larson, if you say this is what

God wants me to do, I'll do it. I won't like it, but I don't want these evil things inside me anymore." Randy lowered his head in prayer. "God, forgive me. Take this pride from me. I surrender it to You."

Randy reached forward with his right arm toward his pastor. The pastor put out his hands, and Randy's fist hovered over them. Slowly Randy's hands opened. Seconds later the edge of the key chain dangled from his fingers, then a portion of the key emerged.

"Pride, I command that you attach to yourself Disobedience and all others under your control," I said. "When you leave, you will take them with you and go to the pit!"

When at last the keys fell from Randy's hand, he screamed and fell back on the floor in violent convulsions. I motioned for the pastors to stand back. The struggle we all witnessed was a battle for Randy's soul, waged over a set of car keys.

With one final hideous scream, Randy fell limp.

Innocuous Actions, Destructive Demons

As I stated earlier, when it comes to demonic matters, *what you don't know can hurt you*. Some sincere exorcists make the mistake of attempting deliverance on the assumption that you can only become demon-possessed by deliberately committing a grievous sin. Consequently they base their approach on getting the person to confess the premeditated transgression that allowed the demons to enter. These well-meaning exorcists aren't aware that demons don't always need a volitional sin to invade someone. In fact, most of those I've met who were demon-possessed had no idea they had done something that brought them into spiritual bondage.

Consider the case of Sally, a woman in her mid-twenties whom I counseled. She had a demon of hatred that caused her to self-mutilate. Her arms were covered with the scars of countless self-inflicted wounds. "I don't want to cut my body," she pleaded to me tearfully, "but I often return to consciousness from a trance to find my arms covered in blood."

What led to her desperate circumstance? One day Sally decided to read her newspaper horoscope out of curiosity. That day's prediction seemed to come true, so she began to read her astrology charts every day. Eventually, a demon of divination entered her. During the exorcism I performed on Sally, I argued with the demon about his right to possess her because of such a relatively harmless act.

"Millions of people read their horoscopes every day and never become demon-possessed," I said to the demon.

The demon gave me a self-satisfied look. "You're right," the spirit agreed, "but she disobeyed what the Bible says about astrology, and that's all we needed!"

"But she wasn't a Christian. She didn't even know that the Bible condemns astrology."

"That doesn't matter! What she did let us in. We only need a sin the size of the head of a pin to enter. Give us any excuse, and we'll come in."

The fact that Sally's demon said he only needed a small sin to possess her shouldn't make us fearful that every sin of omission could lead to demonic possession. Instead, it serves as a warning to walk closely to the Lord and avoid evil at all costs. We should also pray proactively with faith, constantly seeking the Lord to keep us from temptation.

Randy became demon-possessed as the result of an act of childhood curiosity, nothing more. There was no desire on his behalf to serve Satan. Though Randy's occult act wasn't intentional, he suffered the same consequence as if he had been voluntarily seeking Satan.

A naive or seemingly harmless motive is no assurance of spiritual safety. The maxim "Ignorance is no excuse for breaking the law" is as true in the spiritual realm as it is in our physical world. It does no good for a motorist to argue he didn't know what the speed limit was if the patrolman's radar gun caught him speeding. Likewise, violating God's prohibitions about entertaining the occult exacts a spiritual penalty, regardless of whether or not the offender consciously knew that he was doing wrong.

Satan seeks every advantage to overcome any resistance that our human willpower might impart. One of the best ways is by tricking people into doing things they consider spiritually innocuous. Here are a few examples. Susan was fourteen years old when she was given a Ouija board for her birthday. She thought it was just a clever game to find out the future. Andy was sixteen when he became engrossed with the game Dungeons & Dragons. He thought it was a fascinating way to use his imagination to choose characters who could cast spells. Patricia, a twelve-year-old, invited friends to her house for a slumber party where they held séances and stared at candles to talk to the dead.

Susan, Andy, and Patricia became unwitting participants in occult sins. Not one of them wanted a demon, asked for a demon, or were aware when a demon entered them. However, in a spiritual sense they were guilty and thus became open to demonic intrusion. Each of them came to me for help. Over time, through the process of several exorcisms, they were all freed.

If we humans were genuinely aware of who Satan really is and what his true motives are, none of us would toy with the occult. The evil one knows this, so he lures people into situations where they unwittingly become vulnerable to his deception through all sorts of seduction. Then Satan has them where he wants them. He makes them feel powerful, as though they are beating the spiritual odds by doing something God has forbidden without suffering any immediate negative consequences. Many consult psychics, astrologers, and fortune-tellers. They follow New Age trance channelers because they think such phenomena are spiritually harmless, and even helpful.

In Randy's case, he appeared to be innocent on two counts. First, his sin permitting demonic entry was committed while he was a child under the age of moral accountability. Second, he had no occult purpose in his actions. How could Satan possess him?

Most Christians fail to view the battle for souls as a spiritual struggle based on exacting rules of procedure, established at the dawn of creation. The devil is like a lawyer in a cosmic courtroom, arguing his case where God is the judge, eternity is at stake, and the stiffest sentence is banishment forever from the presence of God.

Unfortunately we assume that the spiritual universe functions on a basis of impartiality. If God is just, we reason, surely He won't allow a demon to take advantage of childhood innocence.

HOW THE DEVIL GOT IN MAY NOT BE HOW HE STAYS

Another lesson I learned from Randy is that the spiritual reason that allows a demon access to an individual may not be the demon's means of remaining there. Randy's demon of disobedience entered because of the "light as a feather" game. The demon stayed there because of his pride.

When a demon enters, he immediately embarks on a plan for further demonic invasion. The spirit will tempt the person to commit other sins that in turn allow other demons to enter. As the number of demons grows, they set out to dismantle the spiritual boundaries in the person. In the place of moral consciousness, the demons establish an infrastructure of evil. Like a cancer spreading from one organ to another, the spiritual malignancy extends to every vulnerable aspect of the person's spirit, soul, and body. Often the victim descends to depths of moral depravity that would have been unthinkable prior to the possession of evil spirits.

One person I met, named Larry, was an example of this. Larry grew up in a home devoid of affection from his father, and he became inordinately attached to his mother. His obsessive anger toward his father eventually allowed a demon of rebellion to enter him. Once inside Larry, Rebellion recognized his victim's emotional condition as the perfect setup for a companion spirit of homosexuality. Larry's homosexual lifestyle wasn't the original reason he became possessed; it was the by-product of a long history of internal spiritual decline.

Larry's story makes this point: The counselor seeking to free one from demons should always look for the root sin that led to the initial possession. It may not be obvious. Focusing on other demons that manifest more violent and offensive behavior may be concentrating on a symptom of the victim's spiritual condition rather than its foundational cause. As in Randy's case, both the sin of original entry of Rebellion and the emotional factors that allowed Homosexuality to control him needed to be addressed before Larry was free.

DELIVERANCE

Many people have strange ideas about deliverance from demons. Hollywood and horror books evoke images of a minister in a clerical collar, waving a crucifix and slinging holy water. Those involved are usually depicted as fearful and hysterical. The victim is generally caricatured as hideous and insane, spitting green pea soup and vaulting about the room as if he were catapulted on a supernatural trampoline. The final stage of the struggle is seen as a conflict between the exorcist and the demon.

This fictitious portrayal hides one of the devil's best-kept secrets: The real battle is between the demon and the victim's will. The exorcist is a representative of God, just coaching the proceedings. He may guide the steps of the procedure, but the decisive contest is based on the victim asserting his will to be free. This can be accomplished by the victim's verbal confession of repentance, followed by his spoken command for the demon to leave.

CASTING OUT A DEMON BY AN ACT OF SELF-DELIVERANCE

My use of the term *self-deliverance* has no relationship to the abhorrent use of these words by euthanasia advocates as a euphemism for *suicide*. I'm referring to a process of deliverance that requires less involvement by the principal exorcist. The victim's spiritual growth is sufficient to resist Satan, and all he needs is prayerful assistance and minimal instruction.

The number of victims able to achieve self-deliverance is small. This rare occurrence takes place when weak demons hang on for some undetected reason. The victim, meanwhile, grows spiritually in God's grace. All that's left to accomplish spiritual wholeness is a final expulsion of minor demonic intruders. Deliverance may come without the victim even knowing it immediately, but definite changes will result.

Roberta had been victimized by a satanic cult and came to me for help. I ministered to her for several months and performed at least a dozen exorcisms. All the evil spirits were driven out, except for a small circle of demons that functioned to make Roberta spiritually insecure. Whenever I tried to cast them out, they claimed the right of Roberta's failure to fully trust in her position as a believer.

I spent many hours going through the Scriptures, reminding Roberta of who she was in Christ. I pointed out that the power of Christ's resurrection had raised her spiritually so that she was made to sit in the heavenly places in Christ Jesus (Eph. 2:6). I emphasized Roberta's completeness in Jesus, according to Colossians 2:10. I also encouraged her to believe she could do anything through Christ (Phil. 4:13) and asked her to exert her authority as a believer (Luke 10:19) to stand up to the devil (James 4:7).

Roberta took these lessons to heart and applied them every day. I didn't see her for nearly a year, and when I met with her again, she asked me to see if any spirits were present. Carefully I went through every testing procedure I knew that would arouse and detect demons. From all I could tell at that moment, all the demons were gone.

"I knew it in my heart," Roberta told me, "but it made me feel better to confirm it." Then she explained something peculiar. "I was in church one Sunday morning. I think it was during the time we sing praise choruses. I suddenly felt a sick feeling in my stomach. For a moment I thought I was going to throw up. Then, whatever was in my stomach rose through my chest and into my mouth. The nausea subsided and I yawned. It was a most unusual yawn—not like when one is sleepy. It was as if I had to open my mouth and let something out. At that instant I knew I had gotten rid of those demons."

She went on. "There was a momentary, stabbing pain in my throat and it was over. I know this sounds strange, but I felt as if a ton of weight left my body. In fact, when I got home from church I got out my bathroom scale to see if I'd lost any pounds. I hadn't, of course, but the sensation of weight loss was so real I had to check."

Not every victim of demon possession can be as spiritually successful as Roberta, nor will they experience the same things in the process of relief. Yet I believe more people could be freed if those who seek to deliver them would take the time to minister God's Word effectively. Self-deliverance can be a reality, but it takes time and patience. The benefit is that those who have been self-delivered have a greater possibility of keeping their freedom, because they are less likely to fall back into the same sins that held them in bondage.

CASTING OUT A DEMON BY MODIFIED SELF-DELIVERANCE

Randy was an example of what I call modified self-deliverance. When the final victory came, it wasn't necessary for me to engage in a lengthy dialogue with the demons to verbally command their departure. I did have to tell Randy what to do, and those gathered with us interceded in prayer to create an atmosphere of faith that weakened the evil spirits. When Randy dropped those keys into his pastor's hands, it was the unspoken equivalent of an oral rebuke, denying the demons inside him any further right to stay.

Modified self-deliverance is an approach that involves the will and verbal stand of the victim. It may entail leading the victim in specific prayers, and encouraging the person to make confessional decisions that will break the hold of certain sins. The reward is seeing the one victimized by the devil exercise moral fortitude to claim his own freedom in the name of Jesus!

DEMONIC HINDRANCES TO DELIVERANCE

Most victims of demons are unable to do what Randy did. The spirits' hold is so strong that any attempt by the victim to resist them is met with a severe counterattack. There are several common methods used by demons. One is putting the person into a demonic trance. In this condition a demon manifests and dominates the victim's consciousness so he or she cannot speak or think. Demons also employ distraction techniques such as mental fogging to diminish clarity of thought or the infliction of intense pain, which breaks the victim's concentration.

Certain demons actually go by the name Blocker, which also describes their function. I have dealt with hundreds of demons like this. They belong to a category of evil spirits whose sole purpose is to hinder the progress of the exorcism. They may make the person mute, so he cannot respond to inquiries or pray against the demons. Other blockers will make the victim temporarily blind, which creates a terrifying experience. One blocker I encountered induced a condition of paralysis.

Some demons can produce a comatose state. I have actually dealt with a blocker demon that went by the name Coma. He was not the most powerful demon, but he had a crucial function. In fact, I was unable to deal with any other demon as long as he was around. Whenever I tried to confront a demon in this system, Coma would manifest and literally place the victim in a comatose state.

Once when Coma took over, a medical physician confirmed the true comatose condition. This tactic not only blocked my access to the chief demons I needed to cast out, it also delayed my ability to help. The demon knew the limitations of my busy schedule and would taunt me by threatening to black out his victim and waste what time I did have.

The casting out of Coma came under most unusual circumstances. In the midst of profound frustration, God reminded me of the account in 1 Kings 17, when Elijah revived the widow's son. Verse 17 says the son was so sick "there was no breath left in him." Apparently he had entered some kind of death state, perhaps a comatose condition. The Bible says Elijah "stretched himself out on the child three times" and prayed. Then "the soul of the child came back to him, and he revived" (v. 22).

During the exorcism of Coma, I asked the two ministers who were assisting me, "This may sound bizarre, but I want you to pray earnestly while I stretch myself out over this man three times, just like Elijah did. Help me lay him on the floor, and I'll hold myself up by my fingers and toes over his body. By faith let's believe that our trust in God's Word is going to defeat Coma."

When I stood to my feet after the third time, Coma manifested in a state of rage. I knew by his fury that his right to continue inducing comatose states had been broken, and he was promptly cast out. We were then able to move on to deal with the more important demons who were there by spiritual rights. We had overcome the forces of evil.

THE JOY OF FREEDOM

That spring afternoon in the rural Canadian community Randy claimed such freedom. After he gave those car keys to his pastor, the pastor knelt by Randy's side and prayed softly. "Lord, fill Randy with Your Holy Spirit and make him more of a man than he ever was. Whatever that car meant to him, I ask You to be that and more to him. In place of the pride of Satan, place a humble spirit in his heart that will make him love You more than all the possessions in this world."

It was a benediction to a battle this rural Canadian community wouldn't soon forget. A son in their city had been set free.

Chapter 27

The Power of the Devil

Maria, a sixteen-year-old teenager, left a lasting impression on me. She wore Coke bottle-thick eyeglasses because she was legally blind, and even with those glasses she could only make out shadowy images. She approached me after a church service to ask some questions about her spiritual condition.

As we began talking about some of the problems in her life, the demonic spirit came forth and verbally challenged me. I called for the pastor who led us into his office where we were soon joined by Maria's father.

I was pleased her father could be involved in the experience. Whenever I am dealing with a minor, I always try to include the parents. This serves two purposes. First, it enhances the follow-up because the parents understand more clearly how their child became subjected to evil forces, so they know how to pray for and spiritually encourage their child. Second, parents have a God-given authority to rebuke a demon, which may have greater effectiveness than that of an experienced exorcist.

The extraordinary thing about Maria's demon was the way he expressed himself. He would move Maria's right arm slowly toward her face, grasp her glasses, and take them off. Because he didn't need glasses, he could not see through the heavy lenses.

In fact, the first time the spirit manifested, he spoke with disgust. "I hate these things," he said, pointing to the glasses. "I can't see a thing when she has them on."

"You don't need them to see?" I asked.

"Of course not," the spirit replied, insulted by my question. "It's the only thing I hate about being in this body. I have to put up with her eyesight!"

I reached for a nearby Bible, randomly selected a page, and laid the text on Maria's lap. "Read this," I said.

"Well, I hate reading *that* book, but if it's all you've got . . ." The spirit rolled his eyes in exasperation and proceeded to read the entire page. He paused every few seconds and looked up with a smirk, as if he were pleased to demonstrate that he wasn't limited by Maria's eyesight. Under his control, Maria's eyes functioned with 20/20 vision!

Normally a demon detests the Word of God, but this demon was so proud of his ability to see through Maria's eyes, he somehow overcame his revulsion to Scripture.

Maria's case raises important questions. Can an evil spirit overtake the faculties of a victim and manifest his presence in place of their neurosensory responses? Just what can Satan do, and what can't he do?

What the Devil Cannot Do

CAN DEMONS INVADE THE SPIRIT OF A CHRISTIAN?

When I first became involved in exorcisms, I assumed that a Christian was immune from the torment of demons. I based that assumption on the influence of other Christian leaders who convinced me of this. I had perfected the logic explaining my position:

"The Holy Spirit and an evil spirit can't dwell in the same vessel." "Light and darkness cannot coexist." "Those who cast demons out of Christians are making excuses for sin problems."

I had even given messages to large audiences, boldly declaring that the very idea of a Christian having a demon was heresy. I insisted that Christians claiming to have demons were making excuses for problems of carnality or personal lack of discipline; they were avoiding the tough part of growing in grace and maturing in a deeper understanding of Scripture.

I overcame this theological prejudice when I agreed to pray with a woman named Audrey. She claimed to be a Christian, but said she had demons. I thought perhaps Audrey wasn't sure what it meant to be a Christian. During our discussion several demons manifested. One was a spirit of death. It overtook her, and she looked as though she were comatose. She was lying rigidly on the floor with her hands stiff against her sides. A pastor and I tried to make her as comfortable as possible. We watched to make sure she was breathing. Her pulse slowed until she only wheezed small spurts of breath. I believed that she was going to die if we didn't intervene.

For several hours we maintained a vigil of prayer until Audrey's pulse and breathing were restored and she regained consciousness. I was puzzled. How could a Christian have a demon and be pushed to the point of death? I wasn't sure how to pray for her because I was confused that darkness and light could dwell together.

After Audrey regained consciousness I interrogated the demon. "What part of her do you possess?"

"I don't have her spirit, that belongs to God. But I do have her body. I entered into her before she became a Christian, when she was involved in the occult."

The demon spat, growled, and taunted me, knowing I was unsure of myself. But I took control with the authority of Christ and within two hours I had cast out Death and the other spirits who entered with him. Audrey rededicated her life to Christ and has never again been affected by this life-threatening spirit.

After that experience I began searching the Word of God more diligently about the matter of demons influencing Christians. I discovered that the issue wasn't as conclusive as I had thought. Gradually I understood that my error was based on a narrow understanding of demonic phenomena, and a predetermined reading of Scripture. In my honest moments of contemplation, I realized that those pastors and Bible teachers who had repeatedly reinforced the "Christian can't have a demon" outlook had very little practical experience with the phenomenon. I concluded that, while doctrine is not based on experience, the lack of experiential testimony about such a crucial area of spiritual deliverance was a glaring weakness.

As I began to discuss the subject with others, I learned that theological sentiments are often based on extreme examples Almost everyone opposed to the idea of Christians having a demon could relate one or more horrific stories about exorcism session in which Christians were encouraged to think of their spiritual failures as having a demonic root. They were then told to vomit up demons of everything from morning sickness to nasal congestion—seriously! I had witnessed some of these deliverance sessions. Highly manipulative evangelists preyed on distraught and gullible people who were looking for a quick solution to their spiritual and physical misery.

I have since learned the simple truth that when you belong to God, what Satan cannot invade is your *spirit*. The moment a person is born into the kingdom of God by faith in Christ (Eph. 2:8–9), the spirit is eternally reborn and belongs to God. Jesus declared in John 10:28 that no one has the power to "snatch" us out of God's hand. However, man is a tripartite being (1 Thess. 5:23), and there are aspects of the human condition that Satan *can* afflict. While he is prohibited from touching the spirit of God's saints, nothing prevents him from tormenting the body and soul—if the disobedient conduct of a Christian allows him to do so.

Much confusion about this issue exists because of the use of the word *possession*. The term doesn't appear in the original Greek language of the New Testament. Bible scholars say those who translated the King James edition added this word in order to classify varying degrees of demonic control. More correctly, the words translated "possession" should simply be rendered "demonized," that is, under the influence of a demon. Attempting to be verbally precise about such a supernatural phenomenon is pointless. You can't take something enshrouded in a mystical context and reduce it to a paradigm of human language. That's why we must cautiously use terms associated with demons.

I do use the words *possession, oppression,* and *obsession* to describe varying degrees of control. By *possession* I mean that the spirit is internalized and claims certain legal rights to invade the person's body. Demonic possession never means a Christian's regenerated spirit has been invaded or that the demon owns the human being. It means that his or her soul or body is influenced by a demon. The demon can manifest through the host's faculties—that is see with the eyes, speak through the vocal cords, and even subject the person to a trance state of mental oblivion. Deliverance comes when the demon inside is cast outside.

Oppression occurs when a demon has not entered the victim and cannot manifest through the victim's neurosensory system. It's as if the spirit were sitting on the person's shoulder, constantly harassing him or her, trying to push all the right buttons to make the person do his bidding.

Obsession describes a condition of slightly less control. The spirit can't influence his victim quite as easily as with oppression, but his leverage still exceeds that of "normal" temptations and urges. In both oppression and obsession, freedom comes, not by exorcism, but by a binding of the demon, subjecting it to restraint by a command in Christ's authority.

What about those instances in which a demon manifests in a Christian? In most cases the demon entered before the believer's conversion to Christianity, and the evil spirit continued to control some part of the person's life because the specific occult sin was never renounced. The demon claims squatter's rights.

The metaphor of what happens when territory is conquered in a war applies here. Even though the conflict may be officially ended, enemy snipers refuse to surrender, so they must be hunted down. Their right to remain may be technically voided since the territory is under new control, but that doesn't mean they leave automatically or give up easily. An offense must be mounted to enforce the terms of victory. The exorcist must diligently pursue every avenue of deliverance to be certain that every demonic influence has been conquered.

In this book I have used the term *legal right* with a very specific definition. I am not referring to any spiritually lawful power over a Christian's spirit that a demon may claim. The cross of Christ has canceled Satan's legal rights to the believer. Evil spirits that demonize Christians are invaders, intruding where they do not belong; they have no authority to remain. By legal I mean a spiritual technicality whereby demons argue the letter of the law, presuming that their resistance is legitimate. In a certain sense, their claim is more literally *moral* than *legal*. However, because of the sense of exacting assertion suggested by the word *legal*, I am using it as a way to emphasize the lawyerly manner in which the exorcist must approach whatever claims on the victim the demon may illegitimately avow.

CAN DEMONS FORCE THEIR WILL UPON YOU?

Those unacquainted with spiritual warfare may assume that demonic possession reduces victims to a zombielike state. In this condition, they are slaves to whatever the demon desires. This is not the case.

Satan cannot force his will upon anyone. His only power is the power of persuasion. Even in the worst cases of demonic possession, the evil spirits never totally control the wills of their victims at all times. I once dealt with a man who had committed murder in the name of Satan. In spite of his morally degenerate condition, he had lucid spiritual moments when we had profound discussions about the condition of his soul. Eventually he was able to call upon the Lord for salvation. After this, the demons were cast out easily because he had forcefully exercised his will against them.

In another situation a woman had ascended to the highest ranks of black magic in a satanic cult. To ensure her status she had committed heinous atrocities and had even consented to the human sacrifice of her best friend in order to save her own life.

In the beginning of my dealings with her, spirits would immediately place her in a trance whenever the name of Christ was mentioned. Sometimes it took hours of prayer and fasting to bring her out of the trance. She often lost days at a time when she had no recollection of where she had been or what she had done.

Yet there was a small part of her that Satan was unable to completely overpower. That part grew stronger and stronger as she spent time in prayer and God's Word. Bit by bit, she overcame the darkness with Light, and was able to have lengthier conversations about spiritual matters. After months of encouragement, she completed a prayer of commitment to Christ.

I always tell those bound by demons to call upon that small portion of their will that is not dominated by the devil. In every case, if the victim truly wanted to withstand Satan's power, he or she was able to do so. No matter how evil a person has been, God sovereignly preserves a part of the person's soul. When they respond to God's truth, they are freed from bondage.

CAN DEMONS PHYSICALLY AFFLICT A CHRISTIAN?

To answer the question of whether a Christian can be physically afflicted, we must first explore the means by which demons influence Christians.

Do Christians sin? Of course. First John 1:8–9 says we do. We cannot continue to abide in sin because of the indwelling nature of Christ. Note, however, that in Ephesians 4:23 Christians are admonished to "be renewed in the spirit of your mind." If the mind of the Christian needs renewal, then it stands to reason that when our minds are not renewed, they may be, to some degree, under the control of ungodly forces.

"Present your bodies a living sacrifice," we read in Romans 12:1. This means our bodies may not be completely sacrificed to God, and could therefore be influenced by Satan. The lack of spirituality in the life of a Christian doesn't necessarily mean he or she is possessed. But it does mean that some part of the Christian's nature is open to evil forces.

In Luke 13:16, Christ cast a demon out of "a daughter of Abraham." It's true she wasn't living under the covenant of grace this side of the Cross, but as an Old Testament devotee of God she was spiritually protected by the best that God could offer that side of Calvary. Yet a spirit of physical infirmity demonized her.

In fact the first demon that Jesus cast out came from an apparently devout Jew in the synagogue on the Sabbath. Christ's first exorcism was in a church! The man in Luke 4:33–35 was certainly "possessed," because the demon spoke through his body. Christ told the unclean spirit to "come out of him" (v. 35).

CAN SATAN TAKE YOUR LIFE?

In spite of all that God allowed Job to suffer at the hands of the devil, the Lord drew the line at Job's life. ("Behold, he is in your hand, but spare his life" [Job 2:6].) I have had my own life threatened many times by demons. They have repeatedly told me that my intervention to free souls from Satan would cost me my life. Once it almost did.

During an exorcism, an individual in a demonic trance materialized a knife and pointed it at my throat. (I recognized the knife as the one I kept in a drawer in my office, fifteen miles away! This person hadn't been to my office, and certainly wouldn't have known where the knife was kept.)

I stood motionless as the sharp point of the blade pressed against the skin at my neck and was poised to pierce my Adam's apple. A momentary thrust forward with the blade would have ended my life. There was no question in my mind that the demon fully intended to slit my throat.

Others who were there to assist in the exorcism could not come to my aid because they were afraid the person would kill me. They silently prayed for God's intervention on my behalf, but they stood perfectly still.

The demon pushed me toward a wall until my back was flat against it, with nowhere to turn. "Where is your God now?" the spirit taunted me. "I'm going to kill you and prove that your God isn't as powerful as you say He is. If God is all you claim He is, I wouldn't have this knife at your throat!"

In that moment, as I faced certain death at the hands of a demon, a supernatural composure came over me. "I don't know if God will let you kill me," I responded, "but I do know this. If God allows you to cut my throat, you will. If He doesn't, you won't. Whether or not you kill me is in God's hands, not yours."

The demon's eyes flared ever brighter. He seemed furious that I wasn't pleading for my life.

"We can make a deal," he offered. "I'll spare your life if you back off and leave us alone."

The spirit slowly twisted the point of the blade, and I felt it bore slightly into my skin, piercing the flesh. If I have ever been tempted to reach an accommodation with a demon, that was it. But I knew better. Many people had cautioned me about dealing with demons, fearful my life would be endangered. I had always told them, "The safest place in the world is in the center of God's will. That is the one place where the devil can't harm you." Now my faith in God's Word and His protection was being put to the test.

I have no idea how long I stood immobilized. I suppose it was seconds, though it felt like hours. Beads of perspiration formed on my brow as I quietly prayed. I felt the hands of the demon-possessed person begin to shake, and I wondered if the unsteady way he held the knife might cause him to injure me even if he didn't kill me. I thought of trying to call the person out of the trance, but I determined that even if I were successful, the shock he would experience could thrust his arm forward.

My mind raced. *What if he falls off balance? Suppose he hears a noise or something startles him and his arm jerks forward?*

In the midst of my speculation, unseen hands seemed to restrain the arm of the demon and then pull him backward. As the knife withdrew, I let out a deep sigh. The person suddenly returned from the demonic trance, horrified to find he was holding a knife to my throat. Slowly he stepped back and lowered his arm. I quickly grabbed his wrist and forced the knife to the ground.

God did not allow my life to be taken, but He permitted me to reach the brink of death. My faith was tested to the limit. At that moment I learned that faith isn't a presumptuous conclusion about what we hope God will or will not allow. Rather it is a quiet trust that no matter what God permits the devil to do, He is in ultimate control.

I didn't die that day because my life was in the Lord's hands. The day of my departure from this earthly vessel is appointed by Him. No demon can usurp that authority. When we walk in God's will and seek to acknowledge Him in all our ways, He directs our path. If I had died at the hands of that demon, it wouldn't have been because the demon outsmarted or overwhelmed the Holy Spirit. It would have been because God, in some mysterious way, had chosen to call me home in that fashion.

In almost every exorcism I have conducted, the demons have threatened to kill their victims. Often this threat is made to intimidate the exorcist, in hope the fear of such a tragedy will make him back away. Yet, in the hundreds of exorcisms in which I have been involved, I have never known a victim of demons to be killed or permanently harmed. Just the opposite usually occurs. The threats of the demons have proved to be hollow in the presence of God's glory.

WHAT THE DEVIL *CAN* DO

SATAN CAN DELIVER THE GOODS

Satan's powers of temptation are his most irresistible lure, and he isn't always bluffing. Many times he can fulfill what he pledges. In Matthew, chapter 4, Jesus didn't dispute the tempter's claims of worldly domination. Satan offered Jesus all the kingdoms of this world, and Christ tacitly acknowledged the devil's ability to fulfill that bid.

I've known people possessed by demons who supplied them with drugs, sex, money, and a host of other evils. "Serve me," Satan said, "and all this will be yours." They served him, and he delivered. But that delivery was for a moment and for a huge price. No sinful satisfaction is forever, and the cost is immeasurable. What Lucifer offers in one realm, he extracts at a horrible price in another. People will make compromises with their souls for the most base of reasons.

For example, Marlene was a victim of multiple sclerosis and was confined to a wheelchair. She wanted to walk, but her disease left her unable to control most of her muscles. In desperation she called on the devil. "If God won't heal me, Satan can have my life!" she declared in a fit of rage one day.

Her proposition gave demons the right to possess her. One night I watched her, under demonic control, get out of her wheelchair, walk across a room, and attack two men who were praying for her freedom. While this was happening, she was aware enough to realize Satan had partially made good on his bargain. The devil allowed her to walk—at the price of possession.

We struggled for hours to convince Marlene she had to fully renounce her pact with Lucifer. Part of her wanted to, but another part was gratified that the demons made her muscles capable of doing what they couldn't do naturally. Eventually, I stopped the exorcism because Marlene was not cooperating fully, and I determined we were wasting our time. Victims of possession can only be freed if they truly want liberation at any cost. Any unwillingness to relinquish a benefit the demon appears to give will be a foothold for the demon to continue his activities.

I've prayed for Marlene since then, and I hope she's been freed; but I've never forgotten that she was willing to spend an eternity in hell for exchange for a few moments of walking.

Not everyone's situation is as dramatic as Marlene's. I have known cases of possession in which Satan bargained with people who were timid and offered them an extroverted personality. Others who had been rejected found acceptance in a satanic cult. Or physically unattractive people have suddenly found themselves desired by cult members. But in every case, the trade-off was at a terrible consequence.

Satan cannot truly give what he promises. And he can't make people accept the terms of his contract. He can only allure with assurances of the forbidden. On occasion, one may taste the fruit of his temptation, as Eve did, but the satisfaction will not be lasting.

SATAN CAN CONTROL A CHRISTIAN'S THOUGHTS AND WORDS

Let me explain how Satan can also control the thoughts and speech of a Christian. In Matthew, chapter 16, Jesus had just concluded His explanation to His disciples on the true nature of His earthly mission—that He must suffer and die (v. 21). Peter immediately spoke up in an effort to dissuade Christ from going to the cross: "Far be it from You, Lord; this shall not happen to You!" (v. 22).

The response of Christ was abrupt and stern. "Get behind Me, Satan!" Jesus said *to Peter* (v. 23). I'm not suggesting that Peter was demon-possessed. I am proposing that Peter, while standing in the presence of Christ, was sufficiently influenced that he literally spoke the words Satan wanted him to say. Even more astounding is the fact that earlier, in verse 16 of that chapter, Peter had given the confessional statement of faith on which Christ said He would build His church!

In Acts, chapter 5, Ananias and Sapphira, members of the early church, lied to the apostle Peter. They had sold some possessions to give to the church, then had second thoughts and conspired to keep back a portion for themselves. When Peter asked them what amount they had received for the sale, Ananias and Sapphira lied. What was the source of that lie? The apostle Peter said, "Satan filled your heart to lie to the Holy Spirit" (v. 3). In judgment, God struck them dead. If we accept the assumption that Ananias and Sapphira experienced the new birth in Christ, then how can we explain away the fact that their hearts were filled by Satan to such an extent, they were capable of committing a sin worthy of such abrupt and severe divine judgment.

Satan can, in some instances, take over a Christian's mind and speak through his lips. Demons are in certain instances able to place Christians in a trance state so that the unclean spirit controls psychomotor functions and conscious mental processes. I have dealt with scores of cases of people who were undeniably followers of Christ, and yet demons spoke through them and even violently attacked me. It is disingenuous to suggest that they somehow lost their salvation long enough to let a demon in and then thereafter resumed their Christian walk.

If Satan can control our speech when we are disobedient and fill our hearts with evil when we are rebellious, he may be able to do a lot more to Christians than we would like to admit. What scriptural lessons can we learn from this startling information?

A Christian can be born again and have spiritual victory over the original Adamic sin that eternally separates mankind from God and still have besetting sins (Heb. 12:1)—uncontrolled thoughts, resentment, anger, and bitterness. Salvation must not be confused with sanctification. The Holy Spirit's continuing work of grace is a progressive act of God's desire to draw us closer to Him.

Those who, yet saved, resist this scriptural plea (1 Thess. 4:3) may find they have harbored demonic pockets of activity from their preconversion lives. This message needs a greater emphasis in our churches so that we may set free any of our brothers and sisters in Christ who are suffering the "hangover" of Satan's influence from their former lives of sin.

As kindly as I can say it, those who underestimate what Christians can suffer at the hand of Satan are doing a disservice to the body of Christ. They are consigning sincere Christians to a life of continued demonic influence and causing needless suffering in the lives of those whom the Lord would set free.

Let no one misunderstand me. A Christian cannot be demonized if by "possession" you mean "ownership." The child of God is owned by the Lord. But I will testify that a Christian can be severely influenced by demons and even be inhabited by them. I will also do all that I can in Jesus' name to see that those who are "heirs of God and joint heirs with Christ" (Rom. 8:17) will experience the hope of freedom from demonic bondage.

Chapter 28

Satan Doesn't Play Fair

Tony's Story

According to a recent *USA Today* report, today's runaways are different from a generation ago. The youngsters who hit today's mean streets aren't there because they don't want to go home. Some are afraid to go home, where abusive parents and stepparents sexually molest them. Some have been told to hit the road because one of the parents simply didn't want them anymore. They were either a drain on the family's financial resources or an interference with a parent's lifestyle. Tony's tale is the story of how evil seeks to devour this generation of youth, and how Satan exploits their emotional pain to lure them into indulging in occult ceremonies.

I first became aware of nineteen-year-old Tony through a letter he wrote to me. One page was filled with an elaborately detailed pencil drawing of me in various stages of torture and dismemberment. These depictions were accompanied by line illustrations of satanic symbols: a baphomet (goat's head pentagram), a dagger dripping with blood, a hooded figure with a scythe, and a mutilated Christ figure hanging upside down on a cross.

Tony also inscribed his own aphorisms: "Death to all Christ followers." "I promise to kill my father." "They have taken my soul and suicide is the only solution." And "Hail Satan." Below all of these statements were contradictory but desperate cries for help. Finally in closing, below the words, "Your dead friend, Tony," he wrote, "Help me, I beg you."

A secular psychiatrist might have had a field day analyzing the convoluted and threatening way Tony expressed himself. I saw a plain pattern of rejection and a profound sense of worthlessness.

I prayed earnestly and then answered Tony's letter. That led to a series of phone conversations. A demon manifested during a few phone calls and spoke to me. On one occasion an unidentified spirit made a chilling boast: "Tony made a pact with me when he mingled the blood of animals and children. That gave me full rights to him!"

The fact that I was able to correspond with Tony and talk with him on the phone raises the question: "Why couldn't Tony's demons prevent this from happening?" Couldn't they have overtaken him to prevent him from reaching out for help?

Some people don't understand where demons abide when they aren't actively controlling their victim. Possession isn't a static phenomenon. The person who has a demon may not have that particular demon all the time. If the host is a willing recipient of unclean spirits, and has an open door of access, demons can come and go at will. They don't have to stay in the victim permanently. Satan is not omnipresent; he is limited in his ability to be anywhere he wants anytime he wants.

I've encountered situations where demons, previously identified as possessing the host, were not there at some point in the exorcism. Other spirits in the host acknowledged that the missing demons were outside on another mission. In that case I was able to "lock out" the absent demons and keep them from returning.

Exorcisms are often complex procedures and need to be performed methodically, sometimes over an extended period of time. Not doing so may preclude the opportunity to face an important demon. For example, in one case a demon that was critical to the domination of the victim was absent during the early stages of the exorcism. If I had ended the procedure prematurely, I would never have known about this spirit, and he would have come back later. (I couldn't "lock" him out, since I didn't know about him.) This may explain why some who minister deliverance discover that a person they thought was totally freed once again has demons they never knew about. To keep this from happening, we might ask the Lord to forbid reentrance of spirits who exited without going to the pit.

MEETING TONY FACE TO FACE

I became very concerned about Tony and suggested that I fly into his city for a confrontation with his demons. I arrived a few days later and met Tony, who was accompanied by the pastor of a church he had attended. Tony was short, stocky, and dressed in a leather jacket, black jeans, and a black T-shirt with the slogan "Evil Knows No Boundaries." His head was shaved, except for a punk-style strip down the middle. Silver rings were inserted through three holes in each earlobe.

When he saw me, Tony pulled the lapel of his black motorcycle coat over his face and hid behind it. It took hours of talking before he would sit up straight in his chair and look me in the eye. He was a teenager who believed nobody wanted him—nobody but the devil.

Whenever I tried to talk to Tony his demons came forth and challenged me. After discussing the situation with his pastor, we decided there was no choice but to attempt an exorcism. For four days Tony's pastor and I battled dozens of demons, casting them out one by one.

The pastor was a man of faith and stood shoulder-to-shoulder with me throughout the battle. He had heard about cases of demon possession and preached about demons and the devil, but he had never encountered anything like this. Without him, the struggle for Tony's soul would have failed. Even when he didn't understand why I was taking a particular direction during the deliverance, Tony's pastor gave me his full confidence and prayed unceasingly.

The final struggle was with a spirit who called himself Christ. Whenever he manifested, Tony's right arm shot straight out, stiffened like a "Seig Heil" salute, and his hands formed the sign of Satan (fist clenched except for the first and little fingers extended).

I recognized this as the spirit who had threatened me over the phone. He claimed to have entered when Tony's coven sacrificed an eight-year-old child who had been kidnapped from a playground! "We crucified that child like we did your Jesus," the demon declared. "We pierced the child's hands and ripped open his side." The ghastly deed had been prefaced by the sacrifice of a pig. As a finale, the blood of the two were mixed.

I must pause from Tony's story for a moment to deal with a crucial issue regarding human misunderstanding about what Satan is allowed to do. Certainly the kidnapping and murder of an innocent child doesn't seem "fair." Is Satan obligated to abide by human standards of what seems acceptable?

DOES SATAN ABIDE BY HUMAN STANDARDS?

I recall facing a demon that had possessed a woman since she was five years old. At the time, an elderly male cult member sexually molested her in a deliberate attempt to pass on his spirits to continue the cult heritage.

"What you've done isn't fair!" I protested.

"Fair?" the demon retorted. "Who said that we demons play fair. Fairness is a human ideal you get from your God. To us there are no rules. We do whatever we can to possess a body. You underestimate what we can do, because you can't imagine anything as bad as we are. Why do you think the world is as depraved and violent as it is?"

Demons are dirty fighters. A fallen spirit has no illusions about maintaining some sense of propriety. The only restraint on an unclean spirit is the presence of God's Spirit dwelling in His people and the offensive posture taken by Christians who wage spiritual war against the forces of darkness. Prayer is a powerful weapon in our fight against these principalities.

Hearing about the abduction and murder of a child concerned the pastor and me. We questioned Tony in detail about what happened. He said he wasn't the one who actually got the child, and he claimed he was only an observer of the crucifixion; there was no way he knew exactly who was responsible for the crimes. We encouraged Tony to go to the authorities, though we discovered later that the police showed no interest in Tony's story. Since occult crime is seldom a focus of law enforcement agencies, the criminal activities of satanic cults are not often detected and even less frequently investigated.

Is Human Sacrifice Practiced Today by Satanic Cults?

Though our society would prefer to ignore the reality of human sacrifice, such unthinkable acts to appease occult powers have a well-established history in many ancient cultures. The Mayas, Aztecs, and Incas of Central and South America elevated the practice to such levels of horror that the Spanish conquistadores were able to use this barbarousness as an excuse for genocide. (On special occasions, the pagan priests killed thousands in a single day to ensure the cycles of seasons.) Even today, archaeologists continue to excavate five-hundred-year-old bodies from the icy slopes of the Andean mountains. If the priest did not perform this bloody ritual, these people believed the sun would cease its path through the heavens; therefore the victims of these ritual offerings often went to their fate willingly, considering their death to be honorable. They relished the moment when the Aztec or Incan priest would plunge an obsidian knife into their chests, because they were a propitiation for the entire civilization.

Historical revisionists have made a high-minded attempt to avoid sensationalizing such embarrassing spectacles. To admit that such butchery existed would concede the rationale for missionaries to convert these pagan systems. Even today, in remote sections of Peru and Bolivia where I have visited, consistent rumors insist that the descendants of these primitive priests clandestinely practice the old ways during the outbreak of natural disasters, serious illness, famine, and extreme weather conditions; they believe that the shedding of human blood is the only way to pacify the forces of the mountains and the skies.

The ancients sacrificed to achieve something they needed, such as rain, bountiful crops, or sexual fertility. They also sought to appease the gods they feared. Certain tribes invoked the deities' assistance against an enemy in times of war. Some sacrifices were performed to authenticate devotion or emphasize worthiness.

Contemporary cults use human sacrifice for many different reasons. Devout satanists believe they must break all of God's Ten Commandments, especially the sixth. They leave murder as their grand finale, the ultimate act of allegiance. Other cults systematically use sacrificial murder to fearfully bind members to the cult. On occasion, Satan will manifest himself in some way and call for a human sacrifice to appease his lust for blood, proving he has been "a murderer from the beginning" (John 8:44).

As was the case with Tony's cult, victims of modern devil worshipers are often obtained by kidnapping unattended children, as well as throwaway and runaway kids. In some cults, female breeders are kept to deliver babies for whom there is no record of birth or death. Some cult members consider it a privilege to bear a baby for slaughter.

"Where are the bodies?" the critics cry. Some are burned in ceremonial fires, and the ashes scattered. Satanists may infiltrate a crematorium staff and use the ovens unnoticed. Garbage disposal sites, abandoned mine shafts, and remote lakes serve as dumping places. Other bodies are eaten by acids or ground up in tree-eating machinery. To those still unconvinced that human sacrifice cults can elude authorities, I challenge, "Bring me the body of Jimmy Hoffa." If organized crime could kill a notable person like Hoffa, escape the most intensive of investigations, and leave no trace of his body, why couldn't satanic cults aided by supernatural evil forces do the same?

UNDERSTANDING THE UNPARDONABLE SIN

After we spent several hours praying with Tony about what he had done, we led him in prayers of repentance. Then we proceeded to deal with the demon who called himself Christ. A curious aspect of this exorcism was the physical way the demon enforced his right.

"Tony is mine, he bears my seal," the spirit shouted over and over. When I rebuked that claim, the Christ demon became furious and expressed his legal right even more vehemently. Finally the demon screamed, "Tony is branded forever. He'll never belong to your God."

I called Tony out of the trance. "Have you ever been branded in any way?" I asked.

Tony looked exhausted and his eyes were downcast. He pulled up the right sleeve of his shirt, and with his left hand, pointed to his forearm. Carved into his flesh was a scar with the numbers 666. "Yeah, I did this when they appointed me high priest of the coven." Tony wept out of hopelessness. "The demons are right. I'll never belong to God. You can see for yourself, I'm sealed with their sign."

I explained to Tony that a wound in his flesh was not an irrevocable pact. It was a clever tactic of the devil. Satan often convinces a victim of possession to sign blasphemous statements or to undergo a physical ritual that claims permanent ownership by evil. Then the person is constantly reminded of this vow by the physical evidence. The devil tries to trick people into believing that because they have orally uttered blasphemies, they can never be saved—they have committed the unpardonable sin.

I have often encountered this tactic and found it necessary to explain the real nature of the unpardonable sin. This act, blaspheming the Holy Spirit, referred to in Matthew 12:31, Mark 3:29, and Luke 12:10, does not refer to a specific deed. It implies a continual disobedient attitude toward the Holy Spirit by rejecting the person of Christ and His miracles. This deliberate rejection of His grace continues until the capacity to repent and the desire for God are gone.

This is a deliberate act of unbelief that is not committed in ignorance or haste. The Pharisees to whom Jesus directed this condemnation were experts in the law and had persistently harassed Christ with claims that His miracles were the acts of the devil. Furthermore, they made their accusations immediately after watching Him heal the blind and dumb demoniac.

We can conclude from a thorough review of the scriptural instance in question that the unpardonable sin is descriptive of a spiritual state more than the condition of a single reprehensible act. Those who had committed this sin showed no remorse or repentance toward their sins and displayed no desire to understand the truth of Jesus' words.

Satanic groups try to convince their members that once they have shed innocent blood they can never be forgiven and accepted by God. Such logic is a lie that ignores the substitutionary atonement of Christ who shed His blood to offer us unmerited redemption (Eph. 1:7). There is no crime so heinous or bloodthirsty that it escapes the reach of God's grace.

For those who may feel they have passed beyond the boundaries of God's forgiveness and committed the unpardonable sin,

2 Corinthians 7:10 declares that "godly sorrow produces repentance leading to salvation." "For 'whoever calls on the name of the LORD shall be saved'" (Rom. 10:13) is the promise to those who desire to turn from their wicked ways. The depth of God's love is so unfathomable that He has transformed murderers, adulterers, thieves, and all those who have asked for forgiveness.

ANNULLING THE SEAL OF SATAN

Once Tony realized he was not condemned by the unpardonable sin, we were able to proceed with more resoluteness. I knew that the 666 brand of Satan had to be annulled to remove the legal right of the Christ demon, so I asked the pastor for a glass of water. "Use a paper or plastic cup," I directed, because I had mistakenly handed a glass of water to a demon-possessed person who wanted a drink during a prior exorcism. The spirit promptly manifested, crushed the glass, and tried to injure me with the jagged shards.

When the pastor returned with a cup of water, I held it in my hands for a moment and prayed silently over it. Then I dipped my forefinger in the water and made the sign of the cross over the pink-colored scar of the numbers 666.

I motioned for Tony to take the water. When the cup touched his hands, the Christ demon manifested. His eyes widened and he stared at the cup. "I'm not drinking that!" he yelled. "You can't make me drink that ... that blood!"

"Oh yes I can!" I demanded and moved in closer.

Tony's pastor looked puzzled. He couldn't grasp the demons' revulsion to a cup of water.

I looked at the pastor and explained. "I prayed that the water in this cup would spiritually represent the blood of Christ, so that when I applied it to Tony's brand it would nullify the meaning of the scars."

The pastor was stunned when he understood that the demon,

without my having said a word, saw real blood in that cup. This caused the demon in Tony's body to writhe in torment.

"Grab him," I told the pastor. "Let's hold Tony's head so the Christ spirit can't move it."

He positioned himself to get a better hold on Tony's upper body. I pried open his mouth and forced the contents of the cup down the demon's throat. He screamed and thrashed about violently. Once the contents of the cup had been emptied, the demon went down and Tony returned. He looked suddenly calmer and was docile.

How Do Demons Interact with Other Demons?

During Tony's exorcism, a strange phenomenon occurred. I received a phone call from a young man named Reggie, to whom I had tried to minister deliverance a few weeks earlier. The first time I met Reggie was at a public rally. Reggie came to kill me; he said evil spirits had told him to stab me to death. The attack was thwarted when an alert security guard at the entrance to the auditorium spotted Reggie, sensed he was trouble, and frisked him. The guard removed a six-inch switchblade, hidden in one of the boots he was wearing.

At times Reggie genuinely wanted to be free. On other occasions he appeared unwilling to do what was necessary for his liberty. The timing of his call seemed odd, but I interrupted Tony's exorcism to speak with Reggie; he was in desperate need of help and that's why my office had forwarded the call to me. I took the phone call in a far corner of the room. From the start of the conversation it was obvious that Reggie had not called for help. He was belligerent and verbally abusive. Suddenly one of Reggie's demons manifested.

In my left ear, which was beside the phone receiver, I heard the evil spirit call one of Tony's spirits by name. In my right ear, I heard Tony's demon respond. Yet the voice of Reggie's demon could not be heard in the room. Tony's demon had supernaturally heard Reggie's demon calling out over a distance of more than two thousand miles! It was an uncanny feeling, hearing Reggie's demon call encouragement to Tony's demon, promising that help would be on the way to fight against what I was doing.

Then an even stranger thing happened. I heard Reggie, in his own voice, say, "I'll take any of Tony's demons that want to come into me!" Before I could react, Tony's body jerked and I heard Reggie scream. He laughed and the phone fell silent.

After this incident, I made repeated attempts to contact Reggie, but he never returned any of my calls. To this day I have no idea what happened to him, but I fear the worst since he was willing to receive some of the demons that had possessed Tony.

Not all unclean spirits interact with one another so cooperatively. There is no honor among thieves, and when demons are on the defensive, it's every unclean spirit for himself. When demons are losing the struggle to stay in someone's body, they will fight among themselves to be the last one to go.

My interrogation of weaker spirits in a demonic system sometimes yields valuable information, which is acquired at a fatal cost to the betraying demon. He may be punished by more powerful demons. More than once I have seen weaker demons scream in torment because a more powerful spirit got even with them.

I have also observed demons fighting with one another. Normally they are bound by a vow of evil to cooperate, like a band of robbers who agree on a scheme for thievery and operate in concert. However, if one member of the team should decide to steal from his fellow thieves and take a bigger cut of the action, the others will turn on him. The same is true with demons. I once dealt with a trio of spirits named Murder, Hate, and Revenge. After a time of prayer and fasting, it became obvious to the most powerful demon, Murder, that the forces of God were going to prevail. In some way, Murder "killed" the other two demons. He feared they would confess information affecting his ability to stay in the victim.

On occasion I have coaxed one spirit into doing something that betrays another. Often demons are too intelligent to fall into this trap. However, in the heat of spiritual battle demons can become confused and act unwisely. At certain times I have called on God to send an angel of confusion to disrupt the plans of demons and make them more susceptible to our divide-and-conquer tactics.

THE SMELL OF SATAN

At one point during Tony's exorcism, I noticed a foul odor filling the room. I had heard other exorcists say that pungent odors accompany certain demons, but had only experienced it on a couple of occasions. This time the smell was overbearing, like a combination of sewage and rotting meat.

God spoke to my heart and brought the words of 2 Corinthians 2:15–16 to mind: "For we are to God the fragrance of Christ among those who are being saved and among those who are perishing. To the one we are the aroma of death leading to death, and to the other the aroma of life leading to life."

That Scripture led me to say to Tony's pastor, "I want you to bend over with me and gently blow into Tony's face." Both Tony and his pastor looked at me as if I were crazy. "If God has breathed life into us, and if the life of Christ dwells in us, then by faith we can breathe the aroma of Christ onto a demon," I said to them. The pastor and I drew near Tony's face. Cupping our lips into the shape of an *O*, we softly exhaled. At first there was no reaction. Then Tony started squirming and the Christ spirit came forth, cursing ferociously. The demon appeared to be choking. "Get your breath off me! I can't stand it. It's suffocating me!"

"Keep blowing until he goes down all the way again," I instructed the pastor.

What happened when we blew on the Christ spirit? Demons operate with a mystical worldview, and God may use an evil spirit's supernatural interpretation of a phenomenon to exercise His power.

After a few minutes, Tony returned to consciousness. "What was the most repulsive thing you did at your coven's initiation ceremony?" I asked him.

His eyes rolled from side to side as he tried to concentrate. It took a few minutes before he could remember. Then his face twisted in a grimace. "The entrails," he said. "I had to eat the entrails."

"What entrails?"

"We sacrificed a pig. I had to pull the entrails out with my bare hands and eat them raw. At the time it didn't make me sick; I guess I was under the demon's influence. Afterward, I threw up for hours and was sick for several days."

The Christ demon came back quickly. "So, now you know," he spat put with a sneer. "We got him every way we could. The brand, the human sacrifice, and the curse of the swine."

Now we were getting somewhere. "What's the curse of the swine?" I demanded.

"An ancient curse," the spirit said. "That was our ultimate right to him. I entered when he ate the entrails."

I wondered why that particular deed was so serious, even more serious than the human sacrifice of an eight-year-old child. Then the Lord showed me. Christ cast demons into a herd of swine as proof of His divinity. As a result, the people of Gadara rejected Christ and asked Him to leave their country (Luke 8:26–39). To satanists, ingesting the entrails of a swine was a way of consuming the essence of an antichrist spirit.

WHERE DOES A DEMON GO WHEN HE IS CAST OUT?

I knew what I had to do for Tony's freedom. I bound the Christ demon and asked Tony to kneel facing me. I was about to do something very strange, but I knew in my heart it was right. I have cast out hundreds of demons, commanding every one of them to go to the pit. The exorcism of Tony is the only time I have not cast a demon into the pit (or the "abyss"). Tony's demons were commanded to go into a pig!

Every time I have cast demons to the pit, they have pleaded not to be sent there. I've confronted demons that screamed, writhed, and begged to avoid the pit. As a practical matter, any place a demon doesn't want to go is where I want to send them.

Can demons be sent elsewhere? As mentioned earlier, the demons in the demoniac of Gadara were sent into a herd of swine. In another instance Christ commanded unclean spirits to leave and never return again (Mark 9:25). It might be argued that these demons were implicitly sent to the pit, and that they knew their place of doom without a specific command from Christ. It is also clear from Scripture that some demons, which are now bound in the pit, will be loosed again during the Tribulation period (Rev. 9:1–3).

Why did I cast Tony's demons into a pig? A better question might be, Why did Jesus permit the demons of the demoniac of Gadara to enter a herd of swine? For one thing, those in Gadara were Jews; raising pork was a violation of the Law. Jesus undoubtedly amplified their disregard for God's holy injunction by allowing their illicit source of income to be destroyed. (I suspect that when the pigs plunged over the cliff and into the lake and were drowned, the demons were automatically consigned to the pit.) Just as Jesus reminded the citizens of Gadara of their sacrilege, I reminded Tony's demons of their grave blasphemy.

BREAKING CURSES OF ALL KINDS

Tony's bondage is an example of spiritual slavery rooted in curses. Ancestral curses are often the most serious and may affect descendants for generations. The story of Ray and Cynthia illustrates how serious such spells may be.

Cynthia and Ray had driven more than two thousand miles to meet with me. Normally, I wouldn't have taken a referral for deliverance counseling, but Cynthia and Ray's pastor was a personal friend and he had pleaded with me to consider helping them. Ray was a superintendent in a large Christian school in the northeastern United States. He was considered one of the best in his profession, but a series of strange events had nearly torn his marriage apart.

When Cynthia and Ray walked into my office, I asked them to be seated on a couch. After we exchanged small talk about their long trip, our conversation centered on Cynthia's struggle with demons.

"I never had a serious spiritual problem of any kind growing up," Cynthia said. "My parents were Christians, and I always wanted to marry someone in the Lord's work. That's why it's so hard to imagine that I could have a demon."

"How do you know it's a demon?" I inquired.

"That's what we think it is," Ray added. "Why else would she have tried to jump off that bridge?"

"Your pastor told me about that incident. Please repeat the story for me."

"We had driven down that highway a hundred times on our way upstate and often stopped to admire the beauty of the scenery at Windy Ravine. It's a sheer drop-off, plunging over two hundred feet to a raging river below."

"I don't know what came over me!" Cynthia exclaimed, as she broke into sobs. "I love my husband and children. Why would I want to jump?"

She dissolved into uncontrolled weeping as Ray enfolded her in his arms. I offered a couple of tissues from my desk to wipe her tears and waited patiently for her to regain composure. After several moments she calmed down and continued.

"Something in my head kept telling me to climb over the railing and jump to my death. I knew it was wrong, but the urge was overpowering. If Ray hadn't been there to stop me . . ."

Cynthia broke down again. This time Ray took up the story. "I was so stunned I didn't react at first. I thought she was kidding when she put her foot on the railing and started to pull herself over it. I guess it was the look in her eyes . . . that strange look. I'd never seen it before. It was so evil it frightened me, and I knew I had to grab her."

"Describe that look," I said.

"It flashed into her eyes—just for a few seconds—but I felt I was looking at the devil himself. Someone else seemed to be looking back at me. And that's not all. When I tried to pull her off the railing, she fought back. Afterward, Cynthia told me she didn't remember a thing."

Cynthia broke in again. "I recall Ray stopping the car and suggesting we take a break from the drive to enjoy the scenery for a moment. The fall colors were so beautiful. I remember getting out of the car, and that's it."

There was silence for a moment as they both paused to relieve the tension of their intense account. "What happened after you restrained Cynthia from jumping?" I asked Ray.

"Not much. We were both in a state of shock and got back into the car as quickly as possible and drove off. Neither of us said a thing about what happened the rest of the drive. I suppose I was too confused and Cynthia too embarrassed to discuss it. The subject never came up again until the night that . . ."

Ray paused and looked at Cynthia. He reached out and took her hand as she bit her lip to fight back the emotional pain she was experiencing.

"Have you been to a doctor or some kind of counselor?" I asked.

Both nodded their heads. "Yes, several times," Ray said. "But the night I heard the voice, I was convinced Cynthia's problem is spiritual."

"Is this the male voice your pastor told me about, the one that speaks with a Scottish accent?"

"Yes, and believe me, if you heard it, you'd understand why we're so anxious to see you. It's the scariest thing I've ever encountered, and it comes out of my wife's body. He says his name is the High One, that she belongs to him, and she has to die. The voice goes on and on about now being the time, because Cynthia is the fourteenth."

"The fourteenth what?"

"We don't know."

I saw a faint smirk cross Cynthia's lips as her eyes narrowed slightly. I leaned forward in my chair and fixed my eyes on her. "Who is looking at me? If it isn't Cynthia, I demand in Jesus' name to know who it is."

Ray reassuringly touched Cynthia's arm. For a moment nothing happened, then her muscles tensed and her head tilted back slightly.

"What do you want?" a voice deeper than Cynthia's said with an obvious Scottish accent.

"Are you the High One?"

"I am."

"To whom do you belong?"

"My master, the evil one."

"Satan?"

"Yes, the true lord of the universe."

"How did you come to possess this body?" I asked.

"I've always been here. I was here before she was born."

"Under threat of torment by the angels of God, tell the truth. When did you enter her?"

The High One sighed and gave me an exasperated look. "I told you, before she was born."

I waited for some reaction that would indicate God was executing judgment on the demon for lying, but nothing happened.

"How did you enter before she was born?"

"Through the curse of the elders. She was chosen fourteen generations ago by the Scottish elders. Now she is mine and she must die."

Four hours later, the High One left. In fact, he begged to go, after Cynthia learned of the curse, renounced it, and broke the spell that had been passed down for fourteen generations.

HOW ARE CURSES BROKEN?

A curse is broken in the same way it is established. If the curse was a verbal commitment, the victim needs to verbally renounce the curse. If ritualistic ceremonialism surrounded the curse, the victim needs to go through certain actions that physically and emotionally express the undoing of the curse. If documents were signed, the victim should write a legal statement, voiding the curse.

Curses are exacting, legal arrangements of the spirit world. Just as human contracts contain fine print and carefully crafted language, satanic curses are often filled with minutiae that require a detailed voiding. In some cases, I've discovered that leaving out one phrase or one word can make all the difference. Satan will exploit the smallest thing to keep the curse in effect.

Stacy was a teenager who sold her soul to the devil to join a witchcraft cult. She wanted to gain popularity that she couldn't obtain in her own social circles. Her curse was known as "drawing down the seventh moon." While leading her in a prayer of renunciation, I referred to the curse as the "drawing down of the moon." After a frustrating time of being unable to make the spirit obey my commands, an intercessor who accompanied me suddenly realized I had left out the word *seventh*. That one word made the difference in breaking Satan's bondage of Stacy's life.

Often those who need to break a curse are so emotionally distraught, it's advisable to lead them in a prayer. Don't rush the prayer. Articulate slowly and carefully so that God can direct you at any moment regarding the exact words to be used. If you write down the curse, be sure the person signs it. If it was a blood curse, whereby the person ingested human blood, you may want to partake of Communion with the victim as a symbol of the person's new allegiance to the blood covenant of Christ.

When breaking generational curses, it is helpful to specifically name any blood relatives involved in the curse. If you don't know the names of the participants, be as specific as your knowledge allows. You might have the possessed person say something like, "I renounce all ancestral links to the curse of [name], and subject to Christ all known and unknown blood relatives who trafficked in the occult. If any of my ancestors who are pertinent to the voiding of this curse are unknown to me, I ask the Holy Spirit to bring their names before the throne of God to force Satan's submission to the nullifying of this bondage." Curses upon children can be broken by their parents or whoever has been placed in immediate spiritual authority over them. Curses over wives can be broken by husbands. Children themselves can break the curses of their parents by repudiating the sins of fathers and mothers and claiming a new spiritual heirship as members of God's family.

Don't be surprised by the historical extent of curses. The biblical principle expressed in Exodus 34:6–7 indicates that a minimum of four generations may be involved, and the lineage of Satan's claim could extend much further. Make sure that all spirits associated with the curse are thoroughly interrogated to uncover all those affected by the curse.

CASTING OUT TONY'S DEMONS

I opened my Bible to 1 John, chapter 4, and asked Tony to point the forefinger of his right hand to verse 3: "Every spirit that does not confess that Jesus Christ has come in the flesh is not of God. And this is the spirit of the Antichrist . . ."

"Tony, I'm going to lead you in a prayer. Say each word and phrase after me, and mean it with all your heart."

Tony nodded in agreement. I prayed, "I bow in the name of the Lord Jesus Christ. I receive Him as my personal Savior, and nullify the brand of Satan. I receive the seal of the Holy Spirit, the earnest of my inheritance as a child of God. I renounce the curse of the swine and ask Jesus to forgive me for having eaten of the entrails. I repudiate my position as the high priest of the coven of Satan and command that the spirit of antichrist leave me and enter back into the swine from which he came."

This prayer was not spoken as fluently as I have recorded it here. It actually took nearly thirty minutes to say these few words. Every word was resisted by the demon with violent counterattacks and each mention of Jesus was coupled with profane blasphemies, which we had to constantly rebuke. It took the strength of both the pastor and myself to hold Tony under control until each word of the prayer was clearly enunciated. When at last Tony completed his prayer of confession and repentance, he collapsed from sheer exhaustion, weeping for joy. The curse of his life had turned into a blessing of self-acceptance and a recognition of his worth as a creature loved by God.

Chapter 29

How Satan Steals, Kills, and Destroys

Not long ago I went to see a local theater production. I sat in the darkened theater, stunned by the theme of the performance on stage. The script, written by a gay Jewish playwright, was filled with clichés and stereotypes about Jewish customs. Actors and actresses portrayed an early twentieth-century Russian Jewish community.

A poor, young Jewish man, smitten with love for a rich man's daughter he could never have, slowly went mad. Finally, in desperation, he uttered twice the unspeakable name of God and, according to Jewish tradition, dropped dead. His spirit then became a *dybbuk*, a demon. Unlike orthodox Jews who believe that demons are fallen angels, the Jews in this play believed in the occult cabalistic idea that demons are souls of the departed. According to this belief, these disembodied spirits have unfinished work on earth, which can only be completed by possessing a human body.

The dybbuk of this play entered the body of his beloved as a way of supernaturally bonding their souls. His presence was discovered by the Jewish Council, which convened to conduct an exorcism on her. In their quest to discover how she had become possessed, the rabbis ferreted out the "legal right" of the dybbuk. To do so they summoned the dybbuk's late father from the dead during an elaborate ceremony. According to the play, the boy's father and the girl's father had long ago pledged their offspring to be married, but the girl's father reneged on the pledge. In the end, the rabbis exorcized the dybbuk, the girl subsequently died, and the two disembodied souls found love in the spirit world.

The play troubled me because it repudiated Jewish biblical theology, and it made a hero out of the dybbuk. I was disgusted by this perversion of Jewish tradition, but it prompted a mental journey backward in time to several years ago when I met a woman named Charlene.

A Real-Life Meeting with a Dybbuk

One evening after my message at a Baptist church in the deep South, an attractive thirty-something woman with long blonde hair and a troubled look on her face approached me.

"Mr. Larson, may I have a few moments of your time?" she requested.

I consented and asked the pastor and his wife to accompany me. The four of us sat down in an unoccupied Sunday school classroom.

"You look very disturbed," I commented. "Did something I say tonight upset you?"

"I just got out of the hospital," Charlene said agitatedly. "While I was there, a woman in the bed next to me led me to Christ. When I told her I was being discharged, she suggested that I talk with you if at all possible."

"Why were you in the hospital?"

Charlene stood and reached toward her waist with both hands. She untucked the bottom of her blouse from her slacks and slowly pulled it upward, exposing her midsection. Her entire stomach area looked as if someone had hacked it to pieces with a knife and then sewn it back together with convoluted folds of flesh. I stared at the healing wound, too shocked to respond.

Slowly Charlene lowered her blouse, sat down, and began speaking. "A year ago I came home from a party a little tipsy. I was undressing for bed when it happened."

She paused, and I spoke. "What happened? Did someone attack you?"

Charlene shook her head. "My husband, Stuart, is involved in, shall we say, shady activities. He's Jewish, and years ago he got messed up in a mafialike gang. He fears that someone is trying to kill him, so he keeps a loaded gun in the closet." Charlene pointed her right index finger at her midsection. "For some reason, when I was standing there in the closet, I reached for his gun, placed the barrel against my stomach, and pulled the trigger."

"What were you thinking when you pulled the trigger?"

"I wasn't thinking. In fact, I don't actually remember firing the gun. I only recall seeing the gun and then regaining consciousness just as I pulled the trigger. The next thing I knew, I was awakening in the hospital after surgery." Charlene took several deep breaths. "Can you help me? I need to know why I pulled that trigger and why I still have lingering thoughts of killing myself."

"There are many reasons people are suicidal," I answered. "Some of them are emotional and others are physiological. Have you told all this to a medical doctor and to mental health professionals?"

Charlene wrung her hands nervously and nodded her head affirmatively. "I talked to everybody in the hospital who would listen to me. They put me through all kinds of psychological tests. I spent hours with a shrink. Nobody could find anything in my past that would have made me do this."

"Have you been involved in the occult?"

Charlene shook her head.

"Have any family members practiced witchcraft?"

Again Charlene shook her head no. I concluded that if her

problem had a natural explanation, no one, including me, had found it. I had a sense that she was plagued by serious spiritual problems. Conversely, there wasn't any clear indication Charlene had done something that would give a demon the legal right to take over her consciousness and try to take her life.

I decided to pray to see what God might show me. I instructed the others to kneel with me by Charlene's chair. "Lord Jesus Christ," I prayed, "show us who or what is responsible for the attempt to kill Charlene."

As I prayed, Charlene's body shivered and her left shoulder jerked periodically, but no demons manifested. After several minutes of intense prayer, I was almost ready to send Charlene away. Then the Holy Spirit led me to say something that aroused the enemy. "Thank You, Lord Jesus, that You have come to give us abundant life and deliver us from Satan who comes to steal, kill, and destroy,"

When I said the word *destroy*, Charlene's body stiffened and her thin wispy voice deepened. "Leave me alone. She's mine!"

"Who is speaking? I demand to know—in the name of Jesus Christ." Charlene's head lifted and her eyes opened. It was the same look that I'd seen in Singapore and countless other times since. "Who are you?" I asked.

"I am Suicide."

"By what sin did you enter this body?"

The spirit shrugged its shoulders. "Nothing in particular. She was easy. She didn't have much backbone to say no to anything. We just waited around until the right moment and the door to her soul opened that night when she got drunk. Now that she's mine, you'll never have her. I'm going to kill her!"

I knew this was going to be a tough fight.

HOW DOES SATAN KILL HIS VICTIMS?

"The thief [the devil] does not come except to steal, and to kill, and to destroy" (John 10:10). To fully understand the meaning of this Scripture and what Suicide intended for Charlene, we must first comprehend why a demon needs to possess a human.

Demons are noncorporeal spirits. They have no physical mechanism to express their will. They need a body to accomplish their heinous designs. The devil tries to control the universe and all of its inhabitants. Just as Christians are ambassadors for Christ (2 Cor. 5:20)—His hands and feet to minister the gospel—Satan seeks human emissaries of evil who will spread his teachings. The most effective way to do this is by controlling the faculties of an individual. But while Satan is using a victim for his purposes, he is also bent on destroying and killing them. That is the *only* way he knows how to operate.

DEMONS CAN KILL A PERSON'S EMOTIONAL EXPRESSIONS

When Jesus referred to Satan killing, He was not only alluding to murderous acts by those under demonic control. Satan also destroys those he invades by "killing" the person's core identity. If successful, demons will establish their character as the center of their victims' emotional expressions. The demons will eventually take over almost all emotive responses and act as a filter for all the person experiences.

When the demonic domination reaches that point, the victim may give up and withdraw so that the will of the demons subjugates nearly all of the original person. People give control to demons because they are hiding from their emotions and life.

For example, if someone rejects the victim, the hurt will be amplified by the demons. What might be a minor brush-off will be made to seem like a major rejection. A mild traffic dispute can turn into murder. Demons intensify every feeling as they act out their duty to torment their victims.

Often demons embolden people who otherwise live reclusive lives. Unclean spirits prey on those who are dysfunctional in relationships and withdrawn in crowds. Like a drunk with too much alcohol, the victims of demons develop a boisterous personality with demonic encouragement. They crave the demon like the drunk craves his liquor, though both ignore the consequences.

DEMONS CAN KILL A PERSON'S MENTAL HEALTH

Demons not only kill their victims emotionally, they can "kill" them mentally as well. I am frequently asked if those in mental institutions are demon-possessed. Some may be, but certainly not all. There are many reasons for insanity, including congenital factors, severe illnesses, hormonal imbalances, disease, and trauma. However, my investigations have personally convinced me that some of those who have been labeled mentally ill are, in fact, demonized.

This mental demonization and deteriorations occur in several ways. First, a mentally sound person may be driven to insanity. The demons kill the normal mental processes and leave behind a shattered mind. Second, a demon that mimics insanity may manifest so frequently that mental health professionals presume this demon is actually the person. Third, a demon may facilitate physical infirmities that bring about a physiologically diseased state, which then leads to dementia.

How do you know it isn't a mental problem? I have always approached the possibility of an exorcism cautiously. Most deliverance sessions I've been involved in were the result of a spontaneous demonic eruption that occurred during a conversation or a counseling session. The exorcism wasn't planned. Though I have occasionally dealt with demons as the result of a referral or a request for counseling, such instances are rare. When I have agreed to talk with someone who thinks his predicament might be demonic, I carefully follow a regimen of eliminating all possible explanations other than demonic.

The Roman Catholic Church has strict procedures before a diocese may authorize an exorcism. These include psychological counseling and the insistence that medical advice is sought. Though I don't have a formal checklist, I use an informal process of elimination to explain away demons. Only after I have exhausted every avenue will I suggest that a deliverance may be necessary.

This rigorous approach helps to eliminate the possibility that the person's problems might be mental. However, even if mental aberrations are present, an exorcism might still be in order. Mental illness may be the result of demonic influence, and mental illness can make one susceptible to demons. This "chicken or the egg" question is resolved by acknowledging that it can be either mental illness or demon possession, or both. There are also mental illnesses that have nothing to do with demons.

DEMONS CAN DEADEN THE SPIRIT TO GODLY IMPULSES

In addition to attacking the mind, demons may also seek to 'kill" the spirit by deadening it to godly impulses. I've ministered to individuals who have had their spiritual acuity so numbed they are almost incapable of desiring the things of God. Such individuals may actually think they are beyond redemption. Only persistent biblical counseling will restore them to a state in which they can respond to the Holy Spirit.

In the most extreme example, Satan kills literally by driving the victim of possession to suicide. A demon may so oppress and mentally torment an individual, the person loses perspective on life and despairs to the point of self-destruction.

I was personally acquainted with a pastor who suffered from such oppression. I learned from the pastor's dearest friend that spiritual darkness had haunted him for several years. His mental deterioration was accentuated by demons that tormented him day and night. Unfortunately, this pastor was not part of a denomination that understands and teaches the reality of deliverance, so he didn't know how to pray effectively against these forces.

One Sunday morning before the church worship service, the pastor was acutely despondent. He ate breakfast with his wife and then walked into the bathroom. Moments later his wife heard a loud pop. She thought her husband had dropped something in the bathroom. When she went to see what happened, she found her husband dead on the floor with a gun in his hand.

Did he go to heaven? God alone knows if he was a genuine believer. In the case of Christians who commit suicide, I believe that God judges such people by their spiritual condition when they were last able to think rationally and make spiritual decisions. I also believe that God takes into account the controlling influence of demons that lead to suicide.

Demons also steal from their victims.

How Do Demons Steal From Their Victims?

When Jesus said that Satan steals, you might conclude this refers to individual acts of theft and vandalism. It may, but Satan has other ways of stealing. He steals virginity by sexual temptation, and he steals hope by leaving crushed dreams. Satan purloins the ability to know right from wrong and ravages faith in God and His Word.

The worst damage a demon does is often unseen, as in the case where a demon robs a person of his self-esteem. I have dealt with demonized people who have been encouraged to commit abhorrent acts while under a spirit's control. A teetotaling Sunday school teacher went on drunken binges. A young single woman engaged in promiscuous sex with anonymous men. A housewife took dangerous doses of street drugs.

I once dealt with a demonized young man who came out of a trance state to discover that his body had been used in perverted sex acts by those in a satanic cult. Even though he wasn't directly responsible for these repugnant deeds, he still felt the shame. This resulted in a severe loss of self-respect.

The devil's destruction is complete when the ability to see the world through God's eyes is gone. Moral conscience evaporates and pleasure is taken in corruption. Satan's theft is fully achieved when relationships with loved ones are stolen and the victim of demon possession is isolated to suffer alone, often to contemplate suicide.

CHARLENE SUMMONS HER HUSBAND

For several hours we battled Charlene's demon of suicide. I used every technique at my disposal to weaken the demon. To some extent I succeeded, but the demon belligerently hung on. Then the Holy Spirit spoke to my heart and said, "Get her husband involved." The spiritual impression was so strong it startled me. I wondered what good it would do to involve her husband since he wasn't a Christian, but I couldn't escape what God was telling me.

I explained to Charlene what I wanted her to do. She immediately objected. "You don't understand," she implored. "My husband is a dangerous man. If he doesn't like what's going on here, he might take it out on you."

I insisted that Charlene call her husband, and she finally agreed. While she phoned from another room, the three of us spent an anxious fifteen minutes waiting to hear his response. When Charlene returned, she appeared distressed.

"I told you he'd be angry at being awakened in the middle of the night to come to a Christian church. Please, let me leave. I'll intercept him on the way over here."

I wasn't certain how much of Charlene's desire to leave was her own choosing and how much was the influence of the demon of suicide. Several times she put on her coat to depart and then sat nervously back down to think it over. She rubbed her stomach, fearfully remembering what the demon of suicide had done to her.

We somehow managed to wait it out, and fifteen minutes later her husband, Stuart, entered the room and everyone froze. His dark black hair, solid six-foot-two-inch frame, and piercing dark eyes accentuated all Charlene's warnings. Anger flared from his face, and he exploded as he stepped through the door.

"What are you doing here? You know I've forbidden you to attend church," he yelled. "Who are these people? And what do they want from us? If it's money, tell them to forget it. And which one is the exorcist?"

Charlene pointed at me. Stuart walked over to me, his arms folded in defiance.

"Maybe my wife needs to see a psychiatrist, but she doesn't need you!" he roared. "Perhaps she's schizophrenic or something like that. If it's a mental problem, we'll deal with it ourselves. I can get her the best help in the state, but this business about demons is insane. What do you think this is, the Dark Ages? Whatever you've got to say to me had better be good, and it had better be quick!"

His eyes bore into me and his big arms were crossed in front of him. I stayed calm and spoke clearly and precisely. I told him we were there to help.

Stuart took several deep breaths to calm himself and sat down, still glaring at me. I began my explanation by reminding Stuart what had happened that awful night when Charlene had pulled the trigger of his gun. I spoke to him about her painful recovery in the hospital, but none of this seemed to affect him. His hatred for me was too intense. As I was about to complete my account of the evening, Charlene interrupted.

"Stu, I'm not sure what he's saying is true or not, but please don't be mad. I can't believe these good people would be lying." She gestured toward the pastor and his wife and gently took Stuart's hand. "Go along with this, just for a little while. If you aren't convinced, then we'll leave."

Stuart softened a little and put his arm around Charlene, pulling her close to him. He seemed to genuinely care about her, and I knew that was my one hope of resolving this impasse.

"All right, you've got ten minutes to prove your case. If you can't, we're out of here."

I didn't have time to pray or deliberate about what to do next. I needed wisdom from the Lord quickly, and it came. I commanded the spirit of suicide to manifest. Almost instantly Charlene's back stiffened, and she drew away from Stuart. I recognized the look of Suicide in her eyes.

"Spirit, I take authority over you in the name of Jesus Christ."

Suicide smirked. He knew I was in a difficult situation and he had the upper hand. The Lord drew my attention to the opposite side of the room. This was a Sunday school room for children and a plastic toy container was against the wall.

"Suicide, I command that you get out of that chair, walk across the room, and sit on that toy box." I pointed toward the plastic container. For a moment Suicide did nothing. "In the name of Jesus I summon mighty angels to stand on each side of you and lift you from that chair and force you to the other side of the room."

Suicide's shoulders seemed to thrust upward as if pressure were being applied at the armpits. Almost weightlessly, he stood and staggered toward the toy box with a look of disgust.

Stuart looked confused, but didn't move.

When Suicide finally sat down, I bound him. "I demand that you allow Charlene to return to consciousness. Charlene, I call you forth."

Suicide wasn't sure what I was trying to do and resisted momentarily. Then gradually Charlene came to her senses. When she was fully aware, she anxiously glanced around the room. She reached down with both hands and felt the sides of the toy box.

"Stu, what am I doing over here?" Charlene asked with genuine perplexity.

Stuart lowered his head. "I don't know, sweetheart. Maybe it's hypnosis or something like that."

It was the reaction I wanted. By having the demon take over Charlene's mind and physically move her to another part of the room, I proved to Stuart that something unusual was happening. The look on his face was one of amazement.

"Charlene, please cooperate with me. I need you to do one more thing," I said softly.

Charlene nodded in agreement.

"Suicide, I command that you come to attention."

Charlene's body jerked, and Suicide manifested.

"Look at her husband and tell him who you are!"

For an intense moment Stuart and Suicide glared at each other. Then Suicide spoke. "I'm a dybbuk."

The blood drained from Stuart's face and his body went limp. All his antagonism disappeared, and tears formed in his eyes. He looked directly at me.

"However you want me to help, I'll cooperate. I speak Yiddish, but my wife doesn't understand the language. She's never been around anyone who speaks it." Stuart paused as I waited to find out what he was talking about. "*Dybbuk* is Yiddish for *demon*."

Now that Stuart was convinced that Charlene had a demon, I knew what I had to do. Though it went against all my theological presuppositions, I knew in my spirit that Stuart was the one to cast the demon out of his wife!

CAN SOMEONE WHO ISN'T A CHRISTIAN CAST OUT A DEMON?

Christians aren't the only ones who attempt exorcisms. Medicine men, witch doctors, and all sorts of shamans seek to exorcize evil spirits. In primitive cultures, demons are often believed to be the source of illness, spells, and bad luck. Pagans consort with witch doctors who brew potions and perform spells designed to appease or oppose unseen entities. Certain voodoo ceremonies are designed to expel evil spirits through consorting with "good" spirits. In many cases the clients of such occultists seem to experience phenomena similar to that resembling Christian exorcisms. They also achieve a measure of relief from torment. But the demons have tricked them and will usually revisit their victims when they are out of the limelight.

When the Pharisees accused Jesus of casting out demons by Beelzebub, the prince of the devils, Jesus pointed out that a kingdom divided against itself cannot stand (Matt. 12:25). So what is happening when witchcraft is employed to expel an evil spirit?

Since Romans 12:21 declares that evil is only overcome with good, we know that evil cannot truly cast out evil. What appears to be a legitimate exorcism may only be the unclean spirit temporarily vacating his human residence to give the impression he is gone. As an alternative, the demon may stay but cease certain actions of torment, giving the impression the pagan exorcism was successful. In either case, no true deliverance has occurred.

What bearing does this knowledge have on understanding Charlene's exorcism by her unbelieving husband? While God is not obligated to honor the prayers of the pagan, no matter how sincere he may be, God *does* respect the hierarchy of spiritual order. Ephesians 5:23 points out that the husband is the "head" of his wife, just as Christ is Lord over the church. Certainly such God-given authority is tempered with responsibility. But setting that charge aside, even a nonbelieving husband has divinely given authority over his wife. In this respect, God holds him accountable for her spiritual condition, but He also grants to him the right of bearing her spiritual covering.

"Repeat after me and mean what you say as a chosen one of Israel," I instructed Stuart, whose hands were shaking.

I slowly spoke the words that sealed Suicide's doom. Stuart never took his eyes off the demon as he repeated after me, "In the name of the God of Israel, He who parted the Red Sea, the cloud by day and the fire by night, I take the authority that is mine as the husband of this woman whom God has given to me. We are one flesh and her body is my body. I command that you leave her body and loose her from your desire for death. Go now to the place God has prepared for you, the pit."

With the same resoluteness that Stuart had opposed me when he entered the room, he confronted the unclean spirit. Suicide grimaced, closed his eyes, and left with a scream.

Charlene crumpled forward on the floor. Stuart rushed to her side, knelt by her, and stroked her face. When she came to, they embraced. I sat there amazed that a nonbeliever who had initially denied the reality of demons had successfully helped to complete an exorcism.

When Stuart told the dybbuk to leave his wife, he was not acting on the basis of faith in Christ, and therefore not claiming the sovereign right that would be available to a spirit-filled Christian. He was acting on the basis of conferred authority because of his marital role. Under certain circumstances, a non-Christian may successfully perform an exorcism. In that kind of circumstance, a husband, in conjunction with the authority expressed by a genuine believer, may even evoke the name of Christ as a matter of divine order without personally expressing regenerated faith in the Son of God.

This teaching is not intended to confuse but to encourage those in deliverance to adapt to whatever situation is at hand for the sake of the victim. The night of Charlene's deliverance I might have stubbornly refused her husband's participation. Instead, I welcomed his involvement. This amazing exorcism did not result in Stuart's conversion at that time, but it did achieve Charlene's deliverance. This underscores an important truth: The goal of an exorcism is the freedom of Satan's victim, not conformity to a supposed set of human criteria by which the exorcism must be performed.

God's rain falls on the just and the unjust. He is Lord, and He may choose to heal or deliver a non-Christian in the process of another's freedom from disease or demonic bondage. If these cases cause concern, we must let God be God.

Chapter 30

The Enigma of Demons and MPD

Randall leaned forward and rubbed his knees. He folded his arms across his chest as if guarding himself from further suffering. Tears formed in his eyes. Though he was a grown man in his mid-thirties, his vulnerability made him seem like a child.

"You don't know how much pain I'm in," he said. "I hurt so badly, I want to leave this room and hide somewhere so I can scream." Randall paused as he strained to form his thoughts. "One thing I'm sure of," he said softly, "I don't have multiple sclerosis, even though I have all the symptoms!"

Randall had barely been able to enter my office. He couldn't have made it without leaning on the arms of his wife and his pastor. He had collapsed on my office couch, and it took minutes for him to catch his breath from the ordeal of navigating from the car to inside the building.

"I had M.S. five years ago, but the Lord healed me," Randall insisted. "I refuse to accept the symptoms I now have, and I'm claiming my healing by faith."

I didn't react to his bold statement. I had seen others claim healing from the Lord in the face of severe symptoms. Some were compelled by their own desire. Others were prodded by healing evangelists who didn't want to admit their failures. When people weren't healed by their prayers, they blamed those who had sought healing, saying they were the ones who lacked faith.

Those who claimed healing as Randall did were often audaciously in denial. In some tragic cases, their refusal to seek competent medical help proved to be physically dangerous. By avoiding proper medical treatment, they allowed their condition to worsen, sometimes beyond remedy.

Somehow Randall seemed different. He was sincere, and I was impressed by his confidence. Randall's wife, a shy lady who listened attentively to every word being said, looked worried and a little nervous. Then Randall told me his M.S. symptoms were the result of demonic influence. He pointed to his pastor, sitting next to him, to back him up.

"Pastor Neil says he confronted evil spirits who spoke through me," Randall explained. "He can describe what he's seen and heard. All I know is that God healed me, and the devil is trying to get me to doubt my healing."

Pastor Neil was a portly man, with a graying beard and balding head. He had sat there nodding in agreement with everything Randall said. When it was his turn, he spoke confidently about the deliverance he had attempted.

"I've been through three exorcisms with Randall," he explained. "Each of them seemed successful at the time, but the demons we cast out were all back in a few days. Worse yet, they brought others with them. Some of the new demons were more powerful than the ones we expelled."

As I listened to his narrative, I marveled that the four of us were together under these circumstances. Pastor Neil had contacted me after a series of radio broadcasts during which I talked about spiritual warfare. His daughter had heard the programs and told her father about me. "Maybe Bob Larson is the one who can help you set Randall free," she had suggested.

Pastor Neil asked if I would spend some time with Randall. I had hesitated at first, because of my busy schedule. But when I sensed Neil's sincerity, I couldn't refuse. I had arranged this meeting, hoping to offer some advice that would help them make progress in Randall's deliverance.

My first suggestion was aimed at explaining why the same demons kept coming back. "You probably never found the gate-keeper demon. It didn't matter how many demons you cast out, they didn't have to go to the pit because the gatekeeper kept the door open for them to return."

"Gatekeeper?" Pastor Neil asked.

"Yes, the demon who provides continual access to the person's body or soul. Gatekeepers don't have to be powerful demons. In fact they often aren't. They're just clever. They stay hidden so their role goes undetected. But they're most valuable to the entire evil spiritual system in the person. They control the entry for all the others."

Pastor Neil smiled. "I wish we had known that before. We sure could have saved ourselves a lot of sleepless nights." He patted Randall on the shoulder to encourage him. "Can you tell us anything about the demons we encountered?" the pastor asked.

"Possibly. What were their names?"

"I can't remember them all. Murder, Lust, and Violence were three of the most powerful. There were a couple that seemed to be too serious. They called themselves Regulator and Facilitator. The two strangest were Vivinanda and Sridepok."

"The last two sound like East Indian names. They could be Hindu demons. Randall, have you ever been to India?"

Randall had been struggling to listen to the exchange between me and his pastor. He kept rubbing his knee and elbow joints to assuage the pain. "No," he answered, "and I don't know the first thing about Eastern religions."

His wife looked at him and shook her head in agreement. That puzzled me, but I did have a hunch about two of the other names. "Regulator and Facilitator sound like the identities of multiple personality alters, dissociative states of Randall's consciousness."

"Disso what?" Pastor Neil inquired.

"*Dissociative.* A psychological term used to describe a separate mental and emotional identity when a person's mind has fractured into one or more alternate personalities."

"You mean demons?"

"No, Pastor Neil. Demons are much different from alters, as we call them for short. I can understand your problem accepting the idea of different personalities all abiding in one person's mind and body, but it's real."

The look on Pastor Neil's face indicated he wasn't sure about my diagnosis.

"This is not the first case like this I've seen. I first became aware of multiple personalities nearly twenty years ago when I started ministering deliverance. Back then, no one, including psychologists, was talking about this sort of thing. They certainly didn't have any fancy names for it."

"How did you find out about the alters, as you call them?"

"I was ministering to a man named Phillip who was trying to escape a satanic cult. While I was dealing with demons, an identity surfaced that I could not cast out. It went by a human name— Christopher, a personality that talked and acted like a five-year-old child. That tipped me off."

Randall was now listening intently; he had stopped rubbing his aching muscles. "How did you know for certain that Christopher wasn't a demon?"

"I wasn't sure, until I tried repeatedly to cast him out. I decided to try a different tactic and talked to Christopher as if he were a person. I discovered that Christopher was the name of a child that Phillip's cult had sacrificed. Phillip told me he was the one originally destined to be sacrificed. To avoid being killed, he tricked

Christopher into taking his place. The guilt and remorse so over-whelmed Phillip, he went into dissociative denial. His mind cre-ated an identity, an alter named Christopher, to keep him alive. That way, Phillip didn't have to admit to himself what he had done. After all, Christopher was alive in Phillip's mind and lived as a real identity.

"Randall, I suspect there are several layers to your mind and emotions. The person I'm talking to now may not be the real you. For some reason, the core of who you are is hidden. I want to talk to the Randall we all know."

My abruptness shocked everyone in the room. Talking abstractly about multiple personalities was one thing, but trying to talk to one in Randall was different. Yet if Randall had demons, they were listening to what I was saying and were beginning to develop a counteroffensive to my strategy. If the element of sur-prise was to remain in my control, I needed to confront whatever alters were part of Randall's consciousness.

He immediately straightened and sat back on the couch, look-ing at me intently. "What are you asking of me?"

Randall's wife and pastor looked equally baffled. If nothing else, Randall's sudden reaction indicated I had touched a sensitive point. I probed further. "Something traumatic happened to you, some time, somewhere. Perhaps when you were so young, you don't remember. Your mind may have experienced selective amne-sia and blocked it out. I feel that your thinking and emotions are being regulated carefully; you're under some kind of control by another part of your consciousness."

"You think I'm crazy, is that it?" he argued with a pained sound in his voice.

"I didn't say that. I do think your mind has been fractured by past emotional injury, and the essence of your identity has been submerged. I need the part of you that is hiding to come out."

Randall narrowed his eyes and hugged himself tightly.

Pastor Neil looked at me dubiously. "Randall isn't mentally ill, if that's what you're thinking," he interjected. "He heads one of the ministries to youth in our church. Not only that, he also has a master's degree in educational psychology. In fact, he's only a few hours away from writing his doctoral thesis."

I thought for a moment. *They still don't understand what I've been trying to explain. I've got to make them understand the difference between demons and dissociated alters or we'll never set Randall free.* (Dissociative identity disorder is the result of severe trauma and has been recognized by the American Psychological Association officially since 1980.)

I leaned forward and patted Randall on the shoulder. His body relaxed a little. "I absolutely don't mean Randall is insane," I said to Pastor Neil. "What I'm talking about is a complex defense mechanism that has probably kept Randall sane and alive. Actually, the fact that his mind developed mentally dissociated identities is proof of his intellectual acumen. Only the brightest people are able to do that. I've known people who have hundreds of multiple personalities and each alter has its own set of personal habits and distinctions. Imagine trying to remember every detail of personal behavior, including the likes of all those separate personalities—all using the same brainpower!"

Randall and Pastor Neil seemed relieved. "If there are other personalities inside Randall, how would they differ from a demon?" the pastor asked.

"Think of it in terms of two words: *survival* vs. *destruction*," I explained. "A demon is there to destroy the person. A multiple personality, an alter, is there to facilitate the person's survival. Often the abuse or emotional trauma was so severe that the person who experienced it would have cracked mentally if he had continued living with the memory of what happened. So part of him encapsulates the memory, along with all its feelings, and splits off. That way the rest of the consciousness can go on without having to remember the hurt or the horror, as in the case of Phillip."

Randall's wife spoke. "Who are these personalities you're

talking about? Are they different from the person I know as my husband?"

"Facilitator could be one of them. That doesn't sound like the name of a demon. An alter personality who facilitates would help to smooth over the trauma and minimize the hurt of the memory. Regulator could be some sort of internal mechanism to keep Randall's true feelings under control. That way he wouldn't have to feel any pain from the past."

Pastor Neil stood for a moment and took a couple of steps around the room, as though it helped him to think better. "I understand what you're saying, but how does all of this tie in with demons? I know that I dealt with demons. They were violent and cursed me profanely. That wasn't Randall."

"I agree, it probably wasn't. But the demons could be hiding behind Regulator and Facilitator. They could even be possessing one of these alters."

Pastor Neil shook his head. "Whoa! Wait a minute. Are you saying that a specific alter might have a demon, while the rest of Randall's consciousness does not?"

"Yes, and I'll take it one step further. In the realm of multiple personalities, there are good alters and bad alters. Good alters are the part of the person's consciousness that has acknowledged Christ as Savior. Bad alters, for one reason or another, refuse to make that spiritual surrender. Sometimes bad alters are just spiritually unconvinced identities. At other times these portions of the person are possessed by a demon."

Pastor Neil's frustration was plain as he quickened his striding about the room. "You're telling me that the spirit of a person can be saved, that separate aspects of his consciousness can receive Christ while other aspects reject the Lord? Is that right?"

"Exactly. Our task is to sort through that maze to gain the assistance of the good alters. Then we can attempt to win the bad alters over to God. At that point, we'll be able to distinguish the identities that are demon-possessed and cast them out."

My explanation was interrupted by wailing. Randall, who had been sitting quietly, leaned forward with his head in his hands. His sobbing grew more and more intense until he spoke in a soft, childlike voice.

"I didn't think anyone cared about me. It's been so lonely all these years staying in hiding. But I had to regulate Randall or . . ."

"Or he would have hurt too much?" I inquired.

"Yes," Regulator said between sobs. "I regulate everything about him. When someone says something that hurts him, I don't let him feel the pain. When he's disappointed, I make him believe what happened never really happened. You're not mad at me for doing that, are you?"

"No," I said, "we're not mad at you. In fact, you are very important to Randall's freedom from the demons."

"Are you talking about the dark ones who live in the shadows?"

"Yes. They're not like you. They come from another place and time."

Regulator shook his head. "You can say that again! They appear and disappear. Sometimes there are many of them, and other times just a few." Regulator pulled his knees up under him and hunched his shoulders in fear. "Please don't ask my help to get rid of the dark ones. They frighten me."

"Who can help?" I asked.

Regulator shrugged his shoulders. I glanced at Pastor Neil, who looked totally perplexed at the proceedings. He wasn't alone. I wasn't sure what to do next. More than once I have reached a point in an exorcism where I didn't know what to do. At those times, intercessory prayer is usually the most effective course of action.

I bowed my head and clasped hands with Pastor Neil and Randall's wife. "Lord Jesus, whether You want me to face a demon or alter, bring forth the one who can most help us."

I lifted my head and watched to see what would happen. For a moment nothing. Regulator stared straight ahead, his body still poised in a frightened position. Then he blinked and his face sobered. His body relaxed and he sat erect.

"Let me guess. You're Facilitator. Is that right?"

"I am. But if you think you're getting rid of me—"

"I don't want to get rid of you, and I don't want to get rid of Regulator. I need both of you, but obviously you know some things he doesn't."

"If you're talking about the dark ones, I do. I make certain they don't have any reason to get mad at the rest of us."

"Do you appease them?"

"Let's just say I facilitate everything that goes on internally between those of us who are part of Randall and those who come from the dark world."

"Do you know how the dark ones got there?"

"Yes, but why should I tell you?"

"Because I come from God. I can get rid of the dark ones if you'll help me."

For the next hour Facilitator and I debated his role in Randall's deliverance. Gradually, I was able to convince him to cooperate. His greatest fear was that any assistance he lent would cause the dark ones to retaliate as they had done before. The Holy Spirit had paved the way for our encounter, and I was eventually able to lead Facilitator to Christ. When I did, his attitude changed to one of willingness.

"Do the names Vivinanda and Sridepok mean anything to you?" I asked.

"They are the most powerful of the dark ones," Facilitator answered. "They were here before I arrived. Regulator knows more about them than I do."

"Do you mind if I talk with Regulator?"

"Not at all. I suspect he's anxious to talk to you."

Facilitator closed his eyes, and Randall's body hunched over again in the fearful pose of Regulator.

"I'm glad you're back, Regulator," I said. A slight smile crossed the face of Regulator, but something didn't seem right. I narrowed my eyes, looked sternly, and decided to test my spiritual hunch. "You are Regulator, but you're not the same Regulator we spoke with. You are a dark one."

The demon let out a cackle. "Very clever of you. There are two of us named Regulator. He's part of this body, and I come from my master."

"Spirit, I bind you in the name of Jesus Christ and command that you tell me what you regulate."

"The same thing as my counterpart—his emotions, his perception of things."

I thought for a moment about what the difference between the alter and the demon could be. The answer came. "You regulate reality. You lie to him. You make him believe that what *is not* is, and that what *is* is not."

The demon looked startled. I knew the Holy Spirit had revealed Regulator's purpose to me, because I couldn't have known it any other way.

"Very, very clever. But it won't do you any good. I can twist his mind to make him think what I want to make him think. Even now I'm telling him that you are not truly a man of God. By the time you get back to talking to him, he'll be convinced he's got to keep quiet."

"I demand to know who is under you and what other spirits are in your control."

"Pain, that's all. But that's enough."

"Is pain the one who creates the suffering of the phony multiple sclerosis?"

"My, you are getting this all figured out, aren't you? Of course. Perhaps you'd like to see a sample of what we can do."

Randall's body suddenly jerked and Regulator the demon was gone. I immediately recognized Randall as he doubled over in pain, clutching his right knee. He grimaced for a moment and then said, "I've got to leave. I shouldn't be here. The pain is just too severe."

I remembered the threat of Regulator and dealt with it directly. "Randall, you've been lied to. I know you're not that sure you should be here, and your confidence in me has been shaken. But look at Pastor Neil. You trust him, don't you?"

Randall looked at his pastor and then back at me. I prayed, "I command that angels of God search out and torment the spirit of pain. I bind Pain to Regulator the demon, and command that both of them experience all the torment they've put on Randall. And I increase that torment seven times greater."

My command sent Randall into convulsions. His body twisted and jerked, first in one direction and then the other. He let out a scream. Then he relaxed and Regulator the alter looked at me.

"Do you remember when the dark ones entered?" I asked.

Regulator nodded.

"You've got to tell me how it happened. If you don't, the pain Randall has been gong through will continue, and he may never be free. You don't want that, do you?"

Regulator shook his head. "I was very little, maybe eight or nine. It was Sunday morning, and a missionary visited our church. He asked if there was anyone there who wanted to give his heart to Jesus. If they did, they were supposed to pray with him out loud. I whispered to my mother and asked her if I could pray. My mother laughed. She said I was too little and that I didn't understand."

Regulator began weeping. "But I *did* understand. I loved Jesus. I wanted to give my heart to Him. It hurt so bad when my mother laughed, I decided to regulate my emotions so that I would never be laughed at again. Years later, when I finally gave my heart to Jesus, I did it all by myself so no one would know. But it wasn't the same as that Sunday morning. My mother robbed me of something. It has always hurt me very much, deep down inside." Regulator pointed toward his chest.

I had to seize the emotional vulnerability of the moment.

Without telling anyone what I was doing, I commanded that Regulator the demon come forward. "Spirit, I demand in Jesus' name that you tell me how what I've just heard allowed you to enter this body."

Regulator locked his eyes on me. "Our little friend, the other Regulator, left out one important detail. That Sunday morning speaker was a missionary from India. Some of my kind had followed the missionary to America. They wanted to keep him from winning souls to Christ when he preached. They seized the opportunity. When little Randall decided to regulate his emotions, it gave them the right of entry. You see, by controlling his feelings that way he was actually resisting the Holy Spirit. He didn't realize that, but they did. It gave them all the legal ground they needed."

"Is that when Vivinanda and Sridepok gained access?"

"Yes, they're the . . ."

"You almost slipped and said too much, didn't you? It doesn't matter anyway, because I know they're the gatekeepers."

Regulator was furious. "Even if you know, it won't do any good. I'm not leaving." Regulator cocked his head back arrogantly. "Don't you think it's interesting how one moment in a child's life could lead to years of suffering from a disease that his body really doesn't have?" The demon threw his head back and laughed viciously.

I had learned all I needed to know. Now I needed to have Randall confess the sin of controlling his emotions in response to the Holy Spirit's conviction and deal with the anger toward his mother. He also needed to see past Regulator's lies that allowed the demon to distort his spiritual perception. These tasks took more than an hour.

As I worked with Randall, I also took time to carefully answer all the questions he and Pastor Neil had about multiple personalities. That evening they both got a crash course in understanding a crucial area of ministry that the body of Christ needs to embrace.

WHAT KINDS OF TRAUMA CAN CREATE MULTIPLE PERSONALITIES?

Multiple personality disorder usually begins in childhood because, unlike adults, children can't run from abuse. The only place they can hide is inside their heads. As the victim grows older, the separate personalities become even more autonomous, and each has its own special way of functioning in the everyday world.

The various alters of a multiple system cope internally like pieces of a pie. Each piece has a limited amount of coping power. When that limit is reached, the switch to a different alter may occur. In this way, the many alters that are part of the system absorb the emotional anguish and physical pain of the trauma.

From time to time one particular alter identity may be "out." When this happens, the host body and core personality of the victim's original identity may lose track of time.

Satanic cult programmers sometimes purposely create alters in victims through the use of trauma—both physical and emotional. Triggers are words or symbols that evoke previously implanted responses. For example, a satanic ritual abuse survivor may be programmed so that every time he sees the color red, a self-mutilating alter will come out and cut the body. Some victims are subjected to advance programming and are told they will die on a certain date. In satanic cults certain alter personalities are brainwashed to continue attending ceremonies to assure loyalty to the cult.

HOW IS MULTIPLE PERSONALITY DISORDER TREATED?

The treatment of multiple personality disorder requires a comprehensive approach, combining psychological therapy and spiritual intervention. Once the exorcism is over, multiple personalities must be integrated. The one ministering deliverance should be aware that previously undetected demons may surface during the integration process. These demons use the dissociative state as a shield and may be forced into the open when the alters are identified and have been integrated (or brought back to union with the core personality).

During the process of treating someone with multiple personalities, a Christian clinician should identify all the alters and help the victim work through traumatic issues for healing and restoration. The final task of the counselor is to allow or encourage the alters in the host's mind to fuse and cancel any remaining demonic ground. Because integration may have to weave its way through inaccurate memories, self-abuse, animal alters, foreign languages, and demonic resistance, complete integration often takes months or years.

Multiple personality disorder disrupts the victim's comprehensive identity and total memory system. Traumatized multiples lose contact with the person God meant them to be. It is important that the Christian community provide a haven for those suffering from dissociative disorder by offering them unconditional love and acceptance. If these people are provided understanding and support, they can once again function normally and offer their considerable talents and mental acuity to the body of Christ. Most important, Christians need to be careful about confusing demon possession with multiple personality disorder.

RANDALL'S DRAMATIC DELIVERANCE

Randall's victory over the demonic forces that had invaded him came when he renounced the sin of his childhood—resisting the Holy Spirit by regulating his emotions. I commanded that the spirit of pain be attached to the demon Regulator, and that he be bound to the unclean spirits Vivinanda and Sridepok. Then I cast out all of them together. While these spirits were leaving, they tried to inflict severe pain on Randall by intensifying the symptoms of multiple sclerosis. This tactic forced me to stop several times and allow Randall to recuperate physically before the exorcism could proceed.

When the demons were finally cast out, all the pain Randall had been suffering disappeared instantly and the symptoms of M.S. vanished. Facilitator and Regulator were no longer needed as distinct identities. They merged into the total consciousness of Randall to become part of his conscious resources, which would assist him in dealing with other life problems. Randall walked from the room under his own power without the slightest limp. Because his dissociative condition was not a complex one, full integration was achieved that night through the healing hand of God. Randall was delivered, but more important, Christ healed and restored him to the wholeness God meant his life to be.

Chapter 31

What I've Seen the Devil Do

For many people, demons are mythic figures that adorn medieval, religious paintings or make guest appearances in horror movies. Their supernatural deeds are the stuff of Hollywood film editors and computer animation programmers. In modern parlance, the term *demon* represents a metaphor for whatever plagues or torments a person. Any connection of the word with real supernatural entities is dismissed as a primitive explanation for phenomena that ancient man didn't understand.

Yet demons are very real to me, and should be real to all who believe the biblical accounts of evil spirits. Though all Christians can confront demons, only those submitted to Christ's authority should contemplate this awesome responsibility. An exorcism is no place for the merely curious or those seeking spiritual thrills. And an ordained and properly qualified minister should be present if at all possible.

I've included in this book but a fraction of the demonic deeds I've witnessed. Moreover, if I were to chronicle the most dramatic supernatural demonstrations I've experienced, some might be overwhelmed with the information. I want to be sensitive to that fact. I've tried to include accounts that will best illustrate the ways in which Satan operates. The following incidents should serve as a warning to help you understand the dynamics of spiritual warfare. The first story in this chapter shows how bizarre the devil's tactics can be.

SHOCKING DISPLAYS OF THE DEVIL

More than twenty years after Linda Blair played a fictional character whose head rotated 360 degrees as she spat out pea soup in the movie *The Exorcist*, people still ask me if what happened in that movie was accurately portrayed. Some scenes were reasonably authentic, but the more absurd demonic displays were pure Hollywood hype. I've seen more demonic supernaturalism than any living human I've known, but I have yet to witness arms and legs lengthened like rubber bands, heads spinning like tops, or bodies floating in the air. Contrary to myth and occult legend, Satan doesn't display his power in these ways. What I have seen the devil do is remarkable, nonetheless. Christians should be aware of his deception.

I have observed minor acts of levitation. God allowed me to witness a woman, under demonic attack, thrown about a room as if unseen wrestlers were hurling her in a ring. Two pastors assisted me in the exorcism, and it took the combined physical strength of all three of us to keep her from serious injury. As we firmly held on to her, we felt her limbs and torso being yanked in first one direction, then another. Her muscles weren't taut from straining against us. The force we felt from her body was like magnets pulling her in several different directions at once. This battle went on for fifteen minutes until our petition for angelic assistance prevailed. When she finally collapsed, her body was bruised in places where we had not touched her.

This same woman suffered critical internal injuries, which

were verified by a physician who examined her. Some of the internal lacerations actually required minor surgery and stitches. In one instance, pieces of wire twisted into shapes that represented death curses were found inside her body and had to be surgically removed. The attending physician had no explanation for the phenomenon of finding solid objects, which somehow had passed through her flesh as if they were immaterial.

Another woman with whom I counseled was assaulted by a sexual demon of incubus. During the exorcism, the spirit said he had come to impregnate her with a devil-child. Along with a pastor, his wife, and the woman's husband, I watched her abdomen supernaturally swell until it expanded to the size of a full-term pregnancy. The complete phenomenon took less than an hour. We countered this demonic impregnation with prayer and commanded that Satan's supernatural offspring be aborted. Gradually, her distended abdomen shrank back to normal size. The spirit was angry because, in his words, we had "killed" his child.

Did the woman's womb truly conceive a half-human, half-demon monster? I doubt it, but what would cause a woman's body to react that way? Every medical doctor knows it takes nine months of hormone stimulation affecting muscle tension and skeletal laxity for the female body to accommodate the baby that is ready to be born. Such physiological conditions occurring in a matter of minutes go way beyond the explanation of medical science.

Some of the most vicious demons I've faced were ones that possessed the body of a young woman named Sharon. As a teenager she joined a black magic sect and witnessed the sacrifice of infants. At the age of twenty-five, she contacted me for help to escape the cult she had once zealously served. The truth of God had slowly dawned on her heart, and she was now becoming fearful that she might be the cult's next sacrifice.

Sharon was afflicted with a demon of suicide. At least a dozen times in the last three years, demons drove her to that desperate act. When I ministered to her, unclean spirits repeatedly tried to choke her and kill her by strangulation. These spirits were so powerful that three or four people were required to subdue them physically.

The most dramatic display of her demons took place late one evening as we neared the end of an exorcism. One bloodthirsty demon knew that Christ was much stronger than he and his legions, and he realized his doom was near. As two men and a woman who assisted me prayed and commanded the demons to leave, we watched in horror as Sharon screamed and writhed. Invisible claws ripped her body until dozens of open wounds seeped with blood. None of us could imagine what was happening. We looked at one another with expressions of utter shock and revulsion.

I was not going to let Satan divert us from what God had called us to do. "You must leave, in the name of Jesus. We will not back down," I said.

The demon held on and inflicted more gashes, even though we prayed and claimed the blood of Christ. Sharon's face, arms, and legs were covered with deep, parallel scratches as if the extended fingers of a hand with claws had been scraped across her skin. We knew similar wounds were all over her body, because we could see blood seeping through the clothing she wore.

As the torment grew more intense, the demon's delaying tactic succeeded: Sharon was in so much pain that we had to stop the exorcism. The woman who was present took Sharon into the bathroom, helped her disrobe, and had her stand in the shower to wash off the blood. Though the demon had gained valuable time to regroup, we were able to resume the exorcism the next day. He was eventually defeated and cast out and did not return. We achieved this final victory because Sharon made a commitment to see herself freed, despite the pain.

THINGS I DIDN'T THINK THE DEVIL COULD DO

Through the years I've learned not to underestimate the supernatural capabilities of the devil. About the time I think I know where the line is drawn on what the devil can and can't do, he performs a feat that defies my presumptions. For instance, does the devil have any right to impersonate a servant of God and thereby deceive a victim of possession? I once thought the answer was "No!" but I learned through practical experience my conclusion was wrong.

I've had people with whom I was ministering a deliverance receive phone calls between sessions from a voice they identified as mine. In each case, the voice told them things about their situation that only I would have known. They would converse unknowingly with a demon and would give him important information regarding their deliverance. They had endangered their own spiritual freedom in response to the voice they thought was mine. In some cases, the exorcism was set back days or weeks because of this.

I have even had my physical appearance duplicated by demons. I've received phone calls from people commenting about a recent visit I supposedly made to them. In each case, the victims should have immediately recognized the impersonator because they were told to do something contrary to their spiritual welfare. They obeyed because they were convinced I had actually paid them a visit. The manifestation that they saw seemed credible, not only because of the physical resemblance, but also because the personage again knew things about the victim that only I would have known. Were these human agents of evil who had their appearance altered by a clever makeup artist? Or were these demons taking on physical form and disguising themselves as me? I don't know. But the more important question is "Would God permit a demon or a satanic cult member to do this?"

Some questions are best left unanswered. The more you try to resolve such puzzles, the more paranoid you become. I shrug off such supernatural trickery. I acknowledge what happened, I try to convince the victim of the truth, and then I move forward. It is futile to dwell on how or why the devil does certain things. Such endless speculation does not build faith, and faith is a crucial key to spiritual freedom.

I've also seen the devil mimic the miracles of God through the manipulation of natural laws.

THE CASE OF THE MISSING BRIEFCASE

I am writing this book on a laptop computer. However, before I entered the information age, I wrote my manuscripts in longhand and then had a secretary type them. Without the current technology of hard drives and backup diskettes to protect documents, my only security was to make a copy of the manuscript. One time I overlooked this practice, and the Lord used that oversight to teach me a valuable spiritual lesson.

I was in the middle of writing a book when I was called to minister deliverance to a woman trying to escape a satanic cult. Her pastor and a woman from her church joined us for the exorcism. The book I was writing had a tight deadline, and I kept the only copy of the manuscript with me so I could work on it when I had a spare moment. At a critical point during the exorcism a demon manifested and said, "Let me see that book you're writing."

The request puzzled me. I assumed it was merely a delaying tactic and responded accordingly. "We're here to cast you out, not look at manuscripts. I command that you obey us in the name of Jesus Christ."

The spirit smirked again and looked toward a far corner of the room where the manuscript, which I kept in a small leather pouch, had been lying on a table. Out of the corner of my eye I glanced in the direction of the manuscript. It wasn't there!

The spirit immediately sensed my distress. "Oh, is your book manuscript missing?" he said mockingly. "If this God you serve is so powerful, why didn't He keep us from taking it?"

I searched in vain for some natural explanation. The exorcism was taking place in the victim's home, and only four people were present. When we had entered the house earlier that day, we had walked straight to the victim's living room where the exorcism took place. No one had left the room since we arrived, and no one had passed through. I wondered if this was a phenomenon I had read about in occult literature—an apport, the disappearance of a physical object and its reappearance at another location. I had previously assumed that apports were really accomplished by trickery, and the devil was taking credit for an illusion.

Yet this couldn't be explained in natural terms. I believe that Satan mimics the miracles of God through the manipulation of natural laws. Satan may have insights into Einstein's theory of relativity—the idea that matter and energy are interchangeable. The phenomenon of dematerialization and rematerialization may be accomplished by transforming the matter into energy, which is then reassembled as matter. (If angels could move the stone from Christ's empty tomb, then fallen angels may have similar power.) Obviously, I don't have the final answer on this issue because I can't comprehend the mysteries of the universe. Furthermore, I don't need to know how the devil can do what he does, since my trust is in God who created all that is to show forth His glory (Ps. 19:1).

I'm embarrassed now to admit that, when the manuscript disappeared, my first reaction was one of anger. The demon's taunt was successful. *If I can't trust God to protect that manuscript, can I trust Him to protect me in other circumstances?* I wondered. And then there was the practical question of the imminent deadline.

I was overwhelmed with discouragement. The demon sensed this and knew he had won a temporary victory. With the emotional state I was in, there was no way to successfully continue the exorcism. I was spiritually weakened.

Perhaps I didn't lay the manuscript on the corner table, I thought. *Maybe there was too much on my mind, and I actually put it somewhere else in the room.*

I yanked cushions from the couch and looked underneath. I

moved every object, lifted every sheet of paper, and checked behind every piece of furniture. Even as I conducted my search, I knew it was in vain. A pouch that size holding a thick manuscript couldn't be anywhere else in the room.

Then I began searching elsewhere in the house, from one end to the other. After an hour I returned to the living room and sat dejectedly on the couch. *Why would God permit such a thing at a time when I was in His service?* I wondered.

In the midst of my despair, God's Spirit spoke to my heart. I sensed how ridiculous I had been, frantically running about the house, trying to find the manuscript. I realized the devil was laughing at my predicament and my lack of faith in God. One thought finally passed through my mind: *If God permitted Satan to steal this important manuscript, I have to leave that matter in His hands. God can get that manuscript back for me anytime, anywhere.*

I'm convinced that Satan is often the unwitting accomplice of God's purposes. The devil seeks to bring harm, but what Satan means malevolently God turns to our advantage. As Joseph said regarding the misfortune his brothers brought upon him, "You meant evil against me; but God meant it for good" (Gen. 50:20).

God doesn't toy with us capriciously, but He sometimes lets the devil go further than we think he should to give us an opportunity for spiritual growth. The case of the missing manuscript was my chance to mature in grace and exhibit confidence in God.

I believe God allowed Satan to take that manuscript to see how I would handle it. If I reacted in "the flesh" and tried to get it back by physical means, it wouldn't be returned. If I placed my trust in God, I would give the Lord an opportunity to show that His power is greater than that of the devil. Once I realized this, I stopped looking for the manuscript and prayed.

"Lord, You could have kept the devil from taking that manuscript. If You allowed the devil to take my personal property, I still trust You. Nothing You allow the devil to do to me will shake my confidence."

A peace came over me. I was still concerned about the manuscript, but I was no longer fretting about whether I would get it back. Moments later I felt an urge to walk into one of the bedrooms. I excused myself and headed in that direction. When I stepped inside the room, I saw the pouch lying on top of the bed. I had been in that room minutes earlier and it wasn't there. I walked over to the bed, picked up the pouch, and looked inside. The manuscript was there, not a single page missing.

I returned to continue the exorcism with more faith and power than I had before. Demons that had successfully resisted me before the loss of the manuscript seemed powerless when I commanded them in the name of Jesus. What mattered to me most was not that I had the manuscript, but that my faith in God was restored. I realized, as never before, that my protection from the hand of the enemy is only as good as my trust in God.

This has proved true, even when demons have attempted to kill me.

ATTEMPTS ON MY LIFE

Once, during an exorcism at a remote mountain location, I had to interrupt the proceedings because of a previously scheduled business phone appointment. It was necessary to drive to a nearby town where there was telephone service. Before I left, a demon warned that he would kill me for what I was doing.

After I finished the call about an hour later, I was driving back to the exorcism site. I rounded a curve and almost ran into a large black horse standing directly in my path. I slammed on the brakes, veered to the side, and brought the automobile to a screeching halt. The horse stood motionless. Its dark eyes stared directly at me. I glanced down at my trembling hands, and when I looked back it was gone.

Later, when I returned to the scene of the exorcism, the victim of the evil spirits met me at the door. She broke into sobs and thanked God I had returned safely. "The spirits told me you'd never make it back alive," she explained. "They told me they would use an animal to take your life."

I resumed the exorcism in the confidence that God is in control at all times. When the devil is plotting our destruction, the Lord is protecting us from the secret aims of the enemy. As the psalmist declared, "They have hidden their net for me in a pit . . . / Let his net that he has hidden catch himself; / Into that very destruction let him fall" (Ps. 35:7–8).

THE CASE OF FAILED BRAKES

A year after the black horse incident, I traveled around the world speaking for missionary groups. Just before I left, I was involved in the exorcism of Jonathan, a man who had belonged to a highly secretive black magic cult. I was warned by the demons before they were all cast into the pit that they would retaliate by killing me while I was overseas.

I thought nothing of their threat until I visited South Africa. While there, a Christian businessman loaned me a luxury automobile. I was driving from one church to the next when I approached a busy intersection just outside Johannesburg. I put my foot on the brake pedal and it went all the way to the floor! I saw a car coming into the intersection that would smash into me. Quickly I shifted into low gear and pumped the brake pedal again. The car jerked, slowed slightly, and sailed through the red light.

I squinted my eyes and expected a rough jolt. Within seconds my car came to rest by the side of the road, several hundred yards beyond the intersection. I sat up in the car, opened my eyes, and could not believe I had made it through. God's angels must have spared me a disaster. Before I did anything, I paused to thank God in prayer for His hand of safety in my life.

I found a pay phone and called for a tow truck. Then I made a long-distance call to Jonathan, whose demons had threatened to kill me. "Are you all right?" he burst out. "The demons told me that you would be in a serious car accident today. I've been pacing the floor frantically wondering if you were safe."

Later, when my automobile arrived at the repair shop, the mechanic looked it over and shook his head. "This car has a dual braking system," he explained. "It's rail-safe. If one system doesn't activate, there's an electronic backup. In your case, both systems failed simultaneously. I don't see how that could happen!"

Why did God allow the devil to tamper with the brakes and nearly kill me? I favor a different approach to dealing with what happened. Instead of wondering why God let it happen, I prefer to praise God, knowing that Satan's attempt to harm me was unsuccessful. I may have had a close call, but I wasn't killed or injured. My involvement in spiritual warfare made me vulnerable to the devil's attack, but Satan wasn't able to do what he wanted. God stayed the hand of evil from accomplishing all that the enemy intended.

God has blessed me with discernment concerning spiritistic phenomena, and I never treat the devil's displays as if they are a sideshow. I encounter these demonstrations with the armor of God (Eph. 6:10–17); in fact, I often go through the physical motions of actually putting on the defensive and offensive weapons Paul described in Ephesians.

As I enter into struggles of demonic warfare I always remember that Satan is an impostor. He's a loser, not a winner. He is desperately trying to duplicate God's miraculous power. Like the smoke and mirrors of a Hollywood set, the devil advances his purposes through deception, trickery, and intimidation. I have a healthy respect for what the devil can do, but I also know that, compared to God, Satan dwells with maggots and worms and has been "brought down" to the "lowest depths of the Pit" (Isa. 14:11–12, 15). I do admonish demons, but I am cautious about rebuking the devil myself. Instead, I follow the example of the archangel Michael, who declared to Satan, "The Lord rebuke you!" (Jude 9)

One final story will show you how God can fight these spiritual battles for us by guiding our thoughts and actions.

THE STORY OF THE WHITE HORSE

Janie was dedicated to the devil before she was born. Her parents and grandparents performed a prenatal ceremony, giving Satan all claims to Janie's life. Her earliest memories were of spirits manifesting to her. These demons, who appeared as imaginary playmates, seemed to mean no harm.

That changed when she became a young adult. At twenty years of age her psychic curiosities led to her involvement in a secret occult group that practiced a form of esoteric black magic. Janie was the mistress of the cult's leader and became pregnant by him. When the child was born, the cult forced her to kill the baby as a sacrifice to Satan. This led to multiple personality fragmentation and demonic possession.

I first met Janie when she journeyed far from her hometown to attend a rally where I spoke. She had previously written to me, seeking help for her dissociative disorder. I agreed to see her briefly, but minutes into the conversation, demons manifested. Soon I was involved in a full-blown exorcism. Unfortunately, the deliverance session had to be terminated when I encountered a demon who spoke only in a foreign language. I was unable to deal directly with the spirit without an interpreter. We met again more than a year later for an additional exorcism, which also ended without total victory.

Nearly two years after out initial meeting, Janie contacted me a third time, desperate for help. The demons controlling her had revealed that when her parents dedicated her to the devil, they specified a certain year and a time Janie would be sacrificed. MPD alters inside her were programmed to commit suicide on that date. That day was three weeks away!

"They will take my life," she cried during our phone conversation. "There are parts of me that I can't control. I'm going to die if you don't help me."

I agreed to meet with her at the earliest possible date. Two weeks before her death date, a pastor friend and I met with Janie for a final, six-hour exorcism. After casting out several minor spirits, we learned that the controlling demon was a spirit who referred to himself as "Double-D," a reference to his functions of death and destruction.

"You'll never get past me," Double-D bragged. "I'm going to kill her, and I'll kill you too."

"You'll have to get past him first," I said confidently, gesturing over my shoulder. Terror filled his eyes.

"He's big, isn't he?" I said, believing that I was guarded from the threats of Double-D by a large angel.

"Yes, he is, but I'll still get you somehow," Double-D insisted.

For two hours I did everything possible to weaken Double-D, but got nowhere. I paused in the exorcism and silently prayed for wisdom from God. The demon had been in Janie's life since the prenatal ritual, and the legal ground of his curse was one of the most tenacious I've ever faced.

As I prayed, two things came to mind. First, I remembered that Janie loved horses. Each time we met, she showed me pictures of the many horses she had raised and ridden. The sweater she was wearing that night had a horse knitted on the front. I knew in my spirit that this had a connection with her deliverance, but I couldn't see the correlation.

Then a second image entered my mind. Earlier that afternoon my wife had taken a walk with our daughter in her stroller, and they had stopped in the gift shop in our hotel lobby. My child reached out from the stroller and grasped a small white toy horse. She clutched it so earnestly, my wife wasn't able to leave the store until she purchased it. The rest of that day, my daughter wouldn't let go of that horse. The last thing I remembered seeing as I said good-bye to my wife and child and left to meet Janie was my baby daughter embracing that toy white horse.

God's purpose became clear. I began speaking under the leading of the Holy Spirit, even before all the thoughts of my mind had developed. Without saying a word to Janie or my pastor friend, I reached for my Bible and turned to Revelation, the sixth chapter. I stared into the face of Double-D and read the words of verse 8: "So I looked, and behold, a pale horse. And the name of him who sat on it was Death."

I fixed my eyes on Double-D. "You are the rider of that pale horse."

The spirit responded in shock and defiance. Finally he said, "Now that you know who I am, what are you going to do about it?"

Remember your daughter's white horse, the Holy Spirit spoke to my heart.

The words of Revelation 19:11 came to me: "Now I saw heaven opened, and behold, a white horse. And He who sat on him was called Faithful and True, and in righteousness He judges and makes war."

I quickly flipped through the pages of my Bible to confirm what God had shown me. I commanded Double-D to submerge. The demon knew I was up to something and didn't go down easily, but my persistent commands caused him to cease manifesting.

As Janie came back to herself, I looked at her intently. "I'm going to ask you to do something very unusual. Please cooperate. Your freedom depends on it."

"I'll do anything. I don't want to die."

"Please close your eyes. Relax for a moment and tell me what you see."

My spirit leaped for joy when Janie said, "I see a beautiful pasture with a white horse at the far end of the field."

"What is the horse doing?"

"He's coming my way. He's getting closer and closer."

"Have you ever ridden bareback?"

"Many times."

"When that white horse reaches you, I want you to grab his mane and leap on top of him, and ride away."

A few minutes later tears seeped through Janie's lashes and trickled down her cheeks. A glorious smile filled her face.

"Have you climbed aboard the white horse?"

"Yes! I'm riding away across the pasture."

"Are you alone on that horse?"

Janie smiled broadly and wept for joy. "No! He is riding with me."

"As you ride away, Janie, claim your freedom from the curse of death, in the name of Jesus."

I paused for a moment and then spoke forcefully. "Double-D, your curse over Janie's life has come to an end. I bind both parts of you, death and destruction together, and command that you function as one. Come to attention and face the judgment of God."

Janie's body jolted and Double-D manifested with both arms flailing and legs kicking. It took all my strength and the strength of my pastor friend to restrain the demon's violence.

"You know who's riding with Janie on that horse, don't you? I command that you confess His name!"

"He who is Faithful and True," Double-D screamed.

I handed my open Bible to my pastor friend and pointed to Revelation 19:11.

"Double-D, Christ Himself has come to set Janie free. He rides away with her now, and as she exercises her faith in Him, your curse over her life is ended. Go now to the pit, in the name of the Lord Jesus Christ."

Double-D looked at me calmly. He spoke almost in a whisper with a resolute tone. "I'll make you a deal. Back off now, and you can have what you want. Go ahead, ask anything of me. You know my master has the right to offer you everything in this world. You can have what you wish, if you'll stop now."

Without hesitating, I spoke back. "In Jesus Christ I have all that I need. In Him is fullness of joy and life everlasting. You can't give that, and what you have to give I don't need and I don't want. I rebuke your offer and command that you leave Janie now."

Double-D struggled again, lashing out with his feet and fists. He screamed at the top of his lungs, "No, don't let Him strike me with His sword."

My eyes glanced down to my open Bible: "Now out of His mouth goes a sharp sword . . ." (Rev. 19:15).

Double-D made one last violent lunge, let forth a piercing scream, and left.

God's love and power are always victorious!

Janie slowly regained consciousness. As her eyes opened, a glow spread across her face. "I'm free. I really feel it for the first time in my life." She wiped away her tears with a handful of tissues I gave her. "I must ask you one question. How did you know I've always wanted a white horse? From my earliest memories as a child, I always dreamed that I would someday ride away on a white horse to escape all the evil in my life."

To those who might argue that it seems unfair for an unborn child like Janie to be dedicated to the devil, don't miss the lesson of this supernatural story. As a small child, God put in Janie's heart the hope that someday her deliverer would come. The white horse that she saw through childlike eyes was God's way of foretelling His final triumph.

A POSTSCRIPT

These supernatural stories are extreme examples of how far Satan will go to destroy the lives of those he targets. Most who minister deliverance will never encounter anything near this. By uncovering what the devil can do, we expose his deception. We also reveal the extraordinary efforts of Satan to hold on to his ground in the lives of victims. If the devil cares that much about the souls of those whom he would destroy, how much more must a loving God care about those for whom He died on the cross.

Before you read on, keep this thought in perspective. It's not what the devil did that I want you to remember. Never forget, my message is this: No matter how tenaciously evil tries to hang on to its territory, God always wins in the lives of those who cry out to Him for mercy. The stunning exhibitions of Satan's pitiful power can be overcome by the might of God as demonstrated by the resurrection of Christ!

PART VI

How to Have Deliverance from Demons and the Devil

Chapter 32

The Exorcist

Pastor Cooper, a godly pastor of a small church, was an extremely effective man of God in an exorcism, even though his denomination taught that anyone who did exorcisms was an unscriptural fanatic. If you asked ministers in Pastor Cooper's denomination to describe an exorcism, they would paint a picture of a mentally ill person surrounded by maniacs screaming at the top of their lungs in an atmosphere of total chaos. This group believes that exorcisms are unnecessary in our current dispensation, and that casting out demons was used only as a sign of Christ's divinity. According to their opinion, present-day deliverance is something practiced by wild-eyed fanatics who suffer from an overdose of enthusiasm, unsupported by proper biblical exegesis.

Pastor Cooper didn't harbor those prejudices. When a woman in his church manifested demons, he refused to sign a pledge saying he would cease being involved in ministering deliverance to her. As a result, he was expelled from his denomination, and he was completely ostracized by pastors who had once been his theological comrades.

Pastor Cooper introduced me to the woman whom he had diagnosed as demonic. As a child she had been severely abused. One time her parents locked her in a closet for three days without food or water to punish her. During that time a spirit appeared to her and offered to take over the role of her parents. "She wanted a new mommy and daddy," the chief demon sneered when he manifested during the exorcism. "We were only too happy to oblige her."

This rejection of parental authority gave legal ground for a demon to enter. Freedom for this woman finally came after an all-night session of battling demons. Pastor Cooper, who was in his mid-sixties, fought the demons vigorously. His willingness to risk his ministerial credentials for the sake of one parishioner greatly impressed me. His quiet confidence in the calling of God on his life gave him the courage to do what no one in his denomination had done before. If Pastor Cooper overcame his theological inhibitions to engage in exorcism, any Christian can do the same if he or she is called by God.

Every Christian can and should be ready to cast out demons. However, most don't because Satan has convinced them it's not their calling or it's too dangerous or it's theologically inappropriate. The truth Satan wants hidden is that the necessary authority to demolish demonic strongholds is given to us by the Holy Spirit when we are born again in Christ. Believers in Christ have been crucified, raised, and seated in the heavenlies with Christ far above all demonic powers (Eph. 1:18–2:6). Like a royal title, our authority to deal with the devil is a birthright of our status as joint heirs with Jesus Christ. "I give you the authority to trample on serpents and scorpions," Christ told His disciples in Luke 10:19.

Just as a policeman packs a pistol to prove he has the power to enforce the authority of his badge, Christians have the Holy Spirit as a source of supernatural strength to enforce the authority God has given us in Christ. "You shall receive power when the Holy Spirit has come upon you," Acts 1:8 tells us. But authority and power are pointless without faith.

Where does that faith come from? We're given the source in Romans 10:17: "So then faith comes by hearing, and hearing by the *word* of God" (emphasis added). To the exorcist, faith is a radical confidence that God's Word means exactly what it says and that God is faithful.

I have seen this biblical truth at work on many occasions. I remember one time a demon placed his victim in a trance and caused her body temperature to drop dramatically, nearly to the point of death. Her lips turned blue and her flesh was cold and clammy. By faith I took God's Word literally. The Holy Spirit brought to my mind Psalm 119, verse 105: "Your word is a lamp to my feet / And a light to my path." I spread open the pages of my Bible and held it above the victim's body.

"In the name of Jesus, I command that God's Word shine as a heat lamp on the body of this one whom Satan has attacked. May the radiant warmth of this lamp bring life back to this body," I prayed aloud.

The demon causing this phenomenon manifested and violently tried to rip the Bible from my hands. Those assisting me restrained the interference until God's Word had proved effective, and health and strength were restored to the woman's body.

Christians who are thinking about a ministry of exorcism always ask me about the physical and spiritual dangers. Let's look at those now.

DOES THE EXORCIST FACE PHYSICAL DANGER?

When I first got involved in exorcisms, I presumed that God would unequivocally protect me from physical injury. My naïveté was shattered the day I faced Karen's demon. Karen was a frail, somewhat shy woman whose abuse of prescription drugs had led to severe forms of demonic bondage. The more she relied on drugs to bolster her behavior, the more Satan became entrenched in her emotions.

Our encounter took place in a church meeting room, where only steel folding chairs were available to sit on. I placed my chair directly in front of Karen, as close as possible, so I could stare into the demons' eyes. I assumed that my authority in Christ would allow me to instantly command their obedience.

Yet one of the demons threatened to strike me for rebuking him.

"Sit in that chair. Don't move, you are bound by the Holy Spirit," I commanded.

Before I knew what was happening, the demon tilted his chair back slightly, drew Karen's knees toward her chest, and quickly thrust her feet forward. Karen's feet landed on my chest and knocked me backward off the chair. The steel chair collapsed on the floor as I landed, bruised and embarrassed. With as little show of surprise as I could muster, I picked up the folding chair and sat back down. This time, however, I placed the chair a full three feet away from Karen. I didn't trust God's Word any less, but my prudence had been given a new dose of reality.

On another occasion, while battling a physically violent demon, the Lord brought to my mind Ecclesiastes 4:12, which says, "A threefold cord is not quickly broken." By faith, I went through the motions of binding the demon's arms and legs to the chair with an invisible cord. After that the demon tried in vain to move his arms and legs as if he were struggling against actual bonds on his hands and feet. The demon was literally restrained because I acted on the basis of God's Word.

I have seen this technique work on many other occasions, but there have been times when the procedure failed miserably. In certain instances I called on mighty angels to restrain demons. That, too, has sometimes proved effective, but not always. I've learned that certain kinds of demons can be restrained by verbal authority, and others by literally applying Scripture, as with the instance of the threefold cord. No technique is universally applicable. The strength and ability of each demon must be determined at the time of the exorcism as the Holy Spirit gives insight and wisdom.

During one recent exorcism, the victim of possession was so violent, I could only control her by making her lie flat on her back on the floor. Prayer warriors who had joined with me assisted in the restraint. Two people held each of her legs steady, and two other people held each of her arms. A fifth person sat near the top of her body to immobilize her head so the demon couldn't bang it against the floor and injure her. A sixth person applied pressure to her shoulders to keep the demon from trying to raise her back off the floor.

A deliverance session is emotionally and physically exhausting. If the exorcist has to be involved in the physical restraint of the victim, his focus is distracted from the mental and spiritual struggle taking place. Unless I inadvertently encounter a case of possession alone, I always make sure that others are present to help.

In spite of all my efforts to be cautious, I have come away from exorcisms with bite marks, bruises, and deep scratches. If the victim is a woman, and if I expect the ordeal to be physically violent, I may ask her to trim her fingernails before we start. Demons will try to claw your eyes out or inflict injury with long fingernails, and I was severely scratched several times before I learned to take this precaution.

The most humiliating form of physical assault is being spat upon. More than once I've been drenched in the course of an exorcism. Take for example the case of a woman named Susan, who was a lesbian. When her demon manifested, he expressed his hatred toward my manhood by spitting. It happened so many times I finally got a towel, hung it around my neck, and continuously wiped the spittle from my face.

When Susan periodically came out of the trance and saw the

humiliation I had gone through, sitting there with a wet towel wrapped around my neck, she was deeply touched. The fact that I was willing to suffer personal embarrassment and revulsion on her behalf was a key to her freedom.

When conducting deliverance, avoid presumptions about what the devil can and cannot do physically to the exorcist. My confidence in God is not based on whether a particular demon may injure me in the course of spiritual battle. Even the best-trained soldiers sometimes get wounded in combat. When I am fighting for the freedom of a soul, I expect no less. I always keep in mind the ultimate defeat of the demon. Praise God the question isn't "*If* the person will be delivered," but rather "*When* will that happen?"

DOES THE EXORCIST FACE SPIRITUAL DANGER?

Spiritual competence, not spiritual perfection, is the qualification for being an exorcist. Authority over Satan is based on the righteousness of Christ, not on our spiritual achievements. More than once I've been involved in an exorcism when I didn't feel adequate for the task. Perhaps it was a period of discouragement when my faith was shaken. At other times I entertained feelings of anger or thoughts of carnality.

If the exorcist has unresolved issues between him and the Lord, this will hinder the deliverance: bitterness toward a family member, anger about a disappointment in life, or despair over some unanswered prayer. We are, after all, human vessels subject to all the foibles and failures of our fallen condition. Being involved in the deliverance of a demon-possessed soul reminds us that our only hope for salvation is in the grace of God—not by any good deeds we perform.

If I know in advance I'm going to be involved in a deliverance, I may spend extra time in prayer and engage in a specified period of fasting. If I encounter the exorcism unannounced, I mentally survey my spiritual state. If I feel inadequate at that time, I stop and pray for forgiveness and ask the Holy Spirit to freshly fill my life and cleanse me from any impurities that would hinder the power of God's Spirit from working through me.

Is fasting necessary? Many reference Matthew 17:21, in which Jesus pointed out that certain kinds of demons could only be expelled through prayer and fasting. Some believe this passage means that fasting has some implicit merit. That may be, but the main purpose of fasting is to draw one's attention away from the satisfaction of the flesh and to focus instead on the realm of the spirit. I have fasted several days prior to an exorcism and still found myself with sufficient energy and spiritual focus.

Sometimes in the middle of an exorcism I have stopped the procedure to spend time in prayer and fasting. This renewal can block out distractions and spiritually reenergize the mind and emotions. There is no rule to be followed regarding fasting. It is a spiritual discipline to be utilized whenever God impresses upon the exorcist that the demons require such diligence.

The most important spiritual preparation for deliverance is a constant state of willingness to be used by God. Such a surrendered attitude of availability protects the exorcist from spiritual dangers. Anyone who presumptuously engages in an exorcism should be warned that trying to cast out a demon is dangerous if you are outside the will of God. Exorcism demands a spiritual stamina that is forged by years of trials and testing that have solidified faith in God and His Word.

Could a demon enter the exorcist if he or she were spiritually unprepared? Such fiction was suggested by the movie *The Exorcist.* The priest, unable to achieve deliverance any other way, invited the demon into his own body, which led to his death. The scriptwriter suggested this as a noble act of sacrifice. No biblically grounded exorcist would ever consider such a foolhardy course of action. To the contrary, the true spiritual exorcist has confidence that God can and will set the victim free. This is accomplished through the authority of Jesus Christ, not by the exorcist exchanging his soul for the victim's.

I do want to caution those involved in deliverance to be careful about the individuals who assist you. Consider whether these persons are acting in faith or whether they have offered their services out of curiosity; such selfish motives might make them vulnerable to demonic attack. I always carefully question those who wish to assist, particularly if I am away from home, where I do not know all the people involved.

I warn potential assistants that demons will exploit any lack of unity in the bond of believers engaged in the deliverance. I add, "You could also be subject to mental and emotional harassment if you have unconfessed, serious sin in your lives." Then I ask, "Can you assure me that you are walking closely with the Lord?"

Sometimes potential intercessors have excused themselves because they felt spiritually unprepared. I don't consider this a sign of weakness. I would prefer that an individual admit his shortcomings rather than get involved in something that could prove injurious to both himself and others.

PRACTICAL CONSIDERATIONS FOR AN EXORCISM

Some of the questions I am asked most frequently pertain to practical considerations regarding one's involvement in an exorcism. For example, What does one wear to an exorcism?

If I know in advance, I like to wear comfortable, casual, loose-fitting clothing. The possibility of a physical struggle and a lengthy session warrants that those involved be as much at ease as possible. When I haven't had the privilege of such preparation, I've been involved in exorcisms while wearing a business suit and dress shirt. Several times I've had this clothing torn or stained during a violent exorcism.

What should you take to an exorcism?

ITEMS THAT SHOULD BE PRESENT AT AN EXORCISM

Take your own Bible so you can readily find passages of Scripture. I also recommend having more than one translation available. Many contemporary churches use the New International Version, but I often find that the language of the King James or New King James is better suited to a literal translation of Scripture.

A good concordance is also important. The ones in most Bibles are brief so it is best to have a separate concordance, such as *Strong's Exhaustive Concordance*. The Holy Spirit may bring to your mind certain Scriptures to use in battling the demons, and your ability to locate that Scripture and apply it precisely might depend on a complete, unabridged concordance.

If your ordeal is long and arduous, the victim often experiences extreme thirst. Sometimes light, healthy snacks are helpful if you are breaking your fast. Remember, when David was fighting and his troops were hungry, he went into the house of God and ate the bread off the altar (1 Sam. 21:6; Matt. 12:3–4). This act would normally have been unlawful, but as Jesus pointed out, the human necessity of the moment was more important than abiding by strict legalistic edicts.

I have also found it helpful to have a portable cassette player with tapes of praise and worship music. While taking a break from the ordeal to rest or rethink what is happening, the tapes are a means of torment to the demons and a further invitation for God's presence to be with you.

Make sure that toilet facilities are readily accessible, and never let the victim go into the rest room alone, once the demons have been aroused. If the exorcist is male and the victim is female, it's important to have another woman present who can assist in this regard. If the victim is offended by such seeming immodesty, at least make sure that someone stands next to the bathroom door and that the door is left slightly ajar. I've had demons manifest once the victim was in the bathroom and lock the door. By holding the victim in a trance state, the demons kept the person in the bathroom for hours, and thus stopped the exorcism.

I have also encountered circumstances when a demon tried to provoke suicide while the person was in the bathroom. Medicine cabinets often contain scissors, razor blades, or other sharp objects. Demons will stop at nothing to impede the exorcism, and those ministering deliverance must constantly be on guard for any delaying tactic.

MAINTAINING THE PROPER ATMOSPHERE

Above all, there must be an atmosphere of faith and authority in Christ. Let me share an illustration that underscores this. I once engaged in an exorcism with a woman who channeled evil spirits as a spiritualistic medium. Soon after we started, I was distracted by odd noises, rapping and racket, from outside the room where we were meeting. Doors slammed and I could hear creaks and groans in the building structure.

The more I tried to go forward, the more I was distracted by the presence of demons all around us. Then the Lord showed me what was happening. I was reacting fearfully to the pandemonium encircling us, and this was inhibiting my ability to face the forces of darkness with the authority of Christ. I stopped the exorcism, withdrew for a few moments, and prayed alone that God would restore to me power, love, and a sound mind, according to 2 Timothy 1:7.

By the time I finished praying, the sounds had ceased, and I was able to resume the exorcism successfully. It was then that God also showed me that what the demons were doing to distract me had not ceased. What had stopped was my ability to hear what was going on. The distracting sounds were supernatural, and my spirit was, supernaturally, "hearing" them. I had listened to them through an attitude of fear rather than faith. When I put my spirit in proper alignment with God and began to operate by faith, my spirit could no longer hear them.

In addition, those involved in an exorcism need to be led by the Holy Spirit so that they are absolutely certain their participation is ordained by God. Having determined that, and having approached the deliverance with proper prayer and preparation, each of those seeking to free a soul from Satan will abide in an atmosphere of faith. Satan has already been defeated by Jesus Christ, and we are merely the executioners of God's judgment.

Probably the toughest question to answer is, "When do you know the time is right to start the exorcism?" I agonize over that decision every time I'm involved. Waiting too long gives the enemy an opportunity to build up strength and develop strategy. Prematurely initiating the exorcism can be emotionally traumatic for the victim. Staring into the victim's eyes and commanding demons to come forth can be devastating if it doesn't occur in God's perfect timing. If the exorcism has been planned in advance and the person needing deliverance is aware of what is going to happen, there's no need to delay once everyone is ready to proceed.

Impromptu exorcisms are a different matter. If I am unsure about the presence of demons, or if the victim is edgy about the procedure, I take all the time that is necessary to wait on the Lord for Satan's hand to be tipped. This may be done by spending time in prayer or singing hymns. Such activities create an atmosphere of spiritual intensity that antagonizes demons and causes them to voluntarily come forward without the exorcist having to confront them. In a situation like this, I respond to the reactions of the demons and deal with whatever spirit manifests as a result of what is happening.

As long as the one ministering deliverance proceeds cautiously, and all participants are willingly submitted to Christ, there is no need to be concerned that the timing will be inappropriate. It is crucial that the exorcist begin calmly, quietly, and methodically. Those who rush into an exorcism and make it a noisy, boisterous affair run the risk that spiritual discernment will be lost in the confusion.

Other intercessors around him may pray, but the exorcist should quietly pray to himself, keeping his eyes open and focused on the victim.

Chapter 33

Preparing for an Exorcism

The screams and commotion from the rear of the sanctuary instantly caught my attention. I had just completed addressing a large audience in a midwestern church, and I was answering questions. The outburst sounded like a violent fight of some sort, so I rushed to the back of the church. A half dozen people were standing around a young woman who thrashed about on the floor. They screamed Bible verses and waved their arms in the air as if shadowboxing an unseen foe.

Several of the would-be exorcists knelt by the woman and tried to physically restrain her arms and legs. "You can't have her. We rebuke you in Jesus' name," one yelled. Another added, "Come out of her and go to the pit!"

The girl kicked and fought back all the more aggressively. "She belongs to me. I'm not leaving!" a hideous voice screamed, salting its protests with curses.

The moment those gathered around the girl spotted me, they motioned for me to join them. "Thank God, you're here," one person said. "Now we can get rid of the demons possessing this girl. You'll know what to do."

I acknowledged their pleas for assistance, but something didn't seem right. As politely as possible, I tried to calm down the amateur exorcists. Several cooperated, but the others had no interest in abating their assault on the forces of darkness. They ignored me and screamed all the louder. Quickly I took spiritual authority and insisted that everyone be quiet to bring order to the situation.

The victim regained her composure. She wrapped her arms around her legs, pulled her knees to her chest, and huddled in a corner. She seemed frightened and equally put off by my intervention. I asked everyone to step aside so I could talk to her alone. They reluctantly agreed, and I helped the woman to her feet. We walked to a nearby church pew where she sat down and stared straight ahead, sulking.

The exorcists retired to a far corner of the sanctuary and continued praying. Their boisterous mumblings of threats against the devil were undoubtedly sincere, but I wondered if their prayers were less a petition to God and more a show of defiance toward me.

"What's your name?" I asked.

"Cheryl," the young woman answered. "Are you going to get rid of the demons in me?"

I leaned against the pew next to her. "That depends on whether or not you want me to, and whether or not you have demons."

Cheryl sat up straight with a defiant look on her face. "What do you mean *if* I have demons? Didn't you see what was happening a few minutes ago?"

"Yes, but that doesn't prove you have demons."

"Look, you don't know how humiliating it is to be thrown on the floor and roll around like that. If you really cared, you'd help me instead of questioning me."

Her belligerence indicated I had touched a sensitive nerve. "How do you know you have demons?" I asked.

"Are you calling me a liar? Do you think this is some kind of act?"

"I didn't say that. I just want to know where you got the idea you have demons."

"She told me, the lady in the blue dress," Cheryl said, pointing to a woman in the far corner of the room. "She prophesied over me and said God told her that's why I cut myself."

Cheryl stretched out her right arm and with her left hand pulled back the sleeve of her sweater. Her wrist was crisscrossed with deep gashes, now healed over by scar tissue.

I gently touched her wrist. "How many times have you done this?"

Cheryl was silent for a moment. "Six or seven times, I don't know for sure," she said, shrugging her shoulders.

"What do your parents think about this?"

Cheryl glared at me intensely. "Parents? What parents? I don't know who my dad is, and my mother dumped me in a foster home when I was thirteen."

I was convinced that Cheryl's antics had nothing to do with demon possession. To be certain, I talked with her for another half hour, interspersing my conversation with words and phrases that would normally antagonize a demon. All the while, I did not take my eyes off hers. Not once did I see that look. I knew my test wasn't foolproof, but it was a strong indication that I was on the right track.

"When you were rolling around on the floor a while ago, how did you feel when one of the ladies rebuked the spirit of witchcraft?"

"I wanted it to be gone."

I leaned forward and touched Cheryl's shoulder. "Cheryl, if you were demon-possessed, you wouldn't have heard what that woman said. At the time you were supposedly in a trance with a demon manifesting. You couldn't have known what was going on. But you did, didn't you? You heard every word those ladies said, and you remember everything that happened, don't you?"

Cheryl lowered her eyes slightly, and tears streamed down her cheeks. "You're right. I put on an act. I don't know why I did it."

Cheryl wept and buried her face in her hands. I reached into my pocket and handed her my handkerchief and sat down on the church pew next to her.

"It's okay, I understand. You were just going along with what that woman said, hoping that it would help. Then, the more you went along with it, the more you became the center of attention.

"When people thought you were just a mixed-up girl with emotional problems, nobody took the time to help you. But when they thought you had a demon, they spent hours with you. Cheryl, if I had been through what you've been through, I might have done the same."

Cheryl looked up with a slight smile on her face. She knew that I understood, and she was relieved to finally know the truth.

THE DANGER OF DIAGNOSING DEMONS

Get ready for a shocking statement. Cheryl isn't an exception. I spend more time convincing people they *don't* have demons than I spend casting demons out of people who do have them.

Some people, like Cheryl, are susceptible to the idea that they have a demon because it quickly simplifies all their problems. It lets them avoid the tough task of dealing with an array of emotional problems. And for the overzealous exorcist, a demonic diagnosis is a quick way to help someone. I've met many people who have been through pseudo-deliverances and have been emotionally scarred as a result. The trauma of having people surround you, shouting insistent rebukes, can be mentally disturbing. Worse yet, if the victim of presumed possession goes along with the ruse long enough, she also accepts the false diagnosis, and everyone involved becomes party to perpetuating the lie. Meanwhile, the person's real problem goes unresolved.

After the exorcist determines that the person is truly demon-possessed, the next question naturally is: When is the person ready for the exorcism?

WHEN IS THE PERSON READY FOR AN EXORCISM?

The presence of a demon doesn't necessitate the immediate act of exorcism. Some Christians erroneously assume that if a demon is manifesting and challenging the saints of God, retaliatory measures must be taken right away. In fact, not everyone who has a demon is ready to be exorcised. Three factors affect this decision: the volitional willingness of the victim, the spiritual preparedness of the exorcist, and the weakened condition of the demon.

Not everyone with a demon wants to get rid of him. Codependence with a demon (which we will discuss later in this chapter) or a desire for the temporary benefits spirit possession can offer will prevent some people from seeking help. Even those who want to be free are not always volitionally cooperative. The victims may have been threatened with harm to them or to family members.

Trust is also a big issue. Does the victim really trust the exorcist? Does the victim really trust God? *Wanting* to be free and *willing* to be free are different. The will of the victim is the spiritual battleground on which the war of exorcism is fought. The slightest reluctance can mean defeat.

For example, issues that need to be resolved may arise in the midst of an exorcism. This is where biblical ministry must blend with a sound psychological understanding of how trauma affects the soul. During a recent deliverance session with a woman, I discovered that an act of incest had been committed by her father. The woman lived in denial about the incident. She wanted to be free from the demons, but found it difficult to admit that the father she loved so deeply had violated her as a young child. Her initial unwillingness to admit what happened gave the demons legal grounds for remaining.

The willingness of the victims can also be affected by their

423

feelings toward God. Some have been tormented by cults in which satanists, posing as religious figures, brutalized them. They were raped with crucifixes, forced to drink blood in mock communions, or watched as cult members in clerical garb committed unspeakable atrocities. Logic tells them not to equate these horrible deeds with the exorcism, but on a deep emotional level the link remains. Victims may will to be free, but a full volitional surrender depends on a 100 percent mental and emotional acknowledgment of that.

WHEN TO START AN EXORCISM

The strength of the demon may be the most important factor in determining when to start an exorcism. I've known people whom I refused to help until they matured in the Lord to the point Satan didn't want them any longer. Though every demon insists he won't leave, some are so tormented by the spiritual life of the victim, they will accept any excuse to go. In fact, I've had demons say to me, "We really don't want to be here. One of the higher-ups made us stay, but we're glad to go. We're sick of all this Jesus stuff."

The role of prayer must be impressed upon everyone involved. Those who assist with intercession by praying apart from the action of the exorcism are just as important as those who face the demons and rebuke them face to face. If I can plan the exorcism in advance, I always try to have prayer warriors in another part of the building; they are the ones who worry unclean spirits the most by making them truly sick of all the "Jesus stuff."

The power of the demon can also be affected by things in the victim's life that haven't been dealt with. Unbroken curses, fetish objects still in their possession, and minor occult practices they continue to indulge in will be toeholds the demon exploits. A material object of obsessive greed or an unconfessed anger toward God over some past discouragement will be enough to allow the demon to continue resistance.

Once while conducting an exorcism in my home, I was hampered by a Balinese wooden carving I purchased as a souvenir while traveling in the Far East. While dealing with the primary demon, I noticed he constantly fixed his gaze on this object, which was sitting on a shelf at the far side of the room.

"What's so interesting about that carving?" I demanded to know in the name of Jesus.

"I'm drawing strength from it," the demon confessed.

Without hesitation, I halted the exorcism and built a fire in my fireplace. When the flames were sufficient, I threw in the carving. It was a hot summer day and the intensity of the fire was almost unbearable, but it seemed appropriate for the occasion. As I watched the carving consumed by the fire, the Holy Spirit reminded me of the words of Deuteronomy 7:26: "Nor shall you bring an abomination into your house, lest you be doomed to destruction like it. You shall utterly detest it and utterly abhor it, for it is an accursed thing."

When the last remnants of the carving crumbled into embers, I returned to the exorcism and readily cast out the demon. This experience makes me wonder how many other victims of demonic attack fail to receive their complete deliverance because they or the one ministering to them have harbored some object or action that is displeasing to the Lord.

Some African and Asian masks depict actual demons. Certain sculptures are intended to convey the presence of a pagan deity. Amulets, fetishes, and souvenir pictures that tourists routinely purchase may transmit cures and hexes. Kachina dolls, dream catchers, yin and yang signs, and other occult paraphernalia don't belong in Christian homes. Though such symbols and objects may be considered spiritually benign, any association with them could hinder one's ability to effectively wage spiritual warfare. These comments aren't intended to be judgmental. My concern is to encourage Christians to look around and rid themselves of anything that could assist the forces of evil.

CAN A PERSON BE DELIVERED LONG-DISTANCE?

Several years ago, I received a phone call from someone who purported to be thirteen years of age. She sounded desperate and frightened. Her name was Rebecca and she said she was destined to be a human sacrifice on Halloween. Rebecca called several times over the next couple of days. During one conversation a deeper female voice spoke, claiming to be Rebecca's mother, Catherine. I confronted Catherine about Rebecca's claims, and other voices started speaking to me, some of them in foreign languages. It took days to sort out all the confusion because my only contact was through the phone calls.

I eventually learned that Catherine and Rebecca were actually multiple personalities of yet another identity. And I detected that several of the voices, including one that spoke with a German dialect, were demons. I rebuked the demons, bound them in the name of the Lord Jesus Christ, and cast out several of them. I continued the exorcism via telephone for several days. Yet I was unable to cast out all the demons in absentia. Thankfully, the victim of these unclean spirits received direct personal counseling and deliverance from a compassionate ministry. Many of her alter personalities were integrated and the demons were confronted and cast out.

After this strange incident, I encountered other cases of demon possession that were handled by telephone. Although I would have preferred dealing with these people face to face in a private setting, I had no choice. In most instances I didn't know the true identity of the person, and I had no phone number to contact the person. Consequently, there was no way the person could be followed up by a local counselor. Some of the situations were life-threatening and a delay to pursue more appropriate circumstances could have been fatal. The limited success of these long-distance exorcisms was the best I could do, given the extenuating circumstances.

Some people suffering demonic attacks, who could not travel to meet me in person, pleaded for me to minister deliverance by telephone. I have done so when possible and I am sure those prayers thwarted Satan's plans. However, I know of only one instance when I prayed for someone over the telephone and they were completely freed.

Unfortunately, long-distance exorcisms can give Satan the upper hand. The unclean spirit can manifest and use the victim's body to make him hang up the phone. In addition, without seeing the victim, the one ministering deliverance has no idea when a demon is manifesting unless the spirit speaks. Several times in this book I have noted how important it is for the exorcist to maintain eye contact with the victim. Often, the spirit's presence is first manifested through the eyes. Also, certain spirits evoke specific kinds of body language when they are present, and the exorcist cannot spot these signs over the phone.

The most important reason to avoid long-distance exorcisms is the potential harm to the host. It is common for demons to injure their victims, especially when the spirit knows he is losing the battle. I have dealt with demons who flailed their victim's head about, trying to bang it against a wall or on the floor to cause a concussion. Some demons twisted arms and fingers out of their sockets, or clawed at eyes. On many occasions, I've had to restrain demons from trying to kill their victims. Some have reached for knives, scissors, or other sharp objects to stab the host. One demon tried to hurl the victim's body through a plate glass window. Others have tried to make the victim drink poison or jump out of upper-story windows.

DEPENDENCY ON DEMONS

The case of a woman named Amanda, who lived in a small community in the northwestern United States, illustrates demonic dependency. Amanda was the church organist, a timid, plain-looking woman. Her print cotton dress, decorated in an outdated pattern, reached to her knees. Her straight hair was pulled back into a bun, and she wore rimmed eyeglasses. She spoke with a squeaky voice, and her eyes averted from people's glances. Amanda's schoolmarmish appearance belied the horrible truth about her private existence.

I met her at the conclusion of a speaking engagement when she asked if she could confide in me about a problem. We talked for quite a while before she mustered her courage to tell me what was on her heart.

"I'm an alcoholic, and no one knows it," she said tearfully. "I hide my drinking at home. I teach piano lessons to children and never have to leave the house, except to go to the store to buy groceries . . . and liquor. My piano students don't detect the problem, and I always sober up and get rid of the evidence before my husband gets home. He doesn't suspect a thing."

The longer we conversed, the more it became obvious to me that Amanda's drinking was compulsively controlled by a demon. I know that identifying a demon of alcoholism, or a demon of any other disease or disorder, is suspect to many, so let me discuss that now

DEMONS AND DISEASES

I have dealt with demons of all sorts of illnesses and addictions, from cerebral palsy to schizophrenia and from heroin addiction to compulsive masturbation. This is not to say that such maladies or urges are always the result of a demon. I am not suggesting that anyone afflicted by a physical or emotional weakness is controlled by evil spirits.

My counseling experiences have taught me that demons both exploit physical abnormalities and encourage aberrational behavior. For example, a demon may have known a person was genetically predisposed to alcohol addiction. The demon tempted the person to overindulge in alcohol and then capitalized on the resulting dependency by displaying its functions through the disease's symptoms. Eventually, the distinction between the disease and the demon becomes blurred until both manifest simultaneously.

In the case of a physical infirmity, the demon may mimic the ailments of a disease by afflicting psychomotor and neurosensory functions, or exacerbate the disorder's symptoms until the demon's influence is barely distinguishable from the primary illness. For example, a demon of anorexia would intensify his victim's abhorrent self-image to the point that food avoidance would be a simultaneous demonic and physiological manifestation.

The discerning counselor who encounters a demon manipulating the realm of mental, emotional, or physiological disorders must carefully discern between the sources of natural and supernatural factors afflicting the victim. Sometimes, medical attention may be necessary before an exorcism is attempted. The victim of anorexia may first need intravenous feeding to restore metabolic balance, which will lessen the demon's ability to use his victim's weakness. The alcoholic plagued by a demon may first need to dry out and recover physical strength so the demon no longer can enmesh his function with the features of his victim's disease.

Every disease isn't a demon, but any disease may be exploited or imitated by a demon. Proper medical advice, spiritual insight, and conscientious care for the victim's spiritual insight and condition will direct the exorcist to the right path for restoring total spiritual and physical well-being. In Amanda's case, I immediately told her that I suspected demonic intervention.

AMANDA'S POSSESSION

Amanda did not reject the idea. In fact, she replied, "I know it. I even know when he came in—one weekend a year ago during a drunken binge when my husband was out of town on business. What's difficult about all this is that part of me doesn't want the demon to go."

I led Amanda to a chair and had her sit opposite me while I tried to contact the demon. Calling the spirit of alcoholism forth was easy. He arrogantly presented himself. "What do you want with me?"

"Do you make her drink?"

"Oh, no," Alcohol said, "she does that quite well herself. When she's under my influence, I give her boldness she wouldn't have otherwise."

"What do you mean by that?"

"Look at her. She's pathetic. No personality, no gumption. What can you expect, the strict way her parents raised her, like a nun? She never developed socially. Now, *I* do that for her. That's why she wants me."

I commanded the demon to recede and called back Amanda. "Is it true that you actually like the demon of alcohol?"

"I don't like him in the sense that he's a friend. I like what he does for me. I married my husband because he was the first boy I ever dated. Part of me wants to break out of that mold and live a little dangerously. Of course, I can't do that, being the church organist. But when I drink and the demon takes over, I become someone I've always wanted to be—daring, outspoken. The few people outside the church that I see during the day when I'm drunk tell me they like me. If being that person means having a demon, so be it."

Amanda put her face in her hands and wept. After a few minutes she regained her composure and looked at me decisively. "Thank you for your time, Mr. Larson. I'm sorry to have troubled you. I just can't give up my drinking, and I know that if I don't do that, you can't make Alcohol go."

She stood and walked away. It's one of the few times I've faced a case of demon possession and couldn't proceed to spiritual victory. In every instance where I've found a demon could not be cast out, it was because the demon gave the victim some benefit she wasn't willing to live without.

CAN A PERSON BE DELIVERED WITHOUT KNOWING IT?

Are there cases of people who had demons and were spontaneously set free through some spiritual process other than an exorcism? If someone needs to be freed from demons, and God loves that person enough to want him freed, why couldn't the Lord Himself do the deliverance without the assistance of an exorcist? This is a difficult question to answer since any such occurrence would likely have happened without anyone knowing it. Theoretically, there is nothing biblical to prohibit such a phenomenon, but it is probably very rare. God usually acts through exorcists, just as He acts through Christians to declare His gospel.

God could send an angel to preach to everyone who needs salvation. Or He could manifest Himself supernaturally to convict each soul. Instead, the Scriptures declare that "we are ambassadors for Christ" (2 Cor. 5:20), sent in God's place as human vessels to witness to His saving grace. This is a great mystery of the gospel, that God has condescended to convey the plan of salvation by human instruments.

He works the same way to bring deliverance. "I was in prison and you came to Me," Jesus said in Matthew 25:36. Certainly, those bound by demons are in the worst kind of prison. The exorcist who brings them the truth of God's freedom also ministers unto the Lord. Loving them and speaking words of deliverance to such captives are becoming the hands and feet of Jesus, to walk where He would walk and deliver those whom He would set free.

A FINAL WORD

An exorcism isn't an action, rather it's a process by which the victim of the devil is led from demonic captivity to spiritual wholeness. That bondage may be the illusion of possession (as in Cheryl's case), or it may be an unhealthy demonic dependency. Whatever the circumstances, no force of darkness can forever resist the united effort of a victim who wills to be free and an exorcist who humbly ministers as unto the Lord.

Chapter 34

Anatomy of an Exorcism

Your pulse surges with such intensity, the veins on your neck bulge. Your palms grow sweaty, and your tongue sticks to the roof of your mouth. You're like a sprinter in the blocks, awaiting the words, "Ready, set, go." In this case you fire the starting shot by issuing the demand: "Demon, I command that you manifest in the name of Jesus."

Any exorcism is a trial in spiritual fortitude, but doing it the first time requires an immeasurable step of faith. You've read the suggestions in this book. You've prayed and consulted your pastor and other spiritual leaders. Now, it's down to you and the demon. What if you work up this courage to confront the forces of darkness and nothing happens?

Relax. Everyone who encounters an exorcism for the first time approaches it with anxiety and apprehension. Since you will have prayed about the situation, God will honor your forthrightness, even if your diagnosis is in error. So long as you approach the possible victim of possession with gentleness and understanding—and you have their full cooperation—the rest is up to God.

Sometimes, nothing happens. But that doesn't mean your suspicions were incorrect. Often my first attempt to provoke a demon in a person who is genuinely possessed elicits no reaction. The demon may be away at that moment, he may be in hiding, or he might be powerful enough to resist my initial demands made upon him, especially if I am the least bit hesitant.

How does it feel to be involved in an exorcism? For those who have experienced many of them, it's like a brain surgeon performing one of many thousands of operations; he moves confidently because he understands the precise procedures. Yet the first time he cut open a cranium, his hands were probably shaking so badly, he feared he would injure the patient. With experience and repetition, he mastered the austere technique. For me, after all these years, every exorcism is still a humbling, awesome experience. It confronts my human weaknesses and the limitations of my natural wisdom.

Though every deliverance session has unique characteristics, there is a general flow to the procedure. Like an exploratory medical diagnosis, the initial stages require more questions than answers. The experience might be explained as looking at the jumbled pieces of a jigsaw puzzle that has been dropped on a table. Yet unlike the puzzle, the disparate pieces of an exorcism are invisible, so figuring out how they are interwoven requires a high level of imagination. The unseen must be fathomed by faith.

God *does* give insight as to what to pursue and how far to go. The more we know of how evil men and demons work, the better we are prepared to unravel the problems and apply the truth of the Word of God for healing. It is the truth of Christ and His authority that set prisoners free.

When an exorcism is going well, you feel transported outside yourself into a dimension of the supernatural seldom experienced in any other part of Christian living. As you seek wisdom from the

Lord, God places thoughts into your mind that seem absurd at the time. Don't resist them. Probe, experiment, step out in faith, and remember that each step toward victory leads you deeper into the realm of the nonrational. Be willing to be used by the Holy Spirit in extraordinary ways, without abandoning faithfulness to biblical guidelines.

When an exorcism isn't going well, you will feel intense spiritual stress as if your soul, so some degree, is in a vise grip, with pressure being slowly applied. The exorcist is under constant supernatural attack. The real battleground is the soul of the victim, but your heart and mind are also under assault. I have experienced times when my thinking processes were so tense it was difficult to go from one thought to another. I had to stop the exorcism and step away from the situation to renew my emotional and spiritual energy.

An exorcism can also be the most spiritually exhilarating experience on earth. The Bible comes alive as you see that the forces of evil must obey God's Word. As James said, demons really do believe the truth of Scripture, and they tremble when confronted with God and His Word (James 2:19).

I never leave an exorcism discouraged. I may be disappointed if I was not able to accomplish all that I felt God desired on the pathway to the victim's freedom. However, the obvious presence of the Holy Spirit, which envelops an exorcism, leaves my mind centered on God and His glory, not Satan and his lies.

Others who have been present when I conducted exorcisms tell me that their lasting impression is one of renewed interest in God's Word and greater dedication to faithful Christian living. An exorcism is a microcosmic display of all the scriptural truths we take by faith but are allowed to glimpse in action.

It is amazing what we are privileged to hear, watch, and witness on behalf of the Lord for His glory. Hearing demons scream in torment as they are cast into the pit underscores the reality of eternal punishment and the promise of heaven's home. Observing the hatred that demons have for the blood of Christ gives new meaning to the Atonement.

An exorcism is similar to a masterfully played chess game. We must expect abrupt and unexpected changes in the flow of events as a normal part of the process. Planning ahead is vital. The frustration of the exorcist is the aim of every demon. Staying calm and focused disrupts Satan's strategy.

The basic focus of every exorcism is forcing the demon to acknowledge the authority of Christ and demanding that the unclean spirit acknowledge the authority of the exorcist and the victim. No matter what else happens, these two fundamentals should always occur. Demons must constantly be reminded that God is in control and that the exorcist is confident of eventual victory.

As you have seen from some of the stories in this book, there will be times when the one ministering deliverance gets distracted or discouraged. These are only temporary setbacks in God's purpose of deliverance and healing for the victim. Accept the fact that you are a frail human vessel, totally dependent on the Holy Spirit. Admit the superior knowledge of demons when compared to human understanding. But remember that, in spite of your natural incapacities, God's love for the victim will prevail. Don't ever let these truths leave your mind.

In the hundreds of exorcisms I've been involved in, certain moments stand out. One such instance was the time I methodically eliminated the defenses of a certain demon. Step by step I cornered the adversary until he could no longer resist. Before his final doom was pronounced, the demon looked at me quizzically. "Who taught you the rules?" he asked curiously.

"What do you mean by that?" I asked.

"The spiritual rules that determine what we can and can't do. Someone from our side must have taught you. I've never met anyone who knows the rules as well as you do."

The observation of this evil spirit was more profound than you might realize. While no human being has *all* the answers about how to successfully conduct an exorcism, basic guidelines determine the success or failure of any deliverance.

TEN RULES OF EXORCISM

I've spent a lifetime garnering information about exorcisms, and I'm thankful to share it with you.

Certain aspects of these rules may have been touched on elsewhere in this book. If they are reiterated here it is because I want to emphasize their importance and provide additional details not previously underscored. Here are the ten rules to follow as an anatomy of an exorcism.

1. Bind Lesser Demons to Their Leader

Dealing with demons in aggregate shortens the exorcism process. Demonic systems often have more than one demon assigned to a particular function, so they can be grouped together according to their kind. For example, spirits of lust might work in concert with spirits of pornography and perversion. Another coalition may involve a demon of murder with one of suicide. These could be coupled with a blocking spirit used to induce trance states. Groups of spirits may split into several parts, so groups should be bound together as a whole. Some combinations operate like a wrestling tag team, one taking on the exorcist while the other one rests. All groups of spirits have a hierarchical structure, and those of lower rank function in union with all those above them.

Some spirits will cleverly separate from their function. For example, a spirit of perversion, which causes homosexuality, may be cast out under the name Perversion; however, Perversion may have split off his function so the victim is still plagued by feelings of homosexuality. A spirit of hate, which has been driving his victim to thoughts of murder, might leave under the directive of the exorcist, who casts out the spirit of hate. But by splitting off the function of murder, the victim will continue to suffer as if the spirit of hate had not been expelled.

Complicated? Absolutely. It is difficult to figure out all the details of demon tactics and the procedures of exorcism. The faithful exorcist should not despair. God may give the ability to discern who the spirits are and what they are doing at just the right time. As deceptive as the actions of demons are, God is faithful in leading the spiritually sensitive exorcist to determine how to deal with the many variables. The exorcist is not alone. The Lord Himself promises to bring about Satan's defeat. He is standing by your side every moment of spiritual warfare.

2. Work Through the System

One of the initial goals in an exorcism is to find the pecking order of demons. The arrangement of evil spirits in a demonic system is like that of a military command. Each unclean spirit has jurisdictional responsibility over some part of the emotional and spiritual life of the victim. This network is arranged in a hierarchy of ascending spiritual power. To dismantle this infrastructure, I have found it advisable in some cases to begin at the bottom and work up. That's why I sometimes ask God to reveal which demon is the weakest. Then I attack that particular demon since the other spirits above tend to draw strength from those below them.

There have been times when I started out at the top and worked downward. Those rare occasions were in cases where the demonic system was small. If a dozen or more demons possess a person, the exorcist may want to identify the weakest spirit and start there. More than likely this will be a demon that hasn't been in the victim as long as the others, or it is a demon with a function that isn't totally enmeshed in the emotions of the victim. However, the exorcist may spend a lot of time at lower ranks of demons and be kept from the controlling leader. One must be flexible.

Sometimes demons toward the bottom will reveal secrets about those above them, making the casting out of the ascendant spirits much easier. Spirits at the top are generally more intelligent and powerful demons and less likely to let critical information slip out. Remember, there are biblical ranks of demons that are designated in descending order as thrones, dominions, principalities, powers, and spirits.

Someone should be designated to keep a log of the information received while interrogating the demons. As the internal structure of the victim's demonic system is revealed, list the spirits according to their ranking, cite their right and occasion of entry, and note their legal ground for remaining. Think of the person taking notes as filling the role of a court reporter, ready to read back prior testimony as the jury deliberates its decision.

A lot happens quickly during an exorcism, and sometimes the key to casting out a certain spirit will be related to what another demon, perhaps much lower in rank, revealed in earlier questioning. The written log will help you refer back to crucial facts that otherwise might have been forgotten.

As the end of the exorcism nears, it's wise to consult the log one final time. Go through the list of spirits dealt with and interrogate any left to be certain that no part of the entities listed has missed complete detection. The demons will be forced to give you this information because they must submit to the name of Jesus and His authority.

3. Ask God for Angelic Assistance

I've already given several illustrations of intervention by angelic hosts. As Elisha declared to his servant, "Those who are with us are more than those who are with them" (2 Kings 6:16).

There is biblical precedent for the idea of angels providing help. Daniel, chapter 10, addresses the issue of angelic assistance. Verse 13 indicates that God's messenger was hindered by a demon that delayed the angel from completing his mission for twenty-one days. It is apparent from this reference that demons struggle against angels. Even though angels are more powerful in their uncorrupted state, they still must fight to overcome the resistance of unclean spirits.

How are angels invoked? I am careful to avoid any attitude that would suggest that angels can be whimsically called upon. Asking God for angels shouldn't be treated casually, as if you were calling the family pet. I usually say something like: "I call on the Lord to dispatch mighty angels for assistance in dealing with the demons before me."

Designate the angels' function. Angels may be asked to guard from external demons seeking to interfere. Angels may be requested to bind or restrain the demon to lessen the demon's physical resistance. Angels can also be used to intimidate demons as a way of weakening their resolve. Many times I have halted an exorcism that wasn't going well and issued an edict of this sort: "I command in the name of Jesus that the demon of [demon's name] be confined in a prison and be subject to Christ's judgment until such time as we shall call the spirit forth."

Specific angels may be summoned to deal with certain kinds of spirits. You may ask an angel of truth to torment a lying demon. Be as specific as necessary, but always understand that such a petition is subject to God's will. The Lord is Commander in Chief of heaven's armies, and it is His right to commission angels for earthly assistance. Don't depend upon angels instead of the Lord. Our primary dependence is upon the Lord Jesus, the use of prayer, the presence of the Holy Spirit, and the Word of God.

4. Call Forth Undesignated Demons

Most exorcists encounter times when we aren't sure what to do next. For instance, our knowledge of the demonic network may be limited in the early stages when there is uncertainty about the ranking of the demons. What demons should be commanded to manifest under these circumstances?

The Holy Spirit has taught me a tactic that has been successful in breaking through this barrier. I sometimes employ this trick of the trade to initiate an exorcism if I have no idea what demons are present. I say, "I command to come forth whatever spirit the Lord Jesus has identified to face divine judgment for violating this soul."

After speaking those words, a demon almost always manifests. Then I check to see whether or not this is an interfering spirit. I say, "Are you the demon that *Jesus Christ* has specifically called forth for judgment?"

If the demon acknowledges he isn't the right spirit, command him to be punished for interfering, and then tell him to recede and make way for the correct demon. Do this several times until the specific demon, the one God wants dealt with, comes forward.

Deeper into the exorcism the log can be consulted to decide which demon is next in the succession to be cast out. Even with a detailed log I sometimes ask for the one God wants dealt with, because I sense some spirit needs to be confronted that may not have previously been identified. By summoning the one whom God has appointed to judgment, I am always certain that the time to confront each demon is accurate.

5. Find the Function of the Demon

Knowing the demon's function may be the most important information in understanding how a particular evil spirit should be handled. This puts the exorcist in sync with the parameters for handling each spirit. If the demon is a mind-control spirit, then the exorcist will know to be aware of mind games and intellectual trickery. If the spirit has a name indicating more visceral responses (murder or violence, for instance), the exorcist will be on guard against physical retaliation and also the possibility that the person or his ancestors have committed some violent act.

Knowing the function of the spirit will help the exorcist discover the demon's legal grounds. An example would be a demon of incest. If the victim has said nothing about such a moral dilemma, the chances are the incest demon is exploiting an event that the victim may have denied or suppressed.

It is sometimes advisable to cut the demon off from his function. For example, a demon of false wisdom could be a powerful spirit whose intellectual acumen is crucial to the demonic system. In that case, I would pray, "I take the sword of the Spirit and cut off False Wisdom from his function. I separate the demon from his ability to think and act wisely in the interests of Satan. Having removed the demon from his wisdom, I command that this spirit become foolish and unlearned, and exhibit traits contrary to his function."

Be aware that the function of the demon may not be designated by the demon's actual name. Sometimes the function is hidden because the demon knows that this information will point toward the legal ground by which he remains. A case in point would be a demon of murder. The exorcist might think such a demon's function would be to kill someone. However, murder might also be defined as destroying the emotional capacities of the person, "murdering" their sensitivities. A demon of self-hate might function in several different ways. This kind of spirit could cause masochistic mutilation or influence homosexual behavior. In the first instance the mutilation would be a physical means of demonstrating self-hate. In the second instance the homosexual behavior would be a way of rejecting one's true sexual identity as a means of self-loathing.

6. Employ the Assistance of the Victim

I have written this book from the perspective of the exorcist. The dialogue of each narrative has been shortened to provide the essence of the battles between myself and Satan's demons. I have not included my often-lengthy conversations with the victims. In fact, a great portion of the time spent in many exorcisms is more devoted to talking with and ministering to the one under attack than confronting and rebuking the demons.

Victims are co-combatants and as much a part of the exorcism as I am. Their assertions of moral and spiritual authority are crucial to their freedom. It is futile to tell a demon what to do, unless the command is backed up by the victim's agreement and aggressive resistance to Satan. The exorcism will be unsuccessful without these elements of cooperation.

At times when I have been stymied and uncertain of what to do next, God has often led the victim to suggest a course of action that proved to be the key to lasting victory. I always listen carefully to what the victim has said, because the person is often used by God as much as I am to confront the indwelling demons. Sometimes a victim has said, "This may sound crazy but . . ." and has hesitated to continue. I encourage the person to speak whatever is on his or her mind and to let me, with the help of the Holy Spirit, sort out what to do.

An exorcism is an exercise in encouragement as much as it is an attempt at expulsion. It's a critical opportunity to teach victims about their redeemed authority in Christ and their scriptural position as believers. I often pause during deliverance and give a brief Bible study to build up the victim's faith and understanding. I encourage questions so that they may settle any issues about who they are in Christ.

Demons may battle for control of the person's mind and fog his thinking so he cannot resist. "Focus your thoughts on Christ. Concentrate on the Resurrection. Quote from memory any Bible verses you know," I say to inspire the victim.

If the one receiving deliverance asks for a time of rest, I try to determine whether the person is wavering in her resolve or is genuinely in need of relief from the conflict. A victim's physical and spiritual vitality is necessary, and I am sensitive to the persons condition.

I often meet the victim for the first time prior to the exorcism. My travel schedule does not generally permit me to have a face-to-face follow-up relationship. Furthermore, I am not an academically trained counselor and make no such claims of clinical expertise. My role is that of a spiritual warrior who skirmishes with

Satan when he crosses my path, and the Lord leads me to minister to one who is demonized. I do, however, recognize the critical importance of ongoing professional assistance for those victims who have been freed.

Once a person has been delivered from demons, there are spiritual issues that will take time to resolve. An exorcism "specialist" such as myself may not be the best person to bond with the victim for future rehabilitation. Trained ministers and Christian psychologists who specialize in spiritual warfare need to take over and further assist in restoring mental and emotional health—a task that can take months or years.

Just as the cooperation of the victim is vital during an exorcism, the person's collaboration is important after the last demon is gone. The struggle to achieve freedom, as well as to maintain it, is a battle for the assertion of the victim's will. This goal will be reached by helping the person recognize that his spiritual self-esteem is grounded in Christ.

The victim's whole heart must be turned toward God, and the exorcist must carefully monitor every reaction and answer every concern. The one demonized is in the middle of the fight and can best see how Satan's punches are being thrown. He isn't like an anesthetized hospital patient, where the suffering one's thoughts and wishes are inconsequential to the success of the surgery. A deliverance isn't a one-man or one-woman operation. It's a team effort that requires a shoulder-to-shoulder solidarity that unites the exorcist and the victim in their common war against Satan.

7. Break All Curses

This topic has already been dealt with in regard to ancestral and generational curses, but I want to emphasize the importance of this rule as an integral part of dealing with relational curses. This form of spiritual bondage affects someone as the result of a marital, sexual, or soul-bonding relationship.

While ancestral and generational curses are implemented by blood relatives, spousal curses are also dangerous. Because the husband is head of the wife, his involvement in the occult could affect his marriage partner. A Christian woman married to an unbelieving man who dabbles in the occult should pray, "I submit to my husband according to the Scriptures, except in those cases where he claims a spiritually unlawful right. I break that occult bondage in the name of Jesus and refuse to submit to any forces of evil that would endanger my soul."

Couples involved in a sexual relationship outside of marriage have become one flesh and thus forge a union that can result in demonic subjection. For example, a man sexually cohabiting with a woman who is a witch could fall prey to the demons affecting her. If he comes to Christ, the sexual relationship must be ended and all soul-bonds (which are control mechanisms) broken through prayer. On a lesser level, strong friendships or social and business allegiances with someone involved in the occult could also affect an individual.

Even though the exorcist might not suspect the victim has any ancestral, generational, or relational curses that need to be broken, there is no harm in addressing these issues as a matter of caution.

8. Force the Demon to Tell the Truth or Face Judgment

Scripture clearly indicates that Satan is a liar who cannot hold to the truth (John 8:44; Rev. 21:8). Can the exorcist, then, ever trust what a demon says? We must use spiritual discernment to determine the accuracy of any information provided by a demon. And we should never become involved in any irrelevant conversation. Demons will try to engage the exorcist in all kinds of dialogue as a delaying tactic.

I often say to demons, "I command that you only speak what God allows you to say, no more and no less. I command that you say nothing more than that which is permitted by God to facilitate your expulsion."

Having taken that precaution, how much do I believe of what a demon discloses? I weigh each statement carefully and test it against the Scriptures (1 John 4:1). I also verify the information by comparing it to the demon's other comments to see if it is consistent. I've discovered an additional procedure that has proved valuable. Instruct the demon this way: "I command that the answer you give be held accountable before almighty God and that you be judged if you lie to the Holy Spirit."

Most unclean spirits will be obedient to the truth after they hear this. However, I sometimes have to repeat this command several times. Some demons have such an acute propensity for prevarication that I have to parenthetically command them not to lie before every question and after every answer.

If I suspect a demon has lied to me, I respond, "I hold your answer up before God to be judged by His truth. If you have lied to the Holy Spirit, and if you have misled the servant of God, I ask God to smite you."

Words can't describe the terror I've seen on the faces of demons as God strikes them for their disobedience. They grimace, scream, cry out for mercy, and beg to be relieved from God's torment. Then I might say, "I ask God to stand back and give you another opportunity to speak the truth. If you do not, God will smite you again seven times greater."

Meticulously applying this tactic, often to the point of repetitious boredom, I force demons to abide in some measure of truth. I use the threat of God's judgment as often as necessary to make certain I'm not being misled.

9. Have the Victim Confess the Sin of Demonic Entry

We must keep in mind that God is dealing with the victim to grant freedom and growth. So we also must face the victim with personal responsibility to deal with issues in his or her own life. The victim must apply the truth of God's Word to obtain freedom from the bondage of Satan's lies.

Once a demon's presence, name, and function have been identified, the next step is to remove his right to remain. This is usually grounded in a conscious, willful sin. Have the victim renounce this sin and seek forgiveness through the blood of Christ by a spoken prayer. Demonic resistance is common, and I often have the victim say one word at a time. Just a few sentences of confession may take minutes, even hours. With others, it may come quite freely. This is the demon's stronghold, and he fights tenaciously to stop the prayer. In drastic situations I may halt the prayer to encourage the victim with Scriptures about forgiveness and God's grace.

At this point, distracting demons often interfere. Victims may become nauseous or experience shooting pains. Their minds may be so clouded, they barely know what is happening. I've had victims say things backward or convolute the wording of the prayer.

One woman who had been a high priestess in a mystery cult actually said words of praise to Satan, even though her lips were trying to form a prayer to God. The demonic stratagem was so effective, her ears heard godly words though she was speaking curses. I had to stop exorcising the demon and call forth the mental demon who was twisting her words; then I got rid of him so the prayer could proceed properly.

Sins of demonic entry aren't always acts of a specific place and time. There may be emotional harbors of evil, such as bitterness, jealousy, lust, or covetousness. You may not know the exact time the demon sufficiently exploited this area of life. No matter. Have the victim set the situation right with God. If the demon was misleading, it will soon become apparent. If the confession removes the right of entry, the demon's reaction will readily prove it. He will switch tactics; instead of claiming a legal right, he may start saying he won't leave regardless of what the exorcist does.

10. Make the Demon Pronounce His Own Doom

The exorcist may choose to speak the words of final expulsion, but the Holy Spirit has shown me a more effective way to weaken the demon's final attempt to stay. Have the demon pronounce his own doom. Recite the words and make the demon repeat them. This is the declaration of surrender I use: "I, [demon speaks his own name], acknowledge that Christ is Lord and has risen from the dead to defeat my master, the devil. I renounce all past, present, and future claims to [demon speaks name of his victim] and acknowledge that the one I possess has victory over me in the name of Jesus Christ. I bind to me all parts and portions of myself, and I attach to me any demons under my control. Having no further legal right to stay in this child of God, I lie not to the Holy Spirit, and I go now to the pit!"

Those few words may take many minutes. The demon may repeat phrases at first, but the last six words have to be spoken separately. I've spent an hour getting a demon to say the final word—*pit*.

However long it takes to enforce the capitulation, every moment is to be savored. The long struggle is over, the demon has been defeated, and Christ's promises have prevailed. Now memories of the long struggle fade away. The presence of God's Spirit is overwhelming. My eyes often fill with tears.

It's clear that Satan truly is "like a corpse trodden underfoot" (Isa. 14:19). Jesus has the keys to hell and death (Rev. 1:18) and no weapon formed against the child of God shall prosper (Isa. 54:17). Jesus has crushed Satan under the feet of those who bring the good news!

At the end of each successful exorcism, I am always deeply moved to witness Christ's finished work at the cross. The mystery of the ages, that God loved fallen man so much He sent His Son "while we were still sinners" (Rom. 5:8), seems even more priceless. In the natural realm, angels (faithful and unfaithful) are more powerful and more intelligent than human beings. Yet God has mercifully chosen man, not angels, to be the objects of His grace.

It is Christians who are made "alive together with Christ" (Eph. 2:5) and allowed to "sit together in the heavenly places in Christ Jesus" (Eph. 2:6). While conditionally we do not always deserve such a lofty status, by positional right we are granted what mere human worthiness could never merit.

I once declared to a demon who threatened and taunted me, "In the name of Jesus, I command that you look at me. Gaze into my eyes and see into my soul. What do you see?"

"The righteousness of Jesus!" the evil spirit screamed in dismay. In the realm of spiritual warfare, the truth shines forth.

Christians often give lip service to the words of 1 John 4:4: "He who is in you is greater than he who is in the world." Experiencing an exorcism amplifies this truth. Casting out a demon is only possible because of the Resurrection. It is the empty tomb that allows us to face incomprehensible evil with certainty of victory and the authority of Christ in us, the "hope of glory" (Col. 1:27).

The exorcist and the one to whom he ministers are a team, united with Christ by the sacrifice of His blood. This union with the Savior forms a heavenly combination that no evil spirit can forever withstand. Demons try to run Christians off by reminding them of their fallen nature; but it is the new life in Jesus by which we have been "raised with Christ" (Col. 3:1) that causes evil spirits to flee.

Every believer who has been victimized by the devil needs to acknowledge that no matter what failures beset a believer, the born-again Christian is seated at God's right hand. Knowing who you are in Christ and where you are positioned in His kingdom is a spiritual reality that is sure to doom every demon to defeat.

Chapter 35

Restoration
in the
Name of Jesus

I had been doing exorcisms for only a few years when I met fourteen-year-old Brenda. She spoke to me in the hallway of a Baptist church where I had just concluded a four-day series of lectures. At that time this church was one of the largest in America, and their invitation to speak was an opportunity to expand my ministry. If I received a good word of recommendation from the pastor, I'd be inundated with invitations. I had packed the sanctuary for each day of the seminar. Spiritually, I was elated and awaiting the pastor's endorsement.

"Can I speak to you privately about something?" Brenda asked. "It will only take a moment."

Since this was my last night at the church, many people wanted to shake my hand and express appreciation for my messages. I suspected Brenda wanted to do the same, so I motioned her to the side of the corridor, away from the flow of people.

"What's on your mind?" I asked.

Brenda dropped her eyes and stared at the floor. "It's hard for me to explain. It's embarrassing."

She was short, so I knelt and looked up into her face. Tears streamed from her eyes. "Take a deep breath and steady yourself," I suggested. "Go on when you feel comfortable."

Brenda sniffled and regained her composure. "I read pornography. I'm ashamed afterward, but I can't help myself. Sometimes when I read dirty magazines, I do things to myself I shouldn't. You know what I mean, don't you?"

Brenda's question was direct, but she averted her eyes. My heart was touched by her sincerity. *I'll pray with her and turn her over to the youth pastor to follow up,* I thought. *She was courageous to approach me all alone and talk about something so personal.*

"Brenda, I'd like to say a prayer for you and ask someone to talk with you further. Would that be okay?"

Brenda nodded. "You can tell them about the pornography, but please don't tell them about . . ."

"About what?" I asked.

Brenda closed her eyes and waved her hand across her face with a "never mind" gesture.

"Don't worry," I assured her. "I won't say anything more than you want me to. Take my hand while I pray."

Still kneeling, I reached up and clasped her right hand in mine. "Dear Lord Jesus," I prayed, "thank You for Brenda's honesty, and her desire to deal with this problem. I ask You to cover her in Your blood and—"

"No-o-o-o-o!" The word interrupted my prayer.

I wasn't sure I heard correctly. The "no" sounded like a groan from inside Brenda's body. I opened my eyes and continued. "Lord, I know You love Brenda and will help her overcome this sin, because You are the Son of God and rose victoriously from the dead—"

"No, He didn't!" Another interruption, and this time a scowl appeared on Brenda's face. The words were drawn out in a growl. Her bowed head tilted up, and that look filled her eyes.

I glanced around and saw people were milling about the hallway, exchanging greetings. I didn't want to cause any commotion that would embarrass Brenda, so I took control over the demon "Whoever you are, I bind you in the name of Jesus. Go down now until such time as I call you forth again."

The voice said nothing, but the glare from Brenda's eyes spoke volumes. The demon blinked a couple of times and then Brenda returned.

I stood from my kneeling position and motioned for her to follow me. "I think we need to talk a little more," I explained. "There's an empty room around the corner. Wait there, and I'll be back in a few minutes."

The pastor's office was at the other end of the hallway, so I could keep an eye on the door to Brenda's room. When I arrived at the pastor's office, he was talking to the youth pastor.

"Bob, great message tonight," the pastor said and patted me on the shoulder. "We were just discussing how much we'd like to have you back. That crowd tonight was one of the biggest we've ever had; I think you'll be very pleased at the love offering for your ministry."

"Thank you, that's very kind." I paused, unsure of how to express what I had to say. "I've encountered a situation that I think you'll be interested in," I said, and turned toward the youth pastor. "Do you know a teenager in your church named Brenda?"

"Sure, if it's the same Brenda I'm thinking of. She's short with auburn hair and blue eyes." He looked at the pastor. "Joe's daughter."

"Oh, yes," the pastor acknowledged. "Her dad is one of our deacons. Why do you ask? She's one of my best soul winners."

This won't go over well, I thought. "Pastor, do you mind if I bring her to your office for a few minutes? This is a difficult situation."

He shrugged his shoulders.

"I'll be right back," I said as I walked away.

I returned to the room where Brenda was waiting and asked her to follow me. I would have summoned her father, but this exorcism occurred before I learned how important it is for parents to be present during a child's exorcism. When we reached the pastor's office, Brenda stopped. "I can't go in there and tell him what I've told you. My dad is a . . ."

"A deacon. Don't worry. I already know. I don't want to embarrass you, but you have some very serious spiritual problems, and I feel your pastor and youth pastor need to be present for our discussion. I trust these brothers in Christ."

Brenda's face was flushed and I could tell she wanted to walk away, but she drew in a breath and nodded her head. We knocked on the door, and the pastor opened it. He gave Brenda a shoulder hug and invited us inside. I sat next to Brenda on the couch while the pastor and youth pastor sat opposite us. "Brenda has confided a problem to me, and I'd like the four of us to pray together so she'll have spiritual victory. She may not want to discuss what bothers her right now, but the Lord knows and He'll hear our prayer."

The pastor smiled. "Absolutely. Lead us in prayer," he suggested, motioning toward me.

I nodded and they bowed their heads. I hadn't told Brenda that she had a demon, so she wasn't apprehensive about doing as I asked. I looked at her and began praying. "Our Father in heaven, we come in the authority of Jesus, the name above every name. Thank You that by the power of Your Son's blood we can overcome any sin."

I paused. Nothing happened. Where was the demon who confronted me moments ago, when I had mentioned the blood of Christ?

"Jesus, thank You for defeating the devil at the Cross."

Still nothing. *I'm glad I didn't tell them she had a demon,* I thought. *Maybe Brenda was up to some trick and fooled me.*

I continued my prayer. "Brenda needs to defeat this sin in her life, and I ask You to give her a new filling of Your Holy Spirit and—"

All at once the voice broke in. "There is no Holy Spirit!"

The snarl was clearly from another entity. The eyes of the pastor and youth pastor widened, and they both straightened in their chairs. The youth pastor leaned toward Brenda.

Now the truth is going to be known, I thought. "Who said there is no Holy Spirit? I command, in the name of Jesus, that you tell me who you are!"

Brenda's head tilted up and the demon fully manifested. "I did."

"What's your name?"

"Lust. You can't make me leave. I have a legal right to this body!"

Brenda's mannerisms were gone, and a male personality came over her. Her eyes changed and so did her gestures and expressions.

The pastors watched intently, but said nothing. I felt the presence of God leading me, and I went forward in faith. I proceeded to bind Lust and call forth Brenda. Carefully, I explained to her that she had a demon, and that I needed her cooperation. She said she wanted to be free more than anything, so I continued the exorcism. For nearly an hour I battled the demon of lust, who said he had entered through Brenda's reading of pornography. Methodically, I led her in a prayer of confession regarding her sin; I was sure this would close the door on the demon's right to her.

During the hour I paused several times to ask the pastor if he had any questions or wanted to help in any way. Each time he shook his head and politely told me to continue doing whatever I felt I needed to do.

I longed for prayer support from either of the two men. But despite their lack of involvement, the deliverance went well. Lust put up a fight, but it was mostly intellectual and not physical. The exorcism was done with surprising calm and orderliness. I felt grateful that I didn't have to do something unorthodox that might have raised theological questions. Still, I was getting more uncomfortable by the minute.

I, Lust, renounce my claim to Brenda, and leave now and go to the pit," I instructed the demon to say.

Lust resisted angrily. Brenda was thrown back and forth on the couch. I did my best to hold her arms firmly. Her legs kicked and her head shook furiously, but the pastors did not intervene. I kept her from harming herself or me, but the pastors continued to shrink from the conflict.

"Leave now and go to the pit!" I insisted over and over.

At last, Lust groaned, sighed, and Brenda's body went limp. I propped her against a couple of pillows and waited for her to come around. I looked at the pastor and then at the youth pastor. They did not move toward Brenda to comfort her, nor did they smile with relief at Christ's victory. They sat silently, observing.

This isn't the way most exorcisms end. Usually, the room is filled with exhausted elation. Those involved in the deliverance hug each other or cry. The tension fades as everyone looks at one another like human beings again. The long hours of hearing God's name constantly cursed have thankfully ended.

Brenda regained her composure, and her face was radiant. "Is it over?" she asked.

"I think so. It certainly seems that way, but just to be sure I always—"

"Brenda," the pastor interjected as he stood, "I know your parents must be very worried about you." He reached out for her hand to help her from the couch. "Come with me. We'll call and tell them you were talking with some young people and forgot about the time. I'll drive you home."

"Pastor," I said, "I think we should take a few minutes to see if everything is all right before Brenda leaves. Besides, there are some important instructions I have for her. If you don't mind I'd like to—"

"I do mind," he said firmly with an unsmiling expression. "It's late, and Brenda needs to go home now."

"May I talk with her parents when you call?" I asked.

"No, it's best that I speak with them, as their pastor."

"But I need to explain a little about what happened tonight so they'll know how to help Brenda."

The pastor's face turned stern. "There's no need to tell them anything that went on. What happened in my office doesn't leave this office. Do you understand?" He grabbed Brenda's hand. He looked at me and then at the youth pastor.

The young minister nodded his head in obedience. The pastor was twenty years my senior and one of the most respected church-builders in America, but I stood my ground. If he was advocating some kind of denial, I wasn't going along with it.

"The demon of lust might not be gone," I said. "If he isn't, her problems will be a lot worse since he has been antagonized and threatened. It will only take a few minutes to check for sure. I'm very concerned about her."

Brenda pulled her hand away from her pastor and looked at him, then at me. "If you think it will make a difference, I'll stay. I don't want that evil thing around." She walked back to the couch and sat down. "What do you want me to do?"

"The same thing you've been doing all evening. Listen carefully to what I say, cooperate with all your heart, and pray that Jesus will set you free."

The pastor stood motionless.

Brenda took a deep breath and closed her eyes. "I'm ready. Go ahead."

Why was I so insistent on not letting Brenda leave without further spiritual investigation?

WHAT TO DO WHEN AN EXORCISM HAS ENDED

In a significant number of exorcisms I've conducted, demons went through all the actions of being cast out, but they didn't go. Consequently, I've learned that when an exorcism seems to be over, it's still wise to check, recheck, and then check again to be sure the demon is truly gone. This is not a time for wishful thinking, hoping that everything is okay.

You should ask the victim how he or she feels. This person knows what it is like to have that demon around, and he or she is the best one to evaluate whether the spirit is gone. Ask the victim repeatedly if he or she senses any presence of the demon. The victim may feel hollow inside, because evil once filled spaces now empty in his or her soul. If the victim has any misgivings about freedom, it's better to err on the side of caution.

One way to find out if the demon is still present is to pray for the victim's complete filling of the Holy Spirit. Treat the body as the temple of the Holy Spirit. Dedicate each section of the body to Christ (Rom. 6:12–13). Ask the Lord to force into the open any evil part left behind and to indicate what area of the mind or body the demons might yet try to control. Be thorough. Take time to complete a spiritual diagnostic follow-up before the fruits of victory are fully savored.

BRENDA'S DEMON RETURNS

During the follow-up procedure I knelt before Brenda and addressed the demon again. "Lust, I commanded you to leave in the name of Jesus. If you disobeyed, I demand that you come to attention."

Nothing happened. The pastors stood by the door looking exasperated, and it appeared that my extra effort was foolish. It was obvious they weren't in agreement, so I tossed theological caution aside.

"Lord, I ask You to send strong angels. If Lust hasn't left, may Your angels torment him until he obeys."

Brenda's body jerked, and Lust groaned. He manifested with fury in his eyes.

"Leave me alone! I don't have to go."

"Yes, you do. I commanded you to leave."

"I don't have to leave if I have a right to stay."

"But Brenda confessed her sin of reading pornography. That's how you said you possessed her."

"True."

"Then in Jesus' name I command that you tell me what else we need to know to set her free. May the angels of God torment you more until you quit misleading us."

Lust squirmed in agony. "Okay, okay. Call them off. I'll tell you."

"What's the legal right allowing you to stay?"

"Her father. He's the one."

"The one what?"

"The one who gave her the pornography. He left it lying around the house when she was a little girl. She tried to imitate what she saw in those pictures." The demon looked up at the pastor. "And he's your deacon," the spirit taunted.

That night was one of the most unpleasant I've ever spent. In spite of his reluctance, the angry pastor had no choice but to call the deacon to his office and confront him about the spirit's claims. The proof of what the demon said was the father's contrite admission that he harbored a craving for pornography. I ministered to the father who wept bitterly over his sin. Complete victory came when I led the father in a prayer to cast the demon out of his daughter.

When the exorcism was over, the pastor wouldn't look at me, but he allowed me to spend valuable time cautioning Brenda's father about how to help her heal effectively. Her father thanked me wholeheartedly for the deliverance. He seemed embarrassed in front of the pastor, and the two avoided each other.

THE AFTERMATH OF AN EXORCISM

I explained to Brenda's father that after an exorcism the victim needs special physical recuperation. He or she may sleep for twelve hours or more. The person may awaken the next day with external bruises and internal pain from the actions of the demon who has torn him or her inside (Mark 9:26). The victim is often dehydrated and hungry and will need extra liquids and food.

Emotional rehabilitation is also crucial. A mature counselor should monitor the victim's mental health to address every area of spiritual vulnerability. Some victims will be left with an emotional maturity that is many years younger than their age because they have been spiritually stunted. Those around them need to be supportive and understanding.

Demons of lust, perversion, addiction, and other forms of carnality leave their victims susceptible to the frailties that were points of demonic entry. These areas need to be addressed with a Scripture memory program and serious Bible study. The demon may have been cast out, but the flesh still needs to be overcome daily through trust in God's Word.

If there were demons of rebellion, witchcraft, heresy, or false religions, a dose of strong orthodox Bible doctrine is necessary. The victim must quickly become immersed in teaching that confronts these "doctrines of demons" (1 Tim. 4:1). Banishing error isn't enough. The absorption of truth is crucial to the victim's recovery from the lies he or she once believed.

Those involved in the exorcism face unique challenges following a deliverance. After an initial sharing of the more dramatic aspects of what happened, the discussion should center on positive deliberations about God and His attributes. The spectacular feats of the enemy should not be the focus of the discussions. This tendency is hard to overcome, since some involved in the exorcism may have witnessed this demonic world for the first time. Let them briefly express their amazement, and then turn the emphasis toward what Christ has done. Before the group dismisses, a time of praise and thanksgiving to God is important. The next few days should be spent as much as possible in Scripture reading and quiet contemplation upon the Lord.

The most serious warning to those involved in an exorcism is to be wary of temptations and discouragement. One might think that after such a supernatural experience, they would be on a spiritual high. That exhilaration is short-lived. Satan strikes in such circumstances because he is unexpected. It was shortly after Elijah's great victory over the prophets of Baal on Mount Carmel (1 Kings 18:38–40) that he languished in dejection and asked God to take his life (1 Kings 19:4). I can testify that some of my most difficult struggles occurred after a triumphant exorcism. My emotional and physical exhaustion played into the devil's hands. I have since learned the importance of spiritual vigilance at such times.

THE ILLUSION OF CONTINUED POSSESSION

Can demons return once they are cast out? Those Christ sends to the pit are unable to escape to return. If not cast into the pit, they may reenter under any of three conditions: (1) there was some legal right left (as in Brenda's case), (2) the victim failed to fill his life with God's Spirit and truth, or (3) the victim returned to the same sin that permitted the original possession. Of course, different spirits, other than those cast out, may seek entrance.

I have also encountered another phenomenon that is a copycat of possession, which I call "demonic psychological imprinting." While the demon was internalized, he learned the mental processes of the victim's mind, in the same way a student of neurolinguistics programming masters the detection of physical and emotional patterns. In certain cases after deliverance, the demon can trigger psycho-physiological responses that mimic possession. The demon, though outside, can affect the mind to such an extent that he appears to speak through the vocal cords. The evil spirit uses demonic oppression to trigger past mental patterns to which the victim is still susceptible. The victim may even feel repossessed, but it is an illusion that must be overcome by trust in God's power to keep those who abide in Him free.

THE PATIENT PROGRESS OF HEALING

Almost invariably, past victims become discouraged by how long spiritual reconstruction takes. Although they are exhilarated by the feeling of being freed, they become disheartened when their progress toward spiritual well-being isn't rapid. They must understand that Satan spent months, even years, dismantling the person God meant them to be. In place of their divinely given identity, the devil erected a complex caricature based on carnal impulses and selfish motivation. These negative patterns of behavior have to be reversed through spiritual reconditioning.

Imagine you were told to dismantle the General Motors Corporation. Do you think that by walking into the offices of GM's executives and firing them, you could disassemble a multibillion-dollar organization immediately? Of course not. It would take time to close all the departments, manufacturing plants, and branch offices. Tearing down the infrastructure of evil in the victim's soul and body can be an equally arduous task, except in rare occasions.

One time as I counseled a victim of possession in the aftermath of her deliverance, the Lord brought to my mind Deuteronomy 7:22: "And the LORD your God will drive out those nations before you little by little; you will be unable to destroy them at once, lest the beasts of the field become too numerous for you." The children of Israel didn't defeat all the enemy at once. As they conquered each city, they settled the land and domesticated their surroundings. Once their holdings were consolidated, they moved on to another enemy and followed the same pattern.

This describes the process of deliverance as well as the pace of spiritual reconstruction after an exorcism. Instead of defeating every demon instantly, deliverance comes "little by little." Healing from all that the devil has done must come in God's timing and His way if spiritual rehabilitation is to be complete. In many instances, the assistance of Christian mental health professionals should be sought to further enhance the victim's psychological welfare.

DELIVERANCE ISN'T A DEED

Deliverance isn't a deed; it's a necessary step in total recuperation. Acts 10:38 says that Jesus "went about doing good and *healing* all who were oppressed by the devil" (emphasis added) The goal of an exorcism is not demonic eviction alone. It is also restoration of the victim's soul and body to spiritual wholeness so that they may once again be the person God meant them to me. Ministering healing is as important as bringing emancipation from the forces of darkness.

The entire body of Christ needs to be sensitive to this truth. Often, those delivered from demons find they are ostracized as spiritual lepers. Some Christians cruelly say that the victim was at fault for what happened (which isn't always the case), and therefore must have some inherent weakness that could rub off by association. Others argue mistakenly that the victim might still have demons around that could affect anyone who befriends that person.

But restoring the victim of possession to spiritual wholeness is the responsibility of the church, both local and universal. Real emotional and spiritual healing come when we in the body of Christ humble ourselves, confess our faults to one another (James 5:16), and realize we are all sinners saved by grace. By reaching out to those who have been ravaged by Satan's legions, Christians can serve Christ by extending His compassion to "the least of these," the most hurting among us (Matt. 25:40).

BRENDA'S EPILOGUE

When I said farewell to Brenda and her father, I was deeply troubled in my spirit. The pastor seemed outright antagonistic. I suspected he was theologically disturbed by the exorcism and professionally embarrassed by having to deal with the moral failures of a trusted deacon. In my mind's eye I can still see him standing in the doorway as we left, saying to everyone, "Remember, not a word of what's happened leaves this room. We must not say anything to anyone!"

But what happened did leak out. Perhaps someone overheard the demon's groans in the hallway or someone eavesdropped on the exorcism. The controversy that erupted in the days following besieged the pastor. Finally, he publicly addressed the issue from the pulpit the next Sunday morning.

I wasn't there, but a parishioner sent me a cassette tape of that sermon. When it arrived at my Denver headquarters a few days later, I put the cassette in a tape deck.

"Some of you have heard about an alleged exorcism that occurred at the church last week," the pastor said. "Yes, some very strange things happened, but let me assure you that the theological position of this church hasn't changed. Jesus cast out demons to prove He was the Son of God, and that sort of thing ended with the apostolic age. We don't deal with demons here, and we don't want people around who do. If you think you have a demon, go somewhere else. Our job is to win souls to Christ, not perform exorcisms!"

I hit the off button on the recorder and slammed my fist on the desk. "God, how could You let this happen?" I cried out. "Is this the thanks I get for helping Brenda? Now I'll never speak in a large church like that one again."

I paced the floor in frustration. *What about Brenda?* I thought. *I wonder how she felt after that sermon? She and her father must be horrified. Maybe they doubt what happened. If they do, will the demons exploit their unbelief and find a way to come back?*

My feelings were a mixture of sincere concern for Brenda's spiritual welfare and a selfish reaction to my ego having been bruised.

For the next week I didn't pick up my Bible. I didn't pray. I was angry with God and my fellowship with Him suffered. I may have defeated the demon in Brenda, but I couldn't conquer my own spirit. I was drifting farther and farther away from the Lord, so far that I considered quitting Christian service. Unlike Elijah, I didn't want to die. I didn't have to. I already felt dead spiritually.

Ten days after Brenda's exorcism, a letter from her arrived in the mail.

Dear Mr. Larson,

There are no words to describe how grateful I am for all that you did for me. Slowly, I've been remembering what I went through that night in my pastor's office. I still don't understand all that happened, but I know how I felt when it was over. I still feel the same . . .

I haven't touched a single dirty magazine since that night, and I haven't done that bad thing again. My dad and I have become best friends. We pray and read the Bible together every day. He has changed so much. Mom and he are more in love than ever. She has forgiven him . . .

Tears were streaming down my cheeks. I felt humbled and ashamed.

A lot of people have questions about that night. I just tell them that Bob Larson is the most special person in the world, and that God used you to do some really neat things for me. Thank you for letting God use you. I'll always love Jesus because you cared enough to help me.

Brenda

Brenda had done as much to minister to me as I had done to minister to her and her dad. I put the letter aside and buried my face in my hands. I asked God's forgiveness for my sins of arrogance and self-centeredness.

In the midst of my sorrow Galatians 1:10 came to mind: "If I still pleased men, I would not be a bondservant of Christ."

"Jesus," I cried out. "I'll never again turn my back on someone who is bound by Satan, if You tell me to help him."

What is the legacy of the day in Singapore when I faced my first demon, and that day I read Brenda's letter? I have kept my promise to minister deliverance to those hurting souls God sends to me. I've not been able to help everyone who has crossed my path, and I haven't always had the opportunity to help everyone as much as I wanted. But when God has clearly spoken to my heart to deal with a demon, I've never backed down.

Satan has waged a ferocious counterattack. I have been publicly humiliated by those who said they were doing God a service. I have felt the demons of hell surround me and move in for the kill. My heart has been immeasurably hurt and my spirit has been nearly broken by the lies and deceit of the enemy. And like every Christian, I've failed God more times than I want to admit.

In retaliation for what I've done to the devil, he has struck back to take from me some things I cherished. But the Lord has never allowed Satan to rob me of the things that mattered most: the fellowship of true friends, the love of family, and the grace of God that has kept me in His hands.

I've been blessed! With great suffering has come even greater spiritual bounty. Yes, I have been battered, but I'm still standing, still serving, and still casting out demons *in the name of Jesus.*

Notes

CHAPTER 7

1. Maury Terry, *The Ultimate Evil* (Garden City, NJ: Doubleday, 1987), 511.

2. Vincent Bugliosi, *Helter Skelter* (New York: Norton, 1974), 637.

3. "Night Stalker," *People*, 16 September 1985, 44.

4. Pat Milton, "Drugs Changed Life of Teen Charged in Satanic Killing," *Ft. Worth Star-Telegram*, 15 July 1984.

5. David Breskin, "Kids in the Dark," *Rolling Stone*, 22 November 1984, 30–32.

6. Ibid., 34.

CHAPTER 8

1. "D.C. twilight zone: psychics in demand," *The Denver Post*, 4 December 1988, 1D.

2. Ibid.

3. Russell Targ, Ph.D., International Transpersonal Conference, 10 October 1988.

4. Ibid.

5. Guy Kelly, "Psychics Not Gurus in Turbans," *Rocky Mountain News*, 20 November 1988, 28.

6. See 1 John 4:4.

7 See Gen. 3:5.

CHAPTER 9

1. John Weldon and James Bjornstad, "Fantasy Games People Play," *Contemporary Christian Magazine*, December 1984.

2. Howard Witt, "Teen Suicide, Murders Linked to Fantasy Game," *Dallas Morning News*, 31 January 1985.

3. Gary Gygax, *Official Advanced Dungeons & Dragons Player's Handbook*, TSR Inc. (New York: Random House, 1978), 40.

4. Ibid., 48.

5. James Ward and Rob Kuntz, *Official Advanced Dungeons & Dragons Legends and Lore*, TSR Inc. (New York: Random House, 1984), 9.

6. Ibid., 11.

7. Ibid., 23.

8. Ibid., 26.

9. "The Assault on Role-Playing Games," Game Manufacturers Association handout, 1 March 1988, 1.

10. See Matt. 5:28.

11. 2 Cor. 10:5.

12. Prov. 23:7.

CHAPTER 10

1. *Billboard*, 4 October 1986, H4.

2. John Larrabee, "Slasher Suspect Found Hanged," *USA Today*, 30 November 1988, 3A.

3. *USA Today*, 29 December 1983, 5D.

4. "We're Drawn to Gruesome, Gory Stuff," *USA Today*, 5 April 1984, 2D.

CHAPTER 11

1. Julia Morris and Steve Marshall, "Cult 'Godfather' Hunted," *USA Today*, 13 April 1989, 3A.

2. Ibid.

3. Carl A. Raschke, "Satanism and the Devolution of the 'New Religions,'" *SCP Newsletter*, Fall 1988, 22–29.

4. "1,200 child-abuse deaths cited," *Rocky Mountain News*, 3 March 1989, 50.

5. Chris Lutes, *What Teenagers Are Saying About Drugs and Alcohol* (Wheaton, IL: Tyndale, 1988), 247.

CHAPTER 12

1. Ed Kiersh, *Spin*, August 1988, 24.

2. Ibid., 68.

3. Ibid., 23.

4. Chris Wood, "Suicide and Satanism," *MacClean's*, 30 March 1987.

NOTES

CHAPTER 13

1. "Tracking the Cattle Mutilations," *Newsweek*, 21 January 1980, 16.
2. Larry Kahner, *Cults That Kill* (New York: Warner, 1988), 147–48.
3. Derk Roelofsma, "Battling Satanism a Haunting Task," *Insight*, 1 November 1988, 49.
4. Kevin Diaz, "Police Expert Warns of Satanism," *Minneapolis Star Tribune*, 27 September 1987, 1B.
5. Roelofsma, "Battling Satanism," 48.
6. *Geraldo* telecast of 24 October 1988.
7. Aleister Crowley, *Magick in Theory and Practice* (New York: Castle Books), 95.
8. Richard Cavendish, *The Black Arts* (New York: G. P. Putnam's Sons, 1967), 272.
9. *Nevada Appeal*, vol. 121, no. 86, 23 August 1985.
10. *The Denver Post*, 8 August 1988, 1, 8A.

CHAPTER 14

1. M. Scott Peck, *People of the Lie* (New York: Simon and Schuster, 1983), 204.
2. Ibid., 207.
3. Wade Baskin, *Satanism* (Secaucus, NJ: Citadel Press, 1972), 61.
4. Leslie A. Shepard, ed., *Encyclopedia of Occult and Parapsychology*, (2d ed.), vol. 2 (H–O) (Detroit: Gale Research, 1984), 939.
5. *The Necronomicon* (New York: Avon, 1977), X.
6. Ibid., XXVIII.
7. Ibid., LIII.
8. Ibid., 69.
9. Ibid., 218.
10. Anton Szandor LaVey, *The Satanic Bible* (New York: Avon, 1969).
11. See Matt. 5:39.
12. LaVey, *Satanic Bible*, 33.
13. Prov. 25:21; Rom. 12:20.
14. LaVey, *Satanic Bible*, 33.
15. Ibid., 30.
16. Ibid., 33.
17. Ibid., 67.
18. Ibid., 88.
19. Ibid., 89.
20. Ibid., 90.
21. Ibid., 156.

22. Anton LaVey, *The Satanic Rituals* (New York: Avon, 1972), 14.
23. Ibid., 17.
24. Ibid., 19.
25. Ibid., 57–59.
26. Ibid., 25.
27. Ibid., 77.
28. Ibid., 220.
29. See Prov. 6:16–19.
30. Kahner, *Cults That Kill*, 67–71.

CHAPTER 15

1. See Mark 7:21–23.
2. See Rev. 13:1.
3. *The Book of the Law* (Kings Beach, CA: Thelema), 9.
4. Arthur Lyons, *Satan Wants You* (New York: Mysterious, 1988), 81.
5. John Symonds, "Aleister Crowley," *Man, Myth & Magic, An Illustrated Encyclopedia of the Supernatural* (New York: Marshall Cavendish, 1970) 559–63.
6. *Larson's Book of Cults* (Wheaton, IL: Tyndale, 1982); and J. Gordon Melton, *The Encyclopedia of American Religions* (Wilmington, NC: McGrath, 1978), vol. 2.
7. *The Newaeon Newsletter*, vol. 1, no. 1, 22 December 1977, 1

CHAPTER 16

1. Various portions of this section were compiled with the assistance of J Gordon Melton's book *The Encyclopedia of American Religions*, 179–86, and *Encyclopedia Britannica*, 1986, ed. 15, vol. 25, "Occultism: Witchcraft," 94–96.
2. See Deut. 18:9–14; Lev. 19:31.
3. See Ex. 22:18.
4. See 1 Chron. 10:13.
5. Derk Roelofsma, "Inside the Circle of Witches Modern," *Insight*, 8 June 1987, 91.
6. Margot Adler, *Drawing Down the Moon*, Rev. and Exp. (Boston: Beacon, 1986, 1979), 263, 308–10, 344.
7 Anyone interested in investigating the names and practices of additional witchcraft covens should consult J Gordon Melton's *Encyclopedia of American Religions*
8. Adler, *Drawing Down the Moon*, ix.
9 *USA Today*, 28 October 1986, 1D

10. Judann Pollack, "From Toaster Strudel to McD's Costumes, Halloween is Howling," Advertising Age, 14 September 1998, 4.

11. Lorrie Grant, "Halloween a Treat for Grownups," USA Today 30 October 1998, 1B.

12. Edwin McDowell, "Blookcurdling Capitalism," New York Times, 31 October 1998, B1.

13. Matt. 25:32–33.

14. Adler, Drawing Down the Moon, 112.

15. Cathy Hainer, "The New Face of Witches," USA Today, 29 October 1998, 8D.

16. Jefferson Graham, "'Sabrina' and Hart Bewitch Audiences," USA Today, 18 December 1996, 3D.

17. Cathy Hainer, "The New Face of Witches," USA Today, 29 October 1998, 8D.

18. Silver Ravenwolf, Teen Witch, Llewellyn Publications, St. Paul, MN 1998, back cover.

19. Denise LaVoie, "Witch Guilty of Sex Assault on Child," Rocky Mountain News, 23 August 1996, 44A.

CHAPTER 17

1. "Goodby, Mama Alice," Time, 23 November 1987, 38.

2. USA Today, 12 March 1987, 5D.

3. "Pupil's Absences for Religions Rites Ruled Legitimate," Rocky Mountain News, 8 December 1984.

4. "Mississippi Pharmacist Offers Black Magic to Voodoo Followers," Drug Topics, 3 May 1982, 56.

5. "New Jersey Cop Probes Possible Cult Link to Connecticut Baby's Death," The Press, Atlantic City, NJ, 21 March 1986, 6.

6. "Old Yoruba Customs Draw New Criticism, Newsweek, 7 December 1981.

7. Gary Langer, "Blood-sacrifice Cults Spreading," The Seattle Times, 25 November 1984, 14B.

8. Richard N. Ostling, "Building Bridges in Brazil," Time, 21 July 1980, 43.

9. "Brazil's Bizarre Cults," Newsweek, 27 February 1987, 39.

CHAPTER 18

1. Otto Friedrich, "New Age Harmonies," Time, 7 December 1987, vol. 130, no. 23, 69.

2 Phil. 4:13.

3. Annetta Miller, "Corporate Mind Control," Newsweek, 4 May 1987, vol. CIX, No. 18, 39

4. J. Yuitaka Amano, "Bad for Business," Eternity, March 1986, vol. 37, no. 3, 57.

5. John Bode, "The Forum: Repackaged est," The Cult Observer, April 1985, 5.

6. Bob Larson, *Larson's Book of Cults* (Wheaton, IL: Tyndale, 1982), 275.

7. Bode, "The Forum: Repackaged est," 4.

8. "est Training Changed to the Forum," *The Cult Observer*, February/March 1985, 2.

9. "Erhard's 'Forum': est Meets the Eighties," *Newsweek*, 1 April 1985, vol. 105, 15.

10. Bode, "The Forum: Repackaged est," 4.

11. McMahon, "MLA Selling Controversial Training," *Calgary Herald*, 14 January 1983, A1.

12. Neal Vahle, "Lifespring and the Development of Human Potential," *New Realities*, July/August 1987, vol. 6, no. 4, 22.

13. Pat McMahon, "MLA Selling Controversial Training," 2.

14. Vahle, "Lifespring and the Development of Human Potential," 21.

15. Neal Vahle, "John Hanley: Supporting Others to Produce Results," *New Realities*, July/August 1987, vol. 6, no. 4, 51.

16. Vahle, "Lifespring and the Development of Human Potential," 18.

17. "About . . . Life Training," promotional brochure, n.d., 3.

18. Ibid., 5.

19. Ibid.

20. Insight Transformational Seminars, "Do You Have *All* the Love, Joy, Confidence, Happiness, and Success You Want in Your Life?" *The Awakening Heart Seminar*, promotional brochure, back cover.

21. Montgomery Brower, with Suzanne Adelson and Leah Feldon, "Cult Leader John-Roger, Who Says He's Inhabited by a Divine Spirit, Stands Accused of a Campaign of Hate," *People*, 26 September 1988, 121

22. Ibid., 119.

23. Brower, "Cult Leader John-Roger . . . Stands Accused," 119–20.

24. John-Roger, "The Awakening Heart: The Message of Insight," *The Awakening Heart Seminar*, promotional brochure, 2.

25. Insight Transformational Seminars, biographical note on John-Roger and his organizations, *The Awakening Heart Seminar*, photocopy of promotional brochure.

26. Brower, "Cult Leader John-Roger . . . Stands Accused," 120.

27. Ibid., 119.

28. Michael Murphy, letter from the Esalen Institute, 1.

29. Ibid.

30. George Leonard, "First Visit to Esalen: February 1965," *The Esalen Catalog— 25th Anniversary: The Early Years* (Esalen Institute: Big Sur, CA, 1987), 8.

31. Ibid.

32. Ibid., 8–9.

33. Richard Leviton, "Job's Body: Deane Juhan Is Esalen's Philosopher of Bodywork," *East West Journal*, (January 1988), 61.

34. *The Esalen Catalog—25th Anniversary: The Early Years*, back cover.

35. John Randolph Price, *Practical Spirituality* (Austin, TX: Quartus Books, 1985), 18–19.

CHAPTER 19

1. B. P. Elliot, "Hot Foot Therapy," *US*, 7 May 1984, 14.

2. David Handleman, "Tiptoe Through the Embers," *Rolling Stone*, 26.

3. Carolyn Kortge, "Fighting Fear with Fire," *Register Guard*, Eugene, OR, 18 March 1984, E1.

4. Bernard J. Leikind and William J. McCarthy, "An Investigation of Firewalking," *The Skeptical Inquirer*, vol. 10, no. 1, Fall 1984, 23–26.

5. Ibid., 29–30.

6. Ibid., 30.

7. Ibid., 31.

8. Ibid., 31–32.

9. Ibid., 32.

10. Ibid., 33.

11. Matt. 4:7.

12. Isa. 43:2.

13. Paul Zuromski, ed./pub., *The New Age Catalogue* (New York: Island, 1988) 208.

14. "Discovering Through Inner Quests," product catalog, Institute of Human Development.

15. Heb. 11:1.

16. Gen. 3:1.

17. Rom. 8:28.

18. John W. White, "What Is Meditation?" *New Realities*, September/October 1984, vol. 6, no. 5, 46.

19. Acts 10:38.

20. Matt. 6:7.

21. White, "What Is Meditation?" 50.

22. Ps. 19:14.

CHAPTER 20

1 Gen. 3:4.

2. Lee Aitken, "You Don't Need a Crystal Ball to See That New Age Rocks Are Clearly on a Roll," *People*, 15 June 1987, vol. 27, no. 24, 70.

3. Scott Sutphen, "Increasing Crystal Power," *Masters of Life*, January 1987, 14.

4. Marcia Gervase Ingenito, *National New Age Yellow Pages*, First Annual 1987 Edition, Fullerton, California, 38.

5. "Chatter," *People* 17 May 1976, vol. 5, no. 19, 102.

6. Barbara Brown, "Mind Over Body," *New Realities*, 1980, vol. 3, no. 3, 48–50.

7. Acts 10:38.

8. Ronald Kotzsch, "Acupuncture Today," *East West Journal*, January 1986, 61

9. Paul C. Reisser, Teri Reisser, and John Weldon, *New Age Medicine* (Downers Grove, IL: InterVarsity, 1987), 45.

10. "The Psychic Surgeons—Are They Frauds or for Real?" *Lifestyle*, Calgary Herald, 17.

11. N. O. Brown, "Brazil's Psychic Surgeons," *Omni*, vol. 7, no. 7, April 1985, 96.

12. Paul Zuromski, ed./pub., *The New Age Catalogue* (New York: Island, 1988), 143.

13. "Michio Kushi's New Deal," *East West Journal*, January 1976, 23.

14. "Chatter," *People*, 17 May 1976, 102.

15. Bruce Swain, "Homeopathy on Trial," *East West Journal*, June 1986, 38.

16. Dana Villman and Stephen Cummings, "The Science of Homeopathy," *New Realities*, Summer 1985, vol. 6, no. 6, 50.

17. E. M. Oakley, "The 'Ayes' Have It/Iridology," *New Realities*, November/December 1984, vol. 6, no. 3, 44.

18. Chris Gainor, "Polarity Therapy Restores Body's Energy Balance," *The Vancouver Sun*, 15 September 1982.

19. Polarity Health Institute brochure, n.d.

20. Dr. Randolph Stone, *Health Building: The Conscious Act of Living Well*, CRCS Publications, Sebastopol, California, 1982.

21. Polarity Health Institute brochure, "The Polarity Balancing System: Its Origin and Development," 2.

22. Ibid., 3.

23. Bruce Miller, "Natural Healing Through Naturopathy." *East West Journal*, December 1985, 55.

24 Ibid., 57.

25. Larry Brown, "He's Letting Nature Heal," *Rocky Mountain News*, 15 November 1985, 10.

26. Acts 10:38.

27. Reisser, Reisser, and Weldon, *New Age Medicine*, 45.

28. Rom. 1:24–25.

CHAPTER 21

1. Paul Zuromski, ed./pub., *The New Age Catalogue* (New York: Island, 1988), 216.

2. Owen Davies, "Anti-Matter: Hidden Hoax," *Omni*, May 1985, vol. 7, no. 8, 90.

3. Robert Neubert, "The Institute of Noetic Sciences," *New Realities*, December 1982, vol. T, no. 2, 88.

4. Norm Bowles and Fran Hynds, *PSI Search* (San Francisco: Harper and Row, 1978).

5. Casey McCabe, "CISCOP: Binding Men with Science," *New Age Journal*, October 1985, 11.

6. Col. 2:18 (NIV).

7. Gen. 3:5.

CHAPTER 22

1. *The Denver Post*, 25 August 1978, 6BB.

2. Deut. 29:29.

3. Eric Pement, "Biorhythms: Facts and Fantasies," *Cornerstone*, vol. 7, no. 45, 3–8.

4. Paul Zuromski, ed./pub. *The New Age Catalogue* (New York: Island, 1988), 65.

5. Dan. 2:28.

6. *Washington Post*, 23 October 1983.

CHAPTER 23

1. John Stark, "A Would-Be Mummy Mogul," *People*, 28 July 1986, vol. 26, 85.

2. Ibid., 86.

3. Col. 1:16.

4. Eph. 1:18.

5. John W. White, "What Is Enlightenment?" *New Realities*, March/April 1985, vol. 6, no. 5, 58.

6. Ibid.

7. John 5:24.

8. White, "What Is Enlightenment?" 60.

9. John 8:12.

10. John 1:9.

11. 2 Cor. 11:14.

CHAPTER 24

1. Susan Jean Gifford, ed., *Choices and Connections '88–89* (Boulder, CO: Human Potential Resources, 1987), xxiv.

2. "Introduction" to *A Course in Miracles*, vol. 1 (Framingdale, NY: Foundation for Inner Peace, 1975).

3. James Bolen, "William N. Thetford, Ph.D., Exclusive Interview," *New Realities*, September/October 1984, vol. 6, no. 2, 23.

4. *A Course in Miracles*, 61.

5. Ibid., 69.

6. Letter from foundation for *A Course in Miracles*, 21 November 1984, 1.

7. Clyde Bedell, *Concordex of the Urantia Book* (Santa Barbara, CA: Clyde Bedell Estate, 1986), 21.

8. Ibid., 23.

9. Gal. 1:8.

10. John 16:8.

11. Isa. 40:8.

12. Caryl Matrisciana, *Gods of the New Age* (Eugene, OR: Harvest House, 1985), 15.

13. Gen. 3:4.

14. 2 John 7.

CHAPTER 25

1. Dr. Ed Rowe, *New Age Globalism* (Herndon, VA: Growth Publications, 1985).

2. Richard G. Chrisman, "Letters to the Editor," *Time*, 17 November 1986, vol. 128, no. 20, 7.

3. "More on a New Humanist Manifesto," *The Humanist*, March/April 1973, vol. XXXIII, no. 2, 36.

4. Yuitaka J. Amano, "Bad for Business," *Eternity*, March 1986, vol. 37, no. 3, 55.

5. Paul Zuromski, ed./pub., *The New Age Catalogue* (New York: Island, 1988), 219.

6. Paul Kurtz, ed., *The Humanist Manifesto II* (New York: Prometheus, 1973).

7. Rom. 1:25.

8. Henry Steele Commager, "Declaration of Interdependence," World Affairs Council of Philadelphia, 1975.

9. Doug Groothuis, "The Greening of America," *Eternity*, November 1985, vol. 36, no. 11.

10. Rev. 21:10.

11. John 14:6.

12. Rev. 1:8.

Index

A

A Course in Miracles p.284-286
AC/DC p.67-68
Alcohol p.102
Alternative medicine p.216-220
Angelic assistance p.438-439
Animal sacrifice p.118-120,179,180
Aquino, Michael p.144,145-146
Argenteum Astrum p.150
Arica p.199
Astral projection p.77
Astrology p.268-269
Auras p.272-273
Ayurveda p.247

B

Baby Breeders p.121
Biorhythms p.270-272
Black magic 175
Black mass p.142
Blavatsky, Helena Petrovna p.152
Bloody Mary, Bloody Mary p.74-75

Bodywork p.234
Bonewits, Isaac p.83
Book of Enoch p.134-135
Book of Shadows p.73,113
Branch, Mark p.92
Bundy, Ted p.43

C

Cabala/Kabala p.149
Cabalists p.153
Cabot, Laurie p.156
Carneal, Michael p.70-71
Castaneda, Carlos p.99-100
Cayce, Edgar p.228,251,282
Chi p.223
Chiromancy p.264-265
Church of Satan p.142-145
Chromotherapy p.245-246
Clairvoyance p.77
Clinton, Hillary p.75
Cocaine/Crack p.103
Cognition p.77

Crowley, Aleister p.149-151
Cryonics p.277
Crystals p.220-221
Curses p.2-4,350-357,443-444

D

Dybbuk p.358,359
Demons
    Androgyny p.28
    Common misconceptions p.8
    Definition of p.44-45
    Degeneracy of p.46-47
    Deliverance from p.319
    Dependency on p.427-428
    Diagnosing p.422-423
    Diseases p.428-429
    Fallen angels theory p.45
    Historical references p.45
    In Synagogue at Capernaum p.7
    Influence on children p.48
    Legion p.8
    Mental health p.363-364
    Mongrels theory p 45
    Pre-Adamic theory p.45
    Rank p.25
    Supernatural power p.47-49
Designer drugs p.103-104
Devil
    Temptations of flesh p.43-44
    Existence p.132-133
    What he can do p.334-337
    What he cannot do p.325-334
Dissociative states p.375FF.
Duvalier, Francois ("Papa Doc") p.176
Downers p.103
Dowsing (see water witching) p.266-
    268
Dreamwork p.273-274
Drugs
    Advice for Parents p.104-105
    Common/main drugs p.102 103
    Link with Evil p.101-102
    Link with Satanism p.99-101

Druids p. 156, 157
Dungeons & Dragons p.81-87

E

Egyptian god of the sun p.2
Electromagnetic healing p.221-223
Enlightenment p.279-281
Erhard, Werner (Jack Rosenberg)
    p.192-193
Esalen p.199-20'
ESP p.77
est p.192-193
Evil, definition of p.36-37
Exorcism
    Afterwards p.457-459
    Long distance p.426-427
    Maintaining an atmosphere of
        faith p.416-418
    Preparing for an exorcism p.419-
        422
    Physical danger p.409-412
    Spiritual danger p.412-414
    Ten rules p.436-448
    What to take to an exorcism
        p.415-416
    When is the person ready p.423-
        424
    When to start p.424-425
Exorcist, the p.388,413
Extrasensory perception (ESP) p.252-
    253

F

Firewalking p.203-207
Folk religions p.171-173
Forum, The p.193-194
Friday the 13th/Jason p.91-92
Frost, Gavin and Yvonne p.160

G

Geller, Uri p.254,256
Generational satanism p.2-4,350-
    357,443-444

Global consciousness p.295-296
Global goddesses p.300-301
Global humanism p.296-297
Global pantheism p.297-299
Global sociology p.299-300
Globalism p.294-295
Goddess worship (see global goddesses) p.300-301
Golden, Andrew p.71
Gnosticism p.191
Grimoires: Black Magic Textbooks p.134
Gygax, Gary p.82,83-84

H

Halloween p.165-167
Hanley, John p.194-195
Helms, Sean p.93
Herbology p.246-247
Hermetic Order of the Golden Dawn p.149
Hinduism p.13
Hitler, Adolf p.266
Homeopathy p.236-239
Horror movies p.89-95
Huffington, Arianna p.198
Human Potential Movement p.185-190
Human sacrifice p.120-123,139,142, 342-344

I

I Ching/Book of Changes p.259,261-262
Imagery p.233-234
Incubus p.18,158,160
Insight Transformational Seminars (ITS) p.197
Institute of Human Development p.198
Institute of Transpersonal Psychology p.199
Interdependence p.298
Iridology p.239-241

J

Jesus Christ Superstar p.23
John-Roger p.197-198
Johnson, Mitchell p.71
Jones, Detective Lt. Larry p.101
Jung, Carl p.253

K

Kali, Hindu goddess p.15
Kasso, Ricky p.68-69
Key of Solomon p.134
Kilroy, Mark p.97-98
Kinkle, Kip p.71

L

LaVey, Anton p.137-141,142-145
Legal right p.329
Life Training p.196-197
Lifespring p.194-196
Light as a Feather p.318
Lingam (male phallus) p.13
Loa p.16,178
LSD p.103
Lovecraft, Howard Phillips p.135
Lucas, Henry Lee p.30-34

M

Macumba p.180-181
MacLaine, Shirley p.75,78
Macrobiotics p.234-236
Maharishi Mahesh Yogi p.187
Manson, Charles p. 66-67
Marijuana p.102-103
Maya p.208-209
Meditation p.211-215
Merritt, Andrew p.40-42,44,51-52
Movement of Spiritual Awareness p.197-198
Multiple Personality Disorder (MPD) p.375FF.,384-385
Mummification p.276-277
Music therapy p.227-229

N

Narcisse, Clairvius p.177
National Coalition on Television
 Violence p.81
Naturopathy p.243-244
Necromancy p.86
Necronomicon p.135-136
Neurolinguistics p.207-208
New Age Movement p.81 (see Human
 Potential Movement) p.185-190
New World Order p.301-303
Nightmare on Elm Street/Freddy
 Krueger p.92-93
Nostradamus p.265-266
Nutrition p.234

O

Obsession p.328
Occult crime p.66-70
Oppression p.328
Ordo Templi Orientis (OTO) p.154
Orgonomy p.246
Orixa p.181
Ouija board p.87-88

P

Palmistry p.264-265
Parapsychology p.77,252-254
Parricide p.52
PCP (Angel Dust) p.103
Pentagram p. 162-163
Phallic symbol (Lingam) p.13
Precognition p.77
Polarity therapy p.241-243
Pornography p.43
Possession p.328
Postcognition p.77
Prana p.198
Prevention p.233
Psychic phenomena(PSI) p.75-76,251
Psychic surgery p.229-231
Psychics p.254-258
Psychokinesis (PK) p.253

Q

Pyramid power p.231-234

R

Ramirez, Richard, p.67-68
Reagan, Nancy p.75
Reagan, Ronald p.36
Reflexology p.239-241
Reincarnation p.278-279
Rhine, J.B. p.253,255
Rocky Horror Picture Show p.115
Roland II, Theron Reed "Pete" p.112
Rolfing p.244-245
Rosicrucians p 154
Runes p.274-275

S

Sadhus (Hindu holy men) p.16
"Salvation Settles it All Syndrome" p.8
Santeria p.179-180
Satan
  Limitations p.42-43
  Who he is p.38
Satanic Bible, The p.137-140
Satanic groups p.141-142
Satanic Ritual Abuse p.120-127
Satanic Rituals, The p.140-141
Satanic salute p.73
Satanism, Signs of p.72-73
Schucman, Helen p.284-285
Scientology p.188
Seances p.78
Self-deliverance p.319-320
Self-healing p.233
Self-torture (Bloodless) p.11-16
Sellers, Sean p.106-112,115-116
Serpent and the Rainbow, p.177
Shaw, Dereck p.114
Silva Mind Control p.188
Silver Star, the Inner Order of the
 Great White Brotherhood p.150
Siva (Hindu god) p.16

Slayer p.56,57-62
Spiritualism p.151-153
Stone, Dr. Randolph p.241-242
Sucubus p.160
Sullivan, Tommy p.113-114
Sun worship p.2
Superstitions p.174
Syncretism p.191

T

Tarot cards p.262-263
Tasseography p.263-264
Teenagers (Signs of Satanism) p.72-73
Telepathy p.77
Temple of Set p.145-146
Texas Chainsaw Massacre p.90
Thaipusam p.11-16
Thelema p.149,155
Therapeutic touch p.226-227
Thompson, Eugene Frank p.101
Transcendental Meditation (TM) p.187-188

U

Uppers p.103
Urantia p.286-288

V

Visualization p.190-191,208-211
Voodoo p.175,176-179

W

Walpurgisnacht p.143,144
Warlock p.157
Water witching p.266-268
White slavery cults p.31
Wilson, Colin p.135
Witch doctor 2,16
Witchcraft p.156-163
    Feminism/goddess worship p.161,300-301
    Festivals:
        Beltane p.162
        Esbats p.162
        Lughnasadh/Lammas p.162
        Oimelc/Candlemas p.162
        Sabbats p.162
        Samhain p.162
    Witchcraft Cults:
        Church and School of Wicca p.159
        Church of All Worlds p.160
        Church of Pan p.160
        Church of the Eternal Source p.160
        Church of the Wyccan Rede p.160
        Covenant of the Goddess p.160
        Circle p.160
        Dianic p.161
        Gardnerian p.158-159
        RadicalFaerie Movement p.160
        Religious Order of Witchcraft p.160
Womanspirit p.300
Woodham, Luke p.70

X

Y

Yin and Yang p.223-224

Z

Zombiism p.177

Slaves p.50, 57-62
Spiritualism p.151-153
Stone, Dr. Randolph p.241-242
Sardonyx p.160
Sullivan, Tommy p.113-114
Sun worship p.2
Superstition p.174
Syncretism p.191

T

Tarot cards p.262-265
Theosophy p.263-264
Teenagers (Signs of Satanism) p.72-73
Telepathy p.??
Temple of Set p.145-146
Texas Chainsaw Massacre p.90
Thuggee p.11-16
Thelema p.149,185
Therapeutic touch p.256-257
Thorazine, Eugene Frank p.161
Transcendental Meditation (TM)
p.187-188

U

Uppers p.103
Urantia p.286-288

V

Visualization p.190-191,208-211
Voodoo p.175,176-179

W

Walpurgisnacht p.143,144
Watloo p.157
Water witching p.266-268
White slavery cults p.31
Wilson, Colin p.138
Witch doctor 2.16
Witchcraft p.156-163
  Feminist/goddess worship
  p.161,300-301
  Festivals
  Release p.162

Esbats p.162
Lughnasadh/Lammas p.162
Ostara/Candlemas p.162
Sabbats p.162
Samhain p.162
Witchcraft Cults
Church and School of Wicca
  p.159
Church of All Worlds p.160
Church of Pan p.160
Church of the Eternal Source
  p.160
Church of the Wyccan Rede
  p.160
Covenant of the Goddess
  p.160
Circle p.160
Dianic p.161
Gardnerian p.158-159
Radical Faerie Movement p.160
Religious Order of Witchcraft
  p.160
Womanchurch p.300
Woodham, Luke p.70

X

Y

Yin and Yang p.225-226

Z

Zombies p.177

About the Author

BOB LARSON is an expert on cults, the occult, and supernatural phenomena. He is the host of a daily one-hour radio show, *TALK-BACK with Bob Larson*, heard in approximately 100 cities in the United States and Canada, and host of two weekly television show. He has lectured in more than seventy countries and has appeared on such television shows as *Oprah, Donahue, Montel, Sally Jesse,* and *Larry King Live, and Politically Incorrect.*

Larson is the author of more than twenty-five books, including the novels *Dead Air, Abaddon,* and *The Senator's Agenda,* as well as *UFO's and the Alien Agenda, In the Name of Satan, Satanism: The Seduction of America's Youth, Straight Answers on the New Age,* and *Larson's New Book of Cults.*

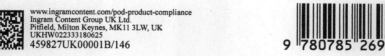